WOMEN IN RELIGION

Mary Pat Fisher

PEARSON
Longman

New York • San Francisco • Boston
London • Toronto • Sydney • Tokyo • Singapore • Madrid
Mexico City • Munich • Paris • Cape Town • Hong Kong • Montreal

Publisher: Priscilla McGeehon
Editor in Chief: Eric Stano
Executive Marketing: Ann Stypuloski
Manufacturing Buyer: Al Dorsey

Library of Congress Cataloging-in-Publication Data

Fisher, Mary Pat, 1943–
Women in religion/Mary Pat Fisher.
    p. cm.
Includes bibliographical references and index.
ISBN 0–321–19481–0 (alk. paper)
1. Women and religion—Textbooks. I. Title.
BL458.F57 2005
200'.82—dc22

                                        2004058389

Credits and acknowledgments of material borrowed from other sources and reproduced, with permission, in this textbook appear on pages 310–318 and page 322.

Please visit our website at http://www.ablongman.com

ISBN 0–321–19481–0
10 9 8 7 6 5 4 3 2 1

This book was designed and produced by
Laurence King Publishing Ltd, London
www.laurenceking.co.uk

Every effort has been made to contact the copyright holders, but should there be any errors or omissions, Laurence King Publishing Ltd would be pleased to insert the appropriate acknowledgment in any subsequent printing of this publication.

Commissioning Editor: Melanie White
Editor and Project Manager: Elisabeth Ingles
Picture Researcher: Sally Nicholls
Designer: Andrew Shoolbred

Front Cover: A Chinese woman prays at Yuantong Si,
a Buddhist temple in Kunming

Photo: Natalie Behring/On Asia

CONTENTS

PREFACE

The subject of women in the world's religions is vast, fascinating, and complex— and full of remarkable personalities. Religions are not isolated, unified wholes; they vary not only from one to another but also internally, through time, place, and factions. The patterns of women's participation are often different from those of men, who tend to hold the positions of leadership. Women's contributions and ways have often been obscured by the predominance of men, so their spirituality may be expressed in alternative, more private means. In the past, none of this was well recorded, but now, with much interest in recovering women's history and analyzing their roles, there is an enormous body of literature about women in religion.

This book is intended to provide an accessible introduction to this variegated mosaic. It gives a balanced view, exploring many perspectives on contemporary issues, including feminist theories and the voices of marginalized women. I have taken a "world religions" approach, with an historical introduction to each major religion, followed by the history of women within the movement and contemporary analysis of the issues raised. To uncover some of the realities of their spiritual lives, I have used women's own voices, allowing them to explain their life experiences and perspectives. Thus the book is lively and relevant as well as descriptive and analytic. Readers of my well-received textbook *Living Religions* have always appreciated its use of real voices, so here I have made extensive use of direct quotations from my interviews with women of many cultures and faiths— some venerated traditional figures, some ordinary contemporary women—because it is only through such "on-the-ground" accounts that a true picture of women in religion begins to emerge.

Women in Religion includes many scriptural passages about women and quotations from other texts with a significant impact on their religious lives, such as the first-century *Lessons for Women* by Pan Chao of China and the fifteenth-century Christian text *Malleus Maleficarum*, which vilified women as witches. Religious founders and scriptures have sometimes been ambiguous in their treatment of women, and within the scope of an introductory text I have tried to unravel some of these ambiguities, such as the Buddha's alleged reluctance to allow women to be nuns and the Prophet Muhammad's relationships with and reported pronouncements on women.

Contents
The first chapter takes an overview of women's religious experiences, regardless of their particular tradition. It looks at issues that emerge again and again, such as

attitudes toward women's bodies and patriarchal restrictions on their religious activities, and introduces various theoretical perspectives on their religious lives. This chapter also introduces the phenomena of women as mystics, healers, and significant spiritual figures.

Tribal cultures vary widely around the globe, but Chapter 2 looks at some common elements in indigenous lifeways. Often they honor female divinities and offer significant spiritual roles for women, particularly as shamans, priestesses, and healers. The chapter addresses some controversial issues, such as genital surgery

Woman at dawn prayers in the sacred Ganges

and appropriation of indigenous spiritual patterns by outsiders, and attempts to see these issues from the point of view of people within the traditions.

Hinduism is difficult to grasp, because it is unfamiliar to people of Western cultures and because there is no single tradition. To help readers move into this complex field, I begin Chapter 3 by tracing the historical roots and pathways of what is generally labeled "Hinduism." I then follow the changing role of women up to the present, in which some are highly regarded as spiritual teachers but historically oppressive conditions continue.

Chapter 4 begins with the lives of Buddha and the women with whom he interacted. It traces the evolution of Buddhism and its major divergent forms, with special attention to how women have fared throughout. Today there is a major thrust toward reviving the orders of ordained nuns and of revisiting Buddhist philosophy through the lens of feminist analysis. After examining these trends, the chapter ends with views of contemporary Buddhist women as teachers and as social activists.

Chapter 5 starts with the common roots of two major religions originating in China—Confucianism and Daoism—and then examines these two paths separately, up to the current situation of women in China and surrounding countries.

Judaism is the first of the three major Western religions that developed from a single root. Chapter 6 follows the position of women in the Hebrew Bible and in later Jewish history. Feminists have played significant roles in Judaism's contemporary redefinition and revival, so considerable space is devoted to feminist theology and liturgical changes, as well as to women's growing leadership in branches of institutional Judaism.

The discussion of women in Christianity starts with the life of Jesus and the Jesus movement, and what we now know about the women who were part of his mission. Chapter 7 then traces the apparent subordination of women within institutional Christianity. It also looks at saints, ascetics, and martyrs. To make the current picture of Christian women intelligible, the chapter examines their leadership roles, their work as activists and social workers, the contributions of feminist theologians, and contemporary issues.

Scholarship on women in Islam is now quite active, so Chapter 8 draws on this research to give a picture of women in Arabia before Islam and then traces what seems to have happened to them during and after the life of the Prophet Muhammad. It looks at the Holy Qur'an and laws pertaining to women in the light of current feminist scholarship, and introduces some of the differing cultures that color the practice of Islam. Feminist activism relating to current issues is described. The chapter ends with an introduction to mystics who have overcome cultural and religious strictures to devote their lives to their Beloved.

New religious movements continue to appear around the world, and Chapter 9 looks at a sampling of those arising in recent centuries, ranging from well-established to contemporary movements, including newer mixtures of religious strands from older traditions. Women play significant roles in some of these newer movements.

Chapter 10 goes beyond this to look at women whose religious paths are not guided by any institution old or new, but rather by their own inner spiritual callings.

Special features

The most salient feature of this book is its frequent use of direct quotations. They appear in the text, in interview boxes, and in excerpts from women's writings, such as Riffat Hassan's important article "Human Liberation is Supported by the Holy Qur'an." Most chapters have biographies of such significant women as the Tibetan Buddhist adept Yeshe Tsogyel and the Christian St. Teresa of Avila. Woven throughout the text, the voices of these real women speak to us across the centuries or across the globe, giving a genuine and meaningful picture of their spiritual experiences and understandings.

The book is illustrated with pictures of both historical and contemporary women from all traditions. They range from my own daughter Marianne with her daughter Maira to the influential contemporary Jewish feminist Judith Plaskow, the Korean theologian Chung Hyun Kyung, a Candomble priestess in a possession trance, and the unclassifiable Kazakhstani woman, Koshi. Other illustrations include a rare photograph of Khadija's Tomb, now demolished, a drawing of the "Altai Princess" found in the permafrost in Siberia, and a Nicaraguan depiction of the Mother creating the world.

At the end of each chapter, there is an annotated list of suggested readings for those who want to explore in greater depth. New terms are printed in bold and defined when they first appear, and a list of these key terms appears at the end of each chapter for study purposes. A comprehensive glossary at the end of the book gives fuller definitions. Chapters on major religions have an historical timeline giving the dates of women who appear in the text.

Acknowledgments

The writing of this comprehensive book has spread across many years and many people have helped. I would especially like to acknowledge and thank Margaret Krebs of California, who generously helped me obtain books not available where I live and conducted two interviews on my behalf, and Galina Ermolina of Siberia, who enthusiastically provided biographical materials, photos, and the interview with a Siberian shaman. My great thanks also go to Elinore Detiger, who arranged my trip to Geneva in 2002 to participate in the Global Peace Initiative of Women Religious and Spiritual Leaders, where I met many of the women doing important work around the globe.

I am very grateful to my excellent team of consultants, not only noted academic specialists but also practicing members of their respective traditions: Dr. Ann Braude, Harvard University; Dr. Vijaya Ramaswamy, Jawaharlal Nehru University; Dr. Michiko Yusa, Western Washington University; Dr. Livia Kohn, Boston University; Dr. Dvora Weisberg, Hebrew Union College; Dr. Rosemary Radford Ruether, Pacific School of Religion; Dr. Riffat Hassan, University of Louisville; and Dr. Christine Gudorf, Florida International University. Rev. Allison Stokes, retired from Ithaca College, offered valuable suggestions on the Christian chapter and Dr. Karma Lekshe Tsomo, San Diego University, on the Buddhist chapter.

Other people have helped in many ways. Alan Nykamp of the Gobind Sadan Institute faithfully typed transcripts of the interviews. Both of my beloved daughters, Marianne Fisher Vandiver and Michelle Fisher Brand, were very supportive in helping to gather materials. Priya translated for Russian-speaking interviewees.

Lyla Yastion, Lenette Partlow Byrick, Alisa Kuumba, Margaret West, Veena Sharma, Sandhya, Sister Metta, Sister Santacitta, Dhammananda, Cuc Nguyen, Sonam Wangmo, Irene Hasapes, Josephine Dalmoro, Mohammed Shariq Rafiq Warsi, Owen Cole, Susan Howard-Azzeh, Amir Hussain, Daya Baweja, Sarah Hartzell, Ann Smith, Elly Pradervand, Jane Sugarman, Bert Gunn, and Lee Bailey shared valuable books, articles, pictures, contacts, and insights. The many women whom I have interviewed have shared their experiences honestly and perceptively. I am so grateful to them all for helping to portray real women's religious lives.

Reviewers of the manuscript were enthusiastic about its form and content, and gave many practical suggestions for improving it. They are: Julye Bidmead, Miami University; Christine Gudorf, Florida International University; Sallie King, James Madison University; Jennifer Manlowe, University of West Georgia; Lynn Ross-Bryant, University of Colorado, Boulder; Claire L. Sahlin, Texas Woman's University; Ana Self Schuber, University of Alabama; Julia J. Sheetz-Willard, Temple University; Ann K. Wetherilt, Emmanuel College; and Steve Young, McHenry County College.

The people at Laurence King Publishers have been a great pleasure to work with, as always. I want especially to thank my faithful longtime editor Melanie White, my brilliant copy-editor Elisabeth Ingles, hardworking photo researcher Sally Nicholls, publishing director Lee Ripley, and designer Andrew Shoolbred. They have all been patient and helpful. I also want to thank Priscilla McGeehon and Eric Stano at Longman for their interest and support in publishing the book.

Although I have worked primarily with women on this project, many men have been supportive and helpful, especially my own beloved father Robert Dix, my husband Edward Fisher, my son Justin Fisher, my sons-in-law Andrew Brand and David Vandiver, and my great teacher, His Holiness Baba Virsa Singh of Gobind Sadan. Babaji has constantly encouraged me in writing this book, as well as helping me to grow spiritually strong and giving me significant spiritual roles to play, for he has great regard for women.

It has been a privilege to write this book. May God bless all who have worked on it and all who will read it.

Mary Pat Fisher
Gobind Sadan Institute for Advanced Studies in Comparative Religion
New Delhi, India

1
WOMEN'S RELIGIOUS EXPERIENCES

We women are all called to be prophets today

KAREN ARMSTRONG

Throughout human history, women have had deep spiritual experiences, have been healers, have had access to enlightened wisdom, and have been willing to devote themselves to the service of others. Each of these women's experiences has been unique. But the spirituality of both women and men has always been expressed within and molded by social systems and religious traditions. In general, these systems and traditions have favored men as spiritual leaders and relegated women to minor roles. Nevertheless, because women as well as men have spiritual experiences, sometimes very powerful ones, there have always been some women who have broken out of the mold.

In this book, we will be looking for women from many cultures who have manifested their spirituality, who have played significant spiritual roles, whether their societies and religious traditions offered them these roles or not. We will look at the cultural and religious constraints that they faced and that women continue to face today in expressing their spirituality. Before conducting this search religion by religion, we will first look at factors that often mold women's religious participation, no matter what their religion.

What is Religion?

Spiritual experience and religion are not necessarily the same thing. In this book we will use the word "**spirituality**" to mean any personal response to dimensions of life that are considered sacred. We will use "**religion**" to mean a particular response to sacred dimensions as shaped by institutionalized traditions. Religion encompasses beliefs, practices, ritual objects, scriptures or oral traditions, and specialists who administer and maintain the tradition. No religious tradition is monolithic or unchanging, but for over a hundred years scholars have been trying to discern the general features of the major "world religions"—institutionalized religious traditions such as Hinduism, Buddhism, Daoism, Confucianism, Judaism, Christianity, Islam, Sikhism, and Baha'i. Many scholars now feel that this approach is too general, divorced from specific political and historical contexts, but it remains a useful framework nonetheless so long as one does not accept its **reified** (concrete) categories as absolute. We will therefore use the "world religions" lens to study women's participation in the largest religions, but we will listen to the voices and stories of real women and also look at less formalized, more localized, or newly evolving spiritual ways.

"Religion" is therefore a somewhat abstract construct; women's experiences are too individual to be so conveniently categorized. This is particularly so because women have often been practicing religion on the fringes rather than in the limelight of religious traditions. Until recently, their experiences have tended to be overlooked in studies of religions.

Patriarchy in Institutionalized Religions

Religion tends to be **patriarchal**—led by men as father figures. The major world religions practiced today have all been founded by men and continue to accord them dominant roles. Religions arise within social systems, the majority of which are already dominated by men, particularly in large-scale societies. Any Buddhist nun is junior to the most junior Buddhist monk. In Islam, the leaders of congregational prayer are always men. In Christianity, though some women have become priests or ministers in some denominations, they are still under the control of male higher authority figures. Religious institutions thus mirror the existing social patterns of control of women by men. Some may even deepen these social inequalities by teaching that women are naturally spiritually inferior or even evil.

Some women accept this situation as the way things are supposed to be. Others struggle to make their voices heard in seats of religious power, but the fact remains that it is mostly men who dictate what women can and cannot do within religious institutions. Women of color perceive this power imbalance as but one further aspect of a larger system of social oppression on the basis of race, class, and culture. Women who are dark-skinned, lower-class, and from less industrialized cultures generally have less say in institutionalized religions than men who are light-skinned, upper-class, and from more industrialized cultures.

Limits on Women's Religious Participation

What effect does this situation have on women's expression of their spirituality? For the most part, they are excluded from roles of authority, though they can and do play supporting roles in some religions. Around the world, it is usually women who clean the holy places, light the ritual candles, prepare food for the ascetics or sacred meals, attend the daily masses, teach the children, and visit shrines to pray for their families. They may also be the secretaries and office managers in religious places. But they are often denied the training or authority to conduct rituals for the community. And even though they may carry on religious rituals at home, the domestic sphere to which their authority is confined is deemed a less holy space than the temple where male priests preside.

Some founders of religions raised the religious status of women somewhat, relative to their previous social conditions, and mitigated their abuse by men. The early days of many religions, before they became institutionalized, are thought to have been empowering for women, for the prophets brought enlightened visions that were to uplift all humanity. But even then, recent scholarship suggests that the gains in power for women were slight and soon lost as the new religion became institutionalized after the death of the founder.

Women's Bodies

A body that has breasts, a vagina, a uterus, and menstrual periods, that can give birth to and suckle children, is a biological fact, like having brown hair or long legs. But the biological features that make it possible for women to bear and nurse children have in most cultures been given great symbolic significance and used to define a constellation of attributes characteristic of the female gender. The **sex** of a person is the biological fact of being female or male; **gender** is a culture's ideas about what it means to be female or male, and what a female or male is allowed and expected to do.

Are there any innate differences between males and females that are totally biologically based and have an actual bearing on their spirituality? Are women more or less likely than men to become enlightened? To be able to adopt an **ascetic** lifestyle (living without worldly comforts, in extreme self-discipline)? To be able to preach? It is difficult to tell, since cultural training so often obscures our natural tendencies. But there have always been women who developed enlightened wisdom, who lived as ascetics, or who were spiritual teachers, even though their religious traditions may have discouraged them from playing these roles, asserting that they were unfit to do so or that their proper sphere was the home. Throughout this book, we will be presenting the stories of many such women.

In many cultures, women's physical characteristics have been eroticized and are considered very alluring. Sometimes women are described as lustful temptresses who will lead men astray from the religious path. Furthermore, the mysteries of the womb and the seemingly magical power to conceive and give birth make women innately different in ways that some men find psychologically unsettling. Women may thus become problems for men, rather than simply fellow human beings. Religious systems established by **patrilineal** societies (based on kinship through the male line) have tried to confine women's sexuality to marriage to avoid confusion about the paternity of a child. One of the ways of doing this has been to portray women as dangerous or evil, in order to warn men away from them except in the socially restricted arena of marriage and family. Some religious traditions require women to cover their bodies and even their faces so that men will not be attracted to them. They may be denied the life of a wandering ascetic since laymen might accost them on the road, or monks might be distracted by them.

Furthermore, while menstrual blood is simply a natural fact of women's bodily existence, many cultures believe that this bleeding is shameful or polluted. This spills over into ideas about women's fitness for religious roles and religious participation. How can a woman defined as a temptress also be a priest and regulate morality? How can a menstruating woman defined as polluted enter places and positions considered holy?

Subject to such negative messages about vaginal bleeding, women who are menstruating or who have just given birth may nonetheless create their own private sacred spaces. A new mother in India may be excluded from the society around her for forty days, since she is considered impure, but she may experience this period of seclusion as a time of quiet and loving bonding with her baby. Many feminists now view their bodies and biological changes as positive and powerful, and they create women-only rituals to celebrate their biological life stages, in somewhat the same way as women in tribal societies have long done.

Women's Non-institutional Spiritual Roles

Though typically marginalized by religious institutions, women in every culture have nonetheless done important spiritual work. Nearly everywhere, women carry on spiritual rituals that take place in the home—lighting the votive candles or *divas*, worshiping the ancestors, painting auspicious designs on the earth. Children watch them and learn about unseen realms. As mothers, women who have given birth to and nurtured children may informally teach them the precepts and values of their religious culture. Grandmothers are also often important in children's spiritual upbringing, imparting whatever faith and enlightened wisdom they have gained over the years. Women are important actors in rituals that mark and give meaning to major life changes: birth, puberty, marriage, death. In everyday, practical ways religions have thus been perpetuated by women, even when they have not been able to officiate at temples.

Consider the memories of Sue Woodruff, Roman Catholic nun and Coordinator of Ministry for her province in Oregon:

Virginia, my mother's mother, carried in her body her Pacific Northwest roots. Her French Canadian and Native American heritage flowed into her prayer. Each evening after supper, Grandma chose one of us to join her in her room for her evening ritual. I treasure the memory of those intimate moments. We carried a pot of tea, two cups, and sometimes a bowl of rice with cinnamon, sugar, and milk. While the tea steeped, Grandma freed her waist-length hair from its topknot. I brushed and brushed her white mane. Meanwhile Grandma began her formal prayers with a reading from Grandpa's French Bible. Memorial cards, yellowing letters, and birth announcements marked favorite passages. After the reading came the prayers to our Mother God in the Chinook jargon of her Columbia River ancestors. Intuitively I knew that although Grandma and I might pray very easily to God our Mother, the Sisters in our parish school would not readily accept this manner of addressing God. So God our Mother remained in our home ritual.

1.1 Marianne and her child Maira. Intimate physical contact with the mother is known to be important in a baby's development

Next Grandma led a family litany in English during which we prayed for each of her thirteen children, her grandchildren, her sister's family, other relatives and myriad of friends. Birthdays, illnesses, deaths, failed crops, journeys, new babies, anniversaries, we prayed for them all. After I had braided Grandma's hair into one long plait for the night, she would pour two cups of tea and we would share secrets and jokes while we sipped. Then with a goodnight kiss, she would send me on my way as she climbed into her bed.[1] ▨

To learn to love, to learn that Someone is listening to one's prayers or that there is a powerful invisible Reality permeating the visible world—these are spiritual lessons that children may receive from their mothers and grandmothers.

A mother herself may also grow spiritually through having a child (fig. 1.1). Dr. Chandra Patel from India observes:

▨ Mothering involves deep, unselfish love… . Throughout babyhood the mother enjoys special intense intimacy with her baby. She nuzzles its neck, kisses its hands, nibbles its toes. Mothering also involves physically caring for the infant—nourishing, nurturing, cleaning, comforting… . It means protecting the infant from hostile environments: testing the bath water, keeping it away from a hot iron or a boiling kettle… . It is said that our basic attitude towards the

INTERVIEW Rosemarie Eble *Emergency Nurse*

I grew up in Newark, New Jersey, in a northern Italian community. I was brought up as Roman Catholic. There was an orphanage that was maintained by a community of sisters—the Sisters of Saint Joseph, of Chestnut Hill. They provided education for the 12 grades.

My goal even from childhood was to try to remain in the presence of God, to try to remember that God is everywhere. The practice of the presence of God was something that the sisters taught us very young. I really do think that most of them were mystics, and probably imparted to me for certain, and probably to most of my peers, a sense of the mystical presence of God. In the 70s and 80s it was considered freaky and downright psychotic if people said things like that. So people who are mystics just didn't say it.

I am now retired from hospital work, but I worked 30 years in critical care nursing. I worked in transplant nursing and hemodialysis before that.

I always was interested in the healing arts, and I've always had and knew that I had a very good brain, and fnd intellectual curiosity very satisfying. So for a long time, I wanted to be a physician. Then I realized that it was the nurse and not the physician that was actually spending time with patients. What the physician was doing was trying to pinpoint the diagnosis so that a range of treatments could be identifed. And it was then the nurse that was actually the one who made that occur. When those concepts became real to me, then I understood that what I wanted was nursing, and not medicine.

The advent of critical care medicine provided nursing the opportunity to do much of the research—the observation and the data collection—so that intensive care units and critical care became a wonderful environment for nurses. But now this was a very complex environment, and as one physician said, "The real talent of a critical care nurse is making sense out of chaos." This organized chaos—all the people who are in emotional crisis—the nurse lives in that environment, whether it is the emergency room, the operating room, the critical care unit, or the ward. But the physician comes in and goes out. So when there is a crisis, the physician arrives in chaos as well. There is an emergency and the physician is notifed. The nurse who is there has to interpret what has occurred, because history becomes important, even in terms of moments. If a person is not conscious right now, but they were five minutes ago—what happened?

Each patient has a mindset as to what they will accept from any therapeutic person. If there is a need for them to accept more than they are willing to right now, then one has to create a bond of trust to try to move them to a point of acceptance.

In the United States, there has been for the past 15 or 20 years the restriction that you can't talk about God. But you can minister. God for me is the reservoir from which I draw. I do not have to say that this is God working through me. Whether the individual to whom I am ministering considers it that way or not is irrelevant to me. And I would hope that they feel cared for—authentically—and that they feel respected when in contact with me, and that they feel comfortable enough to participate in the healing process. By that, I mean that they relax and let their body heal. If they don't trust me, they're not going to sleep. If they don't trust the therapeutic team, they're going to doubt that the medications that we are giving them are really the right ones. They can worry themselves into never getting well.

I think that the intuitive arts are very, very important in therapeutics, and in other professions as well. As a nurse, there was always more to do than there were hands to do it, and more people that needed comforting than you had time to comfort. And at the end of your ability to work, whether it was eight hours or ten hours, suddenly things were done. And you looked back and you said, "God, when did I do that?" Or "How did that resolve?" And you knew that somehow you got superspeed. That was what I always considered my angels helping me. Or my patients' angels helping me. When you had this tremendous urge to get up and check somebody—even though you had just been in there, you've got to go back and do it again. Why did you do it at that particular time? It was no routine thing. And very often when you're very busy, it is only routine that keeps you on track. So you don't want to deviate from routine. That kind of "compulsive behavior" gets things done and is really very benefcial. It's just plain life that convinces one that you have divine help, or angelic help.

Prayer keeps me grounded and real. In my view, spirituality is not gender-based. Spirituality is potentially in each and every person. I think that anyone who has worked in a hospital frame knows that there is another dimension than what is in the procedural manuals.

Rosemarie Eble, interviewed March 7, 2002.

world, as well as towards our bodies, is fashioned early in the way our mother holds us… . Even in those cultures where women are treated poorly, the mother is not denied the opportunity to feed her baby every few hours, and thus revel in the intimacy of the bodily contact that the act of breastfeeding brings.

The insights that occur naturally in the course of mothering are the need to give oneself completely to the physical and spiritual care of the infant, the need to know by empathetic understanding, the need to endure self-discipline, the need to accept the child's development through trial and error, the necessity to love the child not as a possession but as belonging to itself, and the necessity of letting go. These are all spiritual experiences of women which complement and correct the insights of traditional spirituality.[2]

This ideal of motherhood is not universally experienced. Not every home is a safe and nurturing place, nor do all women choose motherhood. Nevertheless, most societies have created rituals to accommodate and shape the profound changes that arise as our relationships with our family and community develop, and women are often central in carrying out these rituals. The helping professions, such as medical care, teaching, psychotherapy, and social work, also offer some scope for the expression of women's spirituality, even in countries where talking openly about spiritual subjects is forbidden. Some religiously pluralistic countries that have made it illegal for the government to promote any one religion have done so by preventing any religious teaching in public institutions. Nevertheless, in her work and her service to others a woman may subtly communicate spiritual values and attitudes or set a spiritual example (see box, p.17).

For many women, communion with unseen dimensions occurs through nature. Gardening is often the province of women. They may have a profound inner connection with the plants, the trees, the earth itself. Prize-winning author Annie Dillard has exceptionally intense, all-senses-alive experiences of the natural world, from microscopic to cosmic dimensions. She writes:

> I walk out; I see something, some event that would otherwise have been utterly missed and lost; or something sees me, some enormous power brushes me with its clean wing, and I resound like a beaten bell... . Something pummels us, something barely sheathed. Power broods and lights. We're played on like a pipe; our breath is not our own.[3]

Women who are artists, craftswomen, poets, writers, composers, or musicians may dip into their inner wells to express their spiritual experiences with less social constraint than women who try to be priests or nuns conforming to patriarchal religious codes. But women's work, whatever it may be, has tended to be socially devalued relative to that of men, so women's creativity has not always been socially rewarded. Over the millennia, how many anonymous women have woven their inner understanding into their rugs, quilts, pots, and wallpaintings and nonetheless died unrecognized?

The American painter Georgia O'Keeffe (1887–1996) was a pioneer who broke through this barrier of anonymity to make bold original statements in her art, going on to win critical acclaim (fig. 1.2). She achieved this by a courageous decision to seek the truth of her own inner experience of simple things— flowers, bones, stark desert scenes:

1.2 Georgia O'Keeffe, *Black Iris III*, 1926. The Metropolitan Museum of Art, New York

> As I looked around at my [early] work I realized that each painting had been affected by someone else. I wondered why I hadn't put down things of my own from my own head. [I thought] "I have things in my head that are not like

what anyone has taught me—shapes and ideas so near to me—so natural to my way of being and thinking that it hadn't occurred to me to put them down." I decided to start anew—to strip away what I had been taught—to accept as true my own thinking.

I found myself saying to myself—I can't live where I want to—I can't go where I want to—I can't do what I want to—I can't even say what I want to—. School and things that painters have taught me even keep me from painting as I want to. I decided I was a very stupid fool not to at least paint as I wanted to and say what I wanted to when I painted as that seemed to be the only thing I could do that didn't concern anybody but myself... .

I was alone and singularly free, working into my own, unknown—no one to satisfy but myself.[4] ▪

Women as Mystics

Both within and beyond institutionalized religions, many women throughout the ages have followed an inner calling to communicate directly with the unseen. This call usually comes unexpectedly, unplanned, bringing a radical shift in awareness. Sickness and difficulties often part the veil, as it were, revealing dimensions of life that are unknown to others. World Religions Professor Lyla Yastion says that her deep spiritual awakening began when she was diagnosed with breast cancer:

▪ Clear now for three years, that experience, the mastectomy and chemotherapy being only outer symbols of the inner instruction of acceptance, even love for the gift of embodiment, for life, for my husband and family, and for other people and creatures which grew in me from that time but I think was deeply seated in my being always. It continues to grow and I pray each day to be open to love's instruction. Since this time of awakening through crisis, I am drawn in what I read, what I teach and experience, to the inner light.[5] ▪

Difficulties can even be embraced and become transformational. As Buddhist nun Pema Chodron writes in *When Things Fall Apart*:

▪ We can use difficult situations—poison—as fuel for waking up... . When anything difficult arises, instead of trying to get rid of it, we breathe it in... . Everything that occurs is not only usable and workable but is actually the path itself... . The trick is to keep exploring and not bail out ... to let things fall apart and let ourselves be nailed to the present moment.[6] ▪

From their awakened inner spiritual reservoirs, women have often performed spiritual services for others, such as healing, guidance, and prophecy. Sometimes outstanding women mystics have been honored as shamans, oracles, or gurus. On the other hand, their insights and power may test institutional boundaries and male dominance. Sometimes their spiritual powers have been misunderstood and feared; they have been treated as madwomen or blamed for bringing bad luck to the community and hideously put to death as witches. In 1486, Christian inquisitors wrote the *Malleus Maleficarum* ("The Hammer of Witches"), a document so anti-female that on its recommendations a great number of people, the majority of them women, were burned as witches, even into the eighteenth century. The *Malleus Maleficarum* states, for instance:

> All witchcraft comes from carnal lust, which is in women insatiable. See Proverbs XXX: There are three things that are never satisfied, yea, a fourth thing which says not, It is enough; that is, the mouth of the womb. Wherefore for the sake of fulfilling their lusts they consort even with devils.... Now there are, as it is said in the Papal Bull, seven methods by which they infect with witchcraft the venereal act and the conception of the womb: First, by inclining the minds of men to inordinate passion; second, by obstructing their generative force; third, by removing the members accommodated to that act; fourth, by changing men into beasts by their magic art; fifth, by destroying the generative force in women; sixth, by procuring abortion; seventh, by offering children to devils....[7]

In fact, women—and men—who have experienced mystical union with the Divine often describe that union in sensual metaphors, for there are no other worldly experiences that approximate the intensity of the divine embrace. Some even feel it as an extraordinarily powerful physical sensation. Consider, for instance, a sample of the poetry of the thirteenth-century German mystic Mechthild of Magdeburg:

> Wouldst thou know my meaning?
> Lie down in the Fire
> See and taste the Flowing
> Godhead through thy being;
> Feel the Holy Spirit
> Moving and compelling
> Thee within the Flowing
> Fire and Light of God.[8]

And the great fifteenth-century Hindu mystic Mirabai, lover of Lord Krishna ("The Dark One"), sang:

> Sister,
> I went into market
> and picked up the Dark One.
> You whisper
> as though it were shameful.
> I strike my drum and declare it in public.
> You say I paid high,
> I say I weighed it out on the scales,
> it was cheap.
> Money's no good here,
> I traded my body, I paid with my life![9]

Most people have not "seen" and "tasted" God, and have not given themselves soul and body to God's service, so they cannot understand the passionate utterances of women mystics. Nevertheless, mystical women are no longer feared. At present in many religions and spiritual movements there is instead a renaissance in spiritual practices that keep open inner communications with the sacred. Barbara Sargent, program adviser for the Kalliopeia Foundation, which gives grants to projects that foster "the innate dignity and creative potential within all people," urges:

> When we don't take time to strengthen our relationship with the Absolute, or God, when we don't take time for meditation, or contemplation, or are not aware of what our dreams might be telling us, we are allowing a build-up of dust to clog our inner pipeline to what is True and Real for each of us individually... . It is only when our inner pipeline to God is clear, when we are surrendered to serve God unconditionally, without thought to our own needs or wants, that the divine energy of life can work through us, can flow through us, into the world and miraculously transform the difficult outer situations.[10]

As we will see, women mystics both known and unknown have arisen within every religious tradition. Spiritual wisdom has often been personified as a woman, such as the Greek Sophia. And the receptivity to what Mechthild calls "the Flowing Fire and Light of God" is a characteristic that has typically been culturally encouraged in women more than in men. In Christianity, Jesus' mother Mary is held up as the highest example of womanhood because she was receptive to the divine Spirit. Many religions regard women as receptive, passive vehicles. In Sikhism, the Gurus taught that we must all become "like women" in order to receive spiritual blessings. Many male mystics have characterized themselves as brides longing for and trying to please their Lord and Master. Both women and men use sexual metaphors of physical self-abandonment to the One they love. Whether this receptivity is an innate characteristic of women or culturally conditioned is hard to determine.

By contrast, some religions deny that women are capable of significant spiritual progress and insist that only those born in a male body may achieve ultimate enlightenment. In Ch'an Buddhism, the word that means the determined, heroic person capable of attaining enlightenment also means "man." But here again, traits such as determination and courage are not necessarily determined by our biological sex.

Women as Ascetics

Another niche has been available to women within some religions: that of celibate ascetics. As in mysticism, this is a niche within which we find well-known religious women with names and histories. In this case, they usually renounce traditional roles within the family as well as possessions and bodily comforts. They do not marry, they do not bear children. To follow this path, they may therefore face strong opposition from their families; they must be very determined to take this relatively unconventional route to spiritual service or enlightenment. If they join an

1.3 Jain nun with mouth-cover to prevent damage to insects, joyous in the midst of austerities

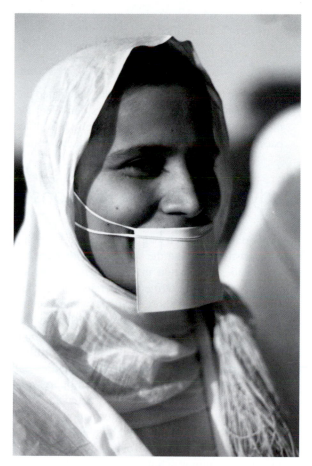

established ascetic order, they may be required to shave their heads and/or cover their bodies completely, thus totally obliterating their femaleness. In some cases, women may take vows of celibacy before they reach the peak of their sexuality—often in the mid-thirties, later than for men—and eventually find themselves in the very awkward position of having to deal with sexual desires they had earlier renounced.

On the other hand, many women find the ascetic life very freeing and happily endure physical hardships and abstinence for the sake of inner bliss, inner communion with the divine power. Women seem just as able as men to handle austerities for the sake of spirituality. In India, where women have traditionally led culturally confined lives, far more young Jain women than men choose the life of ascetics. The Jain nuns (fig. 1.3) sleep on the floor on cardboard, they own only three sets of garments, a few handkerchiefs, and a wooden begging bowl; they endure intense heat and cold, and yet they seem always happy and contented. Contemporary Tibetan Buddhist nun Tenzin Palmo lived for 12 years in a snowy cave in the Himalayas in order to deepen her spiritual practice; today she speaks of the rigors in an offhand way as though they were trifling. The Christian St. Clare was beautiful, wealthy, and highly sought-after, but she gave up everything—even warm blankets and adequate food and sleep—in order to follow joyously the life of "holy poverty" exemplified by Jesus and by her mentor and friend, St. Francis of Assisi. St. Clare was often so weakened by extreme fasting that she could not walk, but yet, as her biographer writes:

> Clare's life of poverty was not a grim, calculated handing over but rather a joyous, easy, impatient flinging aside: lovers don't feel the cold, lovers don't care what they eat—and Clare was a lover, running full tilt toward her Beloved, "with swift pace, light step, unswerving feet, so that even our steps stir up no dust."[11]

Studying Women in Religions

It is important today to try to discover what women have done inside and outside religious institutions, but the search is neither easy nor straightforward. Women's histories and participation in religion have not been well documented. Where women do appear in written materials, one could simply take a descriptive approach, reproducing these writings without comment, or one could take an analytical approach, perhaps coming to different conclusions than the writer.

Contemporary analysis of women's participation in religions is often undertaken from feminist points of view. In general, **feminism** can be defined as the belief that women should have the same opportunities as men, and that relationships should be based on mutuality rather than oppression and hierarchy. It is both an academic approach and a platform for activism. Feminists often aspire to individual freedom and even social transformation. They want to let women speak for themselves rather than be defined by men. This view is a contemporary one, and comes mostly from Western women. When historical materials are analyzed by contemporary feminist scholars, they may discern evidence of patriarchal oppression and inequalities of which women then may have been unaware, or which they may have interpreted in a different way. The same is true of women within religions today. They may not share the belief that women should have equality of opportunity or that, as some feminists believe, women are innately the same as men but have been culturally conditioned to fit a different mold. In this book, we will try to accommodate many women's points of view—including those who are struggling against multiple forms of oppression such as racism and heterosexism, and women of color who would prefer to be called "**womanists**" or in Spanish *mujeristas* rather than "feminists," which they associate with a white Western point of view.

The true picture of women in religions will be elusive and will relate to the social–cultural context of the examiner as well as that of the women being examined. For example, many Western women cringe at the idea of marriages arranged by families rather than the couple themselves. They regard the arranged marriages of other cultures as an indication of religious and cultural subjugation of women. By contrast, many Asian women are quite suspicious of self-arranged "love" marriages, since their failure rate is so high. A recent opinion poll in India showed that even among a sampling of progressive people (90 percent of whom believed that men should help with domestic chores), 74 percent of the women and almost as many of the men said they believed that arranged marriages are more likely to be successful than love marriages.[12]

Or take the contrast between Western feminists and some African perspectives. Professor Oyeronke Oyewumi, who has made a deep study of these differences, feels that the global efforts of Western feminists are actually harmful to the interests of African women. She writes:

> Feminism is primarily concerned with the liberation of women. Given ... historical occurrences and the fact that in many African societies the category woman cannot be isolated raises the question of the relevance and value of Western feminism. In much of Africa, "Womanhood" does not constitute a social role, identity, position, or location. This is because each individual occupies a multiplicity of overlapping and intersecting positions, with various relationships to privilege and disadvantage. In addition, local situations are themselves in a state of flux, given the disproportionate influence of external agents in African life. It would be counterproductive in the African setting to single out gender, which thus far has been elaborated only as a biologistic category—a body-based identity—as the primary source and focus of political agitation... . In its various guises and disguises, feminism continues to be the most avid manufacturer of gender consciousness and gender categories, inevitably at the expense of local categories such as ethnicity, seniority, race, and generation that may be more locally salient... . Western feminism ... is entangled with the history and practice of European and North American imperialism and the worldwide European colonization of Africa, Asia, and the Americas.[13]

Cultural restraints are often confused with religious teachings, and religious teachings themselves may be little understood by people who either come from a different religion or are non-religious. Islam, for instance, is little understood by non-Muslims, and often blanket references are made to the oppression of "Muslim women." Professor Amina Wadud writes:

> The secularists express little or no concern over the centrality of Islamic spirituality to Muslim women nor over the importance of Islam as a dimension of identity. The tendency instead is to accept the determinations of rights, liberation, and agency promoted in many Western women's groups. Although they address serious infractions of the rights of Muslim women in the context of some Muslim governments and conservative religious thinkers, they ignore the negative consequences of this approach... . Under the guise of "equality," women are offered opportunities to do the same as, or be like, men... . Ideally, Islam promotes an equitable experience of complementarity between women and men, who enhance the humanity of each other through sharing experiences and perspectives.[14]

What, then, do women in each religion have to say about themselves? One of the major sources of information about women in religions is written scriptures. Typically, the scriptures of the world's global traditions are written down by males. They say very little about women and use language that suggests that those who are active and significant in religions are men. This is called **androcentric** or male-centered language. When women are explicitly mentioned, it is often apparent that they are expected to remain subordinate to men and that their proper sphere is in the home, not in the temple. Men's experience is what is normal; women's experience is on the fringes, not to be taken seriously. It may be considered irrelevant, superstitious, or even dangerous. If women appear in scriptural stories, they may be there only as men's wives or mothers or as temptresses creating problems for the men. If a language uses gender-specific pronouns, a human being is "he," and even the Supreme Deity is usually referred to as "He." If women read such scriptures, they risk becoming invisible to themselves or perceiving themselves as inferior, unworthy beings. But in many cases, women have not even been allowed or educated to read or study the scriptures.

Finding only a few clues about historical women's spiritual lives from their portrayal in canonical scriptures, contemporary scholars are searching in other places, looking for women's own writings, for instance. These are relatively scarce, for women have not been socially encouraged to speak out in their own voices. The great mystical writings of Mechthild of Magdeburg were almost lost to the world, since she had to struggle not only with the difficulties of putting unworldly expe-

1.4 Artist's rendering of an ancient Altai woman, the "Altai Princess," whose mummifed remains suggest that she was a high spiritual initiate

riences into worldly language, but also with the fact that as a woman of her culture she would be criticized for writing about anything at all. In addition to women's rare writings, there are oral traditions, songs, dances, myths, and archaeological findings that give glimpses of their spiritual lives. A **myth** is a story used by a community to make sense of the universe and to place itself therein. As we will see, such clues have led to theories that there were once **matriarchal** (led by women, with descent through the female line) or, at any rate, goddess-worshiping cultures in which women's spirituality was more highly honored than in the more oppressive patriarchal cultures that followed.

One of the areas where relevant archeological research is being conducted is the Altai area of Siberia in Russia, particularly the Ukok Plateau near the Mongolian border. According to oral tradition, during the time of the ancient Scythians the people who lived there had extraordinary spiritual powers. The permafrost has preserved graves with funerary artifacts and mummified humans from two and a half millennia ago. The mummies are so well preserved that some of their soft tissues are intact, complete with tattoos. One of these has been called the "Altai Princess" (fig. 1.4) by archaeologists who think that she was of the nobility because of the sacral sign of the griffin—a mythical creature with the body of a lion and the head and wings of an eagle—tattooed on her forearm and because of the six chestnut horses that were buried next to her sarcophagus. She was dressed in a thin silk robe with a wide red belt. Scientists think that the belt was the sign of a warrior and a spiritual initiate. In her hands was a larch stick, which is thought to be a very significant ritual tool. It was only put into the hands of the Supreme Heavenly Rulers. And her high headdress with gold decorations may be a sign of her magical powers.

According to a Siberian myth—which like many myths may contain clues to prehistoric realities—the northern Altai region was once very warm. The trees and the grass were always green. But the fish or monster bearing the Earth on its back tipped the planet so that it became very cold and started to snow. To save her children, the Goddess Umai turned their souls to rocks. She was able to save two of her daughters, and escaped with them to the southern Altai. But even there they became frozen. There they remain today as glacial mountains whose summits are the heads of Umai and her daughters, in which the most sacred mountain, Belukha, is home to the spirit of the goddess. Such hints from around the world suggest that women's spirituality may once have been highly honored in some cultures.

Are Women Different from Men?

Debate continues over why women are more or less universally devalued relative to men, a circumstance that precludes their access to religious leadership roles. In many cultures, men are thought to be stronger, more assertive, more logical, and thus better leaders, whereas women are considered frailer, more emotional, and more nurturing, and thus needing protection in the home rather than being projected publicly. But these stereotypes are not universally maintained, so they may be culturally learned. When freed from these expectations, men have shown themselves to be tender, emotionally sensitive, and nurturing, and women to be strong and assertive. Both men and women have been limited by these stereotypes rather than allowed to grow into wholeness. Feminists have therefore often fought for the social equality of females and males.

On the other hand, other feminists have found it more productive to discover and celebrate differences between males and females. Men and women are biologically different in certain undeniable ways. More of women's body parts and processes are given over to the perpetuation of the species, to the extent that menstruating women suffer discomfort and perhaps pain for several days every month as their bodies prepare and then slough off a uterine bed for potential fetuses. As we have already noted, the discomfort and blood of menstruation have sometimes been cited as reasons for denying women important positions, whether secular or spiritual.

As the one who bears children and gives them milk from her own body, the mother is also the most likely candidate to take care of the children until they mature. She thus becomes the primary teacher of those children, inculcating in them the culture's ways and values. These functions are so important to the perpetuation of the society and the species that all cultures have endeavored to keep women in the home. Women have thus been assigned different gender roles from men.

Biologically and culturally different, are women also psychically different? This is an area of great controversy. Anthropologists have found certain kinds of differences that seem to be universal and thus perhaps innate rather than culturally learned: women tend to relate to objects and people, and to do so directly and subjectively; men tend to be more objective and abstract in their approach to the world, relating to things and people less easily. In addition, recent biobehavioral research suggests that men and women respond differently to stress. Under stress, men's hormones push them to "fight or flight" patterns, whereas in women, differing chemical responses to stressful situations (e.g., release of more estrogen and oxytocin than in men) seem to make them more likely to "tend and befriend"—to care for their children and seek the companionship of other women.

Subjectively, women often perceive themselves as being inwardly different from men. In some cases, women have learned to value the ways in which they feel themselves different. For instance, Lenett Partlow of Baltimore, who joins with other African-American and Native American women in using spiritual energies for healing others, observes:

> Working with women holding the same spiritual intention is a most awesome oneness. I don't know if I'll ever be able to adequately express in words what I know from my experiences. The closest I can get to the raw truth of what I know is that women possess a certain, definite power of spirit. When they focus together from the core of their beings, from the womb, from the heart, their magic is tangible. I've had the great blessing of giving birth to and raising three males, along with being married three times now, and while men have their magic, the quality of ours is very different. There's a depth of expression that comes from being fearless together, when absolute trust exists among women. It's as if men are wired with a different spiritual frequency than us, or maybe

it's men in this society. But then I've been in ceremony and fellowship with men of high spiritual consciousness and it's still different. Anyway, what I know about the work we do in communion, in ceremony, in ritual, in prayer, in intention together is powerful, necessary, and essential to life. Now I truly understand that the transformation of the earth plane during this time revolves around the rise of the feminine energy and the restoration of the goddess energy on the planet. We are the womb of creation.[15]

If the above generalizations about women's differences are true, then women may be more suited than men to the transcendent religious experience of oneness with all humanity, without regard for categories. Theology Professor Ursula King describes women as having rich spiritual resources:

There is perhaps first and foremost the immense resource of suffering as a source of strength to overcome adversity and affliction. There are the pain, the tears, the agony, the immense labour in bringing new life into the world and attending with equally immense patience to its slow and imperceptible growth. These are the roots for women's resources of compassion, of insight, and ultimately of wisdom.

There is also women's attention to detail, to the minutiae of life, the faithfulness to the daily round of duties which ensure personal and social wellbeing and make the smooth running of ever so many activities in the world possible and bearable. Then there is women's power of listening, of pacifying, of soothing and healing many a wound and settling many a quarrel and dispute. There is the strength of an encouraging smile and the gentle touch of love, the experience of generous selfless giving, of comfort, warmth, patient encouragement and recognition, the adaptability to people and their personal needs, the caring concern and understanding of others... . It is perhaps for this reason that the French religious thinker Pierre Teilhard de Chardin (1881–1955) expressed the view that on women "life has laid the charge of advancing to the highest possible degree the spiritualization of the earth."[16]

Concepts of the Divine

Some religions describe the supreme spiritual power as being formless, all-pervasive, unnameable, and mysterious beyond human understanding. Nevertheless, we humans often try to relate to it in gendered terms (fig. 1.5). In Daoism (also known as Taoism), for instance, the Dao is like a valley that fills with power by being receptive and yielding, and thus is sometimes referred to as Mother of the World. The imagery may be far more personal: some ancient and indigenous peoples have envisioned and worshiped a great goddess, such as the Great Mother Nu Kwa of China, the Greek earth goddess Gaia, Arinna the sun goddess of Turkey, and Great Spider Woman of the Pueblo people. In Judaism, Christianity, and Islam, there is a general emphasis on ultimate control by a dominating male deity, God or Allah. In devotional forms of Hinduism, the godhead may combine "male" and "female"

1.5 Sergio Velasquez, *Creación*.
A Nicaraguan view of the
beginning of the world

qualities in one being, such as the powerful goddess Durga, or in a male god and
his female consort, such as Lord Shiva and his partner Parvati.

We relate to the Divine according to such beliefs and metaphors, so they have
a great impact on our spirituality. If our metaphors for sacred reality are impersonal—such as an all-permeating, infinite Wisdom, Power, or Light—then we can lose
the sense of ourselves as individuals because there is no finite Thing to which "I"
can relate. If I instead follow a path of devotion to a divine Person, conceived
anthropomorphically (as if having human form), I might relate to the Divine as a
child to a father, thus cultivating a relationship of obedience and awe before his
power. If I think of the Divine as a mother, I might develop a sense of gratitude for
her loving care. If I consider the Divine my friend or my lover, the relationship may
be a very intimate one. But according to Christian theologian Sallie McFague, the
problem is that the metaphors for our multifaceted relationship with the Divine
come to be understood as rigid and exclusive models of the Divine itself. She
writes:

If one accepts that metaphors (and all language about God) are principally
adverbial, having to do with how we relate to God rather than defining the
nature of God, then no metaphors or models can be reified, petrified, or expand-
ed so as to exclude all others. One can, for instance, include many possibilities:
we can envision relating to God as to a father and a mother, to a healer and a

liberator, to the sun and a mountain. As definitions of God, these possibilities are mutually exclusive; as models expressing experiences of relating to God, they are mutually enriching.[17] ■

Challenges to Institutional Restrictions

Given the patriarchal structures and theologies of many world religions, some contemporary women are challenging those structures from within, whereas others are carrying on their spiritual work outside of traditional institutions. There is now considerable encouragement for women to come forward, rather than staying in the background spiritually. Dadi Janaki, head of the Brahma Kumaris organization—a relatively new movement that has grown from a form of Hinduism, that emphasizes personal inner experience, and that is mostly led by women—asserts:

> It is time for women to be able to come back to their original state of self-respect and honor and dignity and to be able to take that power from God. We have developed the habit of coming under the influence of others, allowing ourselves to be submissive to others and allowing ourselves to come into a state of secondary position by and in front of others. I come under pressure and become submissive to someone, I become dependent on someone, as if they, alone, are my support. I get caught by the influence of someone. It is time to renounce these three things. Today I have to let go of something. I will not allow anyone to influence me because I get led into deception if this happens. When I don't have that inner purity and inner power then I become dependent on others. And when I don't have that power of truth to be able to take strength from God, then I become submissive to external things and I don't give myself the time to go into the depth of spirituality. Let me use my time in a worthwhile way, let my thoughts be ones supporting everyone's benefit, let me never allow feelings of hopelessness to come into my nature. And if ever I feel weak, let me be able to take all power from God.[18] ■

Where religious institutions are being challenged by feminists, one of their demands is for more women to be given positions of power. Another is to rewrite liturgies and scriptures to eliminate unnecessarily androcentric language, whether in reference to the divine (God = "He") or to humanity (person = "man"). Beyond these attempts, some feminists are demanding radical reforms within the institutions themselves, perceiving them not only as suppressing women but also as having become empty, irrelevant, and more intent on perpetuating their own power than in empowering and uplifting people whether male or female. They are re-examining the original traditions behind such institutions and often finding them radical, reformist, and inclusive, and they want to bring these qualities back to life.

Others have abandoned the attempt to challenge the status quo and bring meaning back into fossilized patriarchal religions, and are turning toward newer religions in which women play a more significant role and are freer to express their spirituality. A major new thrust is worship of the Great Goddess, which some feel pre-dated worship of a supreme male God in many parts of the world. We shall examine Goddess spirituality in more detail in Chapter 9, but suffice it here to say that some women and men are embracing this way in hopes that it will provide a more liberating, holistic, and meaningful path to ultimate reality. Yet other women are stepping outside any kind of organized religion to explore the spiritual world on their own, an individualistic approach that we will be looking at in the last chapter.

Women and Current Issues

Today's religious women are not only concerned with their own salvation. In many cases, they are deeply troubled by the problems of the planet and want to help. Karen Armstrong, the British historian of Judeo-Christian-Islamic religions and a former nun, recently proclaimed:

> It is time to reclaim religion for compassion, the compassion that has been taught by all great world religions, each one of which has expressed an ideal with its own peculiar genius. We women are all called to be prophets today, to speak for God, for the sacred, for the voices that are being drowned out in the mainstream. We are called to be prophets, not because we have had visions, or seen a great fiery chariot, but because of the suffering and pain and despair of the world.[19]

Spiritual women are thus forming networks today to raise their voices against injustice, against militarism, against religious intolerance, against governmental deception, against violence toward women, against destruction of the planet. They feel they can no longer just remain quietly at home and see their sons and daughters and homelands become victims of sick social systems and distortions of religious sentiments. For instance, theology professor Chung Hyun Kyung exposes how Confucian ethics were twisted to turn 200,000 or so young Korean women into "comfort women" for Japanese troops in the middle of the twentieth century. She writes:

> Any group of women must have their "root story" of what it means to be women in their own specific history and land. African-American women remember stories of slavery, brutal kidnappings, rape, forced breeding and labor, and intentional destruction of their family and dignity. Jewish women remember the story of the Holocaust, Nazism, Hitler, German nationalism, Auschwitz, stripping, the gas chambers, and medical experiments with their bodies. European women remember the story of witch-hunting. In the name of holiness they were captured, tried, tortured, drowned, burned alive. Women from Asia, Africa, Latin America, the Pacific, and former European colonies remember what it means to be "other," "primitive," and "savage" in their own land, slowly losing their language, culture, and memories.[20]

Such horrors continue today, only slightly mitigated by what is hopefully called the "advance of civilization." By contrast, urges Right Reverend Vashti Murphy McKenzie, Presiding Prelate of the African Methodist Episcopal Church:

> Listen to the sound of peace: stability, security, safety. Listen to the sound of peace: harmony, tranquillity, wholeness. Listen to the sound of peace: love, creation, justice, longing. Listen to the sound of peace: respect, acceptance, accountability, responsibility. Listen to the sounds of peace. It is hard to hear the sounds of peace in a world determined for war. It is hard to hear the sounds of peace in a century that has been the bloodiest. Edwin Brooks writes that evil triumphs because of the silence of good men. Allow me to rephrase that and say that peace fails because of the silence of good women.
>
> We must cultivate a kind of compassion for those who are caught up in acts of violence. We must teach our children what the world has failed to teach, that nobody wins war and everybody loses. We must teach our children to be sensitive to the differences and the uniqueness inherent in all of us. All of us have a choice to respond when we are faced with evil, and let us make the choice to respond, to gather the facts and the evidence so that we can act as informed men and women. We must have the courage of our conviction.[21]

In the chapters that follow, we will be delving into the particular situations of women in each of the major religious streams—the socio-political contexts of each religion, their founders' teachings and impact on the condition of women, and how these have changed with time and place. Everywhere we will be listening to women's own voices as much as possible. In the midst of all the constraints they have faced, women everywhere, in all religions, have managed to keep the flame of sacred experience and sacred action alight and to pass it down, still burning, to future generations.

Key Terms

spirituality	patrilineal
religion	feminism, feminist
reified	womanist
patriarchal	androcentric
gender	myth
sex	matriarchal
ascetic	anthropomorphic

Suggested Reading

Christ, Carol P. and Judith Plaskow, eds., *Womanspirit Rising: A Feminist Reader in Religion*, San Francisco: HarperSanFrancisco, 1979, 1992. A classic of feminist writings about spirituality.

Flinders, Carol Lee, *At the Root of this Longing: Reconciling a Spiritual Hunger and a Feminist Thirst*, San Francisco: HarperSanFrancisco, 1998. One woman's personal story of trying to resolve inner clashes between feminist positions and spirituality.

King, Ursula, *Women and Spirituality: Voices of Protest and Promise*, 2nd edn., University Park, Pennsylvania: The Pennsylvania State University Press, 1993. Excellent introduction to contemporary spiritual issues in which women are engaged.

Mananzan, Mary John, Mercy Amba Oduyoye, Elsa Tamez, J. Shannon Clarkson, Mary C. Grey, Letty M. Russell, eds., *Women Resisting Violence: Spirituality for Life*, Maryknoll, New York: Orbis Books, 1996. Feminist theologians from around the world uncover the harsh realities of economic, military, cultural, ecological, domestic, and physical violence and suggest religious perspectives and antidotes to these horrors.

McFague, Sallie, *Models of God: Theology for an Ecological, Nuclear Age*, Philadelphia: Fortress Press, 1987. Deriving from the thinking of a Protestant Christian theologian, this pivotal work carries implications for concepts of the Divine in general.

Mohanty, Chandra Talpade, *Feminism Without Borders*, Durham, North Carolina: Duke University Press, 2003. A corrective to unconscious "Western" bias in feminist studies.

Ortner, Sherry B., *Making Gender: The Politics and Erotics of Culture*, Boston: Beacon Press, 1996. Provocative essays by a major feminist anthropologist examining cultural determination of gender roles.

Raines, John C. and Daniel C. Maguire, eds., *What Men Owe to Women: Men's Voices from World Religions*, Albany: State University of New York Press, 2001. An interesting anthology of male scholars' writings about the gender injustices and restrictions within their own religions.

Reed, Betsy, ed., *Nothing Sacred: Women Respond to Religious Fundamentalism and Terror*, New York: Thunder's Mouth Press, 2002. Research into the links between religious fundamentalism and discrimination and violence against women around the globe.

Sharma, Arvind and Katherine K. Young, eds., *Feminism and World Religions*, Albany: State University of New York Press, 1999. One of a series of books edited by these authors about women in religions, this one examines the situations of women in each religion from contemporary feminist perspectives.

Sharma, Arvind and Katherine K. Young, eds., *Her Voice, Her Faith: Women Speak on World Religions*, Boulder, Colorado: Westview Press, 2003. Prominent women religious scholars write about women in their traditions in their own voices, from a personal as well as scholarly perspective.

2
WOMEN IN INDIGENOUS RELIGIONS

The women and Mother Earth are one

MOHAWK PRAYER

Eons ago, perhaps all religious practices fell into the category that we now call "Indigenous Religions." This is a catch-all term encompassing all remaining cultures, generally tribal, in which local religious practices and beliefs are still alive, usually in close relationship to the land upon which the people live. Religion and everyday life are often so intertwined that the people may have no word for "religion" as a thing apart that occurs only sometimes in temples.

It is not possible to draw a composite picture of all women in indigenous religions today. The cultures and their practices are so extremely varied. Among Australian Aborigines alone, there are over 500 different clan groups with varying lifeways and beliefs, and hundreds of distinct languages. In the jungles of Amazonian Peru, at least 53 different ethnolinguistic groups have been identified. Academically trained observers who also have deep personal experience from having lived a long time in these traditions are rare. Most of the traditions are carried orally, so written records and scriptures are few. These cultures tend to be pockets of small-scale tribal societies with simple subsistence methods, but they are no longer isolated, nor are they living totally according to their traditional patterns. By today, most of them have been influenced or dominated by industrialized cultures and their religions. All are continuing to change; they are not static systems.

Nonetheless, there is clear evidence that women have in the past played important spiritual roles in many of these societies and to the extent that their traditional lifeways have survived, they still do. Indigenous cultures provide some of the world's strongest examples of women as religious leaders, but also, in some cases, evidence of oppression of females in the name of religion.

Overview of Indigenous Religions

One of the distinctive characteristics of these varied cultures is an understanding of their environment as sacred and meaningful. In contrast to the general Western view of a world of inanimate, insensitive things, with which humans can do as they like, tribal peoples tend to see the world as consisting of relatives. There are the

Fish People, the Tree People, the Plant People, the Insect People, the animals who are one's brothers and sisters. The sun may be known as Father or Grandfather, the moon as Grandmother. The Earth is often referred to as Mother; many indigenous societies know that all life has emerged from her womb. The spirits of dead ancestors are still present. Mountains, rivers, lakes, stars—the whole cosmos is a web of interrelationships, with active, albeit unseen and mysterious, spiritual forces everywhere. Everything is in some sense permeated with spiritual power and influential in the lives of the people, who are merely part of the web of life.

To proceed in proper relationship with these unseen forces is essential, for not only are they revered—they may be destructive if not properly respected. Therefore another feature of most indigenous cultures is the presence of **shamans**, the Siberian name for visionary women or men who have direct access to the spirit world and have been specially called and trained to interact with spiritual forces on behalf of the people. Indigenous ways are sometimes referred to as "shamanism," but they do not constitute any global "ism." Each culture has its own rich tradition of myths, rituals, songs, stories, healings, and divination, all of which help to integrate the everyday lives of the people with the sacred cosmic web.

The rich spiritual culture of indigenous peoples is passed down from generation to generation, often added to by new visions and changing according to new circumstances. Inevitably, indigenous cultures and their traditions have been largely obliterated by colonizing powers, and they often now subsist only as small and politically powerless minorities where they had once freely roamed the land. Intermarriage with the colonizers has further diluted the traditions. Nevertheless, some of the ancient ways are still carried in the collective memory, typically passed on only by the old women of the tribe. Cecilia Montero from Peru, who has two master's degrees and works as a psychotherapist in North Carolina, drawing upon her psychic abilities, describes how she was informally taught by her great-grandmother:

My tradition is from the mountains of Peru and it comes from way back as it was passed down in a pure expression as sound. I was taught by my great-grandmother between the ages of two and thirteen. A lot of the instruction was silent. She taught me how to dream her dreams. In the Inca tradition dead people, for example, used to be a part of the life. Some of the elders, after they passed, were kept in the house in a mummified way. So the tradition taught that certain people were to communicate with them. It was our task to learn how to communicate with them. That part of the tradition is what my great-grandmother passed down to me.

When I was little, there were messages from different people in the tradition, and my guess is, from outside the tradition as well. They had simple messages like, "Tell my daughter not to wear that dress today." Simple things like that. It was kind of difficult for me when I was a child—too many people came. But then I learned, and she taught me how to know who was who.

It's not like I am in trance. It's, you know—regular. That's what she taught me. Just like the plants are in the physical plane and they can be one with nature, so too we can hear the spirit world, just like the radio. That's what she said, and it was true.

That's how my teachings began. Understanding. First I had a little chair where I sat, and she wanted me to understand the nature of the chair and the wood that made the chair, and the silence that we practiced, and all of that.[1] ▪

Gender Balance

The spiritual roles that women play in indigenous societies are interwoven with their overall status. Traditionally, it seems that women were often socially powerful in tribal cultures. Many Native American groups were apparently **matrilineal**—that is, they traced their lineages through the mothers, rather than the fathers. Lakota women of the High Plains owned their houses and everything in them and could divorce their husbands just by putting the men's clothes outside the house. Tilda Long Soldier reports, "Among the Lakota, the woman owned her body and all the rights that went with it."[2]

Women tended also to hold considerable political power. In Mexica tradition—the indigenous life of Mexico before the Spanish conquest of 1519—each *Kalpulli*, or community, had two directors: the executive director was usually a man, the administrator usually a woman (fig. 2.1). In groups such as the Iroquois Confederacy and Pueblo tribes, clan mothers chose the male leaders, and still today over a quarter of all council members and tribal chairs for Native American tribes are women. Alice Papineau (De-wa-senta), a contemporary Onondaga clan mother,

2.1 Martha Sole Valois, native spiritual leader from Cuernavaca, Mexico

lists the criteria the women follow in choosing a man to represent their clan as *sachem* in the Grand Council: "First, they cannot have committed a theft. Second, they cannot have committed a murder. Third, they cannot have abused a woman."[3] Most important, for the clan mothers to choose a man as chief, he must have demonstrated his ability to take good care of his immediate family, since he will be responsible for all the wider circles of the family, from clan to nation to confederacy, up to seven generations.

Native womanist Paula Gunn Allen paints a very positive picture of "gynocracies," by which she means "woman-centered tribal societies," in which "**matrilocality** [the tradition by which the husband lives with the wife's community], **matrifocality** [households consisting only of the mother and her children], **matrilinearity** [kinship traced through the mother's side], maternal control of household goods and resources, and female deities of the magnitude of the Christian God were and are present and active features of traditional tribal life." She writes about Native American tribes:

Traditional tribal lifestyles are more often gynocratic than not, and they are never patriarchal…. American Indians are not merely doomed victims of western imperialism or progress; they are also the carriers of the dream that most activist movements in the Americas claim to be seeking. The major difference between most activist movements and tribal societies is that for millennia American Indians have based their social systems, however diverse, on ritual, spirit-centered, woman-focused worldviews.

Some distinguishing features of a woman-centered social system include free and easy sexuality and wide latitude in personal style. This latitude means that a diversity of people, including gay males and lesbians, are not denied and are in fact likely to be accorded honor. Also likely to be prominent in such systems are nurturing, pacifist, and passive males (as defined by western minds) and self-defining, assertive, decisive women… .

In tribal gynocratic systems a multitude of personality and character types can function positively within the social order because the systems are focused on social responsibility rather than on privilege and on the realities of the human constitution rather than on denial-based social fictions to which human beings are compelled to conform by powerful individuals within the society.

Tribal gynocracies prominently feature even distribution of goods among all members of the society on the grounds that First Mother enjoined cooperation and sharing on all her children.

One of the major distinguishing characteristics of gynocratic cultures is the absence of punitiveness as a means of social control. Another is the inevitable presence of meaningful concourse with supernatural beings.

Among gynocratic or gynocentric tribal peoples the welfare of the young is paramount, the complementary nature of all life forms is stressed, and the centrality of powerful women to social well-being is unquestioned.[4]

These generalizations cannot be applied fully to all tribal cultures, especially in the present. Colonization by patriarchal Europeans—which began in the fifteenth century and has continued in more subtle forms up to the present—has typically lowered the status of women. In some traditional cultures women have been feared and denigrated, although their spiritual power may be acknowledged and given some room for expression since women are considered as likely as men to have visionary and healing powers.

Among the great variety of African tribes, religious roles may belong exclusively and separately to women and men, they may be parallel, or they may be complementary. Among Australian Aborigines, whose varied tribes have lived for at least 50,000 years as semi-nomadic hunters and gatherers, each within its own sacred territory, researchers are now discovering that women's secret ceremonies are parallel to those of men. Sometimes men in their own secret ceremonies even try to mimic women's menstrual bleeding by subincision of the penis to make it bleed.

Cross-cultural studies of all religions indicate that the more religion is an integral aspect of life, rather than something institutionalized and separate from daily life, the more women are likely to be involved in it. The more a religion becomes institutionalized, the more women tend to be excluded from significant roles in it. In the various tribal subsistence cultures of the Peruvian jungles, women are able to perform spiritual ceremonies, whereas in the more institutionalized spiritual ways of the Andean mountains, where work, marriage, and ownership of land are based on a complex extended family structure, women can practice ceremonies only with their husbands.

In ancient religions as well as in tribal cultures, women have often been priestesses, prophetesses, visionaries, healers, and ritualists. Theology Professor Ursula King concludes:

> The earlier, more undifferentiated religions—whether prehistoric, archaic or tribal—all share a primal vision characterized by a unitary consciousness within which self, society and nature still form a continuum, an uninterrupted whole. The historical religions, with their breakthrough to individual, reflexive consciousness, lost this basic unity and are all shaped by a fundamental dualism affecting time (past/present; present/future) and space (sacred/profane), cosmos (earth/heaven), self (body/spirit) and society (men/women).[5]

Female Divinity

In indigenous beliefs, the sacred may be recognized as numinous, unnameable, fluid, beyond gender, permeating everything. If its aspects are thought to resemble male and female stereotypes, these aspects may not be seen as separate beings. The Mexica term for Creator is Ome Teotl—the dual principle of creation, which is at once male and female, negative and positive, light and dark.

Nevertheless, indigenous traditions are also filled with significant spiritual powers which are envisioned and named as feminine. The Dine (Navajo), Acoma Pueblo, and Lipan Apache of the southwestern region of the United States have a benevolent Creatrix, known as Changing Woman. The male gods may be capricious in their relationships with humans, but she is always kind. She is mysterious nonetheless, for she represents the process of continual change and rebirth—being young, and then old, and then young again. Girls' first menstruation is highly celebrated in these cultures, in her honor. It is she who brings the rain and also controls fertility or sterility, creating the people from pieces of her own skin. One of the ways in which many indigenous people understand the earth as our sacred Mother, Changing Woman is associated with the perpetual renewal of life, always restoring wholeness, peace, and healing. Her song: "I am the spirit within the earth ... all that belongs to the earth belongs to me. It is lovely indeed."[6]

Native womanist M. A. Jaimes Guerrero sees Changing Woman as a powerful female image for contemporary women, particularly those concerned with restoring biological diversity and indigenous people's sovereignty in their environments. Guerrero writes: "This creatrix is not only about present-day change in these fluctuating and transitional times for indigenous peoples and others, she is also about the restoration and renewal of Native women's rightful authority and leadership for a universal indigenous world view."[7]

Similarly, the Laguna Pueblo people honor a creatrix known as Tse che nako, Thought Woman. She is the power of intelligence and sacred order, bestowing blessings, appearing in many forms from the mesas and forests to the seas. Ascription of creative intelligence to a feminine spiritual power is an indication of the respect that Pueblo cultures in general give to women, who traditionally have shared power with men in Pueblo societies.

Another powerful feminine image among Native American peoples is White Buffalo Calf Woman, who established close relationships between the Lakota and the spirit world. Around 1780, the Lakota were hungry and troubled, for they had been forced out of their native woodlands around the Great Lakes by the Chippewa, who had French military support. The Lakota had migrated to the unfamiliar, treeless plains, enduring great hardships and becoming spiritually miserable. At this time of crisis, a female messiah appeared to two hunters. They had walked far from their camp in what is now South Dakota, searching for buffalo. The next part of the story illustrates the power that the Lakota attribute to women, and also the sexual frankness of many indigenous societies. As Manuel Red Bear tells the story:

They had been out for some time and had walked a whole day's distance from the village. Far out on the prairie, one of the young men saw something moving. It was too far away to see it clearly. As they approached they could see that it was a very beautiful young woman. She had very long white hair, and it covered her naked body like a robe. In her hands she carried sage, and on her back was a bundle. The two men were amazed at finding a young woman so far from any village. One of the young men said that this must be a *Wakan Win* [sacred or mysterious woman] to be out here all alone. He turned his eyes away, because she was naked and obviously Wakan.

Now the beautiful young woman was very close. The other young man thought, "I will have *tawi'nton* [sex] with this woman. There is no one to protect her, and I will have my way with her."

The woman was a sacred woman, and she could read his thoughts. She said, "Come ahead and do with me whatever it is that is in your mind."

Immediately the man with bad thoughts went forward, and the woman lay down with him. As soon as they lay down a mist descended from the sky and covered both of them. The other man fell to his knees in amazement. The sound of locusts came from that cloud, and when it lifted, the young woman was standing there unharmed, and all that was left of the bad man was his skeleton. Snakes slithered in his rib cage. Now the good man was very frightened.

The woman addressed him and said, "Do not be frightened; you are a good man, and you had good thoughts about me. To your village I will bring a sacred relic. Go now and tell them to prepare for me. I will come at first light with a great gift to make their lives easier."[8]

The woman did indeed come to the village, carrying a bundle. The people had nothing to offer her but water, so poor were they, but she accepted it. She then told them that she had come from the Buffalo Nation to give them sacred ways. So long as they followed her instructions, performed the ceremonies, and lived with respect for one another, they would never again go hungry. From her bundle, she gave them the sacred pipe and told them how to use it to communicate with the spirit world. She taught them the rituals of the Sun Dance, the vision quest, the sweat lodge, and the way of taking relatives. She cautioned the men to be respectful toward women, unlike the man with bad thoughts. She instructed the children to be good and obedient to their parents. And she taught the women not only how to be good mothers and grandmothers, but also how to perform important ceremonies: the rites for the dead, the coming-of-age ceremony for girls, and the Throwing of the Ball rite, so that young women's lives would be good. As she left, she rolled on the ground and became a buffalo. Not only do the Lakota still honor these rites today; the values inculcated by White Buffalo Calf Woman persist as the essence of a virtuous life. According to the story—which is at once allegorical but also considered true—she came at a time of great need and transformed the people's lives.

African female deities are less anthropomorphic, conceived as elemental energies, but also illustrate the awesome spiritual power attributed to women. Consider the turbulent goddess Oya, revered in West Africa and by descendants of West African slaves in the Americas. She manifests her force in strong winds, in tornados, in the powerful river Niger, in lightning and fire, in the buffalo. In male-dominated societies, she refuses to be intimidated; her magic is very effective. She is an untamed wife of the male god of thunder and kingship, Shango. The Yoruba portray her association with spirits of the dead by dancing in layer upon layer of strips of different kinds of cloth, all of which billow out wildly with the movement of the concealed dancer. Judith Gleason explains:

Although Oya is associated with pointed speech, most of what she's about is highly secret. Always vanishing, she presents herself in concealment. More abstractly, Oya is the goddess of edges, of the dynamic interplay between surfaces, of transformation from one state of being to another.... To describe and elaborate upon Oya's various manifestations is inevitably to present an idea not commonly thought of when the word *goddess* is mentioned. Oya's patterns, persisting through many media—from air to the human psyche—suggest

EXCERPT At the Center of All is Woman
Paula Gunn Allen

There is a spirit that pervades everything, that is capable of powerful song and radiant movement, and that moves in and out of the mind. The colors of this spirit are multitudinous, a glowing, pulsing rainbow. Old Spider Woman is one name for this quintessential spirit, and Serpent Woman is another. Corn Woman is one aspect of her, and Earth Woman is another, and what they together have made is called Creation, Earth, creatures, plants, and light.

At the center of all is Woman, and no thing is sacred (cooked, ripe, as the Keres Indians of Laguna Pueblo say it) without her blessing, her thinking... .

This spirit, this power of intelligence, has many names and many emblems. She appears on the plains, in the forests, in the great canyons, on the mesas, beneath the seas. To her we owe our very breath, and to her our prayers are sent blown on pollen, on corn meal, planted into the earth on feather-sticks, spit onto the water, burned and sent to her on the wind. Her variety and multiplicity testify to her complexity: she is the true creatrix for she is thought itself, from which all else is born. She is the necessary precondition for material creation, and she, like all of her creation, is fundamentally female—potential and primary.

She is also the spirit that informs right balance, right harmony, and these in turn order all relationships in conformity with her law.

To assign to this great being the position of "fertility goddess" is exceedingly demeaning; it trivializes the tribes and it trivializes the power of woman. Woman bears, that is true. She also destroys. That is true. She also wars and hexes and mends and breaks. She creates the power of the seeds, and she plants them... .

Contemporary Indian tales suggest that the creatures are born from the mating of sky father and earth mother, but that seems to be a recent interpolation of the original sacred texts. The revision may have occurred since the Christianizing influence on even the arcane traditions, or it may have predated Christianity. But the older, more secret texts suggest that it is a revision. It may be that the revision appears only in popular versions of the old mythic cycles on which ceremony and ritual are based; this would accord with the penchant in the old oral tradition for shaping tales to reflect present social realities, making the rearing and education of children possible even within the divergent worlds of the United States of America and the tribes.

According to the older texts (which are sacred, that is, power-engendering), Thought Woman is not a passive personage: her potentiality is dynamic and unimaginably powerful. She brought corn and agriculture, potting, weaving, social systems, religion, ceremony, ritual, building, memory, intuition, and their expressions in language, creativity, dance, human-to-animal relations, and she gave these offerings power and authority and blessed the people with the ability to provide for themselves and their progeny.

Thought Woman is not limited to a female role in the total theology of the Keres people. Since she is the supreme Spirit, she is both Mother and Father to all people and to all creatures. She is the only creator of thought, and thought precedes creation.

Central to Keres theology is the basic idea of the Creatrix as She Who Thinks rather than She Who Bears, of woman as creation thinker and female thought as origin of material and nonmaterial reality. In this epistemology, the perception of female power as confned to maternity is a limit on the power inherent in femininity… .

In Keres theology the creation does not take place through copulation. In the beginning existed Thought Woman and her dormant sisters, and Thought Woman thinks creation and sings her two sisters into life… . [They are] her coequals who possess the medicine power to vitalize the creatures that will inhabit the earth. They also have the power to create the frmament, the skies, the galaxies, and the seas, which they do through the use of ritual magic… .

Iyatiku, Corn Woman, the mother goddess of the Keres, who is called the mother of the people, is in a ceremonial sense another aspect of Thought Woman. She presently resides in Shipap [the spirit world of the dead] from whence she sends counsel to the people and greets them when they enter the spirit world of the dead. Her representative, Irriaku [Corn Mother], maintains the connection between individuals in the tribe as well as the connection between the nonhuman supernaturals and the tribe. It is through the agency of the Irriaku that the religious leaders of the tribe, called Yaya and Hotchin [Mother and leader or chief], are empowered to govern.

The Irriaku, like the Sacred Pipe, is the heart of the people as it is the heart of Iyatiku. In the form of the perfect ear of corn, Naiya Iyatiku [Mother, Chief] is present at every ceremony. Without the presence of her power, no ceremony can produce the power it is designed to create or release. These uses of the feminine testify that primary power—the power to make and to relate—belongs to the preponderantly feminine powers of the universe.

From Paula Gunn Allen, *The Sacred Hoop: Recovering the Feminine in American Indian Traditions*, Boston: Beacon Press, 1992, pp. 13–17.

something like a unified field theory of a certain type of energy that our culture certainly doesn't think of as feminine.[9] ▪

Listen to a traditional song sung by her votaries:

> Darkest forest, deepest obscurity
> which grabs and swallows you in the forest,
> Wind of Death
> tears the calabash, tears the bush.
> Shango's wife
> with her thumb tears out the intestines of the liar.
> Great Oya, yes.

Only she seizes the horns of the buffalo.
Only she confronts the returning dead... .

She burns like fire in the hearth, everywhere at once.
Tornado, quivering solid canopied trees
Great Oya, yes.
Whirlwind masquerader, awakening,
Courageously takes up her saber.[10]

The matrilineal Uzo people of the Niger River delta in West Africa honor a creatrix who has various names; sovereign queen, she gave birth to all humanity from her one breast. Ibibio women of southeastern Nigeria covertly worship the Great Mother who created all beings, including the great god of thunder. She is not spoken of publicly, but women's secret knowledge is that the dominant sex is female, not male.

In Africa, gendered concepts of divinity are elusive and varying. The cultures are themselves quite numerous and varied. But some analysts propose that African variations in gendered concepts of divinity reflect men's ambivalence about women's known power. Another explanation could be that sacred power is itself too elusive to be confined to any human categories. There is also the factor of changing sociopolitical environments. Some deities previously understood as female were transformed into males after contact with patriarchal European colonizers.

Women in Mythology

Given that indigenous cultures have extraordinarily rich treasuries of myths designed to clarify and order human relationships within society and within the cosmos, women inevitably figure prominently in the stories. Sometimes women's misbehavior is blamed for the sufferings of humanity, but in general, women are portrayed as powerful and often positive figures.

Women appear in many myths as cultivators of the soil. Among the Haudenosaunee (Iroquois), there is a traditional belief that the soil will bear fruit only if women are the farmers, for it is they who have the generative power and the most intimate relationship with the earth. Mohawks today pray thus:

We give greetings and thanks to our Mother the Earth—she gives us that which makes us strong and healthy. We are grateful that she continues to perform her duties as she was instructed. The women and Mother Earth are one—givers of life. We are her color, her flesh and her roots.[11]

Many traditional women of the Americas still grow three main crops together: corn, beans, and squash. To the Senecas of northern New York State, they are known as *Dio-he'-ko*, "our true sustenance." The three form a nutritionally balanced diet, and they also support each other ecologically: the beans grow up the corn stalks, and the squash provides ground cover to keep out weeds and retain moisture. Together they are known as the "three sisters," with the belief that they are protected by three spirit sisters who are not to be separated.

Likewise, women in many African tribal cultures provide the basic diet through gardening. Food cultivation—and thus life itself—is dependent on their power. Women's behavior affects plants, animals, and forests. Many stories reveal the important consequences—positive or negative—of woman's every action for the whole community, and thus attempt to shape women's lives so that disaster will not occur and the people will flourish. Not only the young and sensual, but also the old women are respected and even feared because of their magical power.

In this regard, Elder Lucy Swan tells a traditional Lakota story about the end of the world:

There is a very old woman who sits on the edge of a tall bluff. She is quilling a beautiful design on a buffalo robe. The woman is very old, so she tires easily. Beside her sits an ancient dog. He is so old that he has very few teeth. Even though he is old, he is still playful.

Every day the woman quills that buffalo robe. Soon she is tired and falls asleep. When she rests at night, the dog unravels all that she did the day before. If that dog forgets to unravel those quills, or gets too old, the old woman will finish the robe. That will be the end of the world.[12]

2.2 An Eastern Arrente Aboriginal woman contemplates symbols left by her ancestors in Australia's Northern Territory

Among some Australian Aborigines (fig. 2.2), there is a myth suggesting that originally only women had the power to perform sacred rituals, but the men stole it from them. The same myth suggests that women are hypersexual, for its two major protagonists are Sisters whose clitorises—seen as sacred emblems—are so long that they leave trails on the ground. Copulating with their brother, they produce so many children that they populate every place where they stop. Their brother advises that all boy infants should be set on the grass so that they will grow whiskers, but that girls should be covered with a mat to keep their bodies soft and hairless and to protect their sacredness. One day while the Sisters are looking for shells, the brother and their male progeny steal the Sisters' bags containing the sacred drawings and symbols of the Dreaming—the timeless period of Creation. They hear the men singing the sacred songs and fall to the ground, afraid. According to the myth:

They were fearful not of the men, but of the power of the sacred songs. The men had taken from them not only these songs, and the emblems, but also the power to perform sacred ritual, a power which had formerly belonged only to the Sisters. They had carried the emblems and dreamings in their *ngainmara*, which were really their uteri; and the men had had nothing.

The Two Sisters got up from the ground, and the younger one said to the elder, "What are we going to do? All our dilly bags are gone, all the emblems, all our power for sacred ritual!"

But the other replied, "I think we can leave that. Men can do it now, they can look after it. We can spend our time collecting bush foods for them, for it is not right that they should get that food as they have been doing. We know everything. We have really lost nothing, for we remember it all, and we can let them have that small part. For aren't we still sacred, even if we have lost the bags? Haven't we still our uteri?" And the younger Sister agreed with her.[13]

Shamans, Priestesses, Healers

The range of spiritual roles that women have traditionally held in Africa illustrates the common indigenous belief that women are highly spiritual people. In African tribes, women may be priestesses devoted to worship of the deities, mediums for the spirits to speak to the people, diviners forecasting the future, singers of the songs of the spirit, and healers. These roles are often considered especially appropriate since women are thought to be particularly open to spirit possession.

Although all women may be thought to have potential spiritual power in indigenous cultures, there are those who have vastly developed their access to the unseen forces and use that connection to help the people. The call comes to them spiritually to take on this role, and women may accept it only reluctantly, for to be an intermediary between physical and spiritual realms is very demanding, self-sacrificial, and even dangerous. The patterns of their calling and their work are similar around the world, so the same word, shaman, is commonly used to refer to them. The word comes from the Tungusian language of Siberia, where the work of shamans is very ancient and still prevalent today (see box, p. 49).

A shaman may be either female or male. If a woman, she will often wait until the menopause to accept her calling, for her spiritual power is so potent during menstruation that it may cause problems. Usually she is "ordinary" in other ways, continuing to carry on her worldly responsibilities. But being a shaman gives a woman considerable status and freedom, even in otherwise male-dominated cultures such as those of Korea. Among the Mapuche of Chile, the shamans were mostly males when the culture was centered on hunting and war. But since the Mapuche became settled agriculturalists during the last century, most of the shamans are now females, presiding at rituals alongside the male lineage chiefs.

A shaman often works by combining traditional methods with those revealed to her by her spirit helpers, using her own sacred paraphernalia (fig. 2.3). A *Yuwipi* healing ceremony conducted by a Plains Indian holy woman usually begins with a period of fasting and her own spiritual purification in a sweat lodge, in which very high temperatures are provided by heated rocks. Then, either in the sweat lodge or inside the totally darkened house, she marks off the area from which she will contact the spirits, surrounding it with strings of hundreds of small bundles of tobacco and honoring the four directions. She constructs an altar for articles such as prayer pipes brought by the people, horsehair, feathers, shells, and stones, according to her visions.

The person to be healed sits opposite the medicine woman and other family and community members line the walls. All present are "smudged" with the purifying smoke of burning herbs such as sage and sweetgrass. In a bed of sand, the holy woman may draw a design representing a spirit helper, a dream, or the patient. Joining her pipe's stem and bowl, she fills it and offers it to the four winds, the Creator, the sky, and the Mother Earth. Then she explains to the people how her spirit helpers came to her, apologizes for being merely human, and asks the grandfather spirits to forgive her if she makes any mistakes as she attempts to serve as an opening for the spirits. Attendants then tie her thoroughly, with her hands behind her back and blankets covering her body. Thus wrapped and tied, she is laid on a bed of sage leaves. According to her previous instruc-tions, songs are sung with accompaniment of drum and perhaps rattle, to ask for blessings and to invite the spirits. After the people repeatedly sing "Somebody I am singing to is coming… He is coming now," the spirits begin to appear in the darkened space as small blue sparks of light and perhaps the sounds of animals. The patient prays earnestly, while the medicine woman communicates with the

2.3 Isabel Case Borgatta's sculpture *Jaguar Woman* suggests the spiritual power of an indigenous woman associated with her totem animal

spirits. Everyone present is invited to add their prayers for the patient and any other requests they may have. Preferably, they will include the whole of creation, and will end their prayer with the phrase *Mitakuye' Oyasin* ("All my relations").

After the holy woman is untied, she relates what the spirits have said, giving the prognosis for the patient and any instructions for what more should be done. She thanks the spirits and allows them to leave. The sacred pipes are lit and passed around for all present to puff on ritually. Then everyone shares in a feast offered by the patient's family. Tilda Long Soldier and Mark St. Pierre describe the medicine woman's major functions in such ceremonies:

> 1) She has led her people through the entire set of rituals; 2) she has, through personal sacrifice—the sweat, fasting, and being wrapped up—put her reputation and her spiritual well-being on the line; 3) she has achieved a trancelike state; and 4) through that state she has become the instrument of healing and sacred communication. It is her desire, through this ritual, to return the patient back to spiritual balance and harmony. Using methods like these, Indian doctors have cured all manner of disease, from mental problems to cancer.[14]

In contrast to the self-sacrificing life of a true shaman, some contemporary women and men advertise themselves as medicine people but seem to be motivated purely by the desire for money and fame. They are accused by Native tribes of selling pieces of their traditions for profit to non-indigenous people who are fascinated with Native spiritual ways. These pseudo-shamans charge money for their workshops and other offerings, and sometimes earn a good living doing so. The Center for the SPIRIT (Support and Protection of Indian Religions and Indigenous Traditions) maintains that there are well-documented instances of people claiming to be medicine men or women of a particular tribe and charging people vast amounts of money for two weeks of experience in presumably Native teachings, whereas the officially designated speakers for the various tribes are able to refute these claims with some firmness. Ojibwa spokeswoman Lenore Keeshig-Tobias cautions:

> Each tribe has their own unique ways which only they can fully understand. Each tribe has their own sacred ceremonies, songs, dances and prayers which form their own tribal religious ways. These come from each tribe's history, science, environment and all the things which make up our different cultures. I am Ponca because of over 10,000 years of intermingling the lives, blood and history of my tribe upon Ponca land. Every movement and action is blessed with a meaning handed down by generations of ancestors and held within our tribal memory.
>
> I say these things because I want to warn people about some bad things happening to traditional ways. All across Indian country, in every city and state, white people are commercializing Lakota ceremonies. Our ways cannot be bought and sold like bibles. No knowledge, no science, no language, no culture is involved in their pitiful mockery of traditional ways... .
>
> It is time we who value old ways begin to explain to our non-Indian guests that our basic philosophy of respect for the circle of life is opening to the under-

INTERVIEW Maria Amanchina *Siberian Shaman*

In southern Siberia there is a pristine mountainous area known as Altai. Many Russians feel that this area has a special spiritual role for the whole of humanity. Traditional spiritual ways of honoring the spiritual forces in nature are still being practiced there to a certain extent. Before the Revolution of 1917, destructive use of spiritual power had co-existed with positive uses of shamanism, so shaman-istic ways were totally outlawed during Soviet years. Nevertheless, in every village there remained an old woman or old man secretly healing the people and help-ing them in their relationships with the spirits. After *perestroika* in the 1990s, these healers revealed themselves again and began helping the people openly once more.

Among these contemporary Altai shamans, one of the most powerful and well-loved is Maria Amanchina. She was born near the Mongolian border in 1958. Her parents, who were sixth-generation shamans, died when she was a small child. From time to time she had strange visions but did not share them with anyone. Often she felt sick for no apparent reason. When she was 14, she had a lung disease, so serious that she spent a long time in the hospital and nearly died. In the spring she went with some classmates to an old woman for help in passing their examinations. Looking at the young Maria, the woman said, "You are special. You saved yourself, but you are very ill. Come to me again tomorrow and bring your nightgown and a needle with a thread. I will help you, and your diseases will leave you." When Maria came back, the woman blew on the needle and it turned red. She told Maria to fnd the skin of a hare in the chest of her family's old belongings. Maria belongs to the Telyos/Telengit tribe, whose sacred protector is the hare. To the girl's surprise, the skin was there. The woman told her always to keep it as a talisman.

When Maria was nineteen, another old Altai woman told her that she had a powerful gift for healing and needed to develop it in order to help the people, but Maria had never had any such intentions. From time to time, strange images or happenings bothered her, but she decided to ignore them.

Trying to live a normal life, Maria trained as a tailor, married, and gave birth to a son. Her husband then died. Maria is an attractive woman, and many men pursued her. She remarried but then divorced, for the marriage was not happy.

At the age of 32, Maria and some friends went to another old Altai healer to seek her help with their health problems. The old woman asked Maria to leave and to return alone the next day, bringing the hare skin with her. When Maria came, the old woman told her that she was to be a healer, and said, "You know what to do. Listen to your heart and your guardians and come to me again in three years." Not heeding this advice, within a year Maria fell very sick again. This time she went to Kalkin, a storyteller, visionary, and clairvoyant who is respected throughout Altai. Although he is almost blind, he had seen everything in his inner vision, and explained that her illness was a special sign for her. He blessed her, saying, "You are chosen. The coming times will be very difficult for people. Many of them will need your help as a healer and a shaman. The more you help people, the stronger you will become. It was easier in our time. There is much darkness nowadays. Be careful." He gave her a bunch of sacred Altai heather and *tyaikh*, sacred white and yellow ribbons. Since then, they have always been on her altar.

Being blessed by Kalkin, Maria recognized at last that she had no other choice but to heal and protect the people of Altai. She realized why she had been sick in her younger years: she could not protect herself from people's diseases and did not know what to do with her own power. As she began to use it, no one taught her how to heal. She had seen how the old women in the village worked, and she followed the inner guidance of her spiritual helpers. She also followed the traditional shamanic way of protecting people and their homes by going from village to village during September and May at the people's invitation, putting *tyaikhs* in their houses for protection and helping them with their problems.

The first patient whom Maria healed was a woman whose case was so serious that the doctors refused to keep her in the hospital because they had no way to cure her. Maria concentrated on the woman, put her hands above her, and then, as she says, "I scanned all the information of her body. I realized what could help her and found the reason for the illness."

2.4 Maria Amanchina, Siberian shaman, and her healing hut

Another early case was a boy with epilepsy. The boy's mother was so grateful when the boy became strong and completely healthy that she did not know how to thank Maria. The boy's father thus brought a sheep to Maria as a gift. The Altai people believe in Maria's power and come to her with very serious problems. Maria says, "I am sure that if I do not help people I will fall ill again." She possesses such great energy that she must spend it helping the people.

The Altai people live according to the natural rhythms of the sun and the moon. Dozens of people come to Maria on the frst days of the new moon, especially the fourth day, which is considered the most powerful for healing. No one comes during the last days of the old moon, for they are sure that bad energies are stronger on those days. People usually bring her water from a sacred spring. Maria studies the water for some time and then begins to tell them about the problems and life situation of the person, for water is thought to keep information. Or she might instead scan the person with her inner vision to get the information. Often she asks the people to bring a few simple things for the healing, and then whispers a prayer over them. She was baptized in the Russian Orthodox Church when she was 40, and she appeals to Christ for help along with the native Altai deities and nature spirits.

Normally communicative, sometimes Maria sits away from the people, watching a river or a mountain, and at these times, no one dares to disturb her. She may later explain the knowledge she received from the spirits of the place about events that occurred in the area and the people who lived there long ago. Often she performs a special ceremony to worship the spirits of the place, giving them small gifts and speaking to them.

She says of her ways of working, "Nobody can explain the essence of shamanism. God created us shamans to help those in need. It is impossible to teach anyone how to heal people. True shamans are those who are not taught by human beings but get knowledge from God, from nature. They have invisible helpers who do a lot of work for them in forecasting the future, healing, and so on. Every person has a guardian angel, and we deal with them."

"Every plant, every tree, every mountain and river is watching us people. They are expecting love and care from us, for they love us. Their spirits expect respect from us. Altai is the place where different dimensions are very close and interact with each other easily."

Maria Amanchina, from an interview by Galina Ermolina, September 2002.

standing of all races. But if our tribal ceremonies are to survive with meaning and dignity for our children, we must explain to the *wasoci* [white-skinned people] that it is not necessary for them to pretend to be Indian to understand the nature of the circle. How can Lakota children find the same respect for tribal ways our grandfathers handed down to us if hundreds of these pitiful ones are out waving pipes, pouring water, singing songs learned from cassettes and whipping a drum?[15] ■

Women's Rituals

Whereas shamans are individuals called by the spirit and may be either women or men, in many indigenous societies there are certain ceremonies or **rituals** (religious or solemn rites carried out in a prescribed order) that are performed only by women. Among the Lakota, it is women who are responsible for conducting the ceremonies for the dead. They carry out their rituals in a humorous way, feeling that the dead are present and wanting them to enjoy themselves. Women are given this role because it is felt that they are better able to bridge the gap between the living and the spirit world.

In Central America, too, most of the death rites are carried out by older women. Since deceased ancestors can harm their living descendants—can even bring disease and death—it is extremely important that they should be appeased properly. Usually it is the daughters and granddaughters of the dead who must arrange offerings and ceremonies for them. These obligations may last up to fifty years. The big feasts arranged by the women are, as among the Lakota, rather lighthearted, so that the dead as well as the living may enjoy them. The women work collectively, forming a network of support that can best be commanded by older women. After a lifetime of evidence these elders are the most convinced of the value of placating the ancestors. At the end of the obligatory initial period of mourning, which may last up to a year, the bereaved women and their supporters are dunked fully clothed into the sea. When they return home, other women tear their mourning dresses off them, and they then dress in bright colors to mark the end of official mourning. But still they must be alert to any demands from the dead for additional offerings.

In Yoruba society, strong patriarchal rule is somewhat transcended in secret societies of priestesses (fig. 2.5) devoted to various divinities, or *orisha*. The *orisha* themselves are elemental forces that may be considered male, female, or non-gendered, and their votaries may be either female or male. A woman who is a spiritual initiate of a male *orisha* may be spiritually possessed by that deity and may bring messages from him to the people. When this happens, she speaks in his voice, and people must refer to her as "he." She/he commands great respect at such a time; in addition, members of the secret societies of priestesses are not to be hurt or offended by any man. Groups of women also dance through the village during special night ceremonies, acting as messengers of the *orisha* in boldly singing songs exposing the wrongdoings of members of the community. These women are immune from retribution for their critical songs and dances, for the *orisha* are happy that they are maintaining social order. Some of these Yoruba traditions are being preserved not only in Africa but also in the African Diaspora (dispersal of a people round the world) in the Americas, as we will see in Chapter 9.

Australian aboriginal societies are strictly segregated as to sex, and the female camps are run by older women who are respected ritual leaders. They live together because they have the independence of being either divorced, separated, or widowed. These older women are the carriers of the traditional knowledge, which they pass down to the younger generations despite the disruptions of modernization, and through their rituals they attempt to maintain proper relationships among the people and with the land. Ethnographer Diane Bell reports:

2.5 Madame Tano, a priestess from the Ivory Coast, Africa, enters a spirit possession trance, supported by her assistants

Through their *yawulyu* (land-based ceremonies) they nurture land; through their health and curing rituals they resolve conflict and restore social harmony; and through *yilpinji* (love rituals) they manage emotions. In *yilpinji*, as in their health-oriented *yawulyu*, women seek to resolve and to explore the conflicts and tensions which beset their communities. In centers of population concentration where Aborigines now live, jealous fights, accusations of infidelity, and illicit affairs occur on a scale impossible a century ago when people lived in small mobile bands. Thus today, women's role in the domain of emotional management, like their role in the maintenance of health and harmony, is truly awesome.[16]

Genital Surgery

Given the perceived power of women, many cultures have made efforts to contain and shape it. In various countries around the world, including some areas of Africa, females of various ages undergo some form of genital surgery—sometimes referred to as "female circumcision"—often under nonhygienic conditions that may result in infections, hemorrhages, the spread of AIDS, or loss of sexual feeling. Western feminists have sensationalized this practice as a *cause célèbre*, trying to bring international pressure to outlaw what they are calling "genital mutilation," but some African women object that they do not understand the cultures in which they are trying to interfere and that they may be doing more harm than good. Nonetheless, there are also quieter efforts by local African women to eradicate the practice.

Forms of genital surgery range from symbolic piercing or removal of the hood of the clitoris to total removal of the clitoris and/or partial stitching together of the labia (infibulation) to prevent intercourse. The operation may take place as a group ritual involving girls who are too young to judge independently what is happening to them, or it may be chosen by adult women as a form of self-assertion or even sado-masochism. Mothers who have their daughters operated on seem to share a loving belief that the operation is beneficial and even necessary, just as do Western mothers who have their infant sons circumcised. When performed as a group ritual, female genital surgery is part of a series of ceremonies that are thought to establish social roles, beliefs, and cultural preservation. Often there is the implication of controlling women's sexuality by removing one of the main sources of their sexual pleasure. However, women may choose the operation as a sign of chastity to enhance their chances of marriage, to enhance their beauty (if the genitalia are considered ugly), to make the area easier to clean and thus improve hygiene, or to exercise some control over use of their bodies.

It is difficult to generalize about the motivations of those involved, since many African women are culturally constrained from talking about their sexuality, particularly with outsiders. From the perspective of a male scholar of African religions, Professor John Mbiti says that the Nandi people of East Africa regard female genital surgery as a sacred initiation into womanhood. He writes:

> It is believed that if a girl is not initiated, her clitoris will grow long and have branches; and that children of uninitiated women would become abnormal.... Unless a person has been through the ceremony she really is "nobody," "incomplete" and still a "child." In an atmosphere of corporate existence, it is literally impossible for anyone to miss such a ceremony and get away with it. Sooner or later she would become the laughing stock of her relatives and neighbours, and any misfortune befalling her or her family would be attributed to the "missing link" in her ritual growth.... It is a rite of maturation, a dramatization of the break with childhood and incorporation into adulthood. The sex organ is the symbol of life; and cutting it is like unlocking the issues of life, so that thereafter there may be an unblocked flow of life.... Through the initiation ceremony of both girls and boys, the corporate life of the nation is revived, its rhythm is given a new momentum, and its vitality is renewed.[17]

Whatever may be the motivation, the whole society, including the women, commonly participate in this ritual surgery for girl children. In addition to the explanations given above, there are some who say that this initiation prepares women to bear the pain of childbirth. Mercy Amba Oduyoye of Nigeria speaks of Africa as a hostile world continually engaged in a struggle against death, producing communities willing to inflict pain on children to toughen them. Female genital surgery is not simply a manifestation of **misogyny** (hostility to women); boys are also subjected to painful and terrifying initiation rites including circumcision. To survive in the culture, women are trained to be submissive and uncomplaining, in the name of spirituality. The pain suffered by the girl is marginalized, and she learns that her body does not belong to her. Oduyoye questions how this can be considered spirituality:

■ I have come to understand spirituality as "externalizing" the anger and the hurt so that one might look them in the face, say "NO" to them, and thereby be filled with power to struggle for transformation. It is what enables one to break the silence that makes continued dehumanization possible. Spirituality has nothing to do with the perpetration or the acceptance of death and evil.[18] ■

Beginning in 1996, families in some Kenyan villages have replaced female genital surgery with a verbal ceremony, "cutting through words." For one week, young girls are secluded together, and given lessons about their roles as women, hygiene, health, reproduction, self-esteem, and communication skills. At the end of the week, the whole community celebrates the girls' graduation into womanhood. However, this alternative to the physical practice of female genital surgery is as yet unacceptable to many people and many communities. Moralistic campaigns to eradicate the practice are ineffective; only when groups of neighboring villages pledge not to carry out the operations can families be confident that there will be a sufficient pool of men willing to marry their daughters. Otherwise, an "uncircumcised" daughter may be unmarriageable. This situation arises not only among tribal peoples; it is also an issue in some Muslim communities.

Rites for First Menstruation

All indigenous cultures celebrate the landmark time when a girl has her first menstrual period and thus is considered a woman rather than a child, for she has become biologically ready for childbearing. Typically the rites involve a period of seclusion during the menstrual period. Outsiders have interpreted this seclusion as a negative custom growing out of a horror of menstrual blood and the conviction that a menstruating woman is unclean. But these days many feminists are offering different, more positive interpretations of menstrual seclusion and taboos.

Among certain Australian Aborigines, when a girl begins menstruating she is secluded with other women. Rituals are performed in a sacred manner, for the menstrual blood itself is considered sacred, as ordained by the mythical Sisters. When the new woman emerges at the end of her period, she is taken to water at sunrise and the other women duck and splash her playfully. They then paint her body and lead her triumphantly to the community, with an older woman clowning, dancing, and joking in the rear of the procession. Her mother cries as her daughter steps over a row of food, marking her transition to womanhood. Then, as is befitting a woman, the initiate distributes the food.

Navajo people also consider first menstruation a sacred time, created to make intercourse "holy and effective, as the Holy People wanted it to be." They tell the story of Changing Woman, for whom the Holy People arranged a special ceremony when she came of age:

■ At this time, the Holy People were living on the earth. They came to her ceremony, and many of them sang songs for her. They did this so that she would be holy and so she could have children who would be human beings with enough sense to think of themselves and a language with which to understand each other.[19] ▪

For the Mescalero Apache who live in what is now New Mexico, the loving and complex eight-day ceremony that follows a girl's menarche is a vehicle for spiritual blessings and renewal for the whole community and an inspiring introduction for the girl to her spiritual strength and potential as a woman. During the ceremonies, she temporarily becomes the major goddess Isanaklesh and, as such, bestows blessings upon the people. Ever after, she can draw on the qualities of the goddess that have been awakened within herself. Isanaklesh's very name means "Woman of Earth." Covered with life-giving pollen, she is beautiful, kind, wise, and full of spiritual power, or *diye*, which she can use for healing and protecting the people. Through the ceremony, a woman learns how to carry spiritual leadership in her family and community and to live by the virtues that will keep the community alive and harmonious. As Ines M. Talamantez explains: "After her ceremony, she will be a keeper of Apache traditions and the pattern of everyday living in which they will continue to endure. Thus she is not only taught and protected by this ceremony; like Isanaklesh, who gave it, she will also teach and protect her tribe."[20]

The seclusion of a menstruating woman is in many societies considered very important, for her spiritual power is thought to be dangerous during her period. Maria Chona, a traditional member of the Papago culture of the American Southwest, explains common beliefs:

▪ Girls are very dangerous at that time. If they touch a man's bow, or even look at it, that bow will not shoot any more. If they drink out of a man's bowl, it will make him sick. If they touch the man himself, he might fall down dead. My mother had told us this long ago and we knew what had happened in our village.

There was a girl once who became dangerous and she did not tell. They were having a good time that day. All the village was planting in her father's field, and he had given them a meal of succotash. They were eating out in the field, her mother was cooking over a campfire. My mother was there and she said this girl was standing with a bowl in the crook of her arm, laughing and eating. It began to rain. The girl and her sisters ran home to take in the bedding, because we sleep out of doors in the summer and it was on the ground.

There was a crash of thunder. All the eating people stood still and then, from the house of that girl they heard a long sigh. They ran there. All the family were lying stunned on the floor, one sister was blind, and that girl was dead. The men dragged the people out into the rain and the house began to burn. "See," said those people, "what has happened to us." Her relatives buried that girl all alone and no one would go near.... That is why, when the lightning strikes a village, they send for the medicine man to see what woman was dangerous.... They do not punish that woman. It is enough to know that she has killed her friends.[21] ▪

Given such stories about the disasters caused by contact with the spiritual power of menstruating women, in indigenous societies there is generally a hut or lodge of some sort where they can live privately for the duration of their periods. This is not a punishment. Many women actually relish the retreat, particularly since it is often a time of enhanced spiritual sensitivity.

Reclaiming Ancestral Roots

Indigenous women in many cultures are making progress in attaining new levels of ritual participation and leadership, in restoring women's rituals, in uncovering women's religious past in the tradition, and in teaching the religious tradition to new generations. Among Native Americans, for instance, women have helped to take over the Native schools and install Native curricula, imagery, and teachers. They have also helped to establish new higher educational institutions. The Lakota-based Sinte Gleska University, for instance, has a female majority on its Board of Regents.

In the attempt to reclaim their own identities, numerous women in industrial societies are making efforts to rediscover the spiritual ways of their indigenous foremothers. Luanna Neff of Hawaii, who has learned to use traditional chants in her native language, explains:

I went back to tradition. It was actually given to me as gifts, many years ago. To utilize traditional chants today and make them, not valid, but continuous, so that they are used properly, has been the most challenging and the most beautiful thing for me in my own evolution and in understanding the importance of ritual and protocol and connection to your spirituality. In Hawaiian, our chants are not merely song—they are power. The power of the word, the sacredness of sound, may be able to tap into that Source, as a resource to heal land, people, places. For instance, there is a powerful prayer of healing for the land, and it applies to human beings as well. It is a prayer that evokes the idea of clearing chaos, decay, mildew, corruption, things of those sorts, and their being replaced with new shoots, new blossoms that come together and intertwine and are able to grow together.[22]

African-American women are likewise learning to value their foremothers and their spiritual wisdom, suppressed among slaves in the Americas. Music has become one vehicle for this process. Sweet Honey in the Rock is an *a cappella* singing group (voices without accompaniment) composed of women of the African Diaspora. When singing among audiences of black women, Sweet Honey invites them into a ritual communication process in which they will feel safe exploring their cultural and gender identities. One of their songs, called "Breaths," includes these lyrics:

> Those who have died have never ever left
> The dead have a pact with the living
> They are in the mother's breast
> They are in the wailing child

> They are with us in our homes
> They are with us in a crowd
> The dead have a pact with the living.[23]

Quite a few contemporary women whose ancestors are from indigenous cultures claim to have been contacted by the deities recognized by those cultures and to be acting and speaking on their behalf. Nana Okomfohene Korantemaa Ayeboafo traveled to Ghana as a singer with the Arthur Hall Afro-American Dance Ensemble in 1974. As she was dancing with the troupe at a traditional shrine, she reportedly became possessed by a spiritual force and began to speak the Twi language of that area and to dance in their traditional way. Thereafter, she returned to the shrine for seven years to learn the language and traditions of the indigenous people. Then she studied for 20 years with the matriarch Nana Okomfohene Akua Oparebea, who before passing away at the age of 95 transferred her sacred baton to Nana Korantemaa. She says that her mission is to reconnect African Americans with their African family, after centuries of separation and oppression. The chief medium for this work is drumming and dancing under spiritual inspiration.

Similarly, Audri Scott Williams (Nana Akua Sebu) says she receives guidance from her spirit guides, the Grandmothers of the Four Directions. She inspired a small group of people with African and Native American roots to undertake a 64-day hike along the Appalachian Trail, retracing their ancestors' paths along the Underground Railroad and Cherokee Trail of Tears escape routes into the mountains. One of the pilgrims in this "Trail of Dreams," Lenett Nefertiti Myrick, speaks of how they were led by their inner voices rather than by any practical knowledge of how to proceed:

> We were inexperienced hikers with a teaspoon of camping experience between us and not a clue as to what lay ahead, except some mountains and maybe some bears and snakes… . Yet we walked to help our youth remember to dream the dreams that evolve humanity to a higher state of being. We walked to remember our connection with Mother Earth and all our forgotten relations living in the wild. We walked with gratitude, humility, and awe of our ancestors' inexplicable strength.[24]

Under the same inspiration, a group from the African Diaspora traveled from the United States to Ghana, Burkina Faso, and Mali to speak with the indigenous elders and visit the infamous Door of No Return, through which slaves were shipped from their homeland. There, Audri Scott Williams wanted to unleash her anguish and rage against those Africans and Europeans who ripped her ancestors out of Africa and enslaved them, denying their humanity, tearing them away from their cultural roots, destroying their families. But, instead, she experienced the awakening of unconditional love. She says:

> I didn't want to feel it wash over me like the waves rolling onto the sand below me. And yet, it came … slowly, gently, calmly, rocking me in her bosom, giving me permission to feel all that I felt and to usher in the divine spark that gives those moments purpose, my purpose. Right there I committed myself

to be a servant warrior for world peace because, in truth, all the pain and suffering that crept into my consciousness in the slave dungeons was made more profound. Because in my heart I knew and I know that all around the world atrocities are being played out against humanity. Women and children suffer unspeakable violence. People of color are disproportionately afflicted with disease, starvation and unemployment. Religious wars claim lives in the most unmerciful ways. There is much work to be done.

I will forever carry Africa in my heart because I found there the true measure of my heart's capacity for love of life, all life. And now I can never turn my back on our atrocities. I can only walk head first into the mire with love and compassion.[25] ■

Healing of the Planet and the People

Indigenous women everywhere are receiving visions that our planet Earth is in trouble and that indigenous spirituality can help to heal its wounds of environmental destruction and cultural violence. The indigenous peoples have been directly affected by these problems, as victims of genocide and as anguished observers of the ill health of the plants and animals and waters in their environment.

The indigenous people of Aoetearoa, New Zealand, identify themselves by naming their mountain, their river, their land, their tribal and subtribal communities. Te Urutahi Waikerepuru explains the importance of this identity:

■ Knowing these things helps to bring about and to keep together the healing, the wellbeing of our people. We have suffered the loss of our lands, our connection to the land. We belong to the mountains, to the sea, to the forest.

Colonization in the 1800s brought a dominant culture which has systematically taken over the land. With the loss of the land, there has been a tremendous alienation from who we are. As a people we are currently in a renaissance, in a reclamation of regaining our cultural identity, our land, our traditional practices, our healing methods, because without these things we become a lost people, we become invisible, we become submerged into the dominant culture. The loss of the land is a loss to us as guardians and as protectors of the land. We are not owners of the land. The connection we had to the land was a spiritual connection. ■

Despite the assault on their identities and traditional lifeways, the people somehow retained their deepest spiritual value: the power of love. Te Urutahi Waikerepuru goes on to tell a story of a place in New Zealand called Hollyhocka:

■ In 1880, Hollyhocka was opposed by a colonizing group, who sent the militia to annihilate the community. A cannon was brought forward, and the soldiers were there in their strength. All we had left at that time were women and children, because our men had already been taken away. We were left with only old men, women, and children. They went out to the gate and they stood facing the

INTERVIEW Luanna Neff *Healing a Bombed Hawaiian Island*

My practice for the last twenty years has been to heal the land of Kaholawe. This is the current name of that island; it means "the taking." The traditional name for that island is "the shining beacon," "the shining vagina." The symbolism behind taking care of that place, that baby, that womb, that sacred area that has been desecrated, has been the most incredibly healing force for women. The idea of a nation has been built behind taking care of that place.

In 1941, when World War II started [when America entered], the military declared martial law and took off the island all the families that were there—for the purpose of national defence, and to use that place for target practice. So from 1943 up until 1992 or 1993, they bombed that island continuously. All the Pacifc Rim nations were invited to come do target practice there. So there is every kind of ordnance that you can think of on that island.

It has been an incredible practice and challenge for me to keep up with the ceremonies, to put them in line, to utilize them. The ceremonies have been able not only to assist deeply in healing that place, but defnitely also healing our people. It has brought every walk of life together to share in that healing process. There is a group of us who have come to participate in that healing, because it is also symbolic of their understanding, their connection to the land.

Our plants are thriving, and they're all the native Hawaiian plants that we planted there. And not just that we planted—all the old ones that had lain dormant for many years are coming out now on their own. Plant species that we have not seen for many, many, many years are beginning to thrive again. The grasses, all our traditional plants that were used for medicinal purposes as well, are coming back and thriving. And because our ceremonies are based on healing, according to the laws of the land and the environment, we have gods that go along with the process of healing as well. There are four major deities, each with three or four months out of the year in which the energy of that particular deity is thriving. It's a co-creative process.

We stopped the target practice, through the ceremonies and through getting the Congress and our Senators and the political side of this entire struggle to finally come to an agreement that not only did the bombing need to stop—they needed to clean it up as well. We were allotted lots of money to assist in that cleanup of the ordnance off the island, their own exploded bombs. They have far from cleaned it up. They have spent every single last $400 million in a period of three years. It showed us that it is not about the money. It's about the commitment, it's about dedication, it's about something that comes much deeper. You can change the world. The money will come when it needs to, however it needs to, but it need not come. It needs the people. It needs the interaction of the people. And we can do that with our spirits. It was a beautiful hard lesson.

We have a matrilineal society. We went through a lot after the Contact [with colonizers] and yet the tradition still carries through, that core of it—the core of who we are as woman, and our participation and role within society as the one who nourishes. We are the keepers of the sacred sites. The women do that, and the men do, too. They have their own style. Traditionally, the men did the laborious physical work and gathered the deep sea fish, and the women gathered the reef fish and the shellfish on the rocks, and the vegetables. We had a very intricate balance between male and female, and we both had love and respect for each other. From royalty to the common person, everyone had a voice. Everyone had a function. Everyone had a purpose, from the children to the grandparents. They were intricately connected to each other and connected to the land that they lived on.

There came a time, a dark period, which we survived—I am so happy to say— and we are still growing and evolving, putting things in place so we have a solid foundation again. Not that it was ever lost, but it was forgotten for a little while. Now we are in a time where the earth is massively changing, and we are reclaiming our identity, our land, our culture, our traditions. We have always been an evolving people. We have always accepted the best of anything that has ever greeted us on those islands. We are an island state. We are seafaring people who have traveled around the world. We have an intelligence that goes beyond intellect, an intelligence that is deep in knowing, and very connected. It is prevalent in our school systems now, in our forms of government which are changing. The state is actually waiting for us to form our national body so that we may have a body in which to govern ourselves and a voice that is more on an equal basis than how it has been.

I know it looks like a long way to go, but the seeds are all there. And this is the time. We have a prophecy: That which is above will be brought down, that which is below will rise up. And here we are.

Luanna Neff, personal communication, October 2002.

cannon. They sang and they danced, and they gave messages of love to the enemy. The cannon did not go off that day. The soldiers came down from their positions and they were taken by the women and the elders and the children, to partake of a banquet inside the community complex. Such was the strength of love that was shown by the people to the enemy. The symbol of white feathers worn by our people is a symbol of peace. We have many other traditional ways of seeking reconciliation, conflict resolution. The one that works for us is the one of love. And as a people we are working toward bringing it to fruit.[26]

Many indigenous people feel a deep spiritual responsibility toward the places where their ancestors lived and where their bodies were buried. Maria Amanchina, the Altai shaman, believes that one of her duties is to revive the sacred places of the Altai, so that they will again give energy to the people, healing and protecting them. The land of Altai is rich in springs whose waters are considered sacred and healing, as well as sacred spots that are thought to attract positive cosmic energies to the planet. Maria continually advises the people to take care of the graves of their ancestors there. After the mummified body of the "Altai Princess" (see Chapter 1, p. 27) was removed by archaeologists to a museum in Novosibirsk, calamities began to befall the Altai region. Maria has tried to convince the museum to return the "Princess," for many local people feel that she was actually a great shaman who protected the land and people. Maria was allowed to sit near the body in the museum for two hours, and then reportedly removed part of her soul and took it back to Altai, releasing the spirit at a sacred spring. However, she says the Princess tells her that if her body is not soon taken back to her native Altai, there will be strange diseases throughout the world. Indigenous people who receive such spirit messages are working hard, both in spiritual and in worldly ways, to get the artifacts and remains of their ancestors out of museums and back to their resting places.

The relationship between the land and the indigenous people is so intimate and reciprocal that for the sake of cultural survival, these peoples feel they must concern themselves with environmental protection as well as return of their lands, artifacts, and ancestors. Biodiversity, the naturally variegated ecosystem, is as essential for spiritual health as it is for ecological health. Some native women blame patriarchy for colonization and for rape of the land; they feel that, as Paula Gunn Allen asserts, bringing back "ritual, spirit-centered, woman-focused world-views" will bring "life-affirming social change that can result in a real decrease in human and planetary destruction and in a real increase in quality of life for all inhabitants of planet earth."[27]

Key Terms

shaman	ritual
matrilineal, matrilinearity	*orisha*
matrilocality	misogyny
matrifocality	

Suggested Reading

Allen, Paula Gunn, *The Sacred Hoop: Recovering the Feminine in American Indian Traditions*, Boston: Beacon Press, 1986, 1992. A classic, though sometimes over-positive, celebration of Native American womanism.

Beck, Peggy V. and Anna L. Waters, *The Sacred: Ways of Knowledge, Sources of Life*, Tsaile (Navajo Nation), Arizona: Navajo Community College Press, 1977. Realistic introduction to indigenous ways in North America.

Bell, Diane, *Daughters of the Dreaming*, 2nd edn., North Melbourne, Australia: Spinifex Press, 1993. Classic of engaged anthropological research of a feminist scholar who lived among Australian Aboriginal women to try to understand their ways.

Gleason, Judith, *Oya: In Praise of the Goddess*, Boston: Shambhala, 1987. Combining ethnography, poetry, personal experience, and mythology, a multifaceted glimpse into the mysterious world of the Goddess, both in Africa and in the African Diaspora.

Harvey, Graham, ed., *Indigenous Religions: A Companion*, London: Cassell, 2000.

Contemporary scholars examine indigenous cultures across the globe, attempting to portray the people's own explanations of their traditions.

Neitthammer, Carolyn, *Daughters of the Earth: The Lives and Legends of American Indian Women*, New York: Collier Books, 1977. Graphic details and old photographs of Native American women's traditional lifeways, portraying their strengths and their challenges.

Olupona, Jacob K., ed., *African Traditional Religions in Contemporary Society*, New York: Paragon House, 1991. A rather mixed bag of contributions, including both men and women talking about African women's spiritual roles.

Oyewumi, Oyeronke, ed., *African Women and Feminism: Reflecting on the Politics of Sisterhood*, Trenton, New Jersey: Africa World Press, 2003. Essays critiquing Western feminists' attempts to explain and rescue their African sisters.

St. Pierre, Mark and Tilda Long Soldier, *Walking in the Sacred Manner: Healers, Dreamers, and Pipe Carriers—Medicine Women of the Plains Indians*, New York: Touchstone, 1995. Holy women and healers, from stories of and interviews with many Native American women who remember or still live by traditional ways.

Wagner, Sally Roesch, *Sisters in Spirit: Haudenosaunee (Iroquois) Influence on Early American Feminists*, Summertown, Tennessee: Native Voices, 2001. Evidence of the freedoms and strengths of Native American women which inspired nineteenth-century feminists.

3
WOMEN IN HINDUISM

The Sun and Moon are Her Eyes

ASHOK BARAROO

Trying to capture the essence of Hinduism is like trying to eat noodles with a spoon. Pick up something and something else slips away. Women's place within Hinduism is even more elusive. In its fullness lie great treasures of beauty, grace, nobility, elevated spirituality, and extraordinary power, as well as harsh oppressions.

Paths of Sanatana Dharma

What is called "Hinduism" is not a single unified tradition. There is no founder but rather many ways of enlightened wisdom and celebration of the Divine. Nor does the word "Hindu" appear in any of the ancient scriptures. It is a geographic label previously used by foreigners to refer to the people living east of the Indus River, which now lies in Pakistan. The label has been stretched to apply to a great variety of religious paths originating in India thousands of years ago and continuing to evolve today. Some call these ways "Sanatana Dharma"—the eternal way of right-eousness and duty.

Many, but not all, of the ways of Sanatana Dharma are rooted in the **Vedas** or ancient sacred literature of the Indian subcontinent. The oldest of these scriptures were probably written down around 1500–1200 BCE, though according to Indian tradition they are much older. According to archaeological discoveries in the twentieth century, historians have attributed them to Aryan invaders from the steppes of southern Russia who overwhelmed the indigenous Dravidian people with their superior war technologies. Included in the Vedas are entreaties to the deities for worldly blessings and also, probably written later, sublime passages of spiritual instruction from forest-dwelling sages. The tradition that evolved from the Vedas is often referred to as **Brahmanic** Hinduism, for it is a hierarchical, caste-structured way in which only those born into the Brahman (Brahmin) caste, the highest, are considered ritually pure enough to conduct religious ceremonies.

Clues to another, older tradition lie in the ruins of an ancient civilization found in sites such as Harappa and Mohenjo-Daro along the Indus River. Artifacts include images of a deity sitting cross-legged in meditation who resembles Lord Shiva (one of the major gods worshiped to the present) and images of a goddess.

	TIMELINE
c.2500–1500 BCE	Harappan civilization
c.1500–1200 BCE	Early Vedic period
c.1500 BCE	Vedas written down
c.1200–400 BCE	Middle and late Vedic periods
c.800 BCE	Caste system fully developed
c.600–300 BCE	Decline of Vedic religion; growth of Buddhism and Jainism
c.400 BCE–200 CE	*Ramayana*
c.400 BCE–400 CE	*Mahabharata*
c.400 BCE–100 CE	Restrictions on women increased
c.100–400 CE	Late classical period
c.100 CE	*The Laws of Manu* compiled
c 600–1700	*Bhakti* movement
1001	Muslim invasions of India begin
12th century	Virashaivism developed
13th century	Akka Mahadevi
16th century	Mirabai
1527–1707	Mughal rule of India
1857–1947	British rule of India
1896	Sarada Devi succeeds Ramakrishna
1937	Brahma Kumaris management entrusted to women
1950	"The Mother" succeeds Sri Aurobindo
1954	Sri Sarada Math founded
1953	Birth of Mata Amritanandamayi
	Chipko tree-hugging movement begins
1992	Babri mosque destroyed by Hindu extremists
2002	Anti-Muslim violence in Gujarat after burning of Hindu devotees in train

Even today, there are some worshipers of Shiva and of the goddess who do not refer to the Vedas. There are also innumerable non-Vedic village deities—mostly protective goddesses—and local ways of worshiping them. Over time, all these ways have evolved and changed, varying in different regions, historical circumstances, and caste levels.

What, then, do all these ways have in common other than their geographic location? One of the themes that suffuses religious life in India is **Dharma**—an all-pervasive ideal that can be roughly translated as duty, moral order, righteousness, a code for living. Everyone is bound by prescribed duties to family members, to society, and to the Divine. Self-sacrifice is expected to supersede self-interest. These responsibilities are codified in detail in certain scriptures such as *The Laws* *of Manu* (written approximately 100–300 CE), but have been propagated more powerfully by well-known epics, particularly the *Ramayana* (*c.*400 BCE–200 CE) and *Mahabharata* (*c.*400 BCE–400 CE). As we will see, this respect for Dharma has major implications for Hindu women.

Another characteristic of all the paths known as Hinduism is a frank spirituality. India has given birth to so many of the world's religions and religious teachers, even today, that despite the effects of modernization and globalization, almost every conversation there will naturally include some reference to religious ways of thinking. Attitudes toward one's fate, for instance, are conditioned by a widespread belief in **karma**—the effects of one's thoughts and actions, felt not only in this life but also in the next, after reincarnation. Atheism and agnosticism are not popular; most people have some belief that there are unseen forces at work directing everything that happens. Rare is the shopkeeper who does not maintain a shrine to some deity or guru and begin the workday with an act of worship. For most women the sacred is very much part of the domestic sphere. The first thing they do upon rising is to light the holy oil lamp. Public life is continually punctuated by religious festivals.

The Changing Role of Women

Considerable controversy is now raging about the relative position of women in Hinduism. Hindu nationalist factions are trying to portray Hindu women as having always enjoyed great respect, but feminists are attempting to call attention to the existence of not only oppression but also violence against them. Both trends co-exist in the culture, but the extent to which they are religiously motivated is subject to debate.

To begin with the negative, there is a startling sex imbalance in the Indian population because of the preference for male babies. At present, so many female fetuses or infants have been killed that there are only 927 females for every 1,000 males. The main reason given for the preference for males is the burden of the dowry system, in which the bride's family is expected to make exorbitant gifts to the groom's family. The birth of a daughter means a tremendous financial burden for her family. A woman's chief role, according to the cultural tradition, is to bear sons and to serve her husband and in-laws without complaint, no matter how much they may abuse her. There are stories of "dowry deaths" in which women are killed by their in-laws for not meeting all their dowry demands. Widows have little social respect. There are efforts by fanatic factions today to revert to tradition and revive the ideal of **sati**—a practice outlawed by the British in 1857, in which widows were cremated alive on their husbands' funeral pyres, theoretically in the ultimate wifely self-sacrifice, but apparently sometimes forced by their in-laws, who could then claim their husbands' property.

Does such misogyny have any justification in the scriptures? There are prayers for male progeny in the Vedas, such as the following: "Let a female child be born somewhere else; here, let a male child be born" (*Atharva Veda VI*, 2, 3). One of the *Upanishads*—the latest of the Vedic writings, which otherwise contain enlightened teachings—advises that if a wife refuses her husband's sexual advances, he should try to persuade her by coaxing, then by gifts, and finally by beating her with his fists or with rods (*Brhad Aranyaka Upanishad VI*, 4, 7). In *The Laws of Manu*, it is written that "Though destitute of virtue, or seeking pleasure [elsewhere], or devoid of good qualities, a husband must be constantly worshiped as a god by a dutiful wife" (*Manu Smrti V*, 154). Child marriage of girls is recommended: "A man, aged 30 years, shall marry a maiden of 12 who pleases him, or a man of 24 a girl of eight years of age" (*Manu Smrti IX*, 94). Child marriage, which many states have attempted to outlaw, still persists in some communities, perhaps to prevent the shame of female sexual activity outside marriage. Further, according to *The Laws of Manu*, women, like slaves, are not to own any property, and "In childhood a female must be subject to her father, in youth to her husband, when her lord is dead to her sons; a woman must never be independent" (*Manu Smrti V*, 148). Nonetheless, according to Manu, "Where women are honored, there the gods are pleased; but where they are not honored no sacred rite yields rewards" (*Manu Smrti III*, 56). Actually, *The Laws of Manu* should not be considered a monolithic text. There are many versions and many commentaries. The conflation of the various strands as *The Laws of Manu*, which contains conflicting remarks about women, is a problem encountered in the feminist critique of Manu. Furthermore, contemporary Hindus may revere the codes set forth in it as ancient writings, but not necessarily as relevant to life today.

It is not possible to understand women's status without an historical perspective. It appears that women were respected in ancient India, and that this respect was only later eroded. As in other small-scale societies, women and men had complementary roles in early Vedic times (*c.*1500–1200 BCE). The family was the center of spiritual life, and the deities would receive offerings only if the wife was present. Families were patriarchal, but women were essential in certain rituals and may have performed some domestic rituals by themselves. Girls received education and had a say in the choice of their husbands. Male gods were predominant, but there were significant goddesses, such as Usha, goddess of the dawn, Sarasvati, the goddess of learning and embodiment of a major river, and Prthivi, the mother Earth, protectress of the dead. However, by the end of this period, the caste system was developing, dividing people into rigid social levels according to their occupations. Moreover, in the wedding hymn, it was stated that a woman was to be the mother of sons. Throughout Indian history, women's oppression has developed hand in hand with oppression of the lower castes.

During the middle and late Vedic periods (*c.*1200–400 BCE), agriculture spread and states were formed in the valley of the Ganges. In addition to the home rites, elaborate public rituals were conducted by ritual specialists, the male Brahman priests. Most upper-class women were relegated to the home sphere and educated only enough to conduct the home rituals. However, some women did not marry and were instead allowed to study the Vedas and live as ascetics. There were also prominent women intellectuals—Vedic scholars (*Brahmavadinis*) such as Ghosha, Lopamudra, Romasha, and Indrani, and Upanishadic philosophers such as Sulabha, Maitreyi, and Gargi. Gargi, for instance, was the wise and educated daughter of a sage. She participated in philosophical debates and is quoted in the *Brihadaranyaka Upanishad* as raising cosmic questions that the great sage

3.1 Shiva, one of the major Hindu deities, is sometimes depicted in androgynous form—half female, half male

Yajnavalkya refused to answer. An occasional woman may have performed the public rites, judging from rare mention in the Vedas. But the essential provision was that a wife had to be present at the rites with her husband because her spiritual power was required for the deities to give their blessings. If a woman was menstruating, she could not attend a ritual, and therefore it had to be postponed, for the rites were considered useless without her presence.

During the late Vedic period, belief developed in an independent female power called *Sri*, coveted by kings. She brought stability, justice, successful agriculture, rainfall, regal power, nobility, good fortune, bounty, and beauty. Sacred trees were worshiped as her special milieu. Lesser female spirits—*apsaras* and *yaksis*—were perceived in trees, stars, and water. The banyan tree, with its great girth increasing via aerial roots, was worshiped then as today by women as a way to family prosperity, long life (especially for the husband), and fertility (especially for bearing sons).

Upper-class women's status further declined as Vedic religion fell into disfavor and other Indian religions—Buddhism and Jainism—grew in popularity between the sixth and fourth centuries BCE. Threats to Brahman men's influence seem to have resulted in the imposition of restrictions on their women between 400 BCE and 100 CE. Previously valued at least for their fertility and considered the agents of good fortune, Brahman women were now scorned for their perceived impurity and lack of education. Growing oppression of women was codified in *The Laws of Manu* by 100 CE, although those proscriptions were not read by the majority of the populace. Child marriage of girls was recommended to protect their virginity. No longer did they have any say in whom they could marry. Buddhism and Jainism permitted women to be ascetics, but Brahman men closed this door to their women. Women's independence was not tolerated, even in their own homes.

Stabilization of kingdoms after 100 CE brought some improvement in the economy of the Ganges plains, leading to better circumstances for the lowest castes and women. Nonetheless, during the late classical period, from 100 to 400 CE, Brahmans continued to debate whether women and low castes could recite the sacred mantra "*Om*" or achieve spiritual enlightenment and liberation. The great epics portrayed extremely influential role models for women as devoted and self-sacrificing wives—Sita, wife of Ram, and Parvati, wife of Shiva (fig. 3.1). Even the previously independent and powerful goddesses Durga and Kali were transformed into wives of the gods. When her husband died, an upper-caste widow had only two socially approved options: to live an austere life, sleeping on the floor and eating little, or to immolate herself on her husband's pyre as a sati. Nonetheless, stories such as that of Sita, heroine of the *Ramayana* epic, may be interpreted by women as encouragement for being inwardly strong, noble, and independent rather than their husband's submissive servant. Sita chose her own husband by arranging a competition to find the strongest and most intelligent prince. When Ram was exiled to the wilderness, she insisted upon going with him because of her love for him, contrary to his expectations that she could not tolerate the hard life. Abducted by the evil Ravana, she steadfastly resisted his advances. When Ram won her back but then doubted her sexual purity since she had lived in another man's house, she proved herself by demanding that a great fire be built and then passing through it unscathed. She raised her sons independently in the **ashram** (religious retreat) of a great sage, since Ram was still concerned that his subjects would doubt her purity. In some versions of the story, she then willed her own death, requesting the Earth, her Mother, to take her back into Her womb. In these parts of the epic, Sita appears as a powerful heroine whose virtues and strengths surpass those of her godly husband.

The **bhakti** movement, devotional adoration of a deity or guru, which flourished from about 600 CE to 1700 CE, opened a new avenue for women's devotional spirituality, and many women saints appeared on the Indian scene, defying norms of married and family life. **Tantric** texts, mystical writings setting out doctrines involving mantras, meditation, and yoga, emphasized worship of the divine feminine. However, some esoteric "left-handed" Tantric practices—such as prolonged intercourse with orgasm withheld until a tumultuous release of energy through the *chakras*, or centers of subtle energy through the axis of the body— were mostly means of liberation for men, who used lower-class women as their sexual partners. In medieval Hindu temples, women called *devadasis* brought beauty and grace to worship of the deities by singing and dancing, and performed minor functions in temple rites.

During the nineteenth and twentieth centuries, under British rule in India, women's property rights were eroded. According to the controversial research of Professor Veena Talwar Oldenburg,[1] the dowry system was previously an institution run by women, for women, so that they would have some economic status and emergency funds. This was especially true of what is called *streedhan*—parental property given to a bride so that she would have some financial independence from her new in-laws. A bride's family and even her village voluntarily gave her gifts at the time of marriage, in a reciprocal system, and this became a safety net for her. Nothing in the scriptures said anything about secretly killing a woman who did not furnish a sufficiently large dowry, as some Indian families now do. However, claims Oldenburg, the British dismantled the old system of communal property rights and replaced it with private property, to which they controlled the titles. Women did not get titles to land. The colonialists then blamed the subsequent female infanticide and dowry deaths on what they said was inbuilt violence toward women in the Hindu tradition. British Christian missionaries came on a "civilizing mission" to attack "Hindoo social evils." According to Oldenburg, portraying Hindus as barbaric gained public approval in Britain for the colonial domination and destruction of Indian culture during British rule from 1857 to 1947.

This British criticism of mistreatment of women was answered by Brahman reformers, most of them men. They looked back to the Vedas to see if there was any religious justification for practices such as child marriage, polygamy, confinement of women in the home, lack of education for them, shunning of widows, and sati—and if not, declared them later accretions that had no base in classic Vedic tradition. Women themselves joined in the movement toward women's liberation during the twentieth-century struggle for Indian independence. Not only did they join in both Mahatma Gandhi's non-violent resistance and in armed struggles, but they were also active in trying to promote social reforms. To do so, they left their traditional roles in the home in order to help their communities and their country.

When independence was won in 1947, women were formally granted freedom and the right to vote. The Constitution of India granted all citizens the right to education, shelter, dignity, health, food, and work, and declared all people equal. Nevertheless, many women are still malnourished, uneducated, and married very young. Despite legislation to protect them from abuses that have no scriptural justification, domestic violence against women continues. Lower-class women are sometimes said to be freer than those in upper classes, but in fact, they are expected to continue to hide their faces behind their veils in public, even while performing difficult physical labor. On the other hand, many Indian women are now highly educated, and some have become leaders in government and other sectors of public life. Some women have been trained as priests, and in the state of Maharashtra they outnumber male priests.

Modern Indian women thus face traditional expectations that they be dutiful wives, mothers, and daughters-in-law at home on top of their outside duties as employees or executives. Manjula Krishnan, Director for Road Transport for the Government of India, was raised in a liberal family in South India and shares household responsibilities with her husband, to a certain extent. Her mother was also a modern woman, yet she habitually rose early every morning to clean the worship room and decorate it with flowers before beginning her other daily chores. She also fasted for religious holidays. Manjula observes:

She probably fasted to purify her body, but it was never thought of as a spiritual act. It was done because it had to be done. Now I think the Indian woman of today is going through a very difficult transition period. She is liberated and at the same time she is fettered. The traditional idea of duty is strong, but there is a lot of confusion and tension, at least among the women with jobs, who are both working and looking after the household—a lot of confusion in their minds about what is their exact range of responsibilities. They are still very much responsible to their mother-in-law. I felt that I had to give my mother-in-law all the respect that I could. Even though she would criticize or say something, you just had to listen without complaining. It was said to us that you have to respect your in-laws and your elders, so we do it—even today.

My grandmother did a lot of rituals, for her entire life was spent within the household. She came from a very pure Brahmin family. The entire community surrounding her was also Brahmin, and everybody knew what rituals were to be done, so she did them. For example, when a woman has her monthly periods she is not supposed to enter the house. A little outhouse is built for that three or four days, and she stays out. This was observed very strictly, and my mother always stayed out during that period. But when my mother got married, she left her home town and came to a bigger city. She found that she couldn't follow all these rituals—they would hamper her daily routine. We had no out-house to go and stay in, so she said, "Okay, don't enter the kitchen, don't enter the **puja** [worship rituals] room. That's good enough. But do everything else." So you can see there is a dilution. She has made it more liberal. And now that I am married and have my own girls, I cannot say even that, because I can't keep them from entering the kitchen. So I say, "It's okay—you go everywhere, but just don't go into the puja room, don't light the oil lamp."

In a way I feel regretful, because there are so many lovely customs and rit-uals that give meaning to life, and I don't even know them, because my moth-er never did them. Cultural roots are very important, because they give you a grounding in the community and the country in which you are born. At least I had some interest in what my grandmother did, but my children don't even ask that, because they are living in a totally different world. Their children will probably be even more cut away from the roots. And so you're just floating, because you have nothing to hold on to. That's why I go back to my gurus, for they bring you back. Without getting into the negative aspects, they bring you back to the positive aspects of tradition. "Come back to music. Come back to your dance. Go for *satsang* [group sacred singing]," I tell my children, and they listen. Tomorrow they will teach their children the same songs. That's what these gurus do—they bring you back to tradition, without hampering your daily routine, making it more "user-friendly." [2] ■

Worship of the Goddess

From earliest times, Hindu spirituality has included worship of the Supreme via feminine forms and metaphors. Adoration and awe of the Goddess's power have not necessarily elevated the status of human females, and in fact often coexist with social limitations on women. Goddesses are not generally regarded as role models, and they are worshiped by both men and women. An exception is the Sri Chakra, an esoteric symbol of the Goddess that can be worshiped only by Brahman men, not by women.

Rivers are highly revered in India, and since antiquity they have been under-stood as manifestations of cosmic female deities. The mighty Ganges River origi-nates in the heavens and flows down to earth, bringing purifying, fertilizing waters and carrying divine grace. According to a familiar story, Mother Ganges consent-ed to descend to earth only if someone would break her fall, which otherwise would have destroyed the world. The great god Shiva offered to receive her in his matted locks and thus slow her descent. Contemporary environmentalists liken his hair to the forests of the Himalayas through which the Ganges flows and warn that cutting down those forests is leading to disastrous flooding from the river's unim-peded flow. It is believed that water taken from the Ganges has a purifying effect; it can be kept for years without spoiling and is revered as sacred.

3.2 The Goddess Durga, ready for battle to rid the world of demons

Village cultures, which are actually more prominent in the daily lives of most Indians than the upper-caste Brahmanic tradition, inevitably recognize local deities. Most of these are perceived as female. They are not usually thought of as shaped like human women, however. Objects by which they are worshiped may be stones without carving, trees, or small shrines without any anthropomorphic image. Whatever happens in the village, good or bad, is thought to be associated with the local goddess, so people naturally turn to her in prayer so that she will protect her village.

Brahmanic tradition recognizes a great Goddess with an awesome creative power, called **shakti**. When this power spirals serpent-like up the spine, awakening the latent energy of all the subtle centers, it is called **kundalini**. Forms and names of the Goddess are many. A popular contemporary devotional tract explains:

Think of a thousand lotuses blossoming all at once. Think of a thousand suns bursting all of a sudden in the sky. Such is her beauty, such is her radiance. The Sun and the Moon are her eyes, the stars her raiment and the green earth its hem. She is the colour of vermilion, of the hibiscus flower, of the sunset sky—and of blood. She is also white as Hamsa [swan] and the snow on the mountain Himavan. She is in the tongues of flames of the funeral pyre. As Amba she is benign like a mother suckling her child, as Tripurasundari she is an enchantress unequalled in beauty, and as Kali she is terrible as death wearing a garland of skulls; whereas she also incarnated herself as Vaishno, who is as pure as a maiden and nothing can compare with her virgin-powers. Though she is truly formless, now and then she incarnates herself in different forms to destroy the evils of the world.[3] ■

One of the best-known manifestations of the great Goddess is Durga, who appeared as a beautiful woman riding on a tiger, armed by the gods with many weapons (fig. 3.2). They called upon her when the earth was overrun by demons, who challenged the pride of the gods. In an epic battle, she slew all the demons in her terrific rage and then returned the kingdom to the gods, for she had no interest in ruling. She is revered as a warrior, protecting her children and maintaining the balance of good against evil in the cosmos. At the same time, Durga is the compassionate Mother of the Universe, bestowing grace and taking care of her children's everyday lives. She maintains the fertility and creativity of the natural environment, as is apparent during Navaratri, the major nine-day celebration of the Goddess conducted every autumn and at the second Durga Puja every spring. Devotees plant barley seeds in an earthen pot, as if in a womb. By the end of the nine days, the barley has sprouted and the vessel is filled with its tall grass. The Goddess is also worshiped with offerings of nine sacred plants associated with her, such as the leaves of the *bel* or wood-apple tree. Thus her worship incorporates the basics of life: soil, water, trees, plants, seeds. Madhu Khanna, specialist in Goddess ecology, suggests that these age-old remembrances of the natural world offer the possibility of a continuing sacred connection to nature inspired by the Goddess, even under the influence of urbanization:

■ In the ritual capsule of Durga Puja, the plants are treated with love and respect, for they embody a sacred world pregnant with life and meaning. This reverence provides a framework for ethical restraints and control, which function as norms against earth abuse; the ritual creates a silent language of geopiety toward biotic life. This, we have lost.

It is worth noting that, whereas some religious institutions have slowly perished under the impact of invasive modernization, others still struggle to survive. The festival of Durga Puja has shown an amazing resilience and ability to adapt to socioeconomic changes. Recent trends show that, far from disappearing, the festival is becoming ever more popular.[4] ■

The Goddess also has a terrifying aspect, known as Kali, the dark one. She is usually depicted with wild hair and tongue hanging out, wearing severed human arms around her waist and bloody heads around her neck. On her forehead is the crescent moon, symbol of transcendent wisdom. In one version of the epic battle between Durga and the demons, Kali appears roaring from the forehead of Durga. She vanquishes a demon whose every drop of blood turns into a duplicate of him-self—a whole battlefield of clones—by drinking all his blood and devouring all the clones. She is sometimes associated with the god Shiva, inciting him to wild activity, nearly destroying the world in frenzy, or standing and dancing on him when he lies in her path to halt her bloodthirsty rage. Her Tantric devotees sometimes worship her with blood sacrifices—of goats, for instance. She is associated with the darkness and chaos that preceded creation, and also with the destruction that clears the way for new creation. Why then would anyone want to worship her? Perhaps because death and violence are part of life, and without acknowledging and coming to terms with their existence, one cannot see reality clearly. In approaching the Kali aspect, the ego is offered for annihilation. Without this, enlightenment and liberation cannot occur. Another explanation for her devotees' love is that they understand the Mother's fierceness as necessary to protect Her children. The eighteenth-century visionary Ramprasad composed many hymns in Kali's honor, revealing her attraction. For example:

> Kali is naked reality.
> She is the feminine principle, unifying wisdom.
> This simpleminded lover of truth
>   Calls her *my Mother, my Mother*,
> because she is the inexhaustible affection
>   who never neglects her children,
> no matter how heedless or rebellious they may be.
> Wisdom Mother cares for this child
>   More tenderly than human mother,
> yet her creative and destructive actions
>   are startling, wild, unpredictable
> as those of a mad person.
> She is surrounded by swirling energy,
> manifest in various feminine forms
>   as human beings and etheric beings:
> powerful women warriors, peaceful contemplatives,
> terrifying protectresses surrounded by flames.
> Godhead in its three aspects,
> Creator, Sustainer, and Revealer,
> stands humbly before my Mother.
> She is supreme.
>
> This poet urges every human heart:
> "If you wish to be liberated from oppression,
> abandon whatever limits you cling to
>   and meditate on the limitless one
> who wears limitation as a garland of heads
>   severed by her sword of nondual wisdom."[5]

Women as Ascetics and Bhaktis

In the midst of the restraints of Brahmanic Hinduism, there have always been women who have had such powerful inner spiritual experiences that they have broken out of social constraints to live and speak in highly unorthodox ways. To a certain extent, this personal revolt against Brahmanic ritualism even became an accepted spiritual path with the flourishing of the bhakti movement from 600 to 1700 CE.

The highly philosophical teachings of the sages in the *Upanishads* described the Ultimate Reality as formless, but eventually intense devotion to a personified deity became the norm in Hinduism. In this bhakti path, all beings—whether male or female—take a feminine persona before the deity they adore. Many great bhaktis have been women. Some cherish the deity as a mother cherishes her child; some approach the Divine as lover, using sexual imagery boldly as a metaphor to express desire for total union with their Beloved. The great thirteenth-century saint Akka Mahadevi (see box, p.76) sang:

> In our embrace
> the bones should rattle
> in a welding, the welding mark
> even should disappear.
> The knife should enter totally
> When the arrow enters, even
> the feathers should not be seen.[6]

Another of the many historic and significant women ascetics of Hinduism is Mirabai, a sixteenth-century princess of North India at the time when Babur, the first of the six powerful Mughal Muslim emperors in India (1527–1707), was terrorizing the area with invasions from Afghanistan. Mirabai became a Vaishnava—a lover of Krishna in a reformist tradition that taught love for God in the context of love for all people, regardless of caste or creed. So strong did her love for Krishna become that she spent all her time worshiping him with dance and song and having conversations with holy men, even after her marriage, much to the displeasure of her in-laws. When her husband died young, her father-in-law the king ordered her to commit sati, but she refused, for she understood that she belonged only to God. Harassed in the palace, she took to dancing before Krishna's image in the public temple, where saints and scholars held her in great admiration. The king reportedly restricted her to her chamber, where she was given a bed of nails to sleep on, a basket with a snake concealed in it, and a cup of poison. According to her account, all these torments turned into blissful encounters with her Lord. She left the palace and spent the rest of her life wandering and singing the praises of Krishna (often known as "Shyam," the dark one) until, it is said, she merged into his image. Her devotional songs are still popular throughout India, full of the mystical pathos of the lover longing for her Beloved:

> I have sacrificed my life
> Unto the beautiful Shyam.
> For Thy sake, O Shyam,
> I have abandoned worldly shame and family custom.
> Without His sight I find no rest
> And streams of tears fall from my eyes.
> To whom could I speak?
> Who could assuage my pain?
> The river of separation is a powerful stream.
> Says Mira: Harken, Lord, grant me Thy sight,
> For Thy feet are my only support.[7]

BIOGRAPHY   Akka Mahadevi

Akka Mahadevi was one of the outstanding figures in a radical South Indian movement known as Virashaivism that rejected Brahmanical patriarchal norms and casteism, beginning in the twelfth century. The movement was begun by a Brahman man, Basava, who renounced his Brahmanic identity and turned Brahmanic traditions upside-down. He taught that women, with their nurturing and creative powers, and low-caste people, without any burdens of worldly power or wealth, were closer to God than the dominant Brahman males. Under his inspiration, many great female saints arose, composing mystical poetry that is still startlingly fresh today. They were ardent lovers of Shiva as the formless Supreme Principle in a state of repose, whom they worshiped by means of a smooth black oval stone (*lingam*) that they always wore around their necks, except when holding it in their hands as a focus for meditation. Since Virashaivite women were not regarded as polluted, they could worship this *lingam* or perform any spiritual rituals when they were menstruating. In the ultimate stage of spiritual realization, Shiva and Shakti (the creative feminine power) are an androgynous whole (see fig. 3.1); the gender of the devotee is irrelevant.

Akka Mahadevi was totally devoted to Shiva. She had no interest in marrying any worldly male. She sang:

> I have fallen in love, O mother, with the
>   Beautiful One, who knows no death,
>   knows no decay and has no form;
> I have fallen in love, O mother, with the
>   Beautiful One, who has no middle, has
>   no end, has no parts and has no features;
> I have fallen in love, O mother, with the
>   Beautiful One, who knows no birth and
>   knows no fear.
> I have fallen in love with the Beautiful One
>   who is without any family,
>   without any country and without any peer;
> Chenna Mallikarjuna [Shiva], the Beautiful, is my husband.
> Fling into the fire the husbands who are subject
>   to death and decay.[8]

Despite her wishes, a prince fell in love with her because of her great beauty and insisted upon marrying her, threatening to kill her parents if she did not submit. Thus forced into marriage, she set her own conditions: "I shall engage myself in the worship of Shiva as I like. I shall spend my time in the company of devotees of Lord Shiva as I like. I shall serve my **guru** [spiritual teacher] as I like. I shall be with the prince as I like. And I shall forgive only three violations of these conditions." For some time, she spent her days in worship of Shiva and the company of other devotees and unwillingly suffered the lust of her husband at night. But once he had made three mistakes with reference to her conditions, she left him and the palace.

She shed her clothing and lived alone among the caves and streams of a holy mountain associated with Shiva, with only her long hair covering her body. Her nakedness was the ultimate refutation of traditional expectations. Her parents found her and begged her to abandon the austerities of her ascetic life, but she was adamant. Even her husband still tried to win her love, this time by dressing like a Shiva-worshiper, covering his body with ashes. Unsuccessful, he begged other Virashaivites to intercede on his behalf, but when they went to Akka Mahadevi, they found her in such deep meditation that they dared not disturb her. Ultimately, she said to her Lord Shiva:

> I speak not of thee,
> I speak not of me
> Merging in you
> I speak no more.[9]

Tiring of earthly existence in a body which she felt had been sullied by sexual contact with her husband, she prayed to her Lord to free her, and thus she left the body.

3.3 Akka Mahadevi, great ascetic devotee of Shiva

Despite such examples of women who took a very different path from that laid out by religious and cultural patriarchal tradition, their deviance did not seem to empower other women to break free. Instead, they were placed on pedestals as saints rather than as role models for women's daily lives. Nonetheless, there is another aspect of Hinduism that comes into play here: reverence for the spiritual value of celibacy. Madhu Kishwar, editor of *Manushi*, a highly regarded magazine about women's issues in contemporary India, explains:

■ Since, in our culture, people (both men and women) who sacrifice their self-interest for others are given far more respect and reverence than those who pursue their own pleasure without taking the concerns of others into account, the idea of voluntary renunciation in pursuit of a higher goal or for the interest of others continues to have a profound hold on our imagination… . We are still heavily steeped in the old Indian tradition which holds that voluntary sexual abstinence bestows extraordinary powers on human beings… . Even ordinary men and women living a life of voluntary sexual abstinence come to be highly respected. Such women tend to be treated as a special category, are subjected to much less scrutiny and restrictions, and tend to get much greater respect from men provided they don't show signs of sexual frustration. Many of the most revered women in Indian religious history opted out of sexual relations altogether, as the lives of Mirabai, Akka Mahadevi, Lal Ded and many others attest. They are treated as virtual goddesses.

In India, men are trained to fear the wrath of non-consort Goddess figures like Durga, Chandi, and Vaishno Devi. While Sita and Parvati invoke reverence, Durga invokes fear and awe. She is the great saviour from worldly adversity, "Herself unassailable and hard to approach" but someone to whom men also turn for protection. Similarly a woman who rises above being sexually accessible, consort of none, nor in search of a consort, tends to command tremendous awe and reverence.[10] ■

Many well-known male spiritual figures in India have named ascetic women as their successors. For instance, the great nineteenth-century saint Ramakrishna took Sarada Devi as his young bride, but they remained celibate, spiritually absorbed in the Divine, beyond worldly concerns. Ramakrishna in fact worshiped Sarada Devi as the Holy Mother, placing her upon the seat of the deity; she also perceived the Divine as the Mother and saw Her within herself. After Ramakrishna's death, Sarada Devi frequently went into **samadhi** (transcendent spiritual absorption) and had unusual spiritual visions, from which it was difficult for her to return to bodily consciousness. Disciples came for her help, and she seemingly took their burdens upon herself when they respectfully touched her feet. She explained:

■ Some people touch my feet, and that refreshes me wonderfully. Again there are others whose touch gives me a terrible burning sensation. I feel it like the sting of a wasp. Only by applying Ganges water do I get some relief. Once, in the absence of an attending disciple, a rather elderly man came here… . He was very anxious to salute me by touching the feet. I protested and shrank back, yet he did it. From that time I have been almost at the point of death through an unbearable pain in the feet and the stomach. I washed my feet three or four times, still I cannot get rid of this burning sensation… . We are born for this purpose. If we do not accept others' sins and sorrows and do not assimilate these, who else will do so? Who else will bear the responsibilities of the sinners and the afflicted?[11] ■

The world's largest monastic order of women independent of male control—Sri Sarada Math—was founded in 1954 in the name of Sarada Devi by the Ramakrishna Mission. Swami Vivekananda, the great disciple of Ramakrishna, had foreseen that without women's *shakti*, the world could not be transformed, and had ordered the establishment of an ascetic order of women working for "liberation of the self and welfare of the world."[12]

Another ascetic order initiated by a man is still run mostly by women: the Brahma Kumaris World Spiritual University. In 1937, "Brahma Baba," visionary founder of the organization, turned all his assets over to a managing committee of eight young women. They have carried on the mission of teaching meditation, self-growth, and universal tolerance to both men and women so effectively that now there are 3,200 Brahma Kumaris meditation centers in 70 countries. The celibate white sari-clad sisters are distinctive in their serene demeanor. According to the organization:

The soundness of [Brahma Baba's] decision to choose women and young girls as administrators and spiritual teachers can be seen in the increasing recognition of the need for the more traditionally feminine qualities of patience, tolerance, sacrifice, kindness and love as core values necessary for personal growth, human relations, and caring communities.[13]

Women's Rituals

Saints and ascetics aside, ordinary Hindu women play important spiritual roles in their everyday lives. Puja, or worship rituals, are carried on in both temples and homes. In many communities, the day begins with women cleaning and arranging the area and materials for worship of their favorite deities, and perhaps performing the worship themselves—waving oil lamps and incense, ringing bells, offering flower garlands and other plant materials, and chanting mantras to please the deities, for the sake of their families. This may be women's work since they are thought to have a naturally devotional nature. Neelu Kumari (fig. 3.4), a very spontaneous and simple young Brahman woman, speaks of her intimate relationship with the deities she worships:

In my village, worship of God was ladies' work. Gents were to work hard. I have seen Hanuman Ji, sometimes Krishna Ji, and Durga Mata. I saw Kali Mata. Her face was not good, and I was afraid. But she loves me very much, Kali Mata. She came in my dream. I was in big trouble—rain was coming and everybody closed their houses. I said, "May I come inside?" "No." This was my village, but nobody called me to come in. I was weeping. It was dark, night. I was very afraid. Water was up to my knees. I was standing alone. Then one lady came on a cycle. Her clothes were like Rajasthani clothes, but I could not see her face because it was night, very dark. She said, "Sit on the back of the cycle." I sat. "Tell me when your house is coming," she said. We went on and on, but because it was night, I did not find my house. Then I saw Qutb Minar [a Muslim tower in Delhi]. I said, "Oh, my house is behind that." Her voice was very much like a man's. She said, "My house is also near Qutb Minar. Maybe you want to go to my house?" I said, "Okay—no problem." Then day came. She said, "This is the gate of my house." I got off the cycle and saw her face—very black, very black, big eyes. Oooh. She loved me. She said, "Go inside." Then I went inside the courtyard. There was one peepul tree. Then I looked back—there was no

3.4 Neelu Kumari performing *arti* before statues of the deities

lady. I looked everywhere. I said, "Who is she? Where did she go?" Then I woke up. I was very afraid.

Someone told me to go to Kali Temple. I didn't know where it was. After one week, I found it. When I went there, right inside the gate there was a peepul tree—the same tree. I said, "Oh, this is that place. I remember." For one month, I went there. If I didn't go there, she was angry with me. In dreams she came and said, "I won't talk to you." If I did not go, there were very many problems for me.

I also see Durga Mata in dreams. She is very beautiful. But when I see her, she is mixed with Kali Mata, and her face is black. Sometimes she is a small girl. She comes and sits on my lap as I am sitting at the *havan* [sacred fire]. She is small, but she caresses my hair and shoulders, blesses my head and shoulders with her hands. I said, "She is a small girl, and she does this to me?" Then I woke up, and then I understood. She loves very much.

If ordinary people are not devoted to God, they do not know what is this plate of light [waved before the deities in worship, called *arti*]. But this arti gives blessing to all, to all people. One person does the arti and another only stands, and God gives blessings to them both, because the gods and goddesses become happy very quickly. When we do arti, we always say their praises—"You are this, you are this, your nose is very good, your ears are very good, and you destroy the demons." Durga Mata becomes happy very quickly, because she is a very kind lady. Worship should be with the heart. If there is no heart, what is worship?[14] ■

In some parts of India women create clay figures or prepare elaborate ephemeral designs of rice, rice paste, or colored powders on the ground outside their homes for the protection and good fortune of the family and worship of various deities (see box, p. 82). They tend sacred *tulsi* plants in remembrance of the god Vishnu. According to their vows and allegiances, they may sing and dance happily in praise of their favorite deities. Spiritual protection of the family is considered an essential part of women's work, and as indicated before, women are thought to have special potential for intimate connections with the gods and goddesses. Many women also undertake fasts and perform rituals for the good health and long life of their husbands, brothers, and sons, for the family's protection and prosperity, and for bountiful crops.

The Hindu woman's status as a wife is marked by separation from her own family, for she goes to live with her husband's extended family, serving her in-laws and veiling her face from her elder in-laws (fig. 3.5). She is further secluded when she becomes a mother, for her postpartum bleeding makes her theoretically impure. Particularly among the rural poor, delivery of the child is carried out discreetly with the help of a midwife, with the mother expected to endure the pain quietly and to keep herself modestly covered. She spends three days snuggled up with her infant, in old clothes. This period of confinement actually becomes a special opportunity for lifelong bonding. Women in the family prepare foods that will help her regain her strength, and the midwife helps to cleanse and massage the mother and child. The midwife is from the untouchable caste; others avoid touching the baby

3.5 According to Indian cultural tradition, village women keep their faces covered in the presence of their in-laws

EXCERPT   Women's Auspicious Designs
Vijaya Nagarajan

Throughout India, one sees bright vermilion and white-gray marks on surfaces of things, a splash of red and white color dabbed on foreheads and bodies, stones and temples, thresholds, doorways, and houses, which, a few hours later, is worn to a light tincture. The designs range from thin, red U-shaped lines, to three parallel horizontal lines, to a smudge on the forehead, stone, or lance. Designs made of white rice flour are drawn on thresholds of houses and temples. Complex lines loop around a matrix of dots. These ritual markings are some of the most ubiquitous signs of sacredness in Hinduism. The red dot is known, depending on the specific Indian language, as *kumkum*, *bindi*, or *pottu*, among others. The threshold designs, too, are called by various names: *kolam*, *rangoli*, *mandana*, and *alpana*, among others.

Like the *bindi*, *pottu*, and other ephemeral marks of puja [auspicious worship—a house of mourning will not have any of these], the *kolam* is one of many daily rituals that evoke, host, and dehost the divine as guests. The daily creation of the *kolam* requires that Tamil Hindu women rise at dawn every day and draw or paint a rice flour design on the thresholds of their homes, on temples, and at the base of trees. The *kolam* is designed to invite, host, and maintain close relationships with the goddesses Lakshmi and Bhudevi, who will in turn prevent harm, illness, and laziness from entering the household. When a woman draws a *kolam* in front of a coconut or banana tree, she is making a *valipatu* (an adoring welcome) to the *devyam* (divinity) in that tree.

The *kolam* is gradually carried away by the feet of passersby and serves as a feeder of sorts for small animals, including birds, ants, and insects; thus, the *kolam* disappears a few hours after it is made. One of the purposes of the *kolam* is to fulfill the dharmic code, to feed one thousand souls every day.... Its gradual disappearance over the course of the day signifies the notion of reciprocal generosity: the household has "fed a thousand souls," that is, the small birds, ants, and insects that have come to the threshold of the house and grazed on the *kolam*, and, in turn, the gods and goddesses may protect the household. A few hours after a *kolam* is made, bits of it disappear as if it had been bitten into, strange breathing holes appear in the surface of the dirt, where burrowing holes of tiny creatures appear. As the *kolam* is dispersed, it also signifies the departure of the gods or goddesses who had been hosted there. The *kolam* exemplifies the ephemerality of "spirit" in Hindu ideology and the continual need to attract the attention of the divine through various acts of ritual generosity.... .

Establishing relationships with the natural world is a necessary component of relationships in the social and cultural worlds. Whether a ritual involves creating the *kolam*, invoking the goddesses Lakshmi, Bhudevi, or Ganga, sacralizing a tree by undertaking vows toward it, or inviting divinities to take up residence (*kudi*) in a tree, a sacred exchange is established. The *kolam* and its many counterparts belong to a category that I call "rituals of generosity." Through the form of puja, or ritual offerings, one enacts the hope for a particular type of relationship with the divinities. In evoking a generous heart, rituals of generosity circumscribe human relationships in both cultural and natural contexts. According to the classical Tamil text, the *Tirukkural*, giving hospitality from the household to those who ask is one of the ways of attracting the goddess of prosperity.... As in any social exchange, these relationships are predicated on the expectation of mutual ritual generosity—that is, one gives freely and receives gifts in return. Just as we can have generous relationships with human beings, so humans can have generous relationships with trees, rocks, rivers, and other aspects of the natural world.

The *kolam* is a ritual act that physically embodies blessings, or "positive intentionalities," reducing the accumulation of negative intentionalities such as jealousy, envy, or greed. With the *kolam*, women's sphere of auspicious power moves in two directions: outward to the world beyond the threshold, and inward to the home, where it contributes to the stability of the household. Making the *kolam* is like raising the sail on a ship for that day, enabling it to leap forward on its course with a strong tailwind. The positive intentionalities travel from the women's hands, through the *kolam*, through the feet of those passing through its energy field, and into their bodies. In this way, both the tangible *kolam* and the auspicious effects of its creation are carried into the larger world. In an environment of scarcity, where the next meal often seems just out of reach, where the world appears capricious and disorderly and death strikes frequently and brutally, where infertility is a source of private and public grief and child mortality rates are high, the notion of reality takes on a different cast. Life is seen as something precious and rare, like the unanticipated arrival of good fortune. The cruelty and heartlessness in oneself and others must be faced, since immoral behavior is seen as the cause of poverty, misfortune, and other forms of inauspiciousness.

In this context, acts of sacredness and faith in divine relationships signify courage and the hope of regeneration from the brutalities inflicted by nature and other humans. In making the *kolam*, the hope is that the auspicious power embedded within the rice flour and invoked by the ritual will be transferred to the community, generating abundance and goodwill.

From Vijaya Nagarajan, "Rituals of Embedded Ecologies: Drawing *Kolams*, Marrying Trees, and Generating Auspiciousness," in Christopher Key Chappel and Mary Evelyn Tucker, *Hinduism and Ecology*, Cambridge, Massachusetts: Harvard University Press, 2000, pp. 455–65.

and its mother to prevent pollution to themselves—but this convention probably also protects the newborn from infection. Three days after the birth, the midwife bathes the mother and child and they are dressed in clean clothes, with accompanying purifying rituals—such as applying fresh buffalo or cow dung plaster to the floors, if they live in a village, thus creating a clean, dust-proof, and insect-resistant surface. Various ritual measures are taken by the women of the family to protect the baby from the evil eye and to insure its long life, and gifts are distributed, with special celebration if the child is a boy. After forty days the pollution of mother and child is considered spent, and they are reintegrated into the family. Until then, mother and baby spend most of their time in a women's milieu.

A very arduous sphere of ritual action inspired by Hindu tradition is spiritual pilgrimage, in which women participate on an equal footing with men. People walk great distances to visit places that are considered especially holy. Many of these are high in the Himalayas, extremely difficult of access. Snow, avalanches, and landslides kill many pilgrims every year. Nevertheless, the desire to receive the blessings and revere the deities in those places is so strong that ordinary people of all types make the journey, women no less than men. The pilgrims may not be in good physical condition, but their faith sustains them. The most ardent devotees even make the long journeys barefoot, to avoid sullying the purity of the sites. Dr. Veena Sharma, Director of the Prajna Foundation, which attempts to uplift children who live in the slums, served as liaison person for a group of pilgrims to Mount Kailash on the Tibet border. This is the most difficult of all pilgrimages, with a very long route from the Indian side up to Lake Mansarovar at approximately 15,000 feet and then days-long circumambulation of the pristine, snow-clad Mount Kailash— abode of Lord Shiva—through passes of up to 19,000 feet. Dr. Sharma speaks of Lake Mansarovar as being feminine in nature, and of women as pilgrims:

Lake Mansarovar is very deep and sometimes it is very tumultuous. It is always changing and at times it is absolutely peaceful and mirror-like. It is as though it is there to continuously reflect Kailash. Kailash is embedded in its womb, in its reflection. It is never separate from Kailash, just as Shiva and Parvati are never separate. They are always shown as tightly embraced together. Lake Mansarovar is always receiving Kailash into its bosom, and in that way, I look upon it as a feminine principle. This may not be very feminist, but nonetheless I feel the receiving part of it, always bearing within it everything that is around. It is reflecting the clouds and the mountains around. It is as though they are all there within this body and that it is holding them together in its depth. Of course, in the Hindu pantheon the creative principle is feminine. As the creative principle it is never the same. Every moment it is changing. The colors are changing, its ripples are changing. You cannot say "I know Lake Mansarovar," because one moment it will be a dark, deep lake, and another moment it is like a mirror shining forth that you can't even set eyes on.

As you go around the flat and barren perimeter of this lake, you feel that all parts of yourself have dropped away and that you are melting yourself, your mind into the environment, into the lake, as though becoming one with it. That's the way I felt. When there are very clear reflections in the lake, you can't tell the outside from the reflection. It's like an inverse picture of the outer. We are told that the world that we live in is also a reflection, that it's not real. If that is so, then Lake Mansarovar symbolizes that perfectly. It looks very real—the reflection is sometimes more sharp and more tangible and visible than the environment around, which is often hazy. As you go around Mansarovar, all congealed thoughts melt and flow down and become part of this lake, which is supposed to be the mind of Brahma [the Supreme].

[In the pilgrimage] many women did much better than men. There were times when things were difficult and men would be much more complaining—"This was not done properly, that was not done properly," etc., always wanting to put the blame on something or somebody—whereas the women, particularly one or two in this batch, would take up the positive side, support me, and start chanting. In that environment, in those circumstances, they were also going through the same difficulty but they were able to keep up their spirits much more than men were. If my batch is any indication of the others, then women perform very well. They have a certain strength, or it may also be that the women who go on such a journey are women who really are determined. All those who go on such a journey are those who are determined. You may not come back from such a journey. There have been instances where people either cannot bear the rarefied atmosphere, in which breathing becomes difficult, or become lost in snow blizzards. About five years ago the whole batch was wiped out. There was a landslide at night and they were all driven into the fast-flowing river. Not one body was found. Even though many people go on this pilgrimage now, I would still say a certain degree of individuation has to be there.[15] ■

Spiritual Music and Dance

Hindu women were traditionally told that the only path to liberation from **samsara**, the otherwise endless cycles of death and rebirth, was worshipful service of their husbands. However, as we have seen, some women ascetics defied the norm and achieved high levels of spiritual realization through direct devotion to God. This possibility was strengthened by the bhakti movement, which created openings to salvation for everyone, of every caste and gender. Another alternative pathway has been claimed for women as well: the salvatory effects of music and dance.

Until the twelfth century, classical music and dance were considered sacred art forms in India; in addition, the bhakti movement brought enraptured dancing and singing in which erotic metaphors, and sensual movements and voice tones, were used to allude to love of the divine Beloved. Attitudes toward the body were not inhibited, and even royal families took pleasure in displaying their physical beauty. But from the thirteenth century onward, more modest standards of clothing became prevalent, and classical dancing and singing became the province primarily of lower caste males and of females who were ritual dancers in the temples, known as *devadasis* ("servants of God"), or of courtesans who performed music and dance for royalty. Those courtesans transcended the strictures on other women, and could, for instance, become well educated, own property, and adopt children. Eventually, however, these art forms developed the social stigma of vulgarity, particularly under Victorian British rule in India. During the twentieth century, the pendulum swung back toward public acceptance of music and dance as expressions of spirituality, and now instruction in classical dance is highly sought after for the girls of Brahman families as a great cultural asset. Many classical styles are now being revived, including the popular Bharat Natyam and the rare Mohiniyattam dance of south India (see box, p. 86).

INTERVIEW Bharati Shivaji *Mohiniyattam Dancer and Teacher*

I am now 55; I have been dancing since the age of eight. Only one year I did not dance—the time I gave birth to my daughter. I belong to a family of performing artists. My mother is a musician and she was very keen that I should learn music and dance, so I was brought up in an environment where I could only hear and see dance and music in the family. So I suppose that came to me naturally, and by the time I was 12 I made my debut. Dance became a way of life for me.

Some 25 years ago I was able to do research on Mohiniyattam—the dance of the enchantress. It was not a very popular style until recently, so I was given a fellowship to revive the dance form. It was such a beautiful experience to travel all over Kerala [a state of south India] and to interact with the people, to document the musical traditions, the temples, this culture, and the music. It took so many years for me to resurrect the dance. Today it is very popular, and a lot of work has gone into its growth and development.

This particular dance form is very meditative, in terms of the technique and the impact it has on the dancer. It is not one of those dance forms that only involves disciplining the body; Mohiniyattam is discipline of the mind and body, a combination of the mind and body. It demands your entire self to bring out and execute a certain movement. It has to come from within. If you are not involved from within, you cannot do justice to the dance form. You cannot separate the body from the mind.

Mohiniyattam is very demanding, but it looks very simple. It has a direct appeal. The beauty lies in its simplicity. But what is simple, people don't like. It's so diffcult to be simple. Everybody wants everything to be intricate, complicated, and what not. But this, it just touches you in the heart.

Only women do Mohiniyattam. It is the feminine spirit that forms its very basis. By that, I mean that the predominant mood in Mohiniyattam is beauty, and the predominant flavor is grace. Grace and beauty are two very important aspects of feminine nature, isn't it? That is why I say the dance is very much attributed to the feminine spirit that is Devi, the goddess. Devi is generally personifed as

3.6 Bharati Shivaji, who has revived the tradition of Mohiniyattam dance

grace. There are several forms of the goddess. One is the ferocious one, and one is very compassionate, and there is Durga in her militant form, but in general Devi is visualized as all grace and beauty personifed. The guru of grace is Devi herself. That is the inspiration for Mohiniyattam. Even the god Vishnu meditated upon her to disguise himself as an enchantress. Even the gods had to bow to her. There are episodes in Mohiniyattam that describe various gods, like Shiva, Krishna, and Vishnu, as well as Devi, but the foundation is the feminine spirit.

Dance for me is not a body discipline. There are other disciplines which one will have to practice to perfect this discipline—yoga, *pranayama* [breath], meditation. This mind-body combination is what the dance is all about. These preparations are done before the dance, and they are our daily practice. You are experiencing a state of mind. You are oblivious of what is around you and you are deep in the thought of the character or the theme that you are going to enact, create, or choreograph. It is that which makes you dance.

Most of the dance forms in India originate from the *devadasi* tradition. *Devadasi* communities were maintained by the temple authorities. Their main job was to perform dance as part of the temple rituals every evening as an offering to the deity of that temple. So they considered themselves servants of God. "*Deva*" is god; "*dasi*" means servant. They considered themselves married to the deity of that temple where they were employed. They stayed unmarried; they were brides of the Lord. Dance was a main medium of communication with the Lord. It was basically just bhakti, expressed at the human level. It was the soul trying to communicate with the Absolute.

The art forms, the traditions that you see today evolved from that tradition, keeping the same spiritual bhakti mood intact. That remains the same. Maybe from the temple precincts dance has shifted to modern auditoriums today, but the mood remains the same, the spiritual fervor still remains the same.

Bharati Shivaji, from interview, May 21, 2003.

Female Teachers

In the case of exceptional spiritual personalities, some Hindu women have been recognized as spiritual teachers, or gurus. In this role, they transcend the patriarchal system to a great extent, though their devotees tend to regard them as their spiritual mothers. Sarada Devi, successor to Ramakrishna, was known as "the Holy Mother." Likewise, the female successor appointed by the intellectual South Indian spiritual teacher Sri Aurobindo (1872–1950) was called "the Mother." A French woman, she was Aurobindo's great support and companion, and after he died she developed the town of Auroville in India to perpetuate his teachings and to create an international experimental township dedicated to spiritual realization as well as to ecological sustainability and self-governance. Late in her long life, she explained her idealistic world view:

My way of seeing is somewhat different. For my consciousness the whole life upon earth, including the human life and all its mentality, is a mass of vibrations, mostly vibrations of falsehood, ignorance and disorder, in which are more and more at work vibrations of Truth and harmony coming from the higher regions and pushing their way through the resistance. In this vision the ego-sense and the individual assertion and separateness become quite unreal and illusory.[16]

In addition to women who have been chosen by their male gurus to succeed them, there have been women whose spiritual elevation was recognized independently, and around whom people gathered for help. Initially, however, they may have been ostracized for their socially odd behavior. Such was the case with an extremely popular contemporary female guru, Mata Amritanandamayi (b. 1953; fig. 3.7). She was discovered lost in meditation from the time she was a small child. When she was nine her mother fell ill, and all the housekeeping for her large family was put on her shoulders, so she had to leave school and work up to midnight on household chores. The family treated her as a servant, but she reportedly bore their demands cheerfully, always remembering her beloved Lord Krishna, and devoting the rest of the night to meditation, prayer, and songs to him instead of sleeping. Recognizing the sufferings of her neighbors, she listened to their problems, washed their clothes, bathed them, and even carried food to them from her own house, despite angry reactions from her family. As a teenager, she became more and more intoxicated with the Divine, first in the form of Krishna and then as the divine Mother of the Universe. At last she left the abuse of her family and lived outside, oblivious to normal needs of the body for food, sleep, and shelter, and losing consciousness of the outer world for days at a time. Ultimately, she had the supreme experience of enlightenment in which she recognized no difference between her individual self and the Divine. As she said, "Nothing is different from my own formless Self, in which the entire Universe exists as a tiny bubble." She understood herself as the Mother of every being, and over time, villagers who had once rejected her began coming to her for help. She physically embraces each person who comes to her, even lepers, lovingly comforting them and listening to their problems, hour after hour, sometimes all night long. She also gives informal spiritual talks to her devotees, translated into many languages (see box). She is said to have

3.7 Mata Amritanandamayi, extraordinary teacher and spiritual leader

EXCERPT **The Awakening of Universal Motherhood**
Sri Mata Amritanandamayi

At present, most women are asleep. Women have to wake up and arise! This is one of the most urgent needs of the age…. Women in countries where materialism is predominant should awaken to spirituality. And women in countries where they are forced to remain inside the narrow walls of religious tradition should awaken to modern thinking… .

In truth, no external power can possibly obstruct woman or her innate qualities of motherhood—qualities such as love, empathy, and patience. It is she—she alone—who has to awaken herself. A woman's mind is the only real barrier that prevents this from happening.

The rules and superstitious beliefs that degrade women continue to prevail in most countries. The primitive customs invented by men in the past to exploit and to subjugate women remain alive to this day. Women and their minds have become entangled in the cobweb of those customs. Women have been hypnotized by their own minds. Women have to help themselves in order to extricate themselves from that magnetic feld. This is the only way.

Look at an elephant. It can uproot huge trees with its trunk. When an elephant living in captivity is still a baby, it is tied to a tree with a strong rope or a chain. Because it is the nature of elephants to roam free, the baby elephant instinctively tries with all its might to break the rope. But it isn't strong enough to do so. Realizing its efforts are of no use, it fnally gives up and stops struggling. Later, when the elephant is fully grown, it can be tied to a small tree with a thin rope. It could then easily free itself by uprooting the tree or breaking the rope. But because its mind has been conditioned by its prior experiences, it doesn't make the slightest attempt to break free.

This is what is happening to women…. If women really want to, it won't be diffcult to break the shackles—the rules and conditioning that society has imposed on them. The greatest strength of women lies in their innate motherhood, in their creative, life-giving power. And this power can help women to bring about a far more signifcant change in society than men could ever accomplish… .

Amma remembers a story. In a village there lived a deeply spiritual woman who found immense happiness in serving others. The religious leaders of the village chose her as one of their priests. She was the frst appointed woman priest in the area, and the male priests didn't like it one bit. Her great compassion, humility, and wisdom were appreciated by the villagers. This caused a lot of jealousy among the male priests.

One day all the priests were invited to a religious gathering on an island, three hours away by boat. As the priests boarded the boat they discovered, to their dismay, that the woman priest was already seated inside. They muttered among themselves, "What a pain! She just won't leave us alone!" The boat set off. But an hour later the engine suddenly died and the boat came to a standstill. The captain exclaimed, "Oh, no! We're stuck! I forgot to fll the tank!" Nobody knew what to do. There was no other boat in sight. At this point the woman priest stood up and said, "Don't worry, brothers! I'll go and fetch more fuel." Having said this, she stepped out of the boat and proceeded to walk away across the water. The priests watched with great astonishment, but were quick to remark, "Look at her! She doesn't even know how to swim!"...

Women have to fnd their courage. Courage is an attribute of the mind; it is not a quality of the body. Women have the power to fght against the social rules that prevent their progress. This is Amma's own experience. Though a lot of changes have taken place, India is a country where male supremacy is still the rule. Even today, women are exploited in the name of religious convention and tradition. In India, too, women are waking up and springing into action. Until recently, women were not allowed to worship in the inner sanctum of a temple, nor could women consecrate a temple or perform Vedic rituals. Women didn't even have the freedom to chant Vedic mantras. But Amma is encouraging and appointing women to do these things. And it is Amma who performs the consecration ceremony in all the temples built by our ashram. There were many who protested against women doing these things, because for generations all those ceremonies and rituals had been done only by men. To those who questioned what we were doing, Amma explained that we are worshiping a God who is beyond all differences, who does not differentiate between male and female. As it turns out, the majority of people have supported this revolutionary move. Those prohibitions against women were never actually a part of ancient Hindu tradition. They were in all likelihood invented later by men who belonged to the higher classes of society, in order to exploit and oppress women. They didn't exist in ancient India.

In ancient India, the Sanskrit words that a husband used when addressing his wife were *Pathni*—the one who leads the husband through life, *Dharmapathni*—the one who guides her husband on the path of Dharma [righteousness and responsibility], and *Sahadharmacharini*—the one who moves together with her husband on the path of Dharma. These terms imply that women enjoyed the same status as men, or perhaps an even higher one. Married life was considered sacred, for if lived with the right attitude and right understanding, with both husband and wife supporting each other, it would lead them to the ultimate goal of life—Self-realization or God-realization.

In the sacred scriptures of India it is written that a place where women are not worshiped is doomed.

In India, the Supreme Being has never been worshiped exclusively in a masculine form. The Supreme Being is also worshiped as the Goddess in Her many aspects. She is, for example, worshiped as Saraswati, the Goddess of wisdom and learning; She is worshiped as Lakshmi, the Goddess of prosperity, and Santana Lakshmi, the Goddess who gives new life within a woman. She is also worshiped as Durga, the Goddess of strength and power. There was a time when men revered woman as the embodiment of these very qualities. She was considered an extension of the Goddess, a manifestation of Her attributes on

Earth. And then, at some point, because of the selfishness of certain men of influence and their desire for power and dominion over all, this deep truth was distorted and severed from our culture. And thus it was that people forgot or ignored the profound connection between woman and the Divine Mother... .

With this power within her, she can influence the entire world. The principle of motherhood is as vast and powerful as the universe. Anyone—woman or man—who has the courage to overcome the limitations of the mind can attain the state of universal motherhood.

The love of awakened motherhood is a love and compassion felt not only towards one's own children, but towards all people, animals and plants, rocks and rivers—a love extended to all of nature, all beings. Indeed, to a woman in whom the state of true motherhood has awakened, all creatures are her children. This love, this motherhood, is Divine Love—and that is God.

Excerpts from an address by Her Holiness Sri Mata Amritanandamayi for A Global Peace Initiative of Women Religious and Spiritual Leaders, Palais des Nations, Geneva, October 7, 2002.

30 million followers worldwide and has founded a host of charitable institutions, including a college of medicine, an engineering college, medical services, vocational training centers, schools, orphanages, temples, soup kitchens, and a large-scale program to provide housing for poor widows, the handicapped, and the elderly. Matronly and commonplace in appearance but radiating an inner dignity and wisdom, she is empowering women to be priests in the male-dominated tradition.

Hindu Practice in the West

A number of Western women have helped to spread selected aspects of Sanatana Dharma around the globe. In the final chapter, we will discuss the life work of one of the pioneers in this movement, the Russian mystic Madame Helena Blavatsky (1831–1891), who helped to introduce Hindu mysticism to Western audiences and ultimately founded the Theosophical Society.

Hindu techniques of meditation and inner growth are quite popular in the West, and are being propagated by women teachers such as Sri Daya Mata, American successor to Paramahansa Yogananda (1893–1952). His widely-read book *Autobiography of a Yogi* has drawn many Western women and men to India to study contemplative aspects of Sanatana Dharma, and Sri Daya Mata now oversees his Self-Realization Fellowship as a global network with 500 meditation centers in 54 countries.

Ma Jaya Sati Bhagavati, an American teacher, takes an admittedly eclectic approach to spirituality. She was born in a poor Jewish family in Brooklyn, received a vision of Christ who told her to "teach all ways, for all ways are mine," found an Indian guru, Swami Nityananda, was instructed in vision by the Indian guru Neem Karoli Baba, and became a devotee of Kali. She founded Kashi Ashram in Florida, from which she emphasizes social service as an important ingredient of spirituality and personally serves those who are suffering, such as people with AIDS, the homeless, and the poor.

Hatha yoga, the ancient Indian art of physical postures and breathing exercises to help the devotee achieve inner concentration, is often taught in the West without its religious context. Many Western women are thus learning and teaching yoga for health and peacefulness. Kripalu Institute, for example, has trained and certified thousands of yoga teachers, many of them women, and offers a huge menu of specialized self-help courses such as "Safe Yoga for Osteoporosis." Its beautiful retreat center in the Berkshire Hills of Massachusetts has survived the dismissal of its own founder over allegations of sexual relationships that contradicted his emphasis on celibacy.

Much to their dismay, Western women have had to negotiate a minefield of hidden sexual agendas on the part of some self-professed gurus who promote themselves in the West. Surrender to the guru is part of the path, so it is very confusing to a woman when the authority figure suggests to her that sex with him will help her advance spiritually. And those who have joined certain groups—such as the ecstatic Krishna-worshiping movement imported to the United States in 1965 by Srila Prabhupada—find themselves in the midst of patriarchal structures and restrictions on women for which they have no previous cultural conditioning. Nevertheless, the appeal of certain aspects of Sanatana Dharma seems to remain strong in the West for both women and men who are searching for soul-satisfying paths toward inner Truth.

Women and Communalism

In contemporary India, there is a strongly nationalistic political movement called communalism that claims to be trying to restore ancient Hinduism. Its interpretation of Hindu tradition is, however, highly selective and exclusivist. Women are playing strong roles in this movement and are participating in its attacks on the Muslim minority in the country. They claim that Vedic women were quite free and that they lost this freedom because of Muslim invasions and rule (*c.*1000–1707 CE). Thus these women in the nationalist movement are not secluded; rather, in 1992 they were seen actively helping to destroy the Babri mosque in Ayodhya, where the communalist factions want to rebuild a temple to Lord Ram which they think previously existed on the same site. Women led a mob in 1990 that killed hundreds of Muslims and were involved in terrible anti-Muslim violence in Gujarat in 2002. Some leading female politicians and women's political groups are helping to fan these flames of hatred, for the sake of Hindu nationalism.

At the same time that women are waving weapons and shouting slogans in public to support the communalist cause, Hindu communalists are otherwise supporting conservative restrictions on women. Citing scriptural references, they publish books that tell women how they should behave with their relatives, what they should wear after they are married, what to do when they are pregnant, and so forth. One such tract advises a woman to accept harsh treatment from her mother-in-law, to put her husband's comfort before her own, and if he beats her, "The wife should think that she is paying her debt of her previous life and thus her sins are being destroyed and she is becoming pure."[17]

Women and Social Activism

Other contemporary Hindu women are taking activism in quite different directions, such as environmental protection, protection of abused women, and help for the poor. Modern India has had a female prime minister and many prominent stateswomen.

Women are challenging environmental developments such as the mind-bogglingly huge Narmada Dam project, a series of 3,200 towering dams along the Narmada River—revered since ancient times as a goddess, and whose entire 815-mile length was traditionally a major spiritual pilgrimage trail, lined with temples to Mother Narmada and Lord Shiva. Because of the world's largest "water development" scheme, the waters impounded by the Narmada Dam project are inundating the beautiful, fertile, and sacred Narmada Valley and displacing approximately 40 million rural people who previously lived there, for highly questionable gains.

Another prime example of a movement in which Hindu women have been playing leading roles is the Chipko "tree-hugging" movement. Throughout the twentieth century, commercial interests moved into the Himalayan forests to cut down the trees for timber and to clear areas for extracting resources and developing tourism. The peasants living there were badly affected, for the trees had provided them with fuel, food for their animals, wood for their tools and houses, medicines, and food. The modern versions of economic development denied them their traditional subsistence-based community economies. Large-scale logging also led to heavy flooding, landslides, and soil erosion, with destruction of the natural ecosystems. So many trees were destroyed that women had to walk up to 15 miles to find fuel and fodder for their animals. Nevertheless, many of the men were lured by promises of industrial-style development, whereas the women were determined to protect the forests.

The women of the hill villages began to organize, around the spiritual slogan that the Himalayan mountain range is the father and the Ganges River the mother of the mountain people, and that both must therefore be protected. In 1972, a sporting goods company tried to fell 50 ash trees. To stop them, some of the village people—most of them women—tried the strategy of attaching themselves to the trees. They had chosen this method since it echoed a mother's instinctive response: if her child were threatened by a wild animal, she would hug the child to protect it. Again and again, in many locations, women's determined tree-hugging stopped the loggers. Women mobilized to stand by the trees wherever the forests were threatened, although it sometimes meant alienating their husbands and even losing their lives. They recited scriptures, bringing Dharma forward as the basis for informed actions. The women of the Chipko movement are still fighting for environmental protection, organizing reforestation work, and entering the public arena to try to educate the people about the realities of the situation.

Prize-winning writer Arundhati Roy (author of *The God of Small Things*), who considers the huge Narmada Dam project ill-conceived and is trying to limit the damage, proposes that in the twenty-first century perhaps we will become disillusioned with grand self-serving ideas that hurt the weak and voiceless. She implies that it is time to turn away from "masculine" strategies and toward "feminine" ones:

Who knows, perhaps that's what the 21st century has in store for us. The dismantling of the Big. Big bombs, big dams, big ideologies, big contradictions, big countries, big wars, big heroes, big mistakes. Perhaps it will be the Century of the Small. Perhaps right now, this very minute, there's a small god up in heaven readying herself for us. Could it be? Could it possibly be? [18]

In their activist roles, Hindu women are discovering bold inner resources that have long lain dormant beneath the mantle of submissiveness dictated by Brahmanic and cultural mores. Those who are religious-minded can find dharmic justification for their actions, for the essence of Sanatana Dharma is positive action for the sake of the greater common good, not for oneself. Their challenge is to maintain their inner equipoise in the face of the worldly difficulties of trying to help others. Mathioli R. Saraswati is founder of Nandlala Sewa Samiti, which runs orphanages, schools, and charitable trusts for the poor, old, and physically challenged and supports centers for spiritual learning and cultural enrichment. She gives much of her time to compassionate and visionary guidance of a constant flow of people seeking solutions to their illnesses or worldly problems, and looking for spiritual salvation. She says:

Sometimes my ears get tired listening to the sorrows and sufferings of people. Like the unabating sound of the ocean, their voices go on and on within me even when I am alone. When I feel spiritually drained I go to Tiruvannamalai [an ancient temple city in the southernmost part of India] and spend days in total silence. I do no worship or meditation but just let the silence of the place wash over me and rejuvenate me.[19]

Key Terms

Vedas	puja
Brahman, Brahmin	shakti
Dharma	kundalini
karma	guru
sati	samadhi
ashram	hatha yoga
bhakti	
Tantric, Tantrism	

Suggested Reading

Alston, A. J., *The Devotional Poems of Mirabai*, Delhi: Motilal Banarsidass, 1980. Spiritually sensitive English translations of the mystical love poetry of this great saint.

Amritanandamayi, Mata, *Awaken Children!*, Vallickavu, India: Mata Amritanandamayi Mission Trust. Multi-volume series of dialogues with an extraordinary contemporary teacher.

Chappel, Christopher Key and Mary Evelyn Tucker, *Hinduism and Ecology: The Intersection of Earth, Sky, and Water*, Cambridge, Massachusetts: Harvard University Press, 2000. Sensitive articles exploring the relationships between sacred teachings and environmental protection themes.

Ghanananda, Swami and Sir John Stewart-Wallace, *Women Saints East and West*, Hollywood: Vedanta Press, 1955. Appealing collection of biographies of saintly women including 14 Hindu saints.

Hancock, Mary, *Womanhood in the Making: Domestic Ritual and Public Culture in Urban South India*, Boulder, Colorado: Westview Press, 1999. Detailed analysis of the interweavings of tradition, modernity, caste, and politics in women's ritual behaviors in part of South India.

Kinsley, David, *Hindu Goddesses: Vision of the Divine Feminine in the Hindu Religious Tradition*, University of California Press, 1986. Thorough and intelligent study of the mythologies and meanings of various goddesses.

Kishwar, Madhu, *Off the Beaten Track: Rethinking Gender Justice for Indian Women*, New Delhi/Oxford/New York: Oxford University Press, 1999. A collection of thought-provoking articles by the respected editor of *Manushi.*

Mullatti, Leela, *The Bhakti Movement and the Status of Women: A Case Study of Virasaivism*, New Delhi: Abhinav Publications, 1989. Description of a thousand-year-old South Indian tradition in which women are free to study scriptures and teach religious philosophy, are never considered polluted, and not infrequently become saints.

Ramaswamy, Vijaya, *Divinity and Deviance: Women in Virasaivism*, Delhi: Oxford University Press, 1996. Fascinating research into the radical twelfth-century movement in which women and lower-caste people were uplifted to spiritual equality and produced great mystical poetry.

——, *Walking Naked: Women, Society, Spirituality in South India*, Shimla, India: Indian Institute of Advanced Study, 1997. Insightful analysis of "deviant spiritual women" who arose within several historical and regional movements, transcending constraints of the Brahmanic tradition.

Sharma, Arvind, ed., *Women in Indian Religions*, New Delhi/Oxford/New York: Oxford University Press, 2002. The latest female scholarship brought to bear on many Indian traditions, including Hinduism.

4
WOMEN IN BUDDHISM

We must all become great women of the Way

MYONGSONG SUNIM

As Brahmanic Hinduism had become bogged down in caste and gender oppressions in the fifth century BCE, a new path that was potentially more liberating for all beings developed in India under the enlightened wisdom of the Buddha. Many women achieved enlightenment in his path and become teachers of note themselves. After the Buddha's death, monks seemed to return to a more misogynistic treatment of women, but as Buddhism spread and evolved, some Buddhist women reached notable spiritual heights and served as powerful transmitters of the **Dharma**, the moral code for living. In the twentieth and twenty-first centuries, Western interest in Buddhist practice has become quite strong, accompanied by intensive feminist critique of any apparently anti-female biases in the various streams of Buddhism.

Life and Teachings of the Buddha

The roles of women in the life story of the Buddha point to the complexities of women's experiences within Buddhist practice. The man who became known as the Buddha ("Enlightened One") was born approximately 463 BCE in Lumbini (now in Nepal), in the foothills of the Himalayas. According to his birth legend, his noble mother Mahamaya delivered him ten months after he entered her side, miraculously, as a pure white elephant. Just as he was not conceived in the usual fashion, neither did he undergo birth by vaginal delivery. Instead, according to the story, his mother's labor started while she was in the Lumbini garden, and, grasping the branch of a tree, she delivered him painlessly through her side. Whether or not he was perhaps actually a month overdue and was delivered by what was later called Caesarean section, tradition says that his mother died seven days after the birth. He was thenceforth breastfed and adopted by her younger sister, Mahapajapati. The boy was named Siddhartha, meaning "he who has reached his goal."

According to familiar Buddhist stories, Brahmans had prophesied a great future for the boy as either a ruler or a world-renouncing holy man. His father wanted him to succeed him as king. Thus it is said that he arranged a life of supreme pleasure for Siddhartha within the palace compound, making it so attractive that he would never want to leave. Instead, according to legends, Siddhartha

	TIMELINE
c.463–383 BCE	Life of Buddha
c.417 BCE	Establishment of frst nuns' order under Mahapajapati
c.383 BCE	First Council of the Sangha criticizes Ananda for supporting women's ordination
100 BCE–100 CE	Rise of Mahayana Buddhism; *Lalitavistara*, biography of Buddha, written
c.80 BCE	Pali Canon written down in Sri Lanka
c.50 CE	Buddhism transmitted to China and then East Asia
3rd century CE	Sanghamitta Theri ordains royal women of Sri Lanka
8th century CE	Yeshe Tsogyel, Tibetan adept
11th century CE	Overthrow of Sri Lanka eliminates nuns' order there
1200–1253	Life of Zen Master Dogen, who affrms spiritual equality of women
1920 onward	Suppression of Chinese nuns and monks by Communists
1951	Chinese overrun Tibet, destroy monasticism
1976–1988	Tenzin Palmo, British-turned-Tibetan Buddhist, meditates in Himalayan cave
1979	Ayya Khema ordained in Sri Lanka
1979	First four nuns ordained at Forest Sangha Nuns' community, England
1998	Full ordination of 135 nuns from 23 countries in Bodh Gaya
2003	Chatsumarn Kabilsingh ordained as Bhikkhuni Dhammananda

became aware of the existence of sickness, death, and the option of asceticism and decided to devote his life to discovering and eliminating the roots of human suffering. Even though he had married his beautiful cousin Yasodhara and she was pregnant with their first child, he left the palace on the very day that his son was born. Contrary to the expected delight at the birth of a son, he reportedly did not even touch the child and stayed only long enough to name him "Rahula," meaning "bondage." He would not return to see his wife and son for seven years. It is said that Yasodhara put on widow's white clothes, stopped wearing jewelry, makeup, and perfume, and took only two meals a day, adopting a life of asceticism that paralleled that of her absent husband.

The Buddha's teachings about compassion are so strong that it is difficult to imagine that he was ignorant of the pain undoubtedly felt by his wife when he left her. Still, he was clearly driven by a tremendous sense of the importance of his mission for the sake of humanity at large. Renouncing the throne and his family responsibilities, Siddhartha shaved his head, exchanged his fine clothes for the coarse robes of a wandering mendicant, and began his search.

After studying with two Brahman teachers, he lived in the forest for six years as an ascetic, undertaking severe renunciate practices such as fasting, exposing his body to extremes of heat and cold, retaining his breath, and "resting" on a bed of brambles. Despite all his heroic efforts, he did not reach his goal.

Then women re-entered his life in spiritually significant ways, according to the *Lalitavistara* (an influential biography of the Buddha written anonymously in India around 100 BCE–100 CE as the Mahayana path of Buddhism was arising). At that point in his search, Siddhartha was reportedly barely subsisting on a self-imposed daily diet of only one juniper berry, one grain of rice, and one sesame seed. According to the *Lalitavistara*, his dead mother Mahamaya then came to him in a vision and urged him to try a middle path between this extreme asceticism and the princely life of pleasure. He agreed to shift his course, and thenceforth accepted more food, kindly prepared for him by ten young women of the nearby village. Sujata, daughter of the head, was said to have been told by the deities, "Formerly you prayed, 'After partaking of the food prepared by me, may the Bodhisattva attain perfect, supreme, and complete Enlightenment.' Now do what must be done."[1] According to this rather magical biography, Sujata then concocted a blessed rice pudding and offered it to the Buddha.

It was after being thus fed lovingly by a woman and then helped by the Earth Goddess that Siddhartha at last achieved his goal. Sitting under a tree, he meditated with such intensity that he perceived the cause of suffering and the means of ending it. He reportedly entered **nirvana**, the ultimate egoless state of bliss. According to the biographies, Mara, personification of evil, tried to thwart his enlightenment by claiming that Siddhartha had not been generous in his past lifetimes and was therefore unworthy of a high spiritual position. Mara was backed by his devilish armies, whereas Siddhartha was alone. He therefore touched the earth, asking her to bear him witness. According to the story, the Earth Goddess came to his rescue, verifying his generosity and causing the armies of Mara to retreat.

After his enlightenment, the Buddha began his forty-five-year mission as a wandering teacher, living a life of voluntary poverty with a begging bowl. Disciples followed him, and for them he established orders of monks and eventually nuns (about which more later). His basic teaching was the Four Noble Truths: 1. Life inevitably involves suffering. It is imperfect and unsatisfactory. 2. Suffering originates in our desires. 3. Suffering will cease if all desires cease. 4. There is a way to realize this state: the Noble Eightfold Path. The Eightfold Path is a systematic approach to correcting our thinking, speech, actions, and livelihood through skillful retraining and quieting of the mind. The Buddha taught that suffering is a basic fact of human existence because of our ignorance and clinging to what is impermanent. Buddhist scholar Rita Gross gives a concise explanation of the Buddha's chief insights:

Buddhists emphasize that it is *conventional* ways of living, based on grasping and self-cherishing, that are inevitably permeated with suffering, not living itself. If grasping and ego-fixation are left behind, one will experience contentment and bliss. Suffering is the byproduct of grasping, which occurs only because of ignorance. Thus, the most important word in the fundamental Buddhist analysis of existence is not "suffering," but "ignorance." Ignorance of what? Ignorance of impermanence, of the lack of a permanent abiding self, ignorance that there is no essence, soul, or entity that endures through all the flux of experience. Because of this fundamental ignorance, which results in grasping for security and permanence and for assurance that personal identity is everlasting, suffering occurs. When it is fully realized that everything is impermanent, including personal identity, there is no grasping, and, hence, no suffering.[2]

EXCERPT Mindfulness and the End of Suffering
Maechee Pathomwan
Contemporary Head Nun of a Province in Thailand

I was ordained as a nun when I was 12 years old. [First] I learned the meditation where you notice the breath in the abdomen. You become aware that your chest fills with air, your abdomen expands, then you exhale and it is empty. I wanted to see what the outcome of practicing this would be.

Five years later, after graduating from the Dharma study school, I moved to Nanachat, a monastery where I learned the four foundations of mindfulness as the basis for meditation... .

As a young nun I was very afraid of ghosts, so I went to stay in a small hut by the charnel ground. I was gripped by a paralyzing fear several times, but I decided to remain meditating to overcome the fear.

Another time someone had carved a watermelon and put a candle in it and seeing this I feared it was a ghost. However, before running away, I stopped and stood still, looking clearly at that ghost, as my father had suggested, till I realized it was a watermelon with a candle.

The temple where I was staying was famous for being infested by snakes. One day I decided to stay still for three hours, but after ten minutes I felt something cold on my leg. I was afraid it was a ghost and I opened my eyes. I was relieved to see it was only a poisonous snake, so I sat even stiller, as recommended by my teacher when encountering snakes.

From my teacher I learned the "lifting of the palm" meditation. First for three days and three nights I lifted and lowered the palm of my hand until I felt the consciousness in the palm of my hand. Then I practiced 12 days consecutively to see what would happen. Finally I went into a six-month solitary retreat.

Once I decided to sit for three hours watching the rising and falling of the abdomen. I was very concentrated and felt very light and rapturous. Another nun was looking after me. When I opened my eyes after what seemed like ten minutes and asked if the three hours were up, the other nun said that I had been sitting for 18 hours.

There has been a noticeable change in my personality during the course of my life. When I was younger, I was very hot-headed. I used to speak coarse language when I was angry and hit things. As I practiced, that ceased, and there was more refnement and stillness. This is the main thing that has happened to me: developing the ability to watch anger as it arises and ceases with mindfulness and clear comprehension of its causes, and being able to deal with it without having to project it out. I feel that mindfulness, awareness and clear comprehension are very important in my daily life.

The inspiration to enter the monastic life was based on the three refuges [Buddha, Dharma, **Sangha**—the community of monastics and perhaps laypeople]. As my practice grew it became more than an inspiration, because I saw how by practicing with awareness I actually experienced things arising and ceasing. This continues to nurture my faith in Buddhism and in this way of life... .

After we have developed a strong foundation, we can sustain mindfulness for a long time and begin to watch the heart/mind [*citta*] directly. We can watch the reactions and feelings that arise. How does each feeling feel? What are we feeling at the moment of sitting? We try to be aware of the current feeling... .

Because the [citta] is the centre of sensory consciousness, it is also the centre of deflements. It is the place where we can watch desire arise and grasping happen. We have to be able to sustain mindfulness in order to use it to comprehend each feeling as it arises. Then we go beyond the perception of it and understand the cause.

Once we realize deflements happen and we have a place, a centre, where perception, consciousness, feeling and volition happen, then we can practice in a way to watch them cease. Once we know how things are, once we know there is desire, we understand it, we do not grasp it anymore and then it ceases.

By practicing in this way we can watch the arising and ceasing of things, and allow this movement to be as it is. We can see that the root cause of grasping and becoming has to do with anger, greed, lust and hatred. We can notice a certain feeling coming and making contact, and through that very awareness we disengage from it and it ceases.

When we see these feelings clearly, they dissolve. As we see desire happening and ceasing, we can decrease the actual process of grasping as we become more advanced in this technique. Automatically we start to re flect on *anicca* [impermanence], *dukkha* [suffering] and *anatta* [no-self]; how things rise, how suffering comes in the course of life and how it ceases.

We continue to practice in this way; as things come, we watch them, we let them be around until we are able to comprehend exactly how they arose and then take them to cessation. Then we understand the frst noble truth [suffering], the second [the cause of suffering], the third [the end of suffering] and the fourth [the path to end the suffering].

Maechee Pathomwan, from "Serenity and Stillness," in Martine Batchelor, *Walking on Lotus Flowers*, London: Thorsons/HarperCollins, 1996, pp. 53–7.

Creation of an Order of Nuns

As the story has come down to us, the Buddha spent an additional year after his enlightenment, walking and teaching. Then, when his son Rahula was seven years old, he returned to his hometown, on foot, begging along with his disciples. He also visited the palace and eventually had a meeting with his faithful wife Yasodhara, who reportedly expressed her sadness that he had been gone and pleasure that he had come to see her after so many years' absence. According to the biographers, he then told the whole royal family that she had been a wonderful wife to him not only in this life but also in his previous life, making great sacrifices so that he could follow his spiritual calling.

Before the Buddha left town the next day, Yasodhara sent his son to him to claim his heritage. What did the Buddha have to offer him? Enlightenment. Thus he had Rahula ordained as a monk, leaving Yasodhara with neither husband nor son at home.

Mahapajapati, the Buddha's aunt and foster-mother, and his lonely wife Yasodhara then appealed to him to allow them and 500 more royal women to join his mendicant order—in upper-class Hindu society of that time, a highly unusual request. But already Mahapajapati had been exposed to the Buddha's teachings and found them highly appealing. Many royal women whose husbands had left to join the Buddha as monks sought her help and spiritual guidance. But when she requested the Buddha to create an order of nuns and ordain them, he refused. Three times, it is said, she made her request, but each time he refused, saying only, "Please do not ask so." Why? We can only speculate. One theory is that he wanted to spare his aunt and the other royal women the difficulties of the life of a wandering ascetic. Another perspective is that although he was enlightened, he was also a product of his time and culture, and could not imagine women so transcending their traditional responsibilities in the home, or did not want to disrupt society with such a revolutionary move.

In any case, the Buddha then reportedly left on foot for Vesali, some 150 miles distant, to preach there. Undeterred, Mahapajapati and some of the royal women shaved their heads, donned saffron robes like monks, and walked the same distance. She explained to Ananda, one of the Buddha's main disciples, the women's desire to become ordained as nuns. Sympathetic to their cause, Ananda approached the Buddha to make their request. According to the scriptural account, he asked the traditional three times, and was thrice refused. At last, Ananda asked if women are capable of spiritual perfection and enlightenment, and the Buddha asserted that they are. Thus encouraged, Ananda repeated the request as a logical corollary, adding praises of Mahapajapati as the foster-mother of the Buddha who had nursed him from her own breasts. Thereupon the Buddha reportedly agreed to allow women to retire from household life to a houseless existence, on the condition that the nuns should abide by Eight Special Rules, in addition to their other ascetic vows. As for Ananda, he was criticized by the other monks for having opened the way for women to enter the monastic order. It is not known how much of this tale is genuine and how much was invented by the monks who carried the scriptures orally or the monks who first wrote them down over 300 years after the death of the Buddha, in Pali—one of the languages of north India—at a Council in Sri Lanka, thousands of miles away. Nevertheless, the story is an established part of Buddhist belief and the Eight Special Rules are still in effect.

These are the Rules, all of them concerning the subordination of nuns to monks:

1   A nun even of a hundred years' standing should salute a bhikkhu [monk] and rise before him, though he had received the higher ordination that very day.
2   A nun should not spend a retreat in a place where there is no bhikkhu.
3   Every fortnight a nun should ask from the Order of monks the time of uposatha [a weekly assembly of the Sangha, or monastic community] and when a bhikkhu would come to admonish them.
4   The pavarana [a ceremony after the retreat, in which members of the Sangha ask each other's forgiveness for offenses committed] should be held by a nun

in the presence of the Order of both bhikkhus and bhikkhunis [nuns].

5   Major offenses of a nun should be dealt with by the Order of both bhikkhus and bhikkhunis.

6   A female novice, who remains on probation for two years, should receive the higher ordination from both orders.

7   A nun should on no account rebuke or abuse a bhikkhu.

8   Nuns should not give admonition to bhikkhus, but bhikkhus should admonish nuns.[3]

Speculation abounds as to the basis of these rules, which seem quite oppressive when seen out of socio-historical context. At the time of the Buddha, Indian women were totally under men's control and protection. To allow them the freedom of moving through the countryside independently as wandering mendicants, forsaking any family responsibilities, was already such a revolutionary step that the restrictions were perhaps placed on them to make their new status more acceptable both to the monks and to society at large. Some commentators feel that the restrictions were designed according to the thinking and weaknesses of the monks— rather than that of the nuns, who were ready to give up everything in order to follow the spiritual path set forth by the Buddha. It is also likely that the rule forbidding a nun to undertake a spiritual retreat in any place where there is no monk was designed for her protection from rapists.

There is another, perhaps apocryphal, sequel to the story of the creation of the nuns' order. According to the scriptural account, the Buddha predicted that Buddhism would last only five hundred rather than a thousand years now that women had been admitted as ascetics:

> Just as, Ananda, when the disease called mildew falls upon a flourishing field of rice, that field of rice does not long endure, in exactly the same way, Ananda, when women retire from household life to the houseless one, under a doctrine and discipline, that religion does not long endure… . And just as, Ananda, to a large pond a man would prudently build a dike, in order that the water might not transgress its bounds, in exactly the same way, Ananda, have I prudently laid down eight weighty regulations, not to be transgressed as long as life shall last.[4]

The fact that Buddhism is still flourishing almost 2,500 years later, with women more active than ever within it, invalidates this claim traditionally attributed to the Buddha. Women have not, in fact, constituted a blight upon Buddhism, and some contemporary feminists are attempting to reform the tradition, claiming that monks have spoiled its original purity. In Taiwan, there is now a movement to abolish the Eight Special or Chief Rules. Venerable Zhaohui Shi of Hongshi Buddhist Institute reports:

> The Eight Chief Rules (gurudharmas) constitute an evil system that makes women feel inferior and makes men arrogant… . Let there be a reasonable, public debate about whether to keep or abolish the Eight Chief Rules. Hopefully Buddhist male chauvinism can break out of its narrowmindedness and reach full psychological and intellectual maturity. Because its strategy and

critique are sound, the movement to abolish the Eight Chief Rules is heating up. Noted senior monks such as Ven. Xingyun, Ven. Liaozhong, Ven. Jingland, and Ven. Chuandao have spoken out boldly in supporting the movement to uphold justice for the nuns. Another tactic I have promoted is to awaken the nuns' critical sense and psychological freedom, since nuns have long slumbered under the slave mentality produced by their education.[5]

Despite their subordination to the monks, many early Buddhist nuns were spiritual women of great distinction. One of the most respected teachers was Patacara, who endured terrible sufferings. According to the texts, she had eloped with her lover, who was her servant. He was fatally bitten by a snake, her two children died, and her parents and family were all killed. Wild with grief, she roamed without clothes. People beat her with sticks as a crazy woman. At length, she staggered naked into the place where the Buddha was teaching. He firmly told her, "Sister, recover your presence of mind." Pulling herself together, she covered herself, told the Buddha her story, and asked for his help. He told her that she had been suffering immeasurable pain not only in this lifetime but for thousands of births. Recognizing that only the Dharma would save her from this suffering, she requested to be allowed to live as a nun. Eventually, she became enlightened and had thirty disciples of her own; she was well known as a compassionate and inspiring guide to other women. The Buddha praised her as the most observant in the rules of the monastic order. In the collection of writings attributed to the women disciples of the Buddha, she explains her tremendous personal transformation:

With my family destroyed, despised by all, with husband dead, I attained the undying.

The noble eightfold way leading to the undying has been developed by me; quenching has been realized; I have looked at the doctrine as a mirror.

I have my dart cut out, my burden laid down; that which was to be done has been done by me.[6]

Names of numerous other women who were the Buddha's disciples, both nuns and laywomen, appear in the texts. Among them was the laywoman Visakha, the intelligent and wealthy mother of a merchant family, who not only supported the Sangha financially but also gave the Buddha good advice about managing the lives of the monastics—and he apparently listened.

The Buddha clearly stated that women and men have the same spiritual potential. Even though the Eight Special Rules subordinating nuns to monks in the Pali texts are attributed to the Buddha, he also set rules to prevent the monks from using the nuns as their servants, for the women were to have equal rights to time for spiritual practice. The success of the nuns in understanding and practicing the Dharma and achieving enlightenment is described in the Pali texts as "the light of the Sangha."[7]

To help the monastics live harmoniously with each other in a disciplined, simple way that was inspiring to others, and to insure perpetuation of the Dharma, the Buddha gave general rules for living and then reportedly created additional precepts as specific problematic situations arose. Ultimately, monks were given 250 precepts to live by, whereas nuns were given 338 precepts, for the nuns were held to most of the precepts created when the monks misbehaved, plus those created when nuns misbehaved, but not vice versa. Venerable Wu Yin, a Chinese nun from Taiwan, comments on this extra burden for women monastics: "Precepts are the ornaments of a monastic. We voluntarily undertake them in order to train our minds. As nuns, having more precepts only makes us more aware and scrupulous in our actions."[8]

Women's Situation in the Major Forms of Buddhism

With such justice being accorded to women and also to people from the lower castes, as well as the promise of liberation from suffering by one's own determined efforts to control the mind, Buddhism became very popular in India. The Buddha sent his disciples out to teach the Dharma and it spread in many directions. As it encountered local belief systems and cultures, it accommodated them, in a dynamic process of evolution that continues today. In time, three major forms of Buddhism could be distinguished. **Theravada**, "The Way of the Elders," is now prevalent in the southern countries of Sri Lanka, Burma, Thailand, Cambodia, and Laos. It claims to be closest to the original teachings of the Buddha; meditation is the chief focus. The versions that developed in northern and eastern Asia—Nepal, Tibet, Sikkim, China, Korea, Mongolia, Vietnam, and Japan—are collectively known as **Mahayana** ("The Greater Vehicle"). This emphasizes compassion and loving kindness but also contains theistic elements as well as highly abstract constructs, such as the concept of "emptiness" (about which more later). Within Mahayana a distinctive path developed in Tibet, called **Vajrayana** ("The Diamond Vehicle"). It includes esoteric Tantric spiritual practices from India and elements from indigenous Tibetan shamanism. Another branch developed in China, where it is known as **Ch'an** Buddhism, and then flourished in Japan, where it is known as **Zen** Buddhism.

Theravada

Institutionalization of Buddhism began three months after the death of the Buddha, with the convening of the First Council of the Sangha. Five hundred enlightened monks attended. Ananda recited the Buddha's words from memory; another senior monk recited the codes of discipline for the monastic orders, both male and female. However, none of the enlightened women who were disciples of the Buddha were invited. And we know that Ananda was criticized for his request to allow women to enter the monastic order. In other words, as soon as the Buddha—who had apparently made it clear that women and men were spiritual equals—passed on, culturally-based negative views of women became apparent among the monks.

Three hundred years later, the memorized texts were first written down in Pali by monks in Sri Lanka. It is possible that their cultural bias against women informed this process. There are some clearly misogynistic portions describing women as sexually insatiable temptresses, deceitful and foolish—a danger to men trying to follow a renunciate path. But praises of certain Buddhist women were included, as noted above. It was also recorded that when a sceptic asked the Buddha if any of his followers ever truly managed to become free from desire and attachment, and to achieve enlightened wisdom, he replied that many hundreds had indeed done so already, of which there were as many nuns as monks, and as many laywomen as laymen.

According to inscriptions at *stupas* (monuments honoring remains of the Buddha or renowned disciples, built during the early centuries of Buddhism), nuns and monks were allowed to keep their personal wealth, and as many laywomen and nuns as laymen and monks devoted their wealth to building these centers of devotion. However, all of the *stupa*s honor men. When some nuns once tried to build one over the remains of their revered sister, it is written in the texts that a senior monk admonished them and destroyed it before their eyes because their devotions were interrupting his meditation. Even today, women are not accorded much spiritual status in Theravada, and ultimately the lineage of ordained nuns completely died out in this original form of Buddhism.

Mahayana

The Mahayana path is theoretically more sympathetic to women. Arising in India approximately 500 years after the passing of the Buddha and then spreading eastward, it claims to be based on teachings of the Buddha that had previously been hidden because people were not sufficiently enlightened to understand them. Its ultimate philosophical teaching is that everything is empty, even the path to enlightenment. The focus is not on personal liberation from suffering but rather on becoming a **bodhisattva**, one destined to become enlightened, who dedicates his or her own spiritual practice to help all suffering beings. Either a male or a female may be a bodhisattva. The earliest Mahayana scriptures, "The Perfection of Wisdom," teach that all the usual distinctions we make between beings, including male/female, are ultimately empty of meaning. Nonetheless, a leading male disciple of the Buddha quoted in the scripture uses a feminine metaphor for wisdom:

> I pay homage to the perfection of wisdom! She is worthy of homage. She is unstained, and the entire world cannot stain her. She is a source of light, and from everyone in the triple world she removes darkness, and leads them away from the blinding darkness caused by defilements and wrong views. In her we can find shelter. Most excellent are her works. She makes us seek the safety of the wings of enlightenment. She brings light to the blind, so that all fear and distress may be forsaken. She has gained the five eyes, and she shows the path to all beings. She herself is an organ of vision. She disperses the gloom and darkness of delusion. She guides to the Path those who have strayed on to a bad road…. She is the Mother of the Bodhisattvas.[9]

In Mahayana belief, there are three types of Buddhahood. One was exemplified by the historical Buddha whose childhood name was Siddhartha, but he was only one exemplar of this type. The Buddha is a person who perfectly practices the path of Dharma and can guide others on that path. Still bound by the patriarchal cultures

4.1 Kuan-yin, the Chinese bodhisattva of mercy, with the compassion of a mother

in which it was practiced, Mahayana Buddhism proclaimed that one could only become a Buddha in a male's body. Another type of Buddhahood— that of invisible Buddhas and bodhisattvas who are beyond the human level and can be seen only by inner vision—reveres personifications of wisdom and compassion. Here many female figures are found, such as Kuan-yin, beloved in East Asia as the hearer of cries, the bodhisattva of mercy (fig. 4.1). Her gender was initially that of a male, but in many cultures she has become worshiped in female form, as a beautiful mother who will save all who call upon her. The final type is Buddha-nature itself, an abstract, all-pervading, impersonal essence potentially existing in all beings; gender is no issue here.

Women's equal potential for spiritual advancement received a huge boost in Japan from the great thirteenth-century Zen master Dogen, who developed the Soto Zen school in which austere sitting meditation is the main practice. He was sharply critical of discrimination against women. For instance, he said:

In the case of a nun who has received the treasury of the true Dharma eye through transmission, if [the monks of] the four fruitions, *pratyeka-buddhas* [those who achieve enlightenment on their own], and even those of the three wise stages and of the ten holy states pay homage to her and seek the Dharma from her, she should receive their obeisance. By what right are only males noble? The empty sky is the empty sky; the four elements are the four elements; the five *skandas* [aggregates composing human appearance] are the five *skandas*. To be female is exactly the same: as for the attainment of the Way, both [male and female] can attain the Way. Hence both should have high regard for the attainment of the Dharma, and not argue about differences between male and female. Such is the most marvelous law of the Buddha-way.[10]

Zen Buddhism developed from the Chinese Ch'an version. Here from the twelfth century onward there was talk of the equal capacity of males and females for enlightenment. The Ch'an master Ta-hui wrote, for instance, "For mastering the truth, it does not matter whether one is male or female, noble or base. One moment of insight and one is shoulder to shoulder with the Buddha."[11]

A mixed method has been perceived about women within Ch'an Buddhism, however, for the imagery for those who are capable of reaching enlightenment is "masculine," referring to traits of courage, determination, and strength of will. These qualities are not necessarily found only in males, though. In explaining the term *chang-fu*, meaning the heroic person who has what it takes to attain enlightenment, the scholar Chan-jan writes, "One who has seen the Buddha-nature, even if she be a woman, is also called 'man.'"[12]

Vajrayana

When Buddhism was established in Tibet in the eighth century by Padmasambhava, a Tantric adept from India, it was presented as a "civilizing" influence taming the presumably wild, aggressive nature of the indigenous people. In the Bon tradition then prevalent (which itself may have subdued previous indigenous ways of life), the area is filled with vicious spirits and the whole Tibetan landscape is understood as a demoness lying on her back. According to an unusual traditional story, the Buddhist agenda was to put sacred structures at strategic points on top of the demoness to subdue her and thence bring forth the virtues that also exist in the land, making Tibet a "Dharma palace." Feminist scholar Janet Gyatso explains this pervasive legend as a metaphor for suppression of the indigenous religion:

> It is a common pattern: the old site of the indigenous religion is associated with some sort of special configuration in the land, in which the powers of the deep are perceived as having particular force. It is a place connected with spirits, spirits that course in a cavernous underground realm, and are often of a female nature or associated with some overarchingly feminine flavor of spirituality. The incoming religion seeks out those very sites, and builds right on top of them. The new structures obliterate the old places of worship, but gain instant history and sacred power thereby.[13]

Though perhaps somewhat subdued by the importing of androcentric Buddhist institutions from India, the powerful female spirit of Tibet was still evident in the development of Vajrayana Buddhism there. Spiritual practice was open to both women and men, and highly esoteric practices were based on sexual intimacies. People did not need to withdraw to monastic life to seek spiritual goals; householders could also become adepts. Women and men were perceived as having the same fundamental nature and the same potential for enlightenment and development of spiritual powers. Qualities commonly thought of as "masculine" or "feminine" existed in both men and women; the ideal was the balance of these qualities in an enlightened person. This balance of masculine and feminine was symbolized by a male and female in sexual union. The male represents compassion; the female represents wisdom.

A central Vajrayana practice is meditation upon a deity, understood as an embodiment of energy. Some of these are female bodhisattvas; some are **dakinis**, or enlightened female energies from the celestial realm who may appear on earth in human form as **yoginis**, females who have spiritual powers and enlightened wisdom because of their meditation practice. Both men and women may meditate on these manifestations, and many leading Vajrayana men as well as women have been initiated by such female deities.

4.2 White Tara is a figure of devotional contemplation for many Tibetan Buddhists

Dakinis of pre-Buddhist Tibet were thought to be wild and dangerous, drinking the blood and eating the flesh of human corpses. They were also associated with menstrual blood, which made women supposedly impure. With the advent of Buddhism, the dakinis were presumably subdued and developed positive qualities as protectors and teachers of the Dharma. There are many stories of their appearing in disguise as old women, who if recognized as dakinis can impart spiritual guidance.

Most famous of the deities is Tara. She is depicted in elaborate devotional paintings as a beautiful young girl, often with seven eyes. The three eyes in her face symbolize the purity of her mind, speech, and body, and the four eyes in her palms and the soles of her feet symbolize immeasurable compassion, loving kindness, joy, and calm composure. Her graceful hands have thumb and forefinger joined, representing the union of compassionate action and wisdom; the open palms confer spiritual blessings. She also holds a lotus flower, symbol of her freedom from any negativity (fig. 4.2). She is dedicated to compassionately helping anyone who calls on her. Many Tibetan Buddhists recite her praises, including these verses:

> Homage to the liberating one, swift and courageous,
> Whose sight is like instant lightning,
> Who arises from myriad stamens
> Of the lotus face of the Protector of the three worlds.
>
> Homage to her whose face gathers
> One hundred autumn full moons,
> Who blazes with the sparkling light of a thousand stars.
>
> Homage to her whose hand is adorned
> With a blue and gold water-born lotus,
> Who has for her domain giving, effort,
> Asceticism, peace, patience, and concentration.[14]

There are numerous historical women in Vajrayana who were renowned as spiritual teachers. Of these, the most famous is the eighth-century Yeshe Tsogyel. Another is Machig Lapdron, a great eleventh-century mystic who was considered a reincarnation of Yeshe Tsogyel (see box, p. 110). Machig Lapdron had been taught to approach evil with compassion, and to head fearlessly into frightening places. She is celebrated as the developer of the Chod practice, a tool for realizing the emptiness of the self, according to the Perfection of Wisdom (*Prajna Paramita*) scripture. In the Chod practice, the mystic makes an offering of her body. After cutting her attachment to her body and her ego, the practitioner visualizes a wrathful dakini cutting off her head, chopping up her body, and cooking it in a vessel made of her skull, transforming it into nectar which is then offered to all spirits. Then the mystic meditates upon the concept that the offerer, the process of offering, and the beings who have been fed are all empty—void of permanent reality or self-hood. The practice was done in remote, lonely places or in cemeteries, accentuating its frightening quality. Those who did this advanced practice wore other people's used clothing, ate beggars' food, and lived where no one else wanted to go, thus copying the example of Machig Lapdron. She was a highly sought-after teacher and at the age of 52 she proved her wisdom and spiritual power to three pandits (learned men) who had come from India to challenge her ability to develop new teachings within Buddhism. Her Chod ritual is still used as an advanced practice today, accompanied by recitations including these phrases attributed to her:

> Phat!
> O! the unenlightened mind, which looketh upon the apparent as being
>   the Real,
> May it be thoroughly subdued in virtue of religious practices;
> And thus in order to master and thoroughly comprehend
>   the true nature of the Real,
> I resolve to free myself of all hope and of all fear... .
>   Phat!
> This illusory body, which I have held to be so precious,
> I dedicate as a heaped-up offering,
> Without the least regard for it, to all the deities
>   that constitute the visualized assembly;
> May the very root of self be cut asunder.
>   Phat![15]

It should be noted here that even though there have been remarkably strong and wise women within Vajrayana Buddhism, proving their spiritual equality with men by their own great efforts, orders of Tibetan Buddhist nuns today have a much lower status than that of Tibetan Buddhist monks, as will be discussed later.

Contemporary Status and Ordination of Nuns

Although there is no lack of women interested in a life of ascetic spiritual study and service, even today there is relatively little institutional encouragement for them to be ordained. In addition, there is a lack of cultural support in societies where a woman's place is thought to be in the home. In some places, the lineages

BIOGRAPHY   Yeshe Tsogyel

The favorite consort of Padmasambhava, who established Buddhism in Tibet in the eighth century, was Yeshe Tsogyel. She also became a great miracle-worker and teacher in her own right. The branch of Tibetan Buddhism practicing the ways of Padmasambhava and Yeshe Tsogyel is Nyingmapa, "the Old School." Parts of her story were contained in the Nyingmapa histories of Padmasambhava, but in the eighteenth century a Tantric monk incorporated these pieces into an inspired biography of the development of her tremendous spiritual power. Some of its salient details follow.

Daughter of a royal couple, Yeshe Tsogyel was so beautiful that her suitors were ready to fght each other to obtain her. For her part, she wanted a celibate life of spiritual seeking. But her father, ignoring her strong entreaties, tried to avoid the conflct among the lusty rivals by declaring that whoever grabbed her could take her. He dressed her in fne clothes, collected a sizable dowry of provisions, and sent her out of the house. At once, the agent of one rival grabbed her by the breast and tried to pull her away. According to the semi-historical biography, she reported:

> However, I braced my legs against a boulder so that my feet sank into it like mud. To move me was like trying to move a mountain, and no one succeeded. Then those fendish offcials took a lash of iron thorns, and stripping me naked they began to whip me. I explained to them:
>
>> This body is the result of ten thousands years of effort;
>> If I cannot use it to gain enlightenment
>> I will not abuse it with the pain of samsaric [worldly] existence.
>> You may be the noblest and most powerful in Kharchu
>> But you lack the equipment to gain a day of wisdom.
>> So kill me; I care not.[16]

Again they beat her, and took her away. She escaped, but was later recaptured. At last, as war was again threatened by the rivals, the king himself demanded her for his wife. Because of her spiritual faith, he appointed her as custodian of the Dharma. His real desire was not for her but for his own spiritual liberation, so in exchange for the priceless guidance of the great master Padmasambhava, the king offered her to him as his spiritual consort. She and Padmasambhava practiced Tantra together in a remote cave, developing extraordinary spiritual powers during their "ecstatic dance of delight." Thus "enabled to act for the beneft of the seven worlds of the ten directions," she was given the secret name Tsogyel, meaning "White Goddess of Pure Pleasure."

After further practices with a slave whom she bought as her personal consort, she went alone to the edge of a glacier for severe austerities. For instance, she is said to have meditated for a year wearing only a cotton cloth. Then, as her

4.3 Yeshe Tsogyel, the powerful
Tibetan Buddhist adept, who
defied all attempts to prevent
her attaining enlightenment

meditation continued, she stopped eating altogether and wore no clothes at all
for protection from the intense cold and wind. Her body racked with afflctions,
near death, she was saved many times by visionary experiences, including help
from deities and a vision of Padmasambhava instructing her to make herbal
elixirs to sustain her body. She was tempted and tormented by visions of
demons, phantom animals, delicious foods, seductive young men, thunderbolts,
and blizzards—all trying to disrupt her meditation—but she remained steadfast,
singing:

> Since I entered the dimension of dynamic space,
> Reaching the Mind of the Great Mother, absolute, empty being,
> The heart of the ten transcendental perfections,
> Enjoying profound and perfect insight,
> I am not to be cowed by visionary experience.
> Every situation is a play of empty being.... .
> Since I entered the arena of mystic practice
> Arriving at the heart of the Mahayana mysteries,
> Enjoying the identical flavour of pleasure and pain,
> I have no preference for good or bad.
> Both good and bad are lifts to peak experience.[17]

When she returned to her guru, he was greatly pleased that she had never lost
heart, and reportedly made this statement:

O *yogini* who has mastered the Tantra,
The human body is the basis of the accomplishment of wisdom
And the gross bodies of men and women are equally suited,
But if a woman has strong aspiration, she has higher potential.[18]

Considered a female Buddha, she was surrounded by both male and female disciples. She gave herself selflessly for the benefit of the people, bringing a dead man back to life, subduing demons, passing through matter, dancing through space, and hiding bits of wisdom throughout the landscape for future use. When her time on earth was finished, she became a rainbow of blinding light and vanished.

Advanced Tibetan Buddhist practitioners have manifested many extraordinary spiritual powers, so there is no reason to doubt her story. In any case, beliefs about Yeshe Tsogyel serve as one of the world's strongest icons of women's potential for spiritual development and service. There is also a positive value placed on her sexuality, quite in contrast with the usual attempts to control and deny women's sexual power.

of fully ordained nuns have even been allowed to die out completely and it is difficult to restore them because of the Special Rule that nuns must be ordained by both ordained nuns and ordained monks.

Why is full ordination important? Only fully ordained nuns or monks can carry on the responsibilities of leading the Sangha (the monastic community), teaching the followers of Buddhism, and guiding the novices. Novices, who are called **samaneris** in Pali and do not follow as many precepts as those who are fully ordained, may only serve as attendants to their teachers and help in the daily duties such as caring for the prayer hall and classrooms.

Sri Lanka was the first place where an order of nuns was created outside India. In the third century BCE, King Asoka of India sent his well-educated daughter Sanghamitta Theri, a nun, with a group of learned nuns to ordain Queen Anula of Sri Lanka and 500 of her attendants, at the queen's request. Orders of both nuns and monks were well supported by Sri Lankan royalty, and in the fifth century CE a group of nuns went to China to ordain Chinese women as nuns. That lineage is still in existence. But in Sri Lanka, the orders of both nuns and monks disappeared during conquest of the kingdom by an Indian dynasty in the eleventh century, and the nuns' lineage was never reestablished there. Only lay sisters, known as "ten precept mothers," have tried to carry on an ascetic life, but they are usually poor and scattered. The "ten precepts" are the basic vows that are traditionally taken by Buddhist monastics in most lineages: to avoid 1. killing, 2. stealing, 3. sexual contact, 4. lying, 5. taking intoxicants, 6. singing, dancing, and playing music, 7. using cosmetics, ornaments, or perfumes, 8. sitting on high or expensive seats or beds, 9. handling precious substances or money, and 10. eating at improper times (i.e., between the midday meal and the next day's breakfast). In recent years, senior Sri Lankan monks have worked hard to help raise the educational standards of the "ten precept mothers," and have been instrumental in preparing and ordaining a select few as nuns.

Buddhism has existed in Thailand for over 700 years and monks are quite well established, but there has never been an official order of Buddhist nuns there. The closest thing is the life of perhaps 10,000 *mae jis*, women who shave their heads, wear white robes, and live monastically somehow without any ordination, education, or official position within the Buddhist community. They receive no help from laypeople, whereas monks are well supported, since people feel that to feed the monks brings them religious merit. Some of the *mae jis* eke out a living by begging. Despite public disinclination to provide a path to ordination for Thai nuns, a few women such as the well-known intellectual Dr. Chatsumarn Kabilsingh have taken *samaneri* or *bhikkhuni* ordination in Sri Lanka. Dr. Kabilsingh, who became Bhikkhuni Dhammananda in 2003, has struggled to help other Thai women receive higher ordination. *Samaneris* are of higher status than *mae jis* but lower than fully ordained *bhikkhunis*. They are both of lower status than the lowest monks. Bhikkhuni Dhammananda explains how she feels about becoming junior to the most junior monk:

To be ordained means that you have shifted your interest from the outside world to an inside world. My interest now is how to lessen my suffering and how to try to make enlightenment real. Junior or senior gets in our way of practice. The lower we are, the better it is for the practice of letting go of the clinging to this self, the illusive self.[19]

The situation in Burma is somewhat better, for women dedicated to meditation, recitation, and study of the Buddhist texts are referred to respectfully by a title meaning "possessors of moral integrity." They live quietly and simply in ascetic communities, but are not considered fully ordained nuns. Nepal, the birthplace of the Buddha, had no Buddhist monks or nuns until the twentieth century. Now there are perhaps 60 Nepalese nunneries; other nuns live by themselves or in small groups. The younger nuns are trying hard to propagate the Dharma.

In Vietnam, a new monastic tradition was founded in 1946: the Vietnamese Mendicant Sangha. The monks and nuns of this order make a distinctive ascetic vow to keep traveling, changing their living place every three to six months. The late nun Venerable Huynh Lien (1923–1987) worked hard for 40 years despite the ravages of war to develop this new path, of which she was appointed the head nun, and now it includes 1,000 nuns. She tried to raise the quality of nuns by establishing courses for them at a large pagoda, and she also did extensive social work by setting up schools and orphanages, visiting people in prisons and hospitals, and working for peace and equality of women and men. Particularly concerned about the need to help women, she said, "I vow that I will eternally be reborn in a woman's body, because there are countless miserable women in the world, and it will be very easy to be close to them and help them, even though I know it will be a difficult task."[20]

In mainland China, there were an estimated three million monks and nuns before 1920, when the Communists began persecuting them and taking over their temples, monasteries, and nunneries and converting them to secular purposes, such as warehouses and barracks. Monks and nuns had to take off their robes and work in other jobs. After the devastating Cultural Revolution (1966–1976), such oppressive measures diminished, and some of the temples have been restored. The older nuns say that they had continued to practice the Dharma in their own homes. However, among today's more materialistic generation in China there is less interest in spiritual practice and religious values.

In Taiwan, Buddhism seems to date back to the twelfth century. Now nuns outnumber monks there. The nuns are relatively well educated and both religiously and socially active, and they have access to full ordination. According to a major Buddhist publication, four of the ten most influential Buddhist leaders in Taiwan are nuns. They have been cited for their outstanding social contributions, their work as religious leaders, and their efforts to provide new ways for women to express their religious commitment. One of these four nuns is Hiuwan Fashih, founder of Huafan University, an architecture and technology college which now has 600 students. Venerable Hiuwan explains her philosophy of education:

■ Buddha's "natural education" is the process of enlightenment; it is man's [sic] innate nature to reach towards this enlightenment…. The environment for education should be away from the noise and dust of urban areas, among the tranquillity of the woods. Living quarters should be simple and pleasant. The learning environment should be decorated with literary and artistic works, and contain objects conducive to religious thoughts and meditation. Academically, the power of imagination and the quality of compassion should be emphasized….

This age of knowledge explosion and advanced technology seems to be progressing in leaps and bounds. But the more advanced human knowledge becomes, the more lonely and desperate the human mind is. It is time to probe deeply into the exact needs of human beings.

How can young people develop confidence? Purifying their thoughts brings compassion and wisdom, then everything in their environment is seen as valuable and they reach true appreciation of the interdependence of things. In this way young people can contribute to this world, striving and planning for the better development of everything in it.[21] ■

Korea received Buddhism from China in the fourth century CE, and nuns' ordination began soon after that of monks. The 6,000 Korean nuns today live in separate communities without personal property, and many of them practice meditation intensively. They are of high educational standard: high-school graduation is required before ordination, they must use the special higher educational facilities at a women's college, and attend various institutions where they receive lengthy training in Buddhist scriptures.

In Japan, the majority of nuns are practicing austere Zen Buddhism or highly devotional Pure Land Buddhism. Although the nuns take precepts as bodhisattvas, they are not considered technically fully ordained since there were never the required five fully ordained Japanese nuns to pass on any lineage. They serve their communities in temples, where the head priest may be either a monk or a nun. Women were the first Buddhists in Japan, and nuns have always been respected since many of them came from the royal family. The Soto Zen nuns take great encouragement from the egalitarian teachings of the Zen patriarch Dogen, and unlike Japanese monks—many of whom are married and let their hair grow—most of the nuns take pride in maintaining pure traditions of celibacy, shaved heads, and monastic life. They have also made a conscious choice to preserve and practice Japanese artistic traditions, such as flower arranging, calligraphy, poetry writing, sewing, and the tea ceremony. All are approached as spiritual practice, with awareness focused on delicate subtleties of colors, scents, textures, and sounds. Paula Arai observes:

> Today, the arts as a living tradition, combining usefulness and beauty, can be found as central qualities in these Soto Zen nuns' lives…. Nuns' temples and monasteries are some of the few places in contemporary Japan where one can find beauty and discipline cultivated and refined in ordinary activities like removing slippers, peeling apples, and cooking radishes. Soto nuns maintain a relatively traditional lifestyle in the midst of a technologically progressive society with the tea ceremony and flower arranging as integral aspects of many nuns' daily lives. The nuns also help preserve the traditional arts of Japan by teaching them in their original spirit: training for the body, mind, and heart.[22]

Tibet once supported one of the largest concentrations of Buddhist nuns, with large nunneries as homes to many intensely religious women. However, starting in 1951, the Chinese occupation, severe oppression, and the destruction of Tibetan religious traditions have largely destroyed the nuns' order in Tibet itself. Now Tibetan nuns are practicing in exile in many other countries, including nearby India and Bhutan, as well as in the West. The community in exile has thus far been unable to provide accommodation for all nuns seeking to practice, so many of them live with relatives. Many are studying and practicing in the Himalayan areas near the Tibetan

4.4 Sister Santacitta and Ani Tenzin Sangmo, director of Thosamling Nunnery for Buddhist women in Dharamsala, India, hiking to the nunnery with their few possessions

border, such as Dharamsala, India, where the Fourteenth Dalai Lama has established his headquarters in exile (fig. 4.4). Because the nuns are not well funded, the
Dalai Lama himself has taken an interest in helping them and has contributed sub-
stantially to buildings and educational programs for them. Previously, some of the
nuns were living in caves for lack of any other shelter—a very ascetic lifestyle,
given the cold winters in the mountains. Several Western women who have become
Tibetan Buddhist nuns—such as Tenzin Palmo and Karma Lekshe Tsomo—are
raising money to build new communities for the nuns of that area, helping to provide not only minimal shelter, which the nuns build with their own hands, but also
literacy training, Buddhist education, and health care. Tenzin Palmo is fundraising
to create a series of nunneries in the area designed to revive the *togdenma* tradition
of female yogis, who undertake years of austere ascetic practice.

In recent decades, many Western women have taken training and ordination as
Buddhist nuns in various traditions and are practicing, teaching, and spreading the
Dharma very sincerely. What is the appeal of the ascetic life, especially one drawn
from a different culture? Ajahn Candasiri is a Scottish nun in the Forest Sangha
Nuns' Community at Amaravati, in Hertfordshire, England, which was established
along with a forest monastery by the English monk Ajahn Sumedho, disciple of the
famous Thai monk Ajahn Chah. She was one of the first four nuns ordained there
in 1979. When asked why she chose this disciplined path, she answered:

We deliberately put ourselves into a form which prevents us from following all
our desires, in order to see them and to notice how they change. Normally,
when we are caught up in the process of desire, there is no sense of objectivi-
ty. We tend to be totally identified with it, so it is very difficult to see it clearly
or to do anything about it, other than be swept along with it… .

In the monastery it's not so easy to do this any more. We deliberately tie
ourselves down in order to look at the drives, energies or desires that would
normally keep us moving. Now you might ask: But what kind of freedom is
this?—tying oneself down in a situation where one is constantly restrained,
always having to conform? Always having to behave in a particular way; to bow
in a particular way, and at particular times; to chant at a particular speed and
pitch; to sit in a particular place, beside particular people… . What kind of freedom is this?

It brings freedom from the bondage of desire. Rather than helplessly, blindly
being pulled along by our desire, we are free to choose to act in ways that
are appropriate, in harmony with those around us… . The monastic form and
precepts help us to make a peaceful space around the energies of desire, so
that, having arisen, they can then burn themselves out. It is a process that takes
great humility, because first we have to acknowledge that desire is there… .
Whatever the monks and nuns might be going through, they are at least
making the effort to be present with it, bearing it patiently, rather than feeling
that it shouldn't be like that, or trying to make it change… . Then, maybe, rather
than simply reacting to the ignorance of humanity and adding to the confusion
and violence that we see around us, we are able to act and speak with wisdom
and compassion in ways that can help to bring a sense of ease and harmony
among people.[23]

Women from many countries are now working together to improve the status of and opportunities for women within Buddhism. A major international group formed in 1987 is Sakyadhita: Daughters of the Buddha. Its aims are to create communication networks among Buddhist women around the world, to enhance understanding among Buddhists of different traditions, to support and educate women as teachers of the Dharma, to guide and assist those wanting to be Buddhist nuns, to conduct research about women's issues in the Buddhist texts, and to help promote world peace through practice of the Buddha's teachings.

Sakyadhita was instrumental in a major ordination ceremony in 1998 for 135 women from many countries held in Bodh Gaya, India, place of the Buddha's enlightenment. It attempted to revive the fully ordained lineages of nuns through the lineage taken from India to Sri Lanka and thence to China. The historic ordination was led by Venerable Master Hsing Yun, with other senior monks from China, Sri Lanka, Thailand, Burma, Cambodia, Tibet, and Bangladesh. According to the Eight Special Rules said to have been set down by the Buddha, it is only with such support from male ascetics that female ascetics can ever achieve full ordination.

Feminist Analysis of Buddhist Concepts

Buddhism in its varied forms has spread to the West in recent centuries, into cultural settings quite different from those where it originated and first developed. Its spread in the West coincided with the growth of the women's movement, so Western feminist scholars have examined it from their own critical perspectives. According to feminist assessment, Buddhism seems to contain, in its core affirmations, a less patriarchal, more egalitarian impetus than other major religions, and yet in practice it seems to deny that impetus, as illustrated in the foregoing section on Buddhist nuns.

Vajrayana Buddhism, for instance, has come under feminist criticism for the Tantric principle of the joined efforts of a man and a woman to achieve transcendent spiritual insights and powers. Whereas this gender equality was revolutionary at that time and region, some feminists who have adopted Buddhism now argue that a woman is quite capable of achieving enlightenment by herself. Western efforts toward independence for women are inevitably resistant to another central principle of many Asian religions: the importance of a spiritual master as a guide. However, in the past as well as the present, the wise Buddhist master may be a woman rather than a man.

As discussed earlier, feminists are carefully analyzing Buddhist scriptures for androcentrism. Where it is found, they are trying to determine whether the male bias stemmed from the Buddha or from those who later wrote down or conveyed his teachings. For instance, there is a passage in which the Buddha is quoted as advising his disciple Ananda not to look at or talk to women, for, as he reportedly said, "Nothing binds men as strongly as women."[24] The corollary is there for nuns as well—"Nothing binds women as strongly as men"—but since it is usually monks who are doing the preaching, the women's point of view is not mentioned, and instead, women are given the impression that they are impure hindrances. The Thai nun Dhammananda points out that weakness for women is men's weakness, not an indication of any failure on the part of women. She writes:

These texts were recorded by and for monks. Newly ordained monks who have not had any practice are still mentally weak. They are easily swayed by their sensual inclinations, of which women are the major attraction. It is not the women's fault but the monks' weakness. Without women's presence, some monks still have enough problems with the image of women they create in their imagination. No woman can be responsible for the sexual behavior of the monks; the monks themselves have to control their own desires. The enlightened monks are able to practice self-restraint and transcend gender differences. The Buddha himself never had to avoid women, because women no longer appeared to him as sex objects. He was well balanced and had complete self-control.[25]

The Buddha is elsewhere recorded as having advised laymen that "To respect one's mother and one's wife is to be blessed."[26]

Other assumptions in classic Buddhist texts seem to reflect the Buddha's Indian cultural background, such as woman's being a commodity belonging to men rather than being an independent human being. The texts speak of women as suffering from five woes: parting from their family at the time of marriage, serving their husbands, and suffering from menstruation, pregnancy, and childbirth. The first two are Indian cultural expectations; the latter three may be celebrated as life-giving processes rather than regarded as reasons for suffering, depending upon one's conditioning.

According to contemporary research, the well-known assertion that a woman cannot be a Buddha may not have originated with the Buddha but may instead have been added to the tradition in about the first century BCE. Early Mahayana texts hold that a woman may become enlightened by changing into a man. Images of women continued to improve: later Mahayana texts on emptiness and the Buddha-nature of all beings accept that a woman may realize her Buddha-nature in her own female form. Interestingly, the term *tathagatagarbha*, which is usually translated as "Buddha-nature," can be more literally translated as "Buddha-womb" or "Buddha-embryo." These obviously feminine metaphors use women's experience of pregnancy to refer to something that is concealed but can be born, for it is inherent in all things. Nonetheless, most of the histories of renowned Buddhist women reveal opposition from their families, since spiritual development and progress to leadership are not a path that women were expected to follow.

Earlier we looked at possible reasons why the Buddha reportedly laid down eight Special Rules subordinating all nuns to all monks, as a condition for creating the nuns' order. Contemporary research is also questioning whether the Buddha himself actually drew up those rules or whether they were added later by the monks. Mahapajapati and other founding nuns were apparently ordained by the Buddha without any two-year probation period (the sixth rule for nuns), so the scriptural story that she accepted the rules may be a falsification.

Western feminist scholar Rita Gross, having embraced Buddhism, is urging a "feminist revalorization of Buddhism." She explains, "Buddhism as received tradition is not perfect and complete as it is. It needs to be revalorized by feminist insights in order to overcome patriarchal inadequacies and excesses, and to be true to its own vision." Professor Gross proposes that a very strong case can be made for a feminist reconstruction of Buddhism that is a genuine outgrowth of central Buddhist teachings. Two of these are egolessness and emptiness. She points out that gender roles and gender privilege are matters of worldly thinking, not of enlightened thought. If egolessness is the goal, then there is no argument supporting male dominance over women. On the other hand, it is not appropriate to encourage women to be submissive, either. Egolessness is the natural outcome of the realization that there is no permanent self, for everything is ever-changing, impermanent. Gross writes:

> [Egolessness] is not a blank vacuous state of nonperception and nonthinking. It is not an indifferent state of not caring what happens to one's self or others, and it certainly has nothing to do with being so psychologically beaten and victimized that one acquiesces to whatever happens. It has nothing to do with being spineless and indifferent, with being a pushover for others' aggression. An egoless person is quite the opposite of a zombie. Rather, she is cheerful, calm, humorous, compassionate, empowered, and energized because she has dropped the burden of ego.[27]

Similarly, Buddhist texts themselves criticize gender discrimination since it contradicts the principle of emptiness. Ultimately, there is no solid self; all its components are insubstantial, ephemeral, empty of eternal reality. Gross claims:

> "Male" and "female," like all other labels and designations, are empty and lack substantial reality. Therefore, they cannot be used in a rigid and fixed way to delimit people.... Therefore, the Buddha said, "All are not really men or women." ...The level of convention and appearance is the level of gender roles and stereotypes, but at the level of absolute truth, "all are not really men or women."[28]

A caveat: even though feminism has brought lively and deep critique of Buddhist doctrines and practices, there is a feeling among some Asian commentators that Western feminism is a product of a particular culture and cannot be applied to Buddhist women of their cultures.

Contemporary Women as Buddhist Teachers

The number of women who are now teachers of Buddhism is mushrooming in all traditions. In addition to guiding practitioners in many centers, they are busily writing books about understanding and practicing the Dharma in contemporary life. A few of the many examples are described below. Though numerous, Buddhist women teachers have all had to struggle with patriarchal institutions. There is, as yet, no chance of a female Dalai Lama.

We have already mentioned two well-known Western women who have long been Tibetan Buddhist practitioners and teachers: Venerable Tenzin Palmo (fig. 4.5), an English-born nun who spent 12 years in a cave on a traditional Tibetan Buddhist meditation retreat and is now trying to help support Tibetan Buddhist nunneries and re-establish the lineage of *togdenmas*, and Karma Lekshe Tsomo, President of Sakyadhita, the International Association of Buddhist Women, college professor, and initiator of educational projects for Buddhist women in the Himalayas. Among many other contemporary women teachers, Venerable Tsultrim Allione was among the first Western women to be ordained as a Tibetan Buddhist nun, wrote the landmark book *Women of Wisdom* about great female masters in the Vajrayana tradition, and directs the Tara Mandala Retreat Center in Colorado. She observes, from a Western point of view:

What I see is a great flowering of women practitioners. We have made a good start in the West. There are still disturbing notes, like translators who duplicate non-inclusive language in their translations, insisting that "he" means "we" and that "Buddha's sons" means all practitioners. There are still women being exploited sexually by teachers who use their power and mystique, imbued in them by their traditions, to seduce their students. There are still many ways nuns are not treated equally. There are also those who feel bringing these problems up is "dualistic." Mostly, though, such issues are being recognized as problems and are being addressed.

We must hold each other gently in this transition, and seek to provide support and facilitate the passage for those who follow. As first-generation translators and practitioners, we are setting precedence for the future. We have the teachings, we have the path.[29]

4.5 Venerable Tenzin Palmo, whose 12-year retreat in a Himalayan cave is described in the book *Cave in the Snow*

Many meditation centers such as the Insight Meditation Society of Barre, Massachusetts, have been set up in the Theravada tradition, and their teachers include a large number of women. Venerable Ayya Khema, who died in 1997, was very active in establishing pioneering meditation centers for women in Australia, Sri Lanka, and Germany. In Nepal, the elderly nun Venerable Dhammawati established a center run by nuns in Kathmandu, to which some 900 laypeople, mostly women, come on special days of worship. The objectives of the center are to teach Buddhism to laypeople, to raise women's status, to make Buddhist education available for children, and to inspire children to practice Buddhism in their everyday lives. Maechee Pathomwan of Thailand, quoted earlier in this chapter, has been teaching **vipassana** (mindfulness meditation) for decades. The Amaravati and Cittaviveka Buddhist Monasteries in England house many excellent women teachers, whose Dharma talks have been collected and published as *Freeing the Heart.*

In the Mahayana tradition, Myongsong Sunim is the abbess of a Korean nunnery housing 257 nuns. She is highly respected in Korea as one of the foremost teachers of Buddhist scriptures. She explains:

> I prefer to talk about the Dharma in an easy relaxed manner. I try to teach laypeople about living correctly in everyday life. As the lotus flower which grows from dirty mud has a beautiful pure bloom, in the same way, laypeople living in the world can flower like the lotus. If they cultivate a good way of living together they are fulfilling the intention of the Buddha… .
>
> There is no difference between the monks and the nuns. They are both disciples of the Buddha. They are like the two wings of a bird. Our mission in life is to spread the Buddha's teaching… .
>
> I tell all the nuns that they must become awakened beings. By their own accomplishments they must become good knowing advisors. They must not kowtow anywhere they go. We must all become great women of the Way.[30]

In Japan, Buddhist women united during the middle of the twentieth century to demand more egalitarian education and leadership opportunities in the spirit of Dogen's teachings of the spiritual equality of men and women. One of the present teachers who is reaping the benefits of this is Zen Master Aoyama Sundo (b. 1933). She is the abbess of a community training women to be advanced teachers, and she is also the head of a temple where she teaches laypeople and leads well-attended retreats. She often appears on television, speaking about the life of Zen. A cosmetics firm wanted to feature her well-known, unlined face. She refused, explaining that she does not use cosmetics and attributing her "glowing complexion" instead to a life of gratitude, living in the present, and accepting everything that happens as a teaching.

Zen meditation centers have been established in many urban areas around the world, and many of them have women teachers. With or without robes and shaven heads, female Zen masters are providing a profoundly different role model from the ones set out for women by patriarchal cultures, and are inspiring many more women to take up the practice of spiritually mature concentration of the mind in the present, leading to direct perception of reality, without concepts, without illusions, without the tyranny of conditioned thoughts and emotions. The late Roshi Jiyu Kennett (d. 1996), who founded abbeys and meditation groups in Europe and the United States, proposed that "this is a religion for spiritual adults, not for spiritual children, with a big daddy and a big stick."[31]

Buddhist Women as Social Activists

The Buddha did not teach people simply to seek their own enlightenment; his goal was the elimination of the suffering of all sentient beings. In keeping with that goal, Buddhist women around the globe are serving not only as spiritual teachers but also as activists, trying to transform their societies.

There are Buddhist women who are trying mightily to reform Buddhist institutions and make room for women in positions of leadership. Venerable Voramai Kabilsingh (1908–2003), mother of Bhikkhuni Dhammananda of Thailand, quoted earlier, received full ordination in a Taiwanese sub-sect of the Theravada tradition but the male-dominated Thai Buddhist establishment refused to see her as anything but a *mae ji* and insisted that the extinct lineage of Thai nuns could not be restored through ordination from China. Undeterred, she managed the building of a temple by and for Buddhist women, offered education for children, published a monthly magazine, and provided for the needs of refugees and the needy. Her daughter is carrying on the work, particularly helping the large numbers of Thai women who have fallen into a life of prostitution. Dhammananda is a sharp critic of the men who run the Thai Sangha. She writes:

The requirements for a man to join the Sangha are minimal. Virtually any man off the street can become a monk, provided he is not completely blind, severely deformed, or obviously insane. There is no requirement for an educational standard—the majority of Thai monks have only four years of compulsory education (the same as most *mae jis*).... . Buddhist men become monks first, and then study Buddhism. A great many monks do not continue a formal Buddhist education. Many monks are simply uneducated farmers in yellow robes.

These facts do not have much social impact in themselves. But the actual situation in Thailand is that Thai society holds the Sangha in extremely high regard, seeing them as representing directly the Buddha. Whatever monks do, good or bad, laypeople prefer not to interfere, being afraid to lose merit and create negative personal karma by speaking ill of monks.... .

Within the context of the Thai Sangha, we should not be surprised to find cases of monks who emphasize the inferiority of women and the evil karma of prostitutes. They can then suggest that women and prostitutes should make more merit to guarantee better future lives by offering dana [gifts] to the temple. As a result, some temples in the north are richly adorned from the income of prostitutes.[32]

Rita Gross argues that the bodhisattva ideal requires committed Buddhists to actively oppose social injustices. She writes:

The bodhisattva ethic of compassion and universal concern for all beings cries out for the development of a social ethic that includes prophetic social criticism and vision.... . When one realizes how unliberating, how oppressive, economically, politically, psychologically, and spiritually, are some of the dominant forms of social organization and authority, it is hard to imagine being serious about liberation or the bodhisattva path without being involved in social action at some level.[33]

Buddhist women can now be found working to relieve suffering in many forms. Roshi Joan Jiko Halifax is the founder of Upaya, in Santa Fe, New Mexico, an organization of socially engaged Buddhists whose programs for the terminally ill, especially those with AIDS, help them die peacefully. Nuns from the order of Nipponzan Myohoji such as the Japanese nun Jun Yasuda undertake lengthy walks crossing many countries to promote causes such as nuclear disarmament, elimination of injustices to indigenous people, and environmental protection, chanting a major Buddhist text to help bring peacefulness. Sister Chang Khong of Vietnam was active, along with the Zen Master Thich Nhat Hanh, in developing the School for Youth for Social Service, which ultimately engaged 10,000 young people in rebuilding the many facilities destroyed by war in their country.

4.6 Aung San Suu Kyi, steadfast supporter of democracy in Burma, has lived under house arrest for many years

Yet other Buddhist women are putting their lives on the line to protest against unjust political systems. Venerable Ngawang Sangdrol is serving a sentence of 21 years in Tibet for "crimes" beginning with her participation in a peaceful "Free Tibet" demonstration when she was only 13 years old. She has reportedly been beaten and tortured.

One of the most celebrated political prisoners in the world is Aung San Suu Kyi (fig. 4.6). She was awarded the Nobel Peace Prize for her staunchly determined efforts to promote democracy for the people of Myanmar (Burma), but it was presented *in absentia*, since she is often under house arrest by the government, which is trying to limit the activities of her National League for Democracy. Her family has settled safely abroad, but Aung San Suu Kyi chooses to stay in her country, constantly exposing herself to danger for the cause that was begun by her father, who was assassinated. She encourages a courageous life of Buddhist ethics, without limiting them to Buddhism as an institution, as the antidote to corruption and oppression:

■ Within a system which denies the existence of basic human rights, fear tends to be the order of the day.... Yet even under the most crushing state machinery, courage rises up again and again, for fear is not the natural state of civilized man [*sic*]. The wellspring of courage and endurance in the face of unbridled power is generally a firm belief in the sanctity of ethical principles combined with a historical sense that despite all setbacks the condition of man is set on an ultimate course for both spiritual and material advancement. It is his capacity for self-improvement and self-redemption which most distinguishes

EXCERPT **Defining Oneself as Buddhist**
bell hooks
Distinguished Professor of English at City College, New York

Asked to define myself, I wouldn't start with race; I wouldn't start with blackness; I wouldn't start with gender, with feminism. I would start by stripping down to what fundamentally informs my life, being a seeker on the path. Feminist and antiracist struggles are part of this journey. I stand spiritually, steadfastly, on a path of love—that's the ground of my being.

Love as an active practice—whether Buddhist, Christian, or Islamic mysticism—requires that one embraces being a lover, being in love with the universe.... To commit to love is fundamentally to commit to a life beyond dualism. That's why, in a culture of domination, love is so sacred. It erodes dualisms—the binary oppositions of black and white, male and female, right and wrong. Love transforms....

Often black participation in contemplative Buddhist practices goes unnoticed. As a group we are noticeably absent from organized Buddhist events. Many teachers speak of needing to have something in the first place before you can give it up. When interpreted literally to mean the giving up of material privileges, of narcissistic comforts, often individuals from underprivileged backgrounds assume these teachings are not for them. Black folks have come to my home, looked at Buddhist work, and wanted to know, "Give up what comforts?" Since much of the literature of Buddhism directed at Westerners presumes a white, materially privileged audience as the listener, it is not surprising that people of color in general and black people in particular may see this body of work as having no meaning for their lives. Only recently have individuals from marginalized groups dared to interrogate the assumption that the contemplative traditions, particularly those from Asia, speak only to privileged and/or white Westerners....

Critical reflection has been intense within the feminist movement as thinkers have addressed the issue of meaningful spiritual practice within the context of patriarchal culture. Ten years ago if you talked about humility, women would say, I feel I've been humble enough, I don't want to try to erase the ego—I'm trying to get an ego. Now the achievements women have made in all areas of life have brought home the reality that we are as corruptible as anybody else. That shared possibility of corruptibility makes us confront the realm of ego in a new way....

In a culture of domination, preoccupation with victimhood and identity is inevitable. I once believed that progressive people could analyze the dualities and dissolve them through a process of dialectical critical exchange. Yet globally the resurgence of notions of ethnic purity, white supremacy, has led marginalized groups to cling to dualisms as a means of resistance. In the United States we are witnessing the resurgence of forms of black nationalism that say white people are bad, black people are good, white people are inferior, people with melanin superior....

If we are concerned with dissolving these apparent dualities we have to identify anchors to hold on to in the midst of fragmentation, in the midst of a loss of grounding. My anchor is love. It is life-sustaining to understand that things are always more complex than they seem. This is what it means to see clearly. Such understanding is more useful and more difficult than the idea that there is a right and wrong, or a good or bad, and you only have to decide what side you're on. In real love, real union or communion, there are no simple rules.

Love as a foundation also takes us more deeply into practice as action in the world. In the work of Vietnamese Zen master Thich Nhat Hanh we find an integration of contemplation and political activism. Nhat Hanh's Buddhism isn't framed from a location of privilege, but from a location of deep anguish—the anguish of a people being destroyed in a genocidal war. The point of convergence of liberation theology, Islamic mysticism, and engaged Buddhism is the sense of love that leads to greater commitment and involvement with the world, not a turning away from the world… .

To be capable of love one has to be capable of suffering and of acknowledging one's suffering. We all suffer. A culture that worships wealth wishes to deny the fact that when people have material privilege at enormous expense of others, they live in a state of terror as well, with the unease of having to protect their gains, which then necessitates even greater control. That's why we see fascism and a compulsion to control surfacing right now in Europe and the United States. The phrase "New World Order" is significant because it confirms a general sense that life is out of control. Our faith in life is weakened by nihilism. Nihilism is a kind of disease that grips the mind and then grips people in fundamental ways. It can only be subverted by seizing the power that exists in chaos—the power of self-agency, and collective agency, too—the idea, as in Nhat Hanh's work, that the self necessarily survives through linkage with collective community.

All this is tied to reshaping Buddhist practice so that one really sees fundamental change. We all have to have a lived practice. For example, if we see a female who is powerful yet humble, we can learn about the kind of humility that is empowering, and about a form of surrender that does not diminish one's agency. Our conventional ways of constructing identity must be altered in the very way we structure practice and form community… .

A culture of domination like ours says to people: there is nothing in you that is of value; everything of value is outside you and must be acquired. This is the message of devaluation. Low self-esteem is a national epidemic and victimization is the flip side of domination. While revolution must begin with the self, the inner work must be united with a broader social vision… .

We have been led to believe that we can have change without contemplation. Militant resistance cannot be effective if we do not first enter silence and contemplation to discover—to have a vision—of right action. The point is not to give up rage, rather that we use it to deepen the contemplation to illuminate compassion and struggle… .

It serves the interest of domination if the only way we respond to being victimized is by unleashing uncontrollable rage. Then we really are just mirroring the very conditions that brought us into victimization—violence, the conquering of other people's territory. If we talk about burning down other people's property as a "takeover," is this any different than what the United States did in Grenada or Iraq? This is not stepping outside the program, it's mirroring it. The other side of total victimage is rage. Women in the early feminist movement who saw themselves as complete victims were often overwhelmed by blinding rage—the two things go together. They become a dangerous force intimately wedded to the psychology of domination.

A fundamental shift in consciousness is the only way to transform a culture of domination and oppression into one of love. Contemplation is the key to this shift. There is no change without contemplation. The image of Buddha under the Bodhi tree illustrates this—here is an action taking place that may not appear to be a meaningful action. Yet it transforms.

From bell hooks, "Contemplation and Transformation," in Marianne Dresser, ed., *Buddhist Women on the Edge: Contemporary Perspectives from the Western Frontier*, Berkeley: North Atlantic Books, 1996, pp. 287–92.

man from the mere brute. At the root of human responsibility is the concept of perfection, the urge to achieve it, the intelligence to find a path towards it, and the will to follow that path... . Concepts such as truth, justice and compassion cannot be dismissed as trite when these are often the only bulwarks which stand against ruthless power.[34]

The movement begun by the Buddha almost 2,500 years ago in India has spread around the world, and its contemporary renaissance seems to be correlated with the growing appearance of Buddhist women in positions of spiritual leadership and social activism. Born a Christian, bell hooks, for instance (see box, p. 124), is also a student of Buddhist teacher Thich Nhat Hanh, and speaks of herself as standing on "a path of love."

Key Terms

Dharma	Zen Buddhism
nirvana	bodhisattva
Sangha	dakini
Theravada	yogini
Mahayana	samaneri
Vajrayana	vipassana
Ch'an Buddhism	

Suggested Reading

Allione, Tsultrim, *Women of Wisdom*, London and New York: Arkana, 1986. Fascinating biographies of six historical women masters in Tibetan Buddhism by a Western woman who has been living with and studying the religious culture since 1967.

Arai, Paula Kane Robinson, *Women Living Zen: Japanese Soto Buddhist Nuns*, New York/Oxford: Oxford University Press, 1999. In-depth analysis of the lives of nuns at the largest Soto Zen nunnery in Japan.

Batchelor, Martine, *Walking on Lotus Flowers: Buddhist Women Living, Loving and Meditating*, London: Thorsons/HarperCollins, 1996. Personal accounts by 18 women who are Buddhist teachers in Asia and the West.

Cabezon, Jose Ignacio, *Buddhism, Sexuality, and Gender*, Albany: State University of New York Press, 1992. Articles on the relationships between sex, gender, and the practice of Buddhism both historically and in the present.

Dresser, Marianne, *Buddhist Women on the Edge: Contemporary Perspectives from the Western Frontier*, Berkeley: North Atlantic Books, 1996. Interesting examples of the many ways in which Western Buddhist women are interpreting Asian traditions in their different cultural setting, amid the realities of poverty, homophobia, militarism, and racism as well as women's issues.

Farrer-Halls, Gill, *The Feminine Face of Buddhism*, Wheaton, Illinois: Quest Books/Theosophical Publishing House, 2002. Beautifully illustrated, clear descriptions of notable women in Buddhist history and in our time.

Friedman, Lenore, *Meetings with Remarkable Women: Buddhist Teachers in America*, Boston and London: Shambhala, 1987. Lively personal interviews with 17 major female Dharma teachers.

Gross, Rita M., *Buddhism after Patriarchy: A Feminist History, Analysis, and Reconstruction of Buddhism*, Albany: State University of New York Press, 1993. Brilliant analysis of Buddhist history and scriptures from a feminist point of view, in the attempt to restore the original spirit of the tradition and improve its treatment of women.

Kabilsingh, Chatsumarn, *Thai Women in Buddhism*, Berkeley: Parallax Press, 1991. Still fresh and biting critique of the situation of Thai Buddhist women by one of the world's greatest Buddhist feminists, now known as Bhikkhuni Dhammananda.

Mackenzie, Vicki, *Cave in the Snow*, London: Bloomsbury, 1999. Story of the spiritual and physical aspects of Venerable Tenzin Palmo's 12-year retreat in a Himalayan cave.

Tisdale, Sallie, *Women of the Way: Discovering 2,500 Years of Buddhist Wisdom*, San Francisco: HarperSanFrancisco, 2006. Scholarly research is combined with vivid imagined details to portray the lives of many significant women in Buddhism.

Willis, Janice D., ed., *Feminine Ground: Essays on Women and Tibet*, Ithaca, New York: Snow Lion Publications, 1987. In-depth analyses by leading women scholars of issues regarding women and the feminine in Tibetan Buddhism.

Wu Yin, Ven. Bhikshuni, *Choosing Simplicity: Commentary on the Bhikshuni Pratimoksha*, trans. Bhikshuni Jendy Shih, ed. Bhikshuni Thubten Chodron, Ithaca, New York: Snow Lion Publications, 2001. Careful explanations of every aspect of the life of a Buddhist nun.

5
WOMEN IN CONFUCIANISM AND DAOISM

What restores balance and harmony is the most important concern

NOH SOO-BOCK

Long before either Confucianism or Daoism began to form in China as distinct philosophies, beliefs and practices existed that had a major impact on women's lives and continue to have in modern times. It is likely that prehistoric spiritual practices were shamanistic, with both female and male shamans as leaders, but the historical record is that of a strongly patriarchal society, in which only exceptional holy women have been remembered for having transcended cultural strictures. Even then, we find many remarkable women in the existing texts.

Ancient Ways of Chinese Religions

The center of Chinese religious and social life was the family, conceived not only as a nuclear or extended family, but reaching back through generations of forebears. Ancestors were venerated through mandatory rituals known as *li*, with offerings made to them at the home altar. If this connection between living and dead members of the family were to be broken, the family and, by extension, society would be likely to be disrupted. Likewise, marriage was undertaken primarily to carry on the patrilineal succession. Wealthy men often had several wives.

In this process of family continuity, the most important kinship ties were between parents and their sons, rather than between husband and wife. All relationships fell into hierarchical levels that reflected the natural cosmic order, in which Earth is subordinate to Heaven, women to men. A woman was always bound by the "three obediences"—as a girl, to her father; as a woman, to her husband; and as an older woman, to her grown son. In fact, women were not mentioned much in the ancient texts, for even though they were important to the system, they were detached from their blood relatives and were seen primarily as procreators of sons and helpmates to their husbands. Their appropriate and separate sphere was the inner chambers of the home. Men were the active agents in society.

The entire cosmos was composed of an impersonal force with two aspects in eternal interplay: *yin* and *yang*. **Yin** is its dark, receptive, "female" aspect; **yang** is its assertive, bright, creative, "male" aspect. During the Chou Dynasty

*c.*1122–256 BCE	CHOU DYNASTY
	Origin of *I Ching*
403–222 BCE	Warring States period
*c.*551 BCE	Birth of K'ung Fu-tzu (Confucius)
*c.*400–350 BCE	*Daode jing* (Lao-tzi?)
*c.*390–305 BCE	Life of Meng-tzu (Mencius)
370–290 BCE	Zhuangzi
*c.*255 BCE–221/206 BCE	CH'IN DYNASTY
	First Empire established
206 BCE–220 CE	HAN DYNASTY
140–87 BCE	Martial Emperor Wu Ti
	Biographies of Women by Liu Hsiang (77–6 BCE)
	I Ching elaborated
105 CE	Death of Pan Chao
215 CE	Political defeat of Celestial Masters
220 CE	Fall of Confucianism as state religion
265–420 CE	CHIN DYNASTY
317–420 CE	EASTERN CHIN DYNASTY
	Daoism and Buddhism come to fore
415 and 423 CE	"New Code" of Celestial Masters
	Lady Wei Hua-ts'un: Shang-ch'ing school of Daoism
618–907 CE	T'ANG DYNASTY
	Imperial support for Daoism
*c.*700 CE	*Classic of Filial Piety for Women*
960–1279 CE	SONG (SUNG) DYNASTY
1124 CE	Birth of Sun Bu-er
1130–1200 CE	Neo-Confucianism: Chu Hsi
1368–1644	MING DYNASTY
1445	Daoist Canon compiled
1644–1911	QING DYNASTY
1912	Republic proclaimed
1919	May 4th Movement
1949	People's Republic founded; Mao Zedong and Communist Party take control
1966–1976	Cultural Revolution
1978 on	Chinese shift toward capitalism

(*c.*1122–256 BCE), relationships between *yin* and *yang* were specified in the earliest form of the *I Ching*, or "Book of Changes." Based on belief in divination, this became a foundational text for both Confucianism and Daoism, both of which developed during the Chou, and it was elaborated with scholars' commentaries in the Han Dynasty (206 BCE–220 CE). The writings about the hexagrams or six-part figures resulting from throws of the divining objects (usually sticks) were interpreted in the *I Ching* as having deep meanings that may reflect ancient Chinese philosophy, as well as later accretions. The explanation of the hexagram interpreted as "The Receptive" reveals the basic ideas behind women's subordination:

> This hexagram is made up of broken lines only. The broken line represents the dark, yielding, receptive primal power of *yin*. The attribute of the hexagram is devotion; its image is the earth. It is the perfect complement of the Creative—the complement, not the opposite, for the Receptive does not combat the Creative but completes it…. For the Receptive must be activated and led by the Creative; then it is productive of good. Only when it abandons this position and tries to stand as an equal side by side with the Creative, does it become evil. The result then is opposition to and struggle against the Creative, which is productive of evil to both.[1]

In the hexagram interpreted as the Family, the interpretation includes these principles:

> The foundation of the family is the relationship between husband and wife. The tie that holds the family together lies in the loyalty and perseverance of the wife…. It is in accord with the great laws of nature that husband and wife take their proper places…. The wife must always be guided by the will of the master of the house, be he father, husband, or grown son. Her place is within the house. There, without having to look for them, she has great and important duties. She must attend to the nourishment of her family and to the food for the sacrifice. In this way she becomes the center of the social and religious life of the family, and her perseverance in this position brings good fortune to the whole house.[2]

Another early text that later became one of the Confucian Classics was the *Book of Rites* (*Li Ki*). It gave detailed prescriptions for the correct ways of behavior, depending upon the particular relationship, including proper ways of interaction between men and women. The general principle was separation:

> The men should not speak of what belongs to the inside [of the house], nor the women of what belongs to the outside. Except at sacrifices and funeral rites, they should not hand vessels to one another. In all other cases when they have occasion to give and receive anything, the woman should receive it in a basket. If she have no basket, they should both sit down, and the other put the thing on the ground, and she then take it up. Outside or inside, they should not go to the same well, nor to the same bathing-house. They should not share the same mat in lying down; they should not ask or borrow anything from one another; they should not wear similar upper or lower garments.[3]

Upper-class homes were built with exterior quarters for men, interior quarters for women, and they were not to mix. Even between a husband and his wife or wives, according to the *Book of Rites*, contact was limited except during the night. There might also be concubines, but each of them could visit the husband only once every five days, without staying the night. Young children were raised together, but as soon as they began to talk, boys were taught to speak assertively, girls quietly and submissively. Both learned basic arithmetic, but at the age of ten, when boys were introduced to more complicated calculations, girls were consigned for good to the women's apartments, where they were taught by governesses how to be proper women—how to speak and behave in pleasing ways, to be obedient to their superiors, to weave and sew and prepare pickled foods, and to help lay out the ritual objects for ceremonies. At the age of about twenty, at most twenty-three, a woman was married; if no marriage could be arranged, she became a concubine. Women did not live independently but rather took their assigned place in the hierarchy for the sake of general harmony.

In contrast to this highly structured and hierarchical path, presented as the social ideal for upper-class women, from ancient times there also seem to have been women with shamanistic callings. They were useful in divination and spirit possession, in which state they called upon the deities for ceremonial rites, prayed and danced to bring rain, and removed harmful energies. Despite their usefulness, they were not necessarily honored.

Women in Confucianism

The philosophy that is called "Confucianism" by Westerners is known as *Juchiao* ("the teaching of the scholars") in China. It is not the product of one man, nor was his name Confucius. His family name was K'ung. Students who adopted his teachings called him K'ung Fu-tzu ("Master K'ung"). He was born in approximately 551 BCE during the Chou Dynasty, son of a once-royal family who had lost their fortune. When he was twenty-three, his mother died, which sent him into a state of deep mourning. Although he had married and had children, he lived the life of a poor scholar and civil bureaucrat, studying the ancient ceremonial rites (*li*) and imperial institutions. At the time, China was in chaos, with feudal lords holding more power than the kings of the central court, rulers being assassinated by their ministers, and sons murdering their fathers. K'ung Fu-tzu earnestly advocated a return to the ideals found in the scriptures and rituals of earlier times, and he edited and promoted them as what are commonly called the "Confucian Classics" of China's cultural heritage. The *I Ching* and the *Book of Rites* quoted above are among them. Few people accepted K'ung Fu-tzu's ideas during his lifetime, but after the brutal reunification of China during the Ch'in and Han dynasties, a cultured class of bureaucrats arose who took interest in his teachings and ultimately adopted the "Confucian Classics" as the basis for civil service examinations and the models for life as a gentleman-scholar.

The teachings of Master K'ung had been amplified by later commentators, most notably Meng-tzu ("Mencius," *c.*390–305 BCE) and after him Hsun-tzu. Despite differences in their approaches, all agreed on the necessity of developing virtue through self-cultivation and adoption of the ideals attributed to the ancient sages. They argued that these would bring peace and harmony within the family and the state. The most important virtue is that of *jen*, which means benevolence, love, humaneness. It is written as two Chinese characters: one representing a human being, and the other meaning "two." In other words, we exist in relationship to each other, rather than in isolation, and we are to be as kind and responsible as possible in each relationship, keeping in mind our relative positions. Although all relationships in the universe are structured hierarchically, this hierarchy is a matter of harmonious interrelationship rather than of cruel subordination of the inferior by the superior partners. The ideal relationship between husband and wife is established in the marriage ceremony, according to the *Book of Rites*:

> The respect, the caution, the importance, the attention to secure correctness in all the details, and then [the pledge of] mutual affection—these were the great points in the ceremony, and served to establish the distinction to be observed between man and woman, and the righteousness to be maintained between husband and wife… . Thus the ceremony establishing the young wife in her position; [followed by] that showing her obedient service [to her husband's parents]; and both succeeded by that showing how she now occupied the position of continuing the family line—all served to impress her with a sense of the deferential duty proper to her. When she was thus deferential, she was obedient to her parents-in-law, and harmonious with all the occupants of the women's apartments; she was the fitting partner of her husband, and could carry on all the work in silk and linen, making cloth and silken fabrics, and maintaining a watchful care over the various stores and depositories [of the household].
>
> In this way when the deferential obedience of the wife was complete, the internal harmony was secured; and when the internal harmony was secured, the long continuance of the family could be calculated on.[4]

The intricate relationships between the husband and his wives and concubines were also spelled out in some detail, always within the context of hierarchy and mutual responsibilities.

Not only daughters-in-law but also sons were bound to be deferential to the parents, always waiting upon them, and not eating until after the parents had eaten their fill. They should never appear to be tired of waiting, by shifting their balance from one foot to the other, or scratching if they itched, or putting on more clothes if they felt cold. Thus women's subordination occurred within a general atmosphere of complete deference to one's superiors at every level. Upper-class women were to set the standard for society as a whole; lower-class women were also enjoined to put themselves last and others first.

Again, this was the ideal. What if a woman did not comply? Her husband could send her out of the house on any of seven grounds considered disturbing to the success of the marriage—disobeying his parents, lack of a male child, promiscuity, jealousy, having an incurable disease, talking excessively, and theft. She had no right to divorce her husband; even if he died, she had to remain in his family's home, caring for his parents and revering his ancestors. In other words, she was expected to be a saintly figure, tolerating everything humbly, always placing her superiors' welfare above her own wishes, and dedicating her life totally to her husband's lineage. However, both husband and wife were theoretically supposed to be respectful, humble, righteous, and kind with each other. There was no approval for the abuse of women.

When "Confucianism" was adopted as orthodox practice during the Han Dynasty, women were given more attention, which took the form of being supplied with more instructional materials and examples to follow. Foremost among the instructional materials was a piece written by Pan Chao (d. 105 CE), a highly educated woman who was asked to tutor the women of the royal family. In her *Lessons for Women*, she wrote advice ostensibly to her own daughters, who were of an age to be married (see box, p. 134). Her instructions became a classic manual for women. She also advocated equal education for women, but this advice went unheeded.

Another form of writing that had a great impact on women was biographies of exemplary female figures. The *Biographies of Women* written by Liu Hsiang (77–6 BCE), a Han Dynasty Confucian scholar, told stories of women who were highly ethical and followed Confucian principles at great cost, even to their own lives. For instance, he wrote of the widow Po-chi, who was in a house that caught fire. It being night, she refused to leave the house without being accompanied by the matron and the governess, as was proper. The matron at length arrived, but even then, as the flames approached her, Po-chi steadfastly refused to leave. According to the biography, she proclaimed: "The rule for women is that when the Governess has not come, no one can leave the house at night. To transgress a rule of righteousness in order to save one's life is not so good as to keep the rule of righteousness and to die in doing so." Thus she died. According to the biographer, "Thus did Po-chi fulfill to the utmost the duty of wifehood."[5] Such stories were eventually understood not as exceptional cases but as setting principles to which all women were held, by social pressure and by law.

During the Han Dynasty, Chinese emperors attempted to increase and consolidate their territory by war. Taxes to finance this expansionism became so great a burden upon poor farmers that they went bankrupt and were turned into slave laborers. Prisoners were also set to hard labor. The work was so harsh that many men apparently died young and were buried in shallow mass graves. Times were thus apparently hard for men as well as for women. During this period Emperor Wu Ti, the Martial Emperor (140–87 BCE), instituted a legalistic, quasi-Confucian imperial cult in which subjects were to be strictly subordinate to rulers, and similarly, wives to husbands. He decreed that men of the royal court could have up to 14 concubines, and he authorized both prostitution and female infanticide. Other poor women were trained to sing and dance in the court, but they remained of very low status. Feminist scholar Terry Woo offers a theory linking these historical circumstances with the strictures of Confucian philosophy:

If we accept as historically accurate that many more young men were killed than women in ancient China, and that it was in part a surplus of women that made possible or perhaps even "customary" the widespread practices and eventual acceptance of concubinage, prostitution, and female infanticide, then would it not make sense to fight the phenomenon with at least a two-pronged approach? First, to encourage peace through self-cultivation, and virtuous behavior, and to discourage lust among men; and second, to encourage the same kind of peaceful coexistence within a house, and to preserve spheres of influence for women, and to discourage seductive behavior that might aggravate sexual promiscuity. If we therefore accept that the oppression of women

EXCERPT **Lessons for Women**
Pan Chao

Let a woman modestly yield to others; let her respect others; let her put others first, herself last. Should she do something good, let her not mention it; should she do something bad, let her not deny it. Let her bear disgrace; let her even endure when others speak or do evil to her. Always let her seem to tremble and to fear. Then she may be said to humble herself before others.

Let a woman retire late to bed, but rise early to duties; let her not dread tasks by day or by night. Let her not refuse to perform domestic duties whether easy or diffcult. That which must be done, let her fnish completely, tidily, and systematically. Then she may be said to be industrious.

Let a woman be correct in manner and upright in character in order to serve her husband. Let her live in purity and quietness, and attend to her own affairs. Let her love not gossip and silly laughter. Let her cleanse and purify and arrange in order the wine and the food for the offerings to the ancestors. Then she may be said to continue ancestral worship... .

As Yin and Yang are not of the same nature, so man and woman have different characteristics. The distinctive quality of the Yang is rigidity; the function of the Yin is yielding. Man is honored for strength; a woman is beautiful on account of her gentleness... .

Now for self-culture nothing equals respect for others. To counteract frmness nothing equals compliance. Consequently it can be said that the Way of respect and acquiescence is woman's most important principle of conduct. So respect may be defned as nothing other than holding on to that which is permanent; and acquiescence nothing other than being liberal and generous. Those who are steadfast in devotion know that they should stay in their proper places; those who are liberal and generous esteem others, and honor and serve.

If husband and wife have the habit of staying together, never leaving one another, and following each other around within the limited space of their own rooms, then they will lust after and take liberties with one another. From such action improper language will arise between the two. This kind of discussion may lead to licentiousness. Out of licentiousness will be born a heart of disrespect to the husband. Such a result comes from not knowing that one should stay in one's proper place... .

[If wives] suppress not contempt for husbands, then it follows [that such wives] rebuke and scold [their husbands]. [If husbands] stop not short of anger, then they are certain to beat [their wives]. The correct relationship between husband and wife is based upon harmony and intimacy, and [conjugal] love is grounded in proper union. Should actual blows be dealt, how could matrimonial relationship be preserved? Should sharp words be spoken, how could [conjugal] love exist? If love and proper relationship both be destroyed, then husband and wife are divided... .

If people in action or character disobey the spirits of Heaven and of Earth, then Heaven punishes them. Likewise if a woman errs in the rites and in the proper mode of conduct, then her husband esteems her lightly. The ancient book, "A Pattern for Women" [*Nu Hsien*], says: "To obtain the love of one man is the crown of a woman's life; to lose the love of one man is to miss the aim in woman's life." For these reasons a woman cannot but seek to win her husband's heart... .

Decidedly nothing is better [to gain the heart of a husband] than whole-hearted devotion and correct manners. In accordance with the rites and the proper mode of conduct, [let a woman] live a pure life. Let her have ears that hear not licentiousness; and eyes that see not depravity. When she goes outside her own home, let her not be conspicuous in dress and manners. When at home let her not neglect her dress. Women should not assemble in groups, nor gather together [for gossip and silly laughter]. They should not stand watching in the gateways. [If a woman follows] these rules, she may be said to have whole-hearted devotion and correct manners.

From Nancy Lee Swann, *Pan Chao: Foremost Woman Scholar of China, First Century A.D.*, 1932, New York: Russell & Russell, 1968, pp. 83–8.

resulted from political upheavals, the Confucians were merely trying to deal with the circumstances as they best knew how... .

Perhaps Confucius and the early Confucians had wished to emphasize *jen* or benevolent relationship as an antidote to the bullying, violence, and suffering; the stress on the responsibility of the senior partner to the junior one especially, may have been hope, albeit a naïve one, in one means of alleviating some of the most immediate and personal oppression.[6]

In any case, there are clues in the literature revealing that women were not simply meek and passive; at least some of them seem to have played their family roles in active, intelligent ways. The mother of Meng-tzu is said to have begun teaching him when he was still in her womb. When she became a young widow, she changed her residence three times, searching for the proper environment in which to rear her son. When he was married, he complained to his mother that his wife was not properly attired when he burst into her room unannounced. Rather than take his side against the wife, his mother chided him for not giving proper warning before entering.

Another story is told of the mother of a harsh administrator who had people cruelly punished or killed in order to maintain social order. When his mother came from afar to visit him, she refused to go to his official palace, as a sign of her disapproval of his actions. Even when he came to her side, she remained formally aloof, to demonstrate the gap between them. She also criticized him, insisting that he should be kind to the people. So powerful was her influence over him that he relented and changed his ways.

It appears that older, experienced women commanded considerable respect. Even though women were not the social equals of men, Confucianism often presented them as the moral equals, and perhaps expected them to be even stronger than men inwardly. Early in the T'ang Dynasty (608–907 CE), imperial women were influential in politics. When Lady Ch'eng wrote her *Classic of Filial Piety for Women* (*c.*700 CE), she depicted women as the moral guides of men, studying the Confucian Classics and capable of setting such virtuous examples and strategically behaving so gently that the men would improve themselves and forsake their anger. According to this text, if a husband is not acting according to the Way, the wife should not acquiesce in his erroneous behavior. Not only is a woman responsible for setting an example of virtuousness for her husband; she should also be kind to the younger concubines, to her sisters-in-law, the servants, and even the dogs and chickens. Thus harmony and order prevail in the household because of the influence of the virtuous Confucian woman, just as peace and stability prevail in the state if the ruler is characterized by Confucian virtues: "respectfulness, tolerance, trustworthiness in word, quickness [in understanding], and generosity."[7] And for women, staying home in the inner quarters was not necessarily perceived as confinement; rather, the home was a place of secure refuge and peace where they performed their familiar duties and therein were respected and self-respecting.

Neo-Confucianism

Confucianism as a state-supported philosophy collapsed with the fall of the Han Dynasty in 220 CE. Buddhism and Daoism came to the fore in China, and Confucianism remained in the background for many centuries until it was revived in the form of Neo-Confucianism during the Song (Sung) Dynasty, beginning in the eleventh century. Now Confucianism became more ascetic and meditation-oriented, with obsessive emphasis on women's chastity, as rulers attempted to regain the "purity" of their Confucian traditions in the face of Mongolian invasions.

5.1 Shoes for bound feet, carefully prepared for upper-class Chinese daughters by their mothers

Whereas the exemplary women of earlier Confucianism had been wise leaders in their home spheres, under Neo-Confucian influence attitudes toward women became considerably more negative. Now men were seen as the masters of women, who became like slaves in their homes. In the case of a spouse's death, a man could remarry but remarriage was strictly proscribed for women. Thus many widows apparently mutilated themselves or committed suicide rather than submit to sexual contact outside marriage. The most influential developer of Neo-Confucianism was Chu Hsi (1130–1200 CE). In his *Reflections on Things at Hand* he gave this harshly androcentric advice:

Question: According to principle, it seems that one should not marry a widow. What do you think?

Answer: Correct. Marriage is a match. If one takes someone who has lost her integrity to be his own match, it means he himself has lost his integrity.

Further Question: In some cases the widows are all alone, poor, and with no one to depend on. May they remarry?

Answer: This theory has come about only because people of later generations are afraid of starving to death. But to starve to death is a very small matter. To lose one's integrity, however, is a very serious matter.[8]

Footbinding, a form of female mutilation cast as a virtuous act, developed at this point and lasted into the twentieth century. Initially for dancers only, a pair of bound feet became a must if a young upper-class woman were to be considered for marriage; lower-class families could not afford to lose their daughters' labor by near-crippling their movements. Tiny feet—the ideal foot was only three inches long—were thought to be an indicator of morality, as well as the perfection of beauty. Footbinding was practiced by women upon their daughters as a matter of pride. They lavished great care upon stitching their tiny embroidered shoes (fig. 5.1). From the age of five or six, girls' feet were tied and bent so that the instep was gradually forced into a folded arch with the toes downward rather than projecting forward, except for the big toe. Previously free to romp with boy children, girls were then sequestered and taught how to walk with a shuffling gait so that they could balance their body weight over a small area of their reshaped feet.

These confining trends notwithstanding, some women blossomed in literary fields during the Ming (1368–1644) and Qing (1644–1911) dynasties, writing thousands of poems. And from the Song Dynasty onward, women could own property and accumulate personal wealth. Nevertheless, the late imperial period was one of social decline.

Rebellion against Confucianism in Modern China

During the nineteenth and early twentieth centuries, China's political corruption and weakness in a world dominated by other states brought forth many calls for reform. Confucianism was attacked as a cause of the problems, including the mistreatment of women. By then, women's position was very degraded, with wide-spread practice of footbinding (now by the poorer classes as well), female infanticide, and the sale of women for sexual purposes. Particularly in the "May 4th Movement" of 1919, students urged the total abandonment of Confucian culture and its replacement with something more like that of the West. Ultimately intellectuals turned to Marxism, and Mao Zedong (Mao Tse-tung) engaged great numbers of peasants in a struggle to redistribute power from the wealthy to the poor. Chairman Mao said he had hated Confucianism since his childhood because of its emphasis on intellectual study of the Classics, "superstitious" rituals, and oppression of women and peasants. He wrote that men were subjected to domination by the state, the clan authorities and their ancestral temples, and hierarchical religious authorities from the King of Hell and the Emperor of Heaven down to lower spirits and local gods. And:

> As for women, in addition to being dominated by these three systems of authority, they are also dominated by the men [the authority of the husband]. These four authorities—political, clan, religious and masculine—are the embodiment of the whole feudal-patriarchal system and ideology, and are the four thick ropes binding the Chinese people, particularly the peasants.[9]

Once Mao's Communist Party took control of China in 1949, he initiated many changes designed to improve the lives of women, for as he wrote, "Women hold up half the sky." The Marriage Law of 1950 replaced polygamy with monogamy, declared a halt to child marriages, supported free choice of marriage partners and equal rights for women and men, and ended the buying and selling of women for marriage. The option of divorce was made available to both women and men. Groups of men took pledges not to accept arranged marriages or require their brides to have bound feet. The Women's Federation of the Communist Party closed brothels, freeing prostitutes and concubines. Women were educated and brought into the work force in massive numbers. In the new idealism of equality, men and women wore the same styles of simple gray or blue clothing. As mothers found jobs in government-run factories or agricultural communes, their children were put into day care.

Such changes shredded the fabric of family life as it had been structured by Confucian hierarchies, bringing both unaccustomed freedom and new problems for women. Now their traditional place within the sacred community of the family was gone; instead they were expected to feel a near-religious commitment to the state. Furthermore, the intellectual elite was severely attacked and often murdered during the Cultural Revolution (1966–1976), and children even publicly denounced their parents, overturning classical standards of filial piety.

Yet more radical changes occurred from 1978, as China shifted its economic style from socialism toward capitalism. One of the first commodities to be marketed—illegally—was women. This still goes on. Unscrupulous men roam the rural areas, luring women to the cities with promises of jobs, raping them to dishonor and make them feel unworthy of marriage, and then selling them for the equivalent of US $400 to $800, much cheaper than the cost of a marriage. These kidnaped "brides" are held against their will far from home and may not even know where they are, so it is difficult for them to escape. They are considered the reproductive property of the men who have bought them, for sexual gratification and production of sons for their lineage. Some of the buyers are mentally retarded, physically disabled, elderly, or groups of brothers. Captives of the men who buy them, the women are vulnerable to physical restraint, starvation, humiliation, beating, mutilation, and even murder. The government is attempting to stop this traffic, but often local officials do not intervene, considering women the legitimate property of their buyers. Prostitution is also booming, with the increase in tourism and as more and more innocent village girls leave their poor communities to seek economic opportunities in the cities, only to fall into the hands of traffickers supplying sex slaves to pimps. The writer Xinran (fig. 5.2) has documented all this.

Not only are women falling victim to trafficking; many educated but poor young women are also choosing to sell their company and their talents as "escorts" or exclusive "personal secretaries" to businessmen. At the "personal secretary" level, the woman is on call for business purposes as well as sexual favors, and in return the man pays for her clothes, hotel lodging, and travel. Meanwhile, the wives, still trained to be meek and obedient, work hard to help support and take care of the family, but without the Confucian connotations of family as sacred unit. Even the ancestors' tablets are now gone from most homes.

In an attempt to curb the growth of China's vast population, from 1979 the Chinese government pursued a "one child" policy. Families having more than one—or for racial minorities and rural peasants, two—children were subject to very heavy penalties. If the first child was a girl, some parents chose to have her discreetly killed in hopes of later having a boy who would continue the lineage and help in the fields. During pregnancy, modern ultrasound techniques of determining the sex of a fetus are widely used, even in rural areas, so that female fetuses can be aborted. There is therefore a growing imbalance, and now China has only 100 females for every 118 males. The World Health Organization estimates that up to 50 million baby girls have disappeared since the early 1980s. However, the "one child" policy has been so successful in curbing population growth that the government is beginning to modify it, lest the bulk of the population become elderly without enough young people to support them.

Despite the Communist government's attempts to discourage religions, and despite fervent materialism, some-

5.2 Xinran, courageous author of *The Good Women of China: hidden voices*

thing still remains of old Confucian virtues in the ideologies of the Communist Party itself, giving a sort of sacred meaning to living for the sake of others—or at least for the sake of the Party. The 16th National Congress of the Communist Party of China, held in 2002, held up many women delegates for special praise because of their selfless service to others. Among them were teachers devoted to their students, women who worked hard to plant trees in formerly barren areas, model workers noted for their dedication and kindness, and one Ye Xiuying, director of a neighborhood committee in a poor area, praised by the Party Congress as "A Woman Pace-setter." Her Party citation sounds like that of an exemplary wise woman from the Confucian past, but with her loyalties shifted from her family to her community:

> The neighborhood committee Ye works with is in charge of an area located at the joint of urban and rural districts. Among the residents living here, there are more jobless persons, more ethnic minorities, and more people living under the poverty line, making the neighborhood characterized with lower average earning, lower living standard and lower education level. These three "mores" and three "lowers" put this area in an awful mess. When Ye first took the post, she felt a great pressure upon her. After she visited the families one by one and had heart-to-heart talks with them, she realized that hers was a lofty job to help alleviate people's suffering. Eventually, Ye became a trustable friend of the local people. When any of them has a problem, the first person they think about going to is Ye. "Since the Party has put me in this post, I will always do my best," she said.
>
> Ye has a deep understanding of the residents' bitterness and is always ready to offer her help whenever it's needed. She personally takes care of 20 elderly people. While trying hard to get support from the government, she saves every penny of her own money to help these elderly poor.[10]

Nonetheless, even with the revival of certain other religions in China, including Christianity and Buddhism, it is hard to find Chinese women today who would call themselves Confucian, since the philosophy is so deeply associated with patterns that today's women regard as oppressive.

After earlier twentieth-century Western feminist attacks on the worst abuses of women in China, such as footbinding, female infanticide, and concubinage—none of which was supported by K'ung Fu-tzu and his early followers—feminist scholars are now taking a closer look at classic Confucian traditions to sort out which strands may actually have contributed to women's relative well-being in China. Now the feminist critique of Confucianism is coming from Taiwan.

Confucianism Outside the Republic of China

Confucianism survives to a certain extent in other cultures that have been influenced by China. In Taiwan, Confucian values are promoted by the government, which celebrates the birthday of K'ung Fu-tzu on a grand scale. Confucianism is the major religion, along with Chinese popular religion, which is an amalgam of Confucianism, Daoism, Buddhism, and indigenous Taiwanese ways. Reverence for ancestors and emphasis on producing sons to perpetuate the patrilineal family structure still characterize rural life, leaving women without family to call their own until they begin raising their own children and grandchildren. In urban areas, however, life has been changing rapidly for women since the 1970s, with increasing modernization and industrialization. Today's Taiwanese women are more educated, more likely to work outside their homes, and likely to bear fewer children. With women dividing their time between work and home, ritual worship of their husbands' ancestors is declining. More and more, they are finding Confucian traditions constricting. Taiwanese feminists are raising their voices against the defenders of these traditions. One of the leading feminists is Lu Hsiu-lien. She identifies aspects of Confucian tradition that she claims are responsible for Taiwanese women's low status and lack of self-confidence. These are the emphasis on continuing the male lineage (which makes girls nonentities), the submission of women to men at all stages of their lives, the insistence on "feminine" behavior (which Lu says turns women into mere ornaments and keeps them submissive and ignorant), the division between men's public sphere and women's household sphere, and the insistence on female chastity, even for young widows, without a corresponding insistence on chastity for men. She is campaigning for the full recognition and equality of women.

In addition, the Taiwanese feminist anthropologist Lin Mei-jung is arguing that to cling to mainland Chinese traditions is not appropriate for Taiwan, which has its own pluralistic culture. She is highly critical of Confucian values that bring inequalities and double standards for men and women.

Observance of Confucianism also continues in Korea. Confucian ideas spread to Korea during their initial development, and were adopted by the society and government. Many older South Koreans still offer sacrifices before ancestral tablets, and there are some 12,000 male Confucian priests for observances of the traditional rites. Confucian ethics are still strong in Korea, where Confucian organizations are taking a conservative stand on social issues, opposing attempts by women's groups to liberalize laws relating to the family. The Confucians feel that despite influences from Western cultures, it is important to maintain traditional standards of behavior for the sake of social harmony, propriety, morality, justice, education, character development, and humanism even within the changing values of modern industrial society.

Both in China and in Korea, women raised according to Confucian principles of chastity and family honor are not taught anything about sexuality. As in other cultures that sequester girls to preserve their virginity, these societies paradoxically put young women at great risk of sexual violence, against which they have been given no defenses. Innocent girls and women are often violently confronted with the modern realities of sexual abuse, finding themselves in such a shameful and impossible position that some ultimately commit suicide. Korean feminist scholar Chung Hyun Kyung tells the story of one woman whose life finally turned out for the better, but which nonetheless exposes the ugly face of sexual exploitation of Asian women who have been taught from early childhood to be submissive (see box, p. 143).

The Development of Daoism

Whereas K'ung Fu-tzu and other scholars from the Warring States period focused on hierarchical submission to restore order in turbulent Chinese society, other thinkers from the same period of chaos recommended a different way toward social harmony. The path—or paths—that became known as Daoism (previously transliterated as "Taoism") are based on aligning oneself with the **Dao**, the intrinsic power and pattern of the universe. This approach is multifaceted and continually evolving, incorporating philosophy, strategies for governance, ritual devotions to deities, priesthoods, monastic communities, rigorous self-cultivation practices, and methods designed for the attainment of immortality. Its complex canon of over 1,600 volumes, collected in 1445, was rescued from near-oblivion in the early twentieth century and is now being intensively studied by scholars in many countries. Among them are feminists searching for evidence of women in this path, which seems to offer special places for females and "the feminine" that are not found in other religions.

Although Daoism, like Confucianism, has its roots in ancient Chinese traditions, its development as a distinct path is attributed to a mysterious figure known as Lao-tzi. According to legend, he was an older contemporary of K'ung Fu-tzu and was a wise but minor official who at the request of a border guard wrote down 5,000 characters summarizing his philosophy, and then disappeared into the mountains. Scholars have been unable to trace him definitively, or the origins of the book attributed to him, which is usually known in the West as the *Tao te Ching* (*Daode jing*—"Book of the Dao and its Virtue"). Current scholarship suggests that the tract may have been written about 400–350 BCE but could be a compilation of wise sayings rather than the work of one person. Its central teaching is that there is a nameless, changeless, invisible reality to which we can attune ourselves. Daoism specialist Professor Livia Kohn explains:

The Dao is ineffable and beyond human comprehension... . If we try to grasp it, [it] can be described as the organic order underlying and structuring and pervading all existence. It is organic in that it is not willful, but it is also order because it changes in predictable rhythms and orderly patterns. If one is to approach it, reason and the intellect have to be left behind. One can only intuit it when one has become as nameless and as free of conscious choices and evaluations as the Dao itself... .[11]

To harmonize ourselves effectively with this transcendent, unifying force we should be soft and receptive, flowing like water. The *Daode jing* says:

Nothing under heaven
Is softer and weaker than water,
Yet nothing can compare with it
In attacking the hard and strong.[12]

The teachings attributed to Lao-tzi were elaborated by Zhuangzi (*c.*370–290 BCE), and from the Han Dynasty onward, organized as religious schools. Not only was

EXCERPT **"Comfort Women" of Asia**
Chung Hyun Kyung

Her name is Noh Soo-Bock. She was born in a small southern village, Ahn Shim, in Korea in 1921. She was the frst daughter of a poor farmer's family... .

It was during the time of the Japanese colonial occupation in Korea. Because of severe taxation by the colonial government, Soo-Bock's father, a poor landless farmer, could not feed his family even with his back-breaking work. Soo-Bock's memory of her childhood, therefore, was flled with hunger... . She never learned how to read or write the Korean language. Instead, from her grandfather she learned a few Chinese letters and the Confucian way of womanhood, especially the importance of chastity... .

When Soo-Bock became fourteen years old, her parents married her off to a family in the next village. Her parents' poverty forced her into this early marriage. One more mouth in the family meant one more bowl of rice which they could not afford. Following the custom of her time, she obeyed her parents and married a man she had never met. Without knowing him, she slept with him in deep darkness on her wedding night, as all Korean women did in her time. The next day she got up and saw her husband's face for the frst time. He was a leper, and she fainted... .

Fear and disgust flled her life. Ignoring Soo-Bock's pain, her mother-in-law made her work all the time, but she did not give Soo-Bock enough food to eat. Fear and hunger overwhelmed her, and she decided to run away... . [She] fnally arrived at her father's house, the home where she had grown up with her brothers and sister. Her father was so angry with her shaming the family's reputation by running away from her marriage that he chased her away, saying, "If you want to die, go and die in your husband's house. You are not one of our family any longer. You belong to your husband's family."

Weeping, Soo-Bock walked and walked to the nearby big city, Tae-ku, without having any plan or knowing anybody. She became a maid. With the hope that her family might accept her if she had money, she saved all her meager earnings and one year later visited her family again. Her father still did not allow her even to enter the house. Her mother pleaded with him to allow Soo-Bock to stay just one night with her brothers and sister. Her father's response was the same, "Go die in your husband's house." ...

In despair Soo-Bock went back to the big city and became a maid once more... . It was autumn 1942. Soo-Bock went to the well to wash her clothes. It was dusk. When she tried to draw water from the well, four Japanese policemen appeared. First, they asked her for water, then one policeman tried to grab her. When she escaped his advance, other police joined him and tied her with rope, yelling and threatening to kill her... .

Soo-Bock and other Korean women were forced to travel in the bottom level of a Japanese military ship and they sailed for forty days. Then they arrived on a shore with many palm trees. It was Singapore. Upon their arrival they were transported to a military base. The next morning, when they awoke, they found many Japanese soldiers trying to look into their tent…. The Korean women held one another tightly and trembled with fear….

When evening came, thousands of soldiers flled the military feld while Soo-Bock and the other Korean women were forced to go on stage and sing for them. The Japanese soldiers became so excited they began to shout and sing and dance. As soon as the women returned to their tent, a Japanese lieutenant came into Soo-Bock's room and tried to rape her. When she begged him not to, he hit her with his fst and kicked her in the stomach until she fainted. When she regained consciousness, she knew what she had become: she had become a so-called "comfort woman" for the Japanese soldiers….

Korean women had to clean the military bases, wash the soldiers' clothing, and carry their bullet boxes in the morning. Starting in the afternoon and through the night they had to receive Japanese soldiers. Sometimes they received more than sixty soldiers a day. If they resisted, they were stripped and whipped in front of Japanese soldiers in the military feld…. Many of the women started to die of starvation, exhaustion, and venereal diseases, and from their wounds from being battered by the Japanese soldiers….

[Even after Japan's fall] When Soo-Bock heard of the plan of return, she became very anxious. "How can I go back home and meet my family with this dirty body?" she asked…. After many days of agony she decided not to go home, and she ran away from the refugee camp…. A man called Mohammed, a devout Muslim, rescued her and she became a maid in his family. After working in his house in Malaysia and receiving his family's encouragement to work for her own independence, she left for Thailand, landing in Hot Chai, where a new mining business was fburishing. She found a job in a Chinese restaurant there and also met the husband she was to keep for life, a poor old Chinese bachelor, Mr. Chen. He could not marry because he was so poor. It was the frst time in her life that Soo-Bock had felt that strange feeling called "love." In the autumn of 1947, she married him in a lotus fbwer Buddhist temple. For Soo-Bock it was a moment of rebirth. She was determined to bring her own beautiful lotus fbwer of life to bloom out of her muddy past.

Their restaurant business fburished, but Soo-Bock could not become pregnant because of the many rapes she had endured. She persuaded her husband to take a young second wife to give them children. Although he refused her offer in the beginning, he later gave in. They took a young Chinese woman, who gave birth to three children. The two women, their three children, and the one husband lived together happily, helping and appreciating one another….

According to research by a Korean feminist group, the number of so-called "comfort women" from Korea was more than 200,000…. Why is Soo-Bock's story, which happened ffty years ago [she is now in her seventies], still a "root story" for Korean women? Because it is happening here right now in the everyday lives of Korean women and many other Asian sisters. We still have poor fathers who want to get rid of their daughters. We still have fathers, brothers, and comrades who honor our chastity more than our life itself. We still have our leper husband who thinks his maleness can cover any flaws in his life. Even though prostitution is illegal in Korea and many other Asian countries, we still have a state which sells our women's bodies shamelessly, this time in the name of national progress. We still have colonialists who come to our land and destroy poor women's lives in the name of development, the Uruguay Round, GATT, WTO, MTV, CNN, the peacekeeping army, and tourism. We still have capitalists who commodify everything under the sun: our women, our children, our brides, our workers, our earth. And we still have soldiers who call us "a little brown fucking machine fueled by rice".... After the series of wars in Asia, World War II, the Korean War, and Vietnam, Asia became the brothel of the world.... Where the militaristic state, colonialism, the patriarchal family, and capitalism thrive, modern-day comfort women and sexual slavery fourish....

One of the main reasons Western men come to Asia for prostitution or why they buy mail-order brides from Asia is: they want a "real woman," a real feminine woman. They blame the feminist movement in the West. They say there are no more woman-like women in the West because of the feminist movement. Women have become man-like, no more softness, no more vulnerability, no more obedience! So they come to Asia to find small, brown [more natural], soft, vulnerable, obedient, real women....

Why are we a fucking machine? We became a fucking machine because we never have been a subject for the soldiers, capitalists, and colonialists. We have been a machine for them. When Western men made the whole earth into a battlefield and became brutally violent warriors as hunters of the world, they began to mechanize the whole world, including us....

Then where was our subjectivity? Where were our power to resist and our legacy of victory? Are we only the passive victims of complex systems of oppression? ... When Soo-Bock ran away from her leper husband; when she determined not to die and began to eat as much as she could and became extremely obedient to violent soldiers, when she ran away again from the refugee camp in Malaysia and never went home, when she found her work and love in a foreign land, she became an agent, a subject for her own life....

In her old age she told us, "Korean, Japanese, Chinese, Thai are not different. We are all friends!" Where did she find this power of forgiveness? Why did she choose to forgive the Japanese? Was it her Buddhism with its wisdom, compassion, and loving kindness? Or was it her experience of being loved by Malaysian, Chinese, and Thai in her new homeland? I do not know. What I know is she cut the vicious cycle of violence and revenge with her power, which I cannot easily name....

Excerpted from Chung Hyun Kyung, "Your Comfort vs. My Death," in Mary John Mananzan *et al.*, eds., *Women Resisting Violence: Spirituality for Life*, Maryknoll, New York: Orbis Books, 1996, pp. 129–38.

there a philosophical *literati* tradition; Daoists also used intense self-cultivation practices including sexual techniques to become more closely allied to the Dao and perhaps achieve a kind of immortality, plus rituals and prayers for communing with a great pantheon of deities. The famous female adept Sun Bu-er explained the practice of immortality thus:

> Four energies combine to form our perfect reality: the decrepit become vigorous, the senile are rejuvenated, the withered face becomes fresh again, white hair turns dark again, the voice is like a bell ringing. The body is light as a feather, the ordinary skeleton completely transformed, flying up to the highest purity.
>
> If learners in the world establish discipline, maintain stabilization, and produce the light of wisdom, by these three powers they can last forever, treading the movements of energy light and clear, stabilizing transformation so as to transcend to immortality ... neither aging nor dying, peacefully existing forever.[13]

By the great T'ang Dynasty (618–907 CE), high point of classical Chinese culture, Daoism was actively supported by the emperor and there were 1,687 recognized Daoist temples, 550 of which were for women, with many women also serving as initiators, teachers, and transmitters of sacred texts and esoteric methods. During the T'ang, many aristocratic women and men entered communal Daoist religious orders. However, alongside this growing popularity, there were abuses and distortions of the Way, and some of the more dedicated practitioners, both women and men, went into hiding to continue their practices secretly. From early times until today, there have been stories of ascetics hiding in the mountains of China as spiritual adepts.

From the Song (960–1279) to Ming (1368–1644) and Qing (1644–1911) dynasties, Daoism became mixed with Confucian and Buddhist practices, especially among the upper classes. They used Daoist inner alchemical practices, Ch'an Buddhist meditation practices, and Confucian ideals of virtue. At the same time, many more deities were added to the Daoist pantheon, quite a few of them being local ones raised to national prominence and official recognition. At the popular level, there was a growth in communication with the spirits through mediums, many of whom were women. The deities gave them detailed instructions for organizing new cults, ways of venerating the deities, martial arts, and practices leading toward inner alchemical changes and immortality.

Because of civil strife and then suppression by the victorious Communist regime in the twentieth century, Daoism almost disappeared in China. However, it survives in places to which Chinese religions had spread, such as Taiwan and Hong Kong. The two major surviving lineages are the Celestial Masters tradition from the second century CE and the Complete Perfection school from the twelfth century. In Daoist temples, the majority of devotees are women. It is primarily they who chant the names of the deities, participate in their ritual devotions, make offerings to them, and ask for their help, often for the sake of their families.

Daoism has also spread to the West, where some aspects of the Way are packaged as means of healing, inner peace, and spiritual development (such as *Qigong* and *Taiji quan*), and are found in the popularization of *feng shui*, the art of placing houses, rooms, and furniture to maximize the proper flow of energy. There are Daoist temples in the West where rituals, purifications, and exorcisms are conducted. The cryptic *Daode jing* has so fascinated Westerners that the book is second only to the Bible in the number of Western language translations—which vary widely in interpretation.

Feminine Aspects of Daoism

In its philosophy, mythology, and practitioners, Daoism provides unique examples of women's spirituality. According to Catherine Despeux and Livia Kohn, authors of *Women in Daoism*, views of women themselves and what was perceived as "feminine" energy changed over time. They distinguish five different historical versions.

The first of these is the view of the Dao as mother. This concept can be discerned in early Daoism in the *Daode jing*. It elevates the power of *yin*—softness, receptiveness, flexibility, intuitiveness—rather than concentrating on the assertiveness and firmness of *yang* energy appreciated in Confucian tradition. By developing the softer qualities in themselves, both men and women can better approach the mysterious Dao:

> The valley spirit does not die,
> It is called the mysterious female.
> The gate of the mysterious female
> Is called the root of heaven and earth.
> Forever and ever, it exists continuously,
> Use it, yet you'll never wear it out.
>
> Highest goodness is like water.
> It benefits the myriad beings
> And never contends.
> By never contending
> It is without fault.
> It rests in what the multitude disdain,
> Thus it is close to the Tao.[14]

Various metaphors are used here for the Dao: the valley spirit, the mysterious female (or "dark mare"), the gate of the mysterious female (or "door of the dark mare"), the root of heaven and earth. Ellen Chen, who has prepared a scholarly annotated translation of the *Daode jing*, says she personally believes that they all refer to the feminine creative power; the gate of the mysterious female is the way leading back to the invisible womb of creation. When the Dao is seen as mother, her energy is dark in the sense of being shrouded in mystery from men's view, like the sequestered women of the inner chambers in Chinese traditional culture.

The second vision of women, according to Despeux and Kohn, emerged during the Han Dynasty (206 BCE–220 CE). During this period, amassing of *qi*, or vital energy, was promoted under a system of *yin/yang* balancing through ritual intercourse, particularly in the Way of Great Peace and the Celestial Masters traditions. Women were seen as wonderful sources of *yin* energy, which could be tapped by a man when the woman reached climax. For their part, the men tried to withhold ejaculation, with the hope that their own "sexual essence" would rise to their brain and increase their *yang*, thus leading to balanced *qi*. This "sexual vampirism"—in which innocent young women were the preferred partners—was an old practice that existed before Daoism. It was thought to increase longevity and also to lead to balance in the cosmos, for according to ancient Chinese belief, sex was necessary not only for personal health but also for cosmic order. Toward the end of this period, millenarian beliefs were prevalent in these schools, with strict morality, a strong sense of community, and hierarchies based on ritual roles. Some women served as senior priests or libationists, and young women were used in initiation rituals. The Celestial Masters in particular encouraged respect for women. But the Way of Great Peace was demolished during military conflicts, while the Celestial Masters were embroiled in politics and scattered. Their sexual rites were disapproved by the general public, but elements of the path were retained and mixed with other ways.

The third period saw women not as sexual partners but as teachers and masters of secret spiritual techniques for personal and social development. This occurred as the Highest Clarity path was revealed in South China in 364–370 CE, and a "New Code" was revealed in 415 and 423 CE to reform the Celestial Masters path. Honor was accorded women who displayed the traditional virtues of Chinese culture, such as chastity, morality, respect for superiors, and celibacy of widows. Instead of taking young women as sexual partners to increase their *qi*, men visualized sexual union with a goddess who would also be their spiritual teacher.

The fourth period described by Despeux and Kohn began during the T'ang Dynasty (608–907 CE). Now many women adopted a celibate lifestyle as an alternative to life in the mainstream. They entered convents, founded new religious movements, became leaders in ongoing movements, and were respected as healers, prophets, shamans, and mediums. Cults developed around the memory of special women, such as the highly regarded twelfth-century poet and author Cao Wenyi, who wrote commentaries to Daoist texts and after her death appeared at spirit-writing séances. Late in the twelfth century, the School of Complete Perfection developed, with many nuns and abbesses who are still considered the spiritual equals of men.

There have been many female adepts in the esoteric schools of Daoism. Since patriarchal norms prevailed in China, some of these women had to run away from their husbands and in-laws in order to practice. However, as official recognition of Daoism increased, some women were allowed by their families to forsake marriage and instead live a life of meditation and devotion. Others practiced along with their husbands or had Daoist husbands who agreed to their living and practicing separately.

One of the most famous of historical female adepts is Sun Bu-er (see box, right). She gave illuminating teachings on mystical practices, with particular reference to the differences between women and men. Sun Bu-er claimed that women take naturally to Daoist practice because of what she sees as their greater tendency

BIOGRAPHY   Sun Bu-er *Female Adept*

The Immortal Sun Bu-er, known as "Clear and Calm Free Human," was an historical woman born in 1124 CE. She had married and raised three children before she began intense Daoist practice at the age of 51. This pattern of developing maturity and completing one's worldly obligations before undertaking spiritual practice was highly approved in the Complete Reality School. The feeling was that if people left society when they were too young for the sake of spiritual practice, they might not reach their spiritual goal; moreover, retreat places would turn into arenas where people were acting out their unfulflled worldly desires in spiritual costumes.

In the case of Sun Bu-er, her husband was also a Daoist disciple and had, in fact, started practicing before she did. In a dream, he had met Wang Zhe, one of the principal founders of the Pure Serenity School of Complete Reality. After the dream, he met Wang Zhe in person and became his disciple. Once, it is said, Wang Zhe came to his house when he was not at home. The master staggered around as if drunk and then collapsed on Sun Bu-er's bed. Outraged, she locked him inside and sent for her husband. When he returned, he declared that it was impossible, for he himself had been with his teacher elsewhere at the same time. When they opened the room, there was no sign of Wang Zhe. They found him asleep in his hostel.

This indication of the master's power was so compelling that Sun Bu-er became his disciple as well. He taught her the "pure serene way of complete realization." She is also said to have studied with an Immortal Sister who was thought to have been a disciple of Wang Zhe's teacher. After practicing together for some time, Sun Bu-er and her husband lived separately, each leading their own schools. Sun Bu-er elaborated the spiritual discipline for women, initiated many followers, and gave deep teachings in metaphorical poetic form. She wrote, for instance:

> All things fnished,
> You sit still in a little niche.
> The light body rides on violet energy,
> The tranquil nature washes in a pure pond.
> Original energy is unifed, yin and yang are one;
> The spirit is the same as the universe.[15]

According to a twentieth-century commentator, Chen Yingning, "All things finished, you sit still in a little niche" refers to the stage at which the advanced practitioner has so re fned her body that she stops eating anything at all and goes into absolute seclusion—perhaps in a cave against which a boulder has been shoved to keep out people and wild animals. She sits there until the "light spirit" is projected out of her body. Chen Yingning, albeit quite advanced in practice and understanding, is not sure what is meant by this, never having experienced this state—so the rest of the passage is better explained by quoting another poem from Sun Bu-er:

> Brambles should be cut away,
> Removing even the sprouts.
> Within essence there naturally blooms
> A beautiful lotus blossom.
> One day there will suddenly appear
> An image of light;
> When you know that,
> You yourself are it.[16]

to softness and inner stillness, but that they need somewhat different methods than men do because of their physiological differences and greater encouragement because of cultural strictures against spiritual practice for women.

The fifth version of women's spirituality in Daoism developed alongside the fourth, to a certain extent. This is the way of "inner alchemy," which has been the main form of Daoist spiritual practice from the Song Dynasty (960–1279 CE) to the present. In Daoist schools of inner alchemy, the practitioner is taught how to create an inner "womb" and nurture an "embryo" within it—the refined spirit—by means of esoteric practices. Women, already having wombs, are considered to have a natural advantage over men in this practice.

Daoist inner alchemical training is designed to purify, recirculate, and store spiritual energy within the body. Females and males start from a different place, because of their different physiological traits. In some Daoist schools, particularly the Celestial Masters school, men are taught to block the flow of semen and transfer that energy to inner development of "spiritual luminosity"; women are taught to "slay the dragon," menstruation being referred to as the "red dragon"—this unusual practice is described below.

Eva Wong, a contemporary teacher of Daoist arts in the West who grew up in Hong Kong, says she has studied with adepts hidden in the cities and mountains. She describes four stages of female Daoist internal alchemy.[17] The first is to cultivate inner tranquility. This requires shaking off social strictures and being disciplined in spiritual practice, becoming free from sexual desire and erratic moods, and—it is hoped—having families and teachers who are supportive and understanding. The second stage involves transforming the musculo-skeletal structure. Women need to work harder than men to build their muscular strength; Daoist callisthenics and inner martial arts such as *T'ai-chi chuan* are helpful (fig. 5.3). However, women's tendons and spines are more flexible than men's, so they have an advantage for Daoist practices. They also have a more open pelvic area, which is helpful in advanced stages of practice. The third stage is the unique practice of "slaying the dragon"—reversing the generative energy of menstrual blood, transforming it into "primordial vital energy" in the breasts, where it reportedly becomes white like milk, and refining it into "primordial vapor" which is stored in the womb. In the final stage, all distinctions, including distinctions between female and male, disappear, and with mind empty, one merges with the Dao.

While these versions of Daoist female spirituality developed among the spiritual elite, the lay masses of women then and now followed the way of popular religion. They prayed at their family altars, visited temples, and practiced simple ethics—such as compassion, nonviolence, good deeds, and perhaps vegetarianism. As in ancient China, their religious practices support traditional society, family, reverence toward ancestors, and worship of homey deities such as the Stove God and the Village God and those who are thought to protect the family.

Significantly, Daoism offered spiritual leadership roles to women who were otherwise marginalized in traditional Chinese culture. As Despeux and Kohn write:

> While Daoism had little impact on the lives of wives and mothers and offered limited opportunities for spiritually gifted daughters, it made a substantial difference for widows and divorcees. Often shunned by mainstream society, they found an active role as priests and nuns of the religion, which allowed them to attain ranks equal with those of men and live a life of comparative independence and freedom. Similarly, expelled concubines, former courtesans, and aging entertainers could find refuge and a new lease on life inside the Daoism organization, shifting their focus away from worldly involvement and toward the attainment of inner peace. No longer accountable to either parents or husband, these liminal figures posed a threat to Confucian order but offered great opportunity for the Dao. Mature, competent, and often with means of their own, they established convents, served as priests and healers, and contributed greatly to the shaping of Daoist organizations.[18]

5.3 Urban women doing their daily *T'ai-chi chuan* exercises

Female Immortals and Adepts

The extensive pantheon of Daoist deities worshiped both in popular culture and in practices of the adept includes many female figures. From the dim reaches of the shamanistic past emerged the Mother Empress of the West, Xiwang Mu, mother and chief of the pantheon of Daoist Immortals. In her early manifestations, she had disheveled hair and made weird whistling sounds, and her body was part human, part leopard, part tiger. By the Han Dynasty, she had become a peerless beauty living on Mount Kunlun, a paradise in whose orchards grow the peaches of immortality. During the T'ang period she became known as the special protectress of women but was adored by men and women alike as the height of *yin* femininity. Incorporated into the Daoist pantheon, she developed a huge retinue of attendants, messengers, and clerks who helped her with her newly recognized responsibilities of welcoming sages into the immortal realm, teaching emperors and devotees, revealing sacred scriptures to appropriate mortals, and acting as patron for all who undertook longevity and immortality practices (fig. 5.4). According to some esoteric schools, she had many young male lovers and practiced sexual yoga with

5.4 The Daoist Mother Empress or Queen of the West with her attendants

them, but this aspect of her life was generally kept secret. Both men and women need to obtain her permission to enter the immortal realm, the plane of existence for both deities and humans who have attained the privilege of eternal life. It is said that Wu-ti, the Martial Emperor of the Han Dynasty, met the Mother Empress of the West. She offered him seven peaches from a tree that bore fruit only once in 3,000 years. He asked to be given the secrets of immortality, but the next-in-command to the Mother Empress, Lady Shang-yuan, refused, reportedly telling him, "You were born licentious, extravagant, and violent; and you live in the midst of blood and force—no matter how many Daoists you invite here in hopes of immortality, you will only wear yourself out."[19]

Lady Shang-yuan, like the Mother Empress of the West, was an ancient deity who preceded Daoism. The spring planting season was under her control, so she was very important to agricultural and even political success. If an emperor displeased her, he would lose divine support for his rulership, and thus the rains would not come at the right time and the crops would be ruined. By the third or fourth century CE, she and the Mother Empress were adopted as important Daoist deities and acquired large retinues of heavenly helpers.

Over time, many mortal women who had become adepts were elevated to the ranks of the immortals, as described in *The Complete Biographies of the Immortals*. According to this book from the Daoist Canon, one of these is Lady Immortal Ho (Ho Hsien-ku). Daughter of a county magistrate, she lived in a village during the reign of the extremely powerful T'ang Empress Wu-hou (seventh century CE). She was apparently a spiritual adept and was often seen running with a light, quick gait along the mountain paths. After being gone all day, she would return at night with fruit from the mountains for her mother. Once the empress called her for an audience, but on the way to the capital, she simply disappeared into thin air. According to the stories about her, and in keeping with one of the methods of becoming immortal, she eventually ascended bodily to the heavens in full view. She was given the title "Supervisor of the Female Path—the Primal Ruler of the Azure Vapor."

Many women who were locally revered for their spiritual gifts were eventually considered deities. Tung-ling Sheng-mu (Sacred Mother of Tung-ling), for instance, was said to be able to alter her form into any shape and to become invisible at will, for she had attained the Dao. Sometimes she would leave her home in order to heal and help people in need. However, this so enraged her husband that he complained to the local magistrate that she was spending her time battling evil spirits instead of taking care of her own household. She was thence arrested and put in prison. Using her magical abilities, she disappeared from her cell, leaving behind only her shoe. From then on, the people prayed for her help. They built a shrine to her, and according to her biography, a green raven was often seen there. If anyone who had been robbed prayed to her, that raven would lead them to the home of the robber. Thus robbery decreased in the area, and those few who attempted to steal typically met with bad luck, drowned, or were killed by wild beasts.

Women also became powerful teachers and even founders of schools of mystical practice. Both the Yellow Emperor and Lao-tzi, considered the founders of Daoism, were thought to have had female teachers. Lady Wei Hua-ts'un is known as the founder of the influential Shang-ch'ing school of Daoism. She was born into a wealthy family in southeastern China during the Eastern Chin dynasty (317–420 CE). From the time she was young, she delved into Daoist scriptures, practiced methods of breath control, tried various austere diets for their spiritual effects, and became an adept at yogic methods of longevity. She wanted to leave home in order to cultivate the arts of immortality, but her parents refused and instead married her to a nobleman when she was 24. She bore two sons and raised them to adulthood. Then she built a retreat for herself and spent the rest of her life studying and practicing Daoist arts. An immortal master appeared to her and taught her how to merge mystically with the deities and thus become immortal. Having mastered the techniques, when she was 83 she reportedly ascended bodily into the sky. According to her sacred biography, she then undertook further study with the Mother Empress of the West and became known as Lady Wei, Guardian of the Southern Mountains. Her followers built the earliest Daoist retreat communities, in the Mao-shan mountain range of southeast China. Although Shang-ch'ing has not lasted as a separate lineage, the practices she introduced for control of the breath, swallowing of saliva, internal direction of energy flows in the body, and mystical ecstasy are still in use today, and the rituals attributed to Lady Wei are still practiced in monasteries and temples.

The majority of contemporary practitioners of Daoism observe a devotional path; only a minority attempt the mystical ways of inner alchemical transformation. Nevertheless, women seem well suited to these rigorous techniques, and today female successors of Sun Bu-er are still practicing in China, Taiwan, and Hong Kong, even after wars and political oppression. In China, most live as recluses in small, remote temples, but some returned to public temples and nunneries in China after the government eased its restrictions on religions. In Hong Kong, some live as "urban hermits" practicing the mystical arts secretly, even though other women serve openly as clergy in devotional temples. The female Immortals are well-known figures in Chinese cultures, where their stories are subject matter for countless films and operas.

Philosophical aspects of Daoism are of growing interest throughout the world. Some commentators explain that Daoism is ultimately a path for reconciling *yin* and *yang*, for bringing the two into balance, but not by way of the analytical mind that sees differences, separations, categories. Eva Wong and Karen Laughlin write:

According to the Daoist view of the universe, the Dao is the underlying reality of all things. This is a state of nondifferentiation and noncategorization…. The development of constructs such as masculine and feminine or male and female, and of a gender identity rooted in these constructs, reflects a movement away from the original nondifferentiated state of existence. The Daoist path of return to the origin involves overcoming this differentiation and categorization of things. This is accomplished through the development of the intuitive, prereflective consciousness and the shrinking of the conceptualizing and analyzing mind…. Just as valley streams flow into rivers and seas, the Daoist adept loses her identity in the Dao, as self and Dao naturally flow together. No longer an individual with a set personality, she develops a new and wider identity as part of the universe at large.[20]

Key Terms

yin
yang
Dao
qi

Suggested Reading

Chan, Wing-Tsit, ed. and trans., *A Source Book in Chinese Philosophy*, Princeton: Princeton University Press, 1963. A classic source, but like most translations, uses male rather than gender-neutral language where the originals are gender-neutral references to "people" (*ren*).

Chen, Ellen, *The Tao te Ching: A New Translation with Commentary*, New York: Paragon House, 1989. One of many translations of the classic text attributed to Lao-tzi. This one is more literal than poetic, with useful commentaries.

Cleary, Thomas, ed. and trans., *Immortal Sisters: Secret Teachings of Taoist Women*, Berkeley, California: North Atlantic Books, 1989, 1996. An appreciative attempt by a male specialist to elucidate mystical writings of famous Daoist women adepts.

Despeux, Catherine, "Women in Daoism," trans. Livia Kohn, in Livia Kohn, *Daoism Handbook*, Leiden, 2000. An excellent historical survey of women's varying situations within the Daoist path.

Despeux, Catherine and Livia Kohn, *Women in Daoism*, Cambridge, Massachusetts: Three Pines Press, 2003. Extensive analysis of the roles of women and female figures throughout Daoist history.

Kohn, Livia, *Daoism and Chinese Culture*, Cambridge, Massachusetts: Three Pines Press, 2001. Scholarly but accessible study of the complexities of Daoism within its changing cultural contexts.

Kohn, Livia, ed., *The Taoist Experience: An Anthology*, Albany, New York: State University of New York Press, 1993. Textual sources and explanations of the mysteries of Daoism.

Laughlin, Karen and Eva Wong, "Feminism and/in Taoism," in Arvind Sharma and Katherine K. Young, eds., *Feminism and World Religions*, Albany, New York: State University of New York Press, 1999, pp. 148–78. Arguments that female images in Daoism do not necessarily equate with respect for women.

Li, Chenyang, ed., *The Sage and the Second Sex: Confucianism, Ethics, and Gender*, Chicago and La Salle, Illinois: Open Court, 2000. Various scholars attempt to explore whether there is any common ground between patriarchal Confucianism and feminism.

Wilhelm, Richard and Cary F. Baynes, trans., *The I Ching or Book of Changes*, Princeton: Princeton University Press, 1967. Fascinating ancient text and historical commentaries, affording myriad insights into Chinese philosophies.

Wolf, Margery, *Women and the Family in Rural Taiwan*, Stanford, California: Stanford University Press, 1972. An anthropologist's description of women's everyday lives in a patriarchal culture that reveres ancestors and values sons.

Xinran, *The Good Women of China: Hidden Voices*, trans. Esther Tyldesley, New York: Pantheon Books, 2002. True stories of violence against women's bodies and spirits in contemporary China, within the context of patriarchal values.

6
WOMEN IN JUDAISM

Her mouth is full of wisdom

PROVERBS 31: 26

Judaism is an ancient religion that has spread far from its original root. Of the approximately 14 million Jewish people living today, six million live in the United States and four million in Israel. Of these, some may be ethnically Jewish but may not be practicing Jewish spiritual traditions. Judaism is rich in history and is experiencing a contemporary resurgence in some areas, and a strong feminist movement has arisen within the otherwise highly patriarchal tradition.

Development of Judaism

The foundation of Jewish spirituality is the *Tanakh*, or Hebrew Bible. It begins with two different accounts of the creation of the world by God. The first is a very poetic mythical account, in which the earth was "unformed and void, with darkness over the surface of the deep and a wind from God sweeping over the water" (Genesis 1: 2). By God's word were all things created, including human beings, whom God created "in His image ... male and female He created them" (Genesis 1: 27). The second version of the creation story (Genesis 2–3) is thought to reflect an older oral tradition. Compared to the egalitarian first version, Genesis 2–3 presents a religious basis for the subordination of women. God is presented as a male deity who creates a man first and a woman later as a companion to the man. The first woman, Eve, is blamed for humanity's loss of innocence and happiness.

According to the biblical accounts, life goes on in any case, with the people often failing to follow God's commands. Nonetheless, in early Jewish history the people feel they have a special relationship with God, a covenant by which they are granted special favors as God's chosen people, and in which they agree to be obedient to the divine commandments. Adherence to religious laws is to become a central theme in the development of Jewish life.

The chief model for obedience to God is the first patriarch, Abraham, who is thought to have lived some time between 1900 and 1700 BCE. He was born in the ancient city of Ur, now in Iraq, and following God's orders moved his family to Canaan, in what is now Israel. According to the Hebrew Bible, God commanded him to be circumcised as a sign of the covenant between them, by which God agreed to be the divine protector of Abraham and all his descendants. The previous

TIMELINE

c.1900–1700 BCE	Abraham, the first patriarch, and the matriarch Sarah
c.1300–1200 BCE	Moses leads Israelites out of Egypt; Miriam's victory dance
By 1207 BCE	Israelites reach Canaan
961–931 BCE	King Solomon builds the Temple in Jerusalem
c.600 BCE	Huldah the Prophetess urges king to attack Goddess worship
586 BCE	Destruction of First Temple, exile of Jews to Babylon
c.20 BCE–50 CE	Sambathe the Greek poetess
70 CE	Destruction of Second Temple by Romans; Temple worship succeeded by rabbinical Judaism
c.100 CE	Beruriah the wise teacher
c.400 CE, c.500 CE	Israelite and Babylonian Talmuds written down
c.690 CE	Kahinah victorious over Muslim forces in North Africa
1095	Anti-Semitism begins to develop with start of First Crusade
1120	Daughter of Joseph regarded as Messiah
1492	Defeat and expulsion of Jews from Spain
1500 on	Jewish cultural center shifts to Central and Eastern Europe; Rebecca Tiktiner's writings
1690s	Memoirs of Glückel of Hamelin
c.1700	Hasidism develops; Edel, daughter of the Baal Shem Tov
1805	Hannah Rachel born; becomes famous woman rabbi
1812–1847	Life of Grace Aguilar, popular novelist
1860–1945	Henrietta Szold, Zionist leader of Hadassah
1885	American rabbis adopt Reform Judaism from Germany
1919	Emma Goldman jailed and deported for promoting birth control
1930s	Reconstructionism supports religious equality of women
1940–1945	Holocaust in Europe
1947	Partition of Palestine, leading to declaration of Israel as independent state
1973	Ordination of Sally Priesand as first Reform rabbi
1970s	Jewish Feminist Organization arises within Conservative Judaism

inhabitants of Canaan worshiped many deities, but ultimately the Israelites paid obeisance to a single deity, and they perceived their nation as the spiritual center through which the world would discover their God. They were named Israel after the grandson of Abraham, formerly known as Jacob.

During a great famine in approximately the fifteenth century BCE, the 12 tribes of Israel's sons reportedly migrated to Egypt. After several hundred years, they were enslaved by the pharaoh or ruler, who further ordered midwives to kill all male children born to Israelite women. The infant Moses escaped this terrible ruling and was raised in the palace by the pharaoh's own daughter. Troubled by the enslavement of his own people and emboldened by the power of God, he confronted the pharaoh and led his people back to Canaan. During their journey, Moses reportedly ascended a mountain to re-establish the covenant with God. His encounter with God's power was overwhelming. According to the biblical account, God gave Moses the **Torah**: the laws by which the Israelites should live righteously in order to uphold their side of the covenant (the word "Torah" is also used for the first five books of the Hebrew Bible, as well as for the whole body of Jewish teaching and law). As the Hebrews traveled through the desert, they carried a precious Ark representing their covenant with God.

By about 1207 BCE, according to archaeological records, the Israelites had reached Canaan. Ultimately, David, the shepherd boy who became Israel's greatest king, built the prosperous empire of Israel with its capital in the city of Jerusalem. There his son Solomon built a huge Temple to house the Ark of the Covenant and to make offerings to God. After some time, however, the empire became unjust and corrupt and the tribes of Israel were split politically. In 586 BCE, the king of Babylonia captured Jerusalem and destroyed the Temple; many of the people were taken to exile in Babylonia. There they were called "Jews," since they were from the southern Israelite kingdom known as Judah.

From then on, the majority of Jews were scattered in the **Diaspora** (dispersion), in this case geographically separated from Zion, the emblematic holy hill in Jerusalem where the Temple had been built. Those who returned to Jerusalem chafed under four centuries of oppressive Roman rule. Amid fervent apocalyptic hopes that they would be saved by God, who would conquer the evil and reward the good, or perhaps even by an actual **Messiah** or savior, Jewish zealots staged an uprising from 67 to 70 CE against the Romans, who slaughtered them and destroyed the towns of Judaea and the second Temple, leaving only its Western Wall. Still today, Jews stand there and weep in remembrance.

Jewish spiritual tradition gradually changed from sacrificial worship conducted by priests to prayer and study led by **rabbis**, men who taught, made decisions, and created prayers. The Jews met for worship, Torah study, and prayer in **synagogues** (meeting places). From the age of five or six, Jewish males were engaged in deep study of the scriptures. Women were exempted from Torah study, and they also did not count as part of a *minyan*—the ten men needed as a minimal attendance for community worship.

As they studied the scriptures, the rabbis developed a vast body of commentaries and oral traditions, much of which was eventually gathered together into the **Talmud**. There are two major versions, one written down in the land of Israel about 400 CE, the other in Babylonia from 500 CE onwards. The Babylonian Talmud particularly emphasizes study of the Torah as the key to Israel's destiny as a model society based on obedience to the laws of God. And it was especially through prayer and Torah study that a person could experience the *Shekhinah*, the Presence of God.

With the Torah and Talmud and rabbis to guide them in the commands of God, Jews dispersed widely throughout Christian and Muslim cultures during the Middle Ages. They thrived in the high culture of Muslim-ruled Spain until Christians conquered the country and forced them out in 1492. From 1095, Jews were targets of recurrent **anti-Semitic** (anti-Jewish) attacks throughout Europe by

Christians who blamed them for not accepting Jesus as their Messiah and for implication in his death a thousand years earlier. Christians were taught to regard Jews
as a different and vile race that should be avoided and even punished. Many Jews
were forced to convert to Christianity or face death at the hands of the dreaded
Inquisition (established by the Roman Catholic Church to root out heretics), but
the *marranos*, as they were called, were still suspected of remaining inwardly
Jewish. By the sixteenth and seventeenth centuries, some European Jews were
confined to **ghettos**, Jewish-only walled urban areas that were locked at night. In
Muslim-ruled areas, Jews generally fared better, with certain rights as "people of
the book."

Oppression and suspicion notwithstanding, some Jews developed a rich inner
spiritual life, particularly noticeable in the Hasidic tradition. This was a path of
ecstatic prayer which was particularly embraced in Eastern Europe. Even today
Hasidism remains one of the most fervent paths within Judaism. There are also the
varied mystical traditions known as Kabbalah. These include visionary practices,
stories, and revelations of a higher world of light whose sparks can be found here
in the midst of everyday life and can be used to "repair" the evil and chaos of the
world.

Misunderstood and even hated by some Christians for religious and economic
reasons, Jews were eventually subjected to a terrible experience—the genocide that
became known as the Holocaust. Almost six million Jews were murdered by the
Nazis in Germany during World War II (1939–1945). Many European countries
lost more than half of their Jewish population; in Poland, which had been home to
the greatest number of Jews, only 70,000 remained out of a previous total of
3,300,000.

Long before the Holocaust, some Jews were attracted to the Zionist movement,
which aimed to re-establish an independent Jewish state in the biblical land of
Israel. In part, they longed to escape from anti-Semitism, but the movement had
deeper roots in Jewish spirituality and culture: the messianic ideal of ending the
long exile from Zion and reassembling the whole Congregation of Israel, reassert-
ing its sovereignty as a source of blessing for all humanity. There had been a continuous Jewish presence in the area, and during the early twentieth century, Jewish
immigration into Palestine was encouraged by Zionists and allowed by Britain,
which took charge following the division of territories after World War I. Then in
1947, the United Nations decided to partition Palestine into two, one part to be
governed by Jews and the other by Arabs, with Jerusalem as an international zone.
The Arabs of Palestine and surrounding countries did not accept this division, and
violence and tensions have wracked the area ever since.

Women in the Hebrew Bible

Jewish history in the biblical period was dominated by men. But current feminist
scholarship is delving into the roles played by women, using scant references in the
Hebrew Bible, plus the tools of archaeology, anthropology, sociology, literary criticism, women's studies, and modern psychology to try to piece together some idea

of women's lives. Even more obscure are their spiritual lives, but a few hints can be found.

First among the women of the Hebrew Bible is Eve, the mythological mother of all humanity, according to the second Creation story (see box, right). This mythical figure has long been blamed by Christians for the fall of humankind from God's grace. Jews have not been so harsh in their opinion, recognizing human imperfection as a given. And some contemporary women are noting that according to the myth, Eve was the first being in the Judeo–Christian–Muslim tradition to make a choice regarding her destiny, and she chose knowledge over obedience (fig. 6.1). Yet even then, the scriptural passage clearly asserts male dominance over women as a divine commandment.

Then there are the matriarchs of the early period, who are considered the foremothers of both Jews and Christians—Sarah, Rebecca, Leah, and Rachel. Sarah had migrated from her ancestral land to Canaan with her husband Abraham, who was her half-brother. Sarah was long childless. According to archaeological findings, as a well-born woman from Haran, in the Hurrian civilization of Mesopotamia, she was entitled to individual rights that were unique for women of the area. One was the right to offer her personal handmaiden to her husband as a consort and to consider any children from their coupling as her own. She thus gave the Egyptian slave Hagar to Abraham, and they procreated a son, Ishmael. But, the story goes, Abraham and Sarah offered such kind hospitality to three men who visited their tent—thought to be God's angels—that one of them mystically promised that Sarah would herself bear a son within the year. According to the biblical account, she was post-menopausal by then, and "Sarah laughed to herself, saying, 'Now that I am withered, am I to have enjoyment—with my husband so old?'" (Genesis 18: 12). A strange conversation with God followed, in which He accused her of laughing because she had no faith. Sarah thus begins to come to life in the biblical narrative as a person who speaks with God and fears God's displeasure. Sarah indeed gave birth to a son, whom they named Isaac, and to protect his inheritance, she reportedly had Abraham banish Hagar and Ishmael to the desert. But according to the Bible, both women were blessed by God, and while Abraham's descendants multiplied and flourished through Sarah's son Isaac—as the Jewish lineage, and later the Christian lineage—they also multiplied and flourished through Hagar's son Ishmael, who is considered the ancestor of Muslims.

Next of the foremothers described in the Bible is Rebecca. Abraham wanted a wife for Isaac from his native land, rather than a Canaanite woman, so he sent a messenger to Haran. Upon meeting Rebecca at a well, where she graciously served water to both him and his camels, the messenger presented her with a gold nose-ring and gold arm-bands. The messenger explained his mission to her parents—to come back with a wife for Isaac, to whom Abraham would bequeath his considerable wealth. But before agreeing, the parents sought Rebecca's agreement, for, like Sarah, she had her rights. She was willing and was thus taken back to Isaac, who loved her.

Rebecca and Isaac were blessed with twins, but according to the biblical account, the two were fighting even in her womb. God reportedly explained to Rebecca:

EXCERPT The Story of Eve

The LORD God planted a garden in Eden, in the east, and placed there the man whom He had formed. And from the ground the LORD God caused to grow every tree that was pleasing to the sight and good for food, with the tree of life in the middle of the garden, and the tree of knowledge of good and bad.... . And the LORD God commanded the man, saying, "Of every tree of the garden you are free to eat; but as for the tree of knowledge of good and bad, you must not eat of it; for as soon as you eat of it, you shall die."

The LORD God said, "It is not good for man to be alone; I will make a fitting helper for him." …So the LORD God cast a deep sleep upon the man; and, while he slept, He took one of his ribs and closed up the flesh at that spot. And the LORD God fashioned the rib that He had taken from the man into a woman; and He brought her to the man. Then the man said, "This one at last is bone of my bones and flesh of my flesh. This one shall be called Woman [*ishshah*], for from

6.1 Adam and Eve with the apple and the serpent, as depicted by Lucas Cranach the Elder (1472–1553)

man [*ish*] was she taken." Hence a man leaves his father and mother and clings to his wife, so that they become one flesh.

The two of them were naked, the man and his wife, yet they felt no shame. Now the serpent was the shrewdest of all the wild beasts that the LORD God had made. He said to the woman, "Did God really say: You shall not eat of any tree of the garden?" The woman replied to the serpent, "We may eat of the fruit of the other trees of the garden. It is only about fruit of the tree in the middle of the garden that God said: 'You shall not eat of it or touch it, lest you die.'" And the serpent said to the woman, "You are not going to die, but God knows that as soon as you eat of it your eyes will be opened and you will be like divine beings who know good and bad." When the woman saw that the tree was good for eating and a delight to the eyes, and that the tree was desirable as a source of wisdom, she took of its fruit and ate. She also gave some to her husband, and he ate. Then the eyes of both of them were opened and they perceived that they were naked; and they sewed together fig leaves and made themselves loincloths.

They heard the sound of the LORD God moving about in the garden at the breezy time of day; and the man and his wife hid from the LORD God among the trees of the garden. The LORD God called out to the man and said to him, "Where are you?" He replied, "I heard the sound of You in the garden, and I was afraid because I was naked, so I hid." Then He asked, "Who told you that you were naked? Did you eat of the tree from which I had forbidden you to eat?" The man said, "The woman You put at my side—she gave me of the tree, and I ate." And the LORD God said to the woman, "What is this you have done!" The woman replied, "The serpent duped me, and I ate." Then the LORD God [cursed the serpent] … and to the woman He said, "I will make most severe your pangs in childbearing; in pain shall you bear children. Yet your urge shall be for your husband, and he shall rule over you." [God also cursed Adam, so that growing food would be a struggle, and then he would himself return to the dust from which he came.]

The man named his wife Eve, because she was the mother of all the living.

The Book of Genesis, 2: 8–3: 20, *Tanakh—The Holy Scriptures*, Philadelphia, Jewish Publication Society, 1988.

> Two nations are in your womb,
> Two separate peoples shall issue from your body;
> One people shall be mightier than the other,
> And the older shall serve the younger.[1]

It is worth noting that in the biblical narratives, most of the instances in which God speaks directly to women concern forthcoming children—for woman's most important role was as a mother, especially of sons. Based on God's revelation to Rebecca, when Isaac was old and wanted to give his greatest blessing to the first-born son Esau, Rebecca conspired to have the blessing given to Jacob, who emerged from her womb second. When Jacob expressed his concern about deceiving his father, lest he be cursed, Rebecca said, "Your curse, my son, be upon me!" (Genesis 27: 13). She acts as an independent and brave woman of the relatively liberated culture of Haran, and, pregnant, she receives a direct revelation from God and is more obedient to that divine wisdom than to her husband's preference.

Jacob had two wives—his cousins Leah and Rachel—who like his mother and grandmother came from Haran, a culture that accorded women freedoms not known in other areas. Rachel, being barren, exercised the same option that was available to Sarah as a Hurrian woman: she sent her maidservant to her husband in order that she might bear children for them.

Many women appear here and there throughout the biblical narratives, often playing strong roles but not dwelt on at length by the narrators. Women in the Hebrew Bible are often depicted as using all the resources at their disposal—spirituality, beauty, cleverness, bravery, family connections—to succeed in protecting their families and their clans. Those who are of most interest in our consideration of women's place in Jewish spirituality are the prophetesses and wise women, for there were no female priests.

In Jewish tradition, a prophet or prophetess is a person who speaks on behalf of God. One of the foremost prophetesses of interest to Jewish women today is Miriam, sister of Moses. According to the Bible, she courageously saved her infant brother from death by putting him in a basket among the rushes in the Nile River, where he was found and adopted by the daughter of the pharaoh; Miriam cleverly arranged for his wet-nurse to be his own mother. After Moses led his people to freedom through the parting of the Red Sea, it was Miriam who led the women in a victory dance with tambourines. But when she and Aaron, her other brother, compared their gift of prophecy with that of Moses, by way of complaining about the woman he married, God reportedly appeared to them and said that while as prophets they could see visions, God appeared openly, "mouth to mouth" to Moses (Numbers 12: 8). For her boldness, Miriam was struck with leprosy, whereas Aaron was not. Contemporary feminist leader Judith Plaskow quotes from the many poems that have been written about Miriam: "This is the Miriam who knows the validity of her own revelation. It is the Miriam who insists to her brother, 'We have both been chosen./What you witness on the mountain/cannot lie without the miracles/below.'"[2]

Huldah is mentioned as being a prophetess in such a matter-of-fact way—as though it was not unusual for a woman to have this spiritual gift—that scholars speculate that there may have been many more prophetesses who are not mentioned. Among those known is Deborah, apparently a very spiritually and politically powerful prophetess, for it is written in Judges 4: 4-5: "Deborah, wife of Lappidoth, was a prophetess; she led Israel at that time. She used to sit under the Palm of Deborah, between Ramah and Bethel in the hill country of Ephraim, and the Israelites would come to her for decisions."

With the Israelites living under fear of Sisera, commander of a Canaanite army reportedly armed with 900 iron chariots, Deborah gave God's order to Barak to gather 10,000 men and challenge Sisera, and she would deliver him and his army into Barak's hands. Barak refused to go without her, so she agreed to accompany him, saying, according to the biblical narrative, "However, there will be no glory for you in the course you are taking, for then the Lord will deliver Sisera into the hands of a woman" (Judges 4: 9). As she had promised, the entire enemy army was killed, except for Sisera. He was killed by another woman, Jael, who enticed the fleeing commander into her tent under pretense of protecting him and then drove a tent peg through his skull as he slept.

There are several "wise women" who appear briefly in the narratives, again in such a way that one can imagine that there were other wise women in Israelite culture. They do not utter prophetic words from God; rather, they seem to be sought out as skilled mediators who use proverbs and rhetoric to convince others to take a particular course of action.

A few women appear in leading roles, most notably Queen Esther, to whom an entire book is devoted in the Hebrew Bible (see box, right). Long afterward, from the fourteenth century CE, she was adopted as a role model by *marrano* women. Cut off from male-centered Jewish traditions for hundreds of years, the *marrano* women led prayers, performed marriages, and developed secret ceremonies based on Esther. Rabbi Lynn Gottlieb has written a poem giving them a voice, as they worshiped in Christian churches contrary to their inner desires:

> And the seasons pass
> saintly Esther
> my soul stays hidden
> speaking softly
> words praising Adonai
> time forgetting time
> eyes forgetting light
> we hide in order to survive
> living in brief moments
> whispering the truth to shadows
> I am a woman and a Jew
> Saintly Esther
> How did you endure those long months
> Of living what you were not
> Of embracing what you loved not.
> As I enter this house of wood and stone
> give me
> your poor handmaiden
> strength enough to pass through
> this night of fear.[3]

In addition to women in the biblical narratives, there are references to the apparently beloved earlier goddess called "Queen of Heaven"—mostly referring to efforts to keep the Israelites from continuing to worship Her and their other traditional gods. The new God, Yahweh (eventually recognized as the sole God of Israel), was stern, invisible, and separate from His creation; He was worshiped and placated in temples by means of animal sacrifices. The older deities were seemingly worshiped more intimately, through iconic objects, sacred groves, and pillars in consecrated sites. When the prophet Jeremiah harangued the Hebrews for neglect-

EXCERPT   The Story of Esther

King Ahasuerus ruled over a vast empire, from India to Ethiopia. Once he held a grand banquet for all the nobles and officials of his empire. For 180 days he displayed all the riches of his kingdom, and then for seven days he gave a huge feast for all those living within his fortified city. Liquor was plied without any restrictions. On the seventh day of this revelry, he sent his eunuchs to bring his Queen Vashti to him, so that he might display her beauty to all the people. However, she refused to come. Furious at being so spurned, the king decided to replace her with a new queen chosen from among the virgins of all the provinces under his rule.

Among those summoned was Esther, also known as Hadassah. She was an orphan who had been adopted by a Jew named Mordecai, whose lineage traced back to the Jews sent into exile in Babylon. Esther was his uncle's daughter… . When Esther's time came to be presented to the king, he loved her most of all and chose her as his new queen.

Meanwhile, Mordecai sat at the palace gate but never revealed his relationship to Esther; she, too kept silent about her Jewish roots, as Mordecai had instructed her. Sitting at the gate, Mordecai learned that two of the king's eunuchs had become angry and were plotting to assassinate the king. He told Esther, who reported their plot to the king. King Ahasuerus had them impaled on stakes.

Highest among the courtiers was Haman. When he passed the palace gate, Mordecai refused to bow to him, even though everyone in the city had been ordered to bow to Haman. Infuriated, Haman proposed to King Ahasuerus, "There is a certain people, scattered and dispersed among the other peoples in all the provinces of your realm, whose laws are different from those of any other people and who do not obey the king's laws, and it is not in Your Majesty's interest to tolerate them." At Haman's urging, the king agreed to send instructions throughout his realm that these people—the Jews of the diaspora—should be destroyed on a particular day.

Mordecai donned the sackcloth and ashes of mourning, and sent a message to Queen Esther to intercede with the king on behalf of the Jews. She sent this message back to Mordecai: "All the king's courtiers and the people of the king's provinces know that if any person, man or woman, enters the king's presence in the inner court without having been summoned, there is but one law for him— that he be put to death. Only if the king extends the golden scepter to him may he live. Now I have not been summoned to visit the king for the last thirty days."

The biblical account continues: "When Mordecai was told what Esther had said, Mordecai had this message delivered to Esther: 'Do not imagine that you, of all the Jews, will escape with your life by being in the king's palace. On the contrary, if you keep silent in this crisis, relief and deliverance will come to the Jews from another quarter, while you and your father's house will perish. And who knows, perhaps you have attained to royal position for just such a crisis.' Then Esther sent back this answer to Mordecai: 'Go, assemble all the Jews who live in Sushan, and fast in my behalf; do not eat or drink for three days, night or day. I and my maidens will observe the same fast. Then I shall go to the king, though it is contrary to the law, and if I am to perish, I shall perish!'

"On the third day, Esther put on royal apparel and stood in the inner court of the king's palace, facing the king's palace, while the king was sitting on his royal throne in the throne room facing the entrance of the palace. As soon as the king saw Queen Esther standing in the court, she won his favor. The king extended to Esther the golden scepter which he had in his hand, and Esther approached and touched the tip of the scepter. 'What troubles you, Queen Esther?' the king asked her. 'And what is your request? Even to half the kingdom, it shall be granted to you.' 'If it please Your Majesty,' Esther replied, 'let Your Majesty and Haman come today to the feast that I have prepared for him.' The king commanded, 'Tell Haman to hurry and do Esther's bidding.' So the king and Haman came to the feast that Esther had prepared."

Esther again requested the king, "Let Your Majesty and Haman come to the feast which I will prepare for them; and tomorrow I will do Your Majesty's bidding." Full of pride, Haman boasted to his family of his great power and had a high stake set up for the impalement of Mordecai, who still infuriated him by not bowing as he passed.

That night the king could not sleep, so he had the records of the court brought out and read to him. Thus he discovered that it was Mordecai who had denounced the eunuchs who were plotting to kill him, so he gave him the highest honors. As for Haman, when he and the king came to Esther's feast, the Queen requested, "If Your Majesty will do me the favor, and if it pleases Your Majesty, let my life be granted me as my wish, and my people's as my request. For we have been sold, my people and I, to be destroyed, massacred, and exterminated. Had we only been sold as bondmen and bondwomen, I would have kept silent, for the adversary is not worthy of the king's trouble."

Thereupon King Ahasuerus demanded of Queen Esther, "Who is he and where is he who dared to do this?" "The adversary and enemy," replied Esther, "is this evil Haman!" The king ordered that Haman be impaled on the stake that he had erected for killing Mordecai, and accepted Queen Esther's request that Haman's order against the Jews be rescinded. Today this great reversal of the Jews' fortunes thanks to Queen Esther's courage is celebrated yearly as Purim.

From the *Book of Esther*, in *Tanakh—The Holy Scriptures*, Philadelphia: Jewish Publication Society, 1988, pp. 1457–61.

ing Yahweh, and thus risking exile from Zion, they reportedly replied that everything was fine so long as they were worshiping the Goddess. Women were apparently included in ways of worshiping Her, as we can glimpse from the biblical account:

▪ Thereupon they answered Jeremiah—all the men who knew that their wives made offerings to other gods; all the women present, a large gathering; and all

WOMEN IN JEWISH HISTORY   **167**

the people who lived in Pathros in the land of Egypt: "We will not listen to you in the matter about which you spoke to us in the name of the LORD. On the contrary, we will do everything that we have vowed—to make offerings to the Queen of Heaven and to pour libations to her, as we used to do, we and our fathers, our kings and our officials, in the towns of Judah and the streets of Jerusalem. For then we had plenty to eat, we were well off, and suffered no misfortune. But ever since we stopped making offerings to the Queen of Heaven and pouring libations to her, we have lacked everything, and we have been consumed by the sword and by famine. And when we make offerings to the Queen of Heaven and pour libations to her, is it without our husbands' approval that we have made cakes in her likeness and poured libations to her?"[4] ■

Maacah, the favorite wife of King Solomon's son Rehoboam, had so much influence with her husband that he installed an image of the Goddess Asherah in the Jerusalem Temple itself. However, after Rehoboam's reign, reformist Yahwists attacked Goddess worship, under guidance from the prophets and urgings of the Jerusalem priests. King Josiah (639–600 BCE) was told by the prophetess Huldah that Yahweh, the jealous God of Israel, would bring disaster upon the Israelites because they had forsaken Him and worshiped other gods, including Asherah (fig. 6.2). Here we see that even the strong women of the Bible were part of a patriarchal system, for the prophetess Huldah reportedly upheld the will of the male deity

6.2 An early goddess figure excavated at Tell el-Duweir, southern Levant

Yahweh against those worshiping the Goddess. The king thus had all cult images burned, their shrines desecrated and destroyed, their priests slain on their own altars, their sacred pillars smashed. He seemed particularly intent on eradicating all traces of Goddess worship. He had the statue of Asherah removed from the Temple, burned, ground into powder, and spread as dust on the graves of her devotees.

Judaism became thoroughly monotheistic, with its God perceived in masculine terms. Only a few hints remain in the Hebrew Bible of worship of the feminine—as in Proverbs, where Wisdom is personified as a female.

Women in Jewish History

Although Jewish history is usually written as the history of men, contemporary research has turned up evidence of many great Jewish women. There is no one stereotype; many vibrant individuals have been rediscovered. What follows is only a sampling.

During the early rabbinic period, women's voices and stories contributed to the open forums through which the Talmud was created. One of the most outstanding women quoted in the Talmud was Beruriah. Living during the second century CE, she was the wife of the well-known Rabbi Meir but was also considered a wise teacher in her own right. She is said to have daily studied 300 laws. A famous story revealing her inner strength and spiritual wisdom is told about the time when her two sons died. It was the Sabbath day, and she did not want to disturb her husband's peace of mind, so when he asked where their sons were, she put him off with vague answers. When the rabbi had finished the final prayer marking the end of the Sabbath, she began a strategic dialogue asking him:

> "Some time ago I was entrusted by a friend with some jewels for safekeeping and now he wants them back. Shall I return them?"
>
> "Of course," answered Rabbi Meir, "the jewels must be returned."
>
> Beruriah then took him to where their dead sons were lying. When he collapsed and cried she gently reminded him: "Did you not say we must return to the owner the precious jewels he entrusted to us? The Lord has given, the Lord has taken. Blessed be the name of the Lord."[5]

Sadly, it seems that Rabbi Meir used his own wife to test prejudices against women. He supposedly sent one of his disciples to tempt her sexually, and when she recognized her weakness, she committed suicide.

In the Diaspora communities, Jewish women lived amidst more egalitarian ancient cultures, such as those of Persia and Greece. In Greece, some of the Sibyls, or prophetesses, seem to have been Jewish. Of these, the writings of Sambathe have been preserved. She used the conventions of Greek epic poetry to exalt Jewish history and spirituality, as opposed to polytheistic, nature-oriented Hellenist traditions, and exhorted Hellenized Jews to return to their own monotheistic religion:

> Why do you offer gifts in vain to the dead and sacrifices to idols?
> Who had led your soul astray thus?
> Who had talked you into deserting the great God?
> Oh, stand in awe before the name of the Father of all creatures.[6]

In North Africa, where Diaspora Jews were living as nomadic farmers and warriors, Kahinah emerged in the seventh century as a powerful chieftain and prophetess. Ultimately, she pulled together many disparate groups and led them to victory against a prince who was seeking to convert Africa to Islam by force. After five years of her rule, which led to unprecedented unity in the area, she was again attacked by the prince's Arab forces. To discourage them, she ordered all the cities in the area to be destroyed, but the Arabs kept fighting nonetheless and she herself was killed in battle. Her dying command to her sons was to surrender. They and most of the Berber tribes of the area eventually converted to Islam.

In Egypt of the ninth to thirteenth centuries, women seem to have been economically active, working and trading outside their homes. In Baghdad, a dispute over taxation led to a ruling that all Jewish men were to be imprisoned. Amid this difficulty, in 1120 CE a young woman known to posterity only as "the daughter of

Joseph" had a vision of the prophet Elijah. Because Jews have traditionally considered Elijah the harbinger of the Messiah, the Jewish community in Baghdad began regarding this woman as their Messiah. The Muslim caliph threatened to kill her by fire but then relented when he, too, had a dream that convinced him that she was the Messiah. He spared her, ordered that the Jewish men should be released, and rescinded the controversial taxes.

During the Middle Ages, when Jews were being killed by zealous Christian Crusaders and expelled from many countries, Jewish women nonetheless used their inner resources to carry on businesses (see box, p. 170) and contribute to the preservation of Jewish tradition by funding book publishing and supporting synagogues. Some were themselves noted scholars of the Bible and Talmud. One of these, Bat HaLevi ("daughter of the Levite"), was beautiful as well as learned, so when she gave lectures at the Baghdad Talmudic Academy, she spoke behind a screen or from a separate room so that the male students would not be distracted from their study of the Law.

The cultural center of Judaism shifted in the Diaspora, but by the beginning of the sixteenth century it was well established in Germany, Poland, and nearby Slavic countries, where the universal language, based on German dialects, of these Central and Eastern European Jews was Yiddish. Women had never been encouraged to study Hebrew, the language of the Bible, but in Yiddish-speaking congregations, a woman sometimes led the other women in prayer in the balcony of the synagogue and prayed their own supplicatory prayers, or *tkhines*—some of them apparently written by the women themselves—in the midst of their domestic tasks. Some of these *tkhines* concerned the particular religious duties of women: making *hallah* (ceremonial bread), lighting the candles for the family on Sabbath Eves and festivals, and observing sexual separation from their husbands during menstruation and ritual bathing afterward. In addition to the often touchingly personal *tkhines*, beautiful poems and moral lessons from Torah study were written in Yiddish by Rebecca Tiktiner of Poland, who died approximately 1550. She shared the fruits of her spiritual experience and Torah study with others so that they could drink from the same well:

> I had seen. In my heart I meditated. With my voice I called out. Here, I have now come. And today I walked. And a well of fresh water I found. And I discovered the big stone from the well, and from it I drank. And I was still thirsty. And I said in my heart. I will go and I will bring. To all my near ones. And my bones will rejoice. That they will drink for the length of their days. To fulfill what is said: drink blessed water and you will be blessed by the Blessed. And so with those who are sheltered in Your shade... . All my good, all, is from You. And my resting place is after [in] You.[7]

The mystical revival movement known as Hasidism developed in the eighteenth and nineteenth centuries, particularly in Poland, around the great mystic and story-teller known as the Baal Shem Tov. Under his charismatic influence, poor and un-educated people became as honored as learned scholars of the Torah and Talmud; what mattered more was inner closeness to God. In this atmosphere, some women's spirituality was particularly appreciated. Edel, the joyful daughter of the Baal

BIOGRAPHY Glückel of Hamelin

The memoirs of a remarkable German Jewish mother of twelve children, written starting in 1690 to help ease the sleepless nights after her husband's death, provide a fascinating and detailed picture of the rather hazardous lives of Jews of those times, who though sometimes wealthy nonetheless were at the mercy of non-Jewish government functionaries. Glückel of Hamelin (Hameln in German), who had a gift for writing as well as for business matters, managed to clear the heavy debts left by her beloved husband of 30 years, marry off her children well, save her son from his foolishness in commerce, and survive the bankruptcy of her second husband. Although she apparently traveled extensively and was heavily engaged in business transactions, her family was always her central concern and her religious faith sustained her through all emotional crises.

Despite Glückel's inner strength, she was bound by religious custom to observe restrictions such as staying physically separate from her husband during her menstrual periods. This was unfortunately the case as he was dying. Glückel reported this in a brief, matter-of-fact way, never questioning the righteousness of the restriction. She also revealed her culturally conditioned conviction that she was a weak woman:

> I said to my husband, "Dearest heart, shall I embrace you—I am unclean?" For I was then at a time I dared not touch him. And he said, "God forbid, my child—it will not be long before you take your cleaning." But, alas, it was then too late… .
>
> The days, my beloved children, that the dear friend of my heart lay dead before me were not as bad as those that followed. Then it was my grief deepened hourly. But in His mercy the great and good God at length brought me patience, so that I have taken care of my fatherless children as far as a weak woman can, bowed with afflction and woe.

Glückel wrote her book of memoirs for her descendants, who then preserved it for nearly 180 years until it was published. She did not intend it to be a book of morals, but her upright character shines through her narrative. Discounting her own wisdom, she faithfully referred her children to the scriptures and the traditional values by which she lived:

> We have our holy Torah in which we may fnd and learn all that we need for our journey through this world to the world to come. It is like a rope which the great and gracious God has thrown to us as we drown in the stormy sea of life, that we may seize hold of it and be saved.
>
> The kernel of the Torah is, Thou shalt love thy neighbour as thyself. But in our days we seldom fnd it so, and few are they who love their fellow-men with all their heart—on the contrary, if a man can contrive to ruin his neighbour, nothing pleases him more.

The best thing for you, my children, is to serve God from your heart, without falsehood or sham, not giving out to people that you are one thing while, God forbid, in your heart you are another. Say your prayers with awe and devotion. During the time for prayers, do not stand about and talk of other things. While prayers are being offered to the Creator of the world, hold it a great sin to engage another man in talk about an entirely different matter—shall God Almighty be kept waiting until you have fnished your business?

Moreover, put aside a fixed time for the study of the Torah, as best you know how. Then diligently go about your business, for providing your wife and children a decent livelihood is likewise a mitzvah—the command of God and the duty of man. We should, I say, put ourselves to great pains for our children, for on this the world is built, yet we must understand that if children did as much for their parents, the children would quickly tire of it… .

Above all, my children, be honest in money matters, with both Jews and Gentiles, lest the name of Heaven be profaned.

Glückel, *The Memoirs of Glückel of Hameln*, trans. Marvin Lowenthal, New York: Schocken Books, 1932, 1977; quoted matter from pp. 151–4, pp. 1–3.

Shem Tov, was revered by her father's followers, who felt that the *Shekhinah* (God's presence) was upon her face. Her son became the successor to the Baal Shem Tov and her daughter Feige became famous for her spiritual understanding. Other noted Hasidic women had their own devotees, because anyone who was thought to be close to God—and therefore able to intercede with Him on behalf of others—naturally developed a following. One of these, Hannah Rachel of Poland (b. 1805), had a deep mystical experience and became a famous woman rabbi whose community built her a synagogue and an apartment from which she preached Sabbath sermons to male rabbis and scholars.

Living amidst European cultures, Jews became drawn into the Enlightenment, when religion and secular culture began to part company. For some this was the *Haskalah*, through which European Jews tried to become more assimilated, rather than maintain their traditional religious identity. In England, women were a significant part of this movement, calling for reform and liberation from aspects of Jewish tradition that seemed stifling, as well as acceptance of Jews by the Christian majority. In their extensive writings, many Jewish women of nineteenth-century England took the stance that if they could receive better education and greater freedom within the Jewish community, they would not be a threat to men, but remain within the domestic sphere, expressing their spirituality in their roles as homemakers and primary carers of children.

One of the most significant of these English writers was Grace Aguilar (1816–1847), whose ancestors came from the matriarchal Sephardic tradition of Spain and Portugal in which Jews secretly maintained their traditions while outwardly converting to Christianity to escape the Inquisition. In this milieu, Judaism was passed down through women, since men's traditional spheres—the synagogues and schools—could not function. Aguilar's 12 novels and tracts were

6.3 Zionist leader Henrietta Szold consulting with kibbutz pioneers around 1940

extremely popular with the reading public, selling hundreds of thousands of copies. In her book *The Women of Israel*, she described biblical women as being like the Victorian feminine ideal—modest, home-centered, and honorable.

As anti-Semitism again menaced the lives of European Jews in the twentieth century, many emigrated to the United States but made efforts to support Jews elsewhere. One of the most tireless workers for the ideal of a Zionist homeland in Israel was Henrietta Szold (1860–1945; fig. 6.3). As influential leader of the large Zionist women's philanthropic and cultural organization Hadassah, she appealed to other Jewish women to work for positive social change. In 1915 she wrote, "The Jew and his Judaism must be perpetuated and can be perpetuated only by their repatriation in the land of the fathers… . It will yield sanctuary, refuge, and protection in the days of readjustment soon to dawn, we hope." In her seventies, Henrietta Szold created a huge project that shifted some 11,000 young European Jews to agricultural settlements in the relatively safer land of Palestine. "In Zion," she wrote, "there is a sanctuary, the refuge that has been established by Jewish pioneers, with the sweat, blood, and labor of those who believe."[8]

Many of the pioneers who helped to develop Israel as a nation were women. They emigrated to Palestine and worked alongside men in construction, in unions, and in the communal agricultural settlements, or *kibbutzes*. The Labor Movement painted an idealized picture, as described by one writer: "None is more beautiful than the pioneer woman, wearing a light plain dress and a simple cloth hat adorned by curls, as she ascends the mountain path in the bright sun of Eretz Israel towards the huts of her commune, or as she does her work in the greenhouse."[9] Nevertheless, women's roles were still largely defined by their traditional family responsibilities, with men as the leaders of society. There were some notable exceptions, such as Golda Meir (1898–1978), who became Prime Minister of Israel, but women had no spiritual authority outside their own homes.

Meanwhile, Jewish women were becoming leaders in social reform movements in the United States. Emma Goldman, radical proponent of birth control and unionization, was jailed and ultimately deported from the United States in 1919 after demonstrating to women that they could prevent pregnancy. The feminist movement included many Jewish women, and eventually they turned their attention toward Judaism itself as a largely patriarchal institution in need of reform.

Traditional Jewish Laws Concerning Women

For a traditional Jew, whether man or woman, every aspect of life is covered in precise detail in the *mitzvot*, or commandments. Many of these are given in the books of the Hebrew Bible; others are elaborations and clarifications of rights and obligations that have been developed by the post-biblical rabbinical traditions. Formulation of these laws into the **halakhah**, or Jewish legal system, has been the exclusive province of men, but it seems that the rabbis attempted to make some provisions for women's rights.

According to cultural customs of biblical times, women were limited in all spheres except the home, which was the center of the community. There was a powerful expectation that Jewish women fulfill the roles of marriage and motherhood. Great importance was also given in the Bible to ways of preparing food that was spiritually acceptable, and these restrictions were managed by women. The final chapter of the Book of Proverbs is devoted entirely to the qualities of a capable wife, as reportedly enumerated by the mother of a king. Such a wife is always good to her husband and wins his confidence by her proper conduct of food-shopping, spinning and weaving, land acquisitions, vineyard planting, business management, and charitable giving. Moreover:

> She is clothed with strength and splendor;
> She looks to the future cheerfully.
> Her mouth is full of wisdom,
> Her tongue with kindly teaching.
> She oversees the activities of her household
> And never eats the bread of idleness.[10]

Despite the value placed on good wives, biblical women had no property rights; all inheritance passed through the male lineage. As was common in customs of the area, men could have many wives. Only a man could initiate divorce. A man could marry a virgin simply by having sexual relations with her. Adultery was defined in terms of men and their sexual honor: if a man had intercourse with another man's wife, or his mother, or his daughter-in-law, both he and she were to be put to death. If a wife willingly had sexual relations with another man or even if her husband jealously suspected that she may have done so, a priest was to administer the *sotah* ritual, giving her bitter water to drink. If she was innocent, it was supposed that she would not be harmed; if guilty, "her belly shall distend and her thigh shall sag; and the woman shall become a curse among her people" (Numbers 5: 27).

Such laws were tempered somewhat by rabbinical legal decisions and by changing cultural customs. The *sotah* ritual disappeared. Marriage became a public ceremony with obligations of husband to wife. The rabbis of the post-biblical period spelled out certain female rights, and women were granted all rights to sexual satisfaction. They were allowed, but not encouraged, to study the Torah; this was the province of men. In the eleventh century, laws allowing polygamy were suspended in Europe (though they continued among Jews in West Asia—Turkey, Iraq, Iran, Lebanon, Syria, Palestine—through the mid-twentieth century). Divorce became a more complicated procedure with provisions for protection of the woman. Talmudic decisions make it clear that women—as well as minors and slaves—are obliged to say certain ritual prayers, because everyone needs the mercy of God.

Nevertheless, women still were not counted in constituting a *minyan*, the quorum for public worship. To avoid diminishing the men's honor or distracting them from their worship, women were not allowed *aliyah*—the privilege of going up to the Torah in a synagogue to read it or say ritual blessings over it before it is read aloud. Menstruating women were traditionally considered ritually impure, and therefore unfit to engage in ritual ways of approaching God. Like any Jew who had skin diseases, or who had touched a dead body, they were to withdraw from the community and then undergo ritual purification in water—*mikveh*—before returning to society and to sacred duties.

Contemporary Changes

It must be noted here that like other religions, Judaism is not monolithic. Over time, various branches have developed from the same ancient roots, with several liberal movements emerging during the nineteenth and twentieth centuries. Women's issues have often been high on the agenda. Some of the major points for more egalitarian treatment of women are the right to be called up to the Torah, to be counted in the *minyan*, to initiate divorce, to have equal rights in carrying out the commandments, and to be rabbis and cantors.

There is a feminist movement even within Orthodox Judaism. Strict Orthodox Jews feel that they are closely following the Bible and Talmud, as well as the traditional rabbinic legal decisions. Within Orthodoxy are found both mystics and rationalists, both exclusivists who withdraw from contact with secular Jews and enthusiasts such as the Lubavich Hasidim who are trying to reach as many Jews as possible with their message. In general, Orthodox women today live within a pattern of traditional gender roles, with home and family their primary sphere, while men are the religious and social leaders. Sexuality is strictly confined to marriage, and Orthodox Jewish women are constrained by rules of modesty not to sit near or socialize with men other than their husbands or relatives. If women come to the synagogue for congregational prayers on holy days, they may be shielded from men's view by a screen. They are to avoid sexual contact with their husbands during and after menstruation and after childbirth. Nevertheless, Orthodox women have led the search for knowledge about Judaism; they were in the forefront of efforts to organize prayer and Talmud study groups for women. For certain public observances that they must attend, women may be in some congregations counted as part of a *minyan*. Orthodox feminists Tova Hartman and Tamar H. Miller Halbertal observe:

Orthodox feminism must not be seen only as a women's movement for solving the "women's problem." Discrimination and the silencing of women in the tradition are problems for all of *klal yisrael*. Orthodox feminism asks what it means to be *nivrah betzelem* [created in the image of God]... . Our success—without knowing what the final product will look like—will be measured against how completely we enlist the whole community to join the struggle. I look forward to the day that our rabbis, husbands, fathers, and sons feel spiritually compromised in a community where *kavod hatzibur* [respect for the congregation] means the absence of women.[11]

The liberal Reform movement emerged from nineteenth-century Germany as an effort to help modern Jews appreciate the relevance of their religion in today's changed world. The traditional emphasis on *halakhah* has given way to ideals of independent choice in matters of faith. Traditional restrictions on menstruating women and the partition between men and women in synagogues have been largely set aside. Preference has been given to moral commandments over rituals, absolute authority is not assigned to the Bible, divine revelation is understood as progressing rather than fixed in the past, and homosexuality is accepted as a natural orientation of some women and men. If women want to, they may do whatever men do, including publicly reading the Torah, being included in the *minyan*, wearing *talit* (prayer shawl) and *tefillin* (boxes with scriptural passages bound to the arm and forehead) for prayers, and serving as cantors or rabbis. The first woman rabbi to be ordained, Rabbi Sally Priesand, was trained in a Reform institution and ordained in 1973. At the four campuses of Reform Judaism-based Hebrew Union College in the United States and Jerusalem, 27 percent of the ranked faculty members are now women, including four full professors. Dvora Weisberg, who is one of them, explains her fascination with Torah study, traditionally a male preoccupation:

Torah is sometimes referred to in Jewish textual tradition as a path. Study of Torah is for me an attempt to follow that path, which I believe leads toward God... . When I study, I feel that I am an active participant in a process that began with the Jewish people, an ongoing search for God's will and our place in the universe... . On the simple level, the Talmud is a human product and thus articulates the beliefs of its authors... . While these men may have seen their work as an attempt to understand the will of God, I do not have to accept their understanding as infallible. Love of Torah need not be blind love.[12]

176 WOMEN IN JUDAISM

The Conservative movement attempts to remain faithful to traditional rabbinical Judaism and its practices (including the avoidance of physical contact between husband and wife during her menstruation), while at the same time acknowledging changes in the Jewish way of life since the Enlightenment. Historical-critical approaches to scriptural understanding have been adopted, and the Jewish Feminist Organization arose within the Conservative movement in the 1970s, seeking "nothing else than the full, direct, and equal participation of women at all levels of Jewish life."[13] In 1983, Conservative Judaism accepted education and ordination of women as rabbis, although acceptance of this provision is left to individual synagogues.

Yet another modern movement is Reconstructionism, which like its parent group, the Conservative movement, defines Judaism as an evolving religion that should continue to adapt to the needs of the times and of the people. From its beginnings in the 1930s in the United States, Reconstructionism has supported equality of women within Jewish life as one of its core commitments. Its founder, Mordecai Kaplan (1881–1983), devised a new prayerbook that omitted passages denigrating women and non-Jews. Women participate fully in Reconstruction synagogues. The first female Reconstructionist rabbi, Sandy Eisenberg Sasso, was ordained in 1974.

Seminaries of these three relatively modern alternatives to Orthodox Judaism—Reform, Conservative, and Reconstructionist—all accept women as cantors. This is a highly meaningful position. Not only does the cantor lead the musical aspects of worship, but according to Jewish tradition she or he is the Messenger of the Congregation and the Master of Prayer. She or he is the one who pleads to God for the congregation's needs, as their representative. As women move into this position, the age-old pattern of male dominance in worship is surely affected.

Feminist Theology

Having had some success in entering previously male domains, so that women may participate equally in congregational worship, Jewish feminists have now turned their attention to the religious tradition itself—its ways of viewing God, the Torah, and Israel—with the goal of making it more humane. In the sacred literature, God has been described largely in aggressive, hierarchical masculine terms; some feminists are seeking other metaphors for the Eternal One that are more appealing to women and that may enhance the spiritual understanding of both men and women. They are trying to find substitutes that evoke a sense of community, of the Power that is within and around us everywhere, ever empowering us, rather than above us, dominating us.

Having women as rabbis helps to cut through the tendency to think of God as a male. Theologically, Judaism does not assign any gender to God; to do so is considered a form of idolatry, which is anathema to this monotheistic tradition. But images of God as an old man with a white beard tend to persist until congregants are faced by a female representative of God. As Rabbi Laura Geller explains:

When Jews encounter a rabbi who is a woman, it forces them to think about God as more than male or female. It provokes them to raise questions that most Jews don't like to confront: what or who is God? What do I believe about God? That primary religious question leads to others. How can we speak about God? What are the appropriate words, images and symbols to describe our relationship to God? Does the English rendering of Hebrew prayers convey the complexity of God? How can we change language, images, and symbols so they can convey this complexity? … The ordination of women has brought Judaism to the edge of an important religious revolution. I pray we have the faith to push it over the edge.[14]

Women are becoming active participants in *midrash*—the ongoing process of interpretation of the Bible. They are paying attention to what has been left out of it, reconstructing the voices and feelings of biblical women, such as what Sarah felt when Abraham attempted to kill their son, thinking that this was what God wanted of him.

Jewish feminists are looking at problematic aspects of Jews' understanding of their relationship to God, such as the idea of themselves as chosen people, and as vassals of a jealous Lord who demands circumcision of male infants as a mark of His ownership. They see that this model is derived from literature written exclusively by men. Some feminist theologians suggest that a more appropriate model of the divine–human covenant is one of partnership, in which the people and God are working together to bring wholeness to the world. They envision an ideal society in which everyone has responsibility for actively building a humane community, all are honored, and none are left out. Whether men and women would have the same roles in this ideal society, or whether their roles are distinctly different but complementary, is still a matter of deep discussion.

Another unsettled issue concerns women's sexuality. During biblical times, the sexuality of women was a force to be controlled, for the sake of the patriarchal family, but sexual impulses were regarded as normal and, within marriage, good. The biblical "Song of Songs" openly links sexuality with sacredness. Feminist scholar Judith Plaskow (fig. 6.4; see box, p. 178) observes:

One of the profoundest images of freedom and mutuality in sexual relations that the Jewish tradition has to offer is at the same time its central image of the connection between sexuality and spirituality. Unlike the Garden of Eden, where Eve and Adam are ashamed of their nakedness and women's subordination is the punishment for sin, the Garden of the Song of Songs is a place of sensual delight and sexual equality. Unabashed by their desire, the man and woman of these poems delight in their own embodiment and the beauty surrounding them, each seeking the other out to inaugurate their meetings, each rejoicing in the love without dominion that is also the love of God.[15]

During the shaping of rabbinical Judaism, more negative attitudes entered the tradition, perhaps because of new social and economic realities in the Diaspora. In rabbinical literature, women's bodies were regarded with disgust—the uterus was described as "place of rot," and even the glance of a menstruating woman was

EXCERPT God-language
Judith Plaskow

A feminist critique of Jewish God-language begins with the unyielding maleness of the dominant Jewish picture of God.... God's maleness is so deeply
and firmly established as part of the Jewish conception of God that it is almost
difficult to document: it is simply part of the lenses through which God is seen.
Maleness is not a distinct attribute, separable from God's anger or mercy or
justice. Rather, it is expressed through the total picture of God in Jewish texts
and liturgy. God in the Jewish tradition is spoken of in male pronouns, and
more importantly, in terms of male characteristics and images. In the Bible, God
is a man of war (Exodus 15: 3), a shepherd (Psalms 23: 1), king (for example, I
Samuel 12: 12; Psalms 10: 16), and father (for example, Jeremiah 3: 19, 31: 9).
The rabbis called him "father of mercy," "father in heaven," "king of all kings,"
and simply "he." Every blessing invokes God as lord and king of the universe, and
throughout the liturgy, he is father God and God of our fathers, lord of hosts,
and king of the earth....

Female images that might balance the prevailing male metaphors exist
in Judaism, but—except in the marginalized mystical tradition—they must be
ferreted out as a tiny minority strand. Isaiah, for example, is one of several
biblical writers who uses images of God as mother (42: 14, 66: 13), and feminist scholars have been at pains to point out that God appears in the Bible as
wet-nurse and midwife, and provider of water and food. But while these attributes are an important reminder that God is not literally male, and they provide
resources for the construction of alternative imagery, they are not picked up in
the liturgy and are vastly overshadowed by masculine terminology. Like the
mystical notion of the *Shekhinah* as God's female presence, they have had
virtually no impact on the dominant image of God....

Obvious and innocuous as male God-language has come to seem,
metaphors matter—on both an individual and social level. Though long usage
may inure us to the implications of our imagery, religious symbols are neither
arbitrary nor inert. They are significant and powerful communications through
which a religious community expresses a sense of itself and its universe.... The
male images Jews use in speaking to and about God emerge out of and maintain a religious system in which men are normative Jews and women are
perceived as Other. Drawing on the experience of only some who stood at
Sinai, they validate a community that is hierarchically structured.

Judith Plaskow, *Standing Again at Sinai: Judaism from a Feminist Perspective*,
San Francisco: HarperCollins Publishers, 1990, pp. 123–5.

poisonous. God was imagined as a non-sexual male; female images of God were banned for they suggested unacceptable linkage of God with women's dangerous sexuality. Women were seated separately from men in synagogues to avoid distracting the men from their worship; they were not called up for *aliyah*, to protect the "honor" of the congregation. Intercourse was defined as a holy obligation of man to woman, who was assumed to have her own sexual desires, but only within marriage. Women's bodies were considered unclean during menstruation and for a week afterward, until they bathed in a *mikveh*, so intercourse was forbidden during this long period every month.

6.4 Judith Plaskow, influential feminist theologian

After this tradition of being considered the tempting and sensual Other, contemporary feminists who want to honor their Jewish roots have attempted to study Jewish attitudes toward sexuality and to revalue and celebrate women's bodies from a woman-centered perspective. For instance, writer Blu Greenberg, who is both a dedicated Orthodox Jew and a feminist, in examining the historical reasons for and contemporary practice of *mikveh* in detail, notes that according to biblical laws some of the water in the *mikveh* must be from natural sources, such as rain, the ocean, or a lake. She thus finds positive value therein:

Purification through the living waters symbolizes a renewal, a re-creation, a regeneration of the life forces. As such, purification was considered a privilege, not a burden. To concretize this, there was a tangible communal reward: access to the sanctuary (and, later, the Temple), where one could bring a sacrifice and find oneself in the presence of God, who gives life.[16]

Feminist Liturgy

To help bring women as full partners into deep relationship to God and to the rest of the Jewish community, many feminists have invented new celebrations of stages of women's lives, have redefined older spiritual practices, and have written liturgies that avoid male language in referring to God and to human beings. Some of these liturgies and rituals are being practiced in informal prayer and study groups, where traditional legal constraints do not apply.

When daughters are born, for instance, in place of the circumcision ceremony that celebrates the birth of a boy, a baby-naming ceremony may take place to

6.5 At her Bat Mitzvah, a girl is expected to read from the Torah scroll, a special privilege

welcome the girl child into the sacred covenant with God. The traditional boys' Bar Mitzvah ("son of the commandment") is now often paralleled by a Bat Mitzvah ceremony for girls at the age of 12 or 13 (fig. 6.5). Menarche and menopause are brought to light and spiritually celebrated; miscarriage and widowhood are handled with compassion. Rosh Hodesh, the celebration of the beginning of each lunar month, has become the focus for many women's groups. Members are creating rituals to celebrate the new moon and their lives as Jewish women, in which traditional acts such as baking special bread, lighting a fire, and suspending work are given positive meanings. *Mikveh* (see box, right) is being profoundly redefined.

The Passover Seder has become an important focus for feminist rituals. It is one of the major rites in the Jewish calendar, evoking the story of the Exodus, in which the Israelites were freed from oppression. This story resonates with women's experiences of oppression within the patriarchal tradition, so in 1975 three women in Haifa organized a feminist Seder whose general pattern has been adopted by Jewish feminists in the United States. It follows the traditional order, but adds the stories of women, remarks on their historical and present oppression, and encourages them in their journey toward independence and self-discovery.

Jewish women's prayer groups are meeting in non-hierarchical circles as part of contemporary attempts to revitalize Jewish worship, to make it consonant with contemporary culture, and to rebuild the sense of spiritual community which so long sustained the scattered Jewish nation. These circles have creatively taken old traditions and made them fresh and relevant today. Rabbi and storyteller Lynn Gottlieb, for instance, has written a new inner spring-cleaning ritual based on women's traditionally thorough house-cleaning rituals in preparation for Passover. It is designed to remove all inner negativity, just as Jewish women traditionally threw out the last remnants of winter:

EXCERPT **Mikva Dreams**
Mierle Laderman Ukeles

In all the gentleness of continuing love, she goes to the Mikva [*mikveh*]. The Mikva waters hit above her breasts when she is standing up. The waters have pressure in them. She pushes into it as she comes down the steps. When she leaves, it seems as if the waters softly bulge her out, back to the world. No, she doesn't want to tell you about it. It is a secret between her love and herself. The Mikva is square. The water is warm, body temperature. Sometimes there are layers of cool water at the bottom. A square womb of living waters.

She goes in, naked, all dead edges removed—edges and surfaces that have come in contact with the world. Nails, loose hair. She has scrubbed herself. All foreign matter removed. A discipline. Is it possible to cleanse oneself completely? What if she looked into a microscope? Would she fnd foreign matter? The standard is the world of the naked eye. The Mikva is for her intrinsic self. Her self-self. Nothing else: no traffc with the world, no make-up with the world. The blood stopped fbwing a week ago. She is the moon. The blood carried away the nest for an unfertilized egg. Her body gets ready every month—builds a nest come hell or high water. If the egg isn't caught and doesn't catch, the nest unravels bit by bit, and the body gets rid of it. Shucks it. A non-life has occurred. Shall she call it a death? She won't because of sister-friends who have had abortions for a million sorrowing reasons. What's one egg? She can't bear that many children. Overpopulation, desires for limits, human endurance, etc. etc. etc. etc. etc. Money education, other kinds of life-giving to do.

But it is an event of non-life. An egg's funeral. A formal procession in measured amounts of time, not rushed; so-and-so number of days. Men don't bleed regularly. That's a simple fact. If they bleed, something is wrong. Women do bleed regularly. It's not an androgynous fact. Much as the artist loves androgynous facts. It is a separating fact. Also children. Only women bleed regularly. Regularly they are involved in either new life or non-life. The Mikva separates one from the other.

In all the glory of continuing love, the Mikva is a taste of Heaven. She tumbles down into the water, like a fetus, and is reborn to life. Old surfaces gone, non-life gone. Life is holy, to be understood as holy and separated from Death, from dead parts. She is always holy—but she causes a separation to be made between life and non-life.

Choose life the Holy One tells her and she does.

Mierle Laderman Ukeles, "Mikva Dreams—A Performance," in Ellen M. Umansky and Dianne Ashton, eds., *Four Centuries of Jewish Women's Spirituality: A Sourcebook*, Boston: Beacon Press, 1992, p. 219.

Removing the *Hametz* [leavening agent]
In the month of *nisan*
with the death of winter
and the coming of spring
our ancient mothers
cleaned out their houses... .

So we labor all women
cleaning and washing
now with our brothers
now with our sons
cleaning the inner house
through the moon of *nisan*.

On the eve of the full moon
we search our houses
by the light of a candle
for the last trace of winter
for the last crumbs grown stale inside us
for the last darkness still in our hearts... .[17]

More difficult than inventing new ceremonies for women and developing women's prayer groups is to change the liturgies used in mainstream congregational and family worship. For example, "Miriam's cup" may be added to family Passover Seder rituals. It is filled with water symbolizing the miraculous well that God granted to Miriam the prophetess to sustain the Israelites during their sojourn in the desert. Liturgical language is also being changed. The feminist argument is that if all humans are created in the divine image, male and female, as in the biblical creation story, liturgy should express this divinity of all people rather than using exclusively male language. They note that the most holy name of God used in the Bible—"YH WH"—has no implications of gender. Without vowels, unutterable, the letters suggest "EXISTENCE."

Where liturgies nonetheless use male references and pronouns in speaking of humans and God, one strategy has been to modify the English translation of Hebrew texts to more gender-inclusive language, but to leave the Hebrew untouched. The English version may, for instance, say "All people shall praise you" instead of "All men shall praise you," and refer to the "God of all generations" or "God of our ancestors" rather than the "God of our Fathers." Some of the biblical foremothers may be named as well as the forefathers. Those who defend the preservation of the Hebrew unchanged maintain that traditions should be kept intact, whereas in fact liturgies based on biblical texts have historically been subject to alterations to avoid hurting the sensitivities of the community. In trying to unravel the complexities of changing liturgical language, Rachel Adler has found that there is a "thicket" of fears involved. She lists some of the issues evoked:

What is the service of the heart? To whom is it addressed? What is the force of its words and why do they arouse such passions in us? Given that prayer words are not about ordinary reality, do they have truth constraints? Will we feel loss for the words we no longer say? What is the force of the metaphors with which we reach toward God? Can feminine metaphors be applied to the God of Israel? What does "woman" mean, and how will its meanings be reflected in the language of prayer? How will we discover the new words and how will we write them on our hearts?[18] ■

Women in Contemporary Judaism

Having come through the Enlightenment (which questioned faith), the Holocaust (which wrenched many survivors away from faith), and modernism (which ignores religious faith), many Jews define their Jewish identity in a secular way that may not include observance of Jewish religious customs, much less traditional laws. For women, there may be additional difficulty in embracing Judaism as a spiritual identity, for while it speaks to women inwardly, it may limit them outwardly. Gail Shulman writes:

■ Despite my being a feminist who is not a traditional Jew, it is my very Jewishness which is at the root of my feminism. Feminism is a prophetic movement concerned with justice for the oppressed, compassion for those who suffer, a sense of history, of community, of righteousness, and the courage to live in opposition... . My feminism is enriched by and rooted in my Judaism, and so the two are in a sense inseparable; yet I do not feel accepted by the very tradition that has formed and informed me, for it fails to support and affirm the women that I and many other feminists have become.[19] ■

Despite the increasing participation of women in all branches of Judaism, at some point most modern Jewish women have been faced with the continuing patriarchal assumptions of traditional Judaism. When the first and thus far only Russian-born woman rabbi in the former Soviet Union, Nelly Shulman, appeared in Belarus in 2000 to lead the Jews of a remote village in worship, one of the elderly male council members sighed, "Well, a woman is better than nothing."[20] Susannah Heschel, an influential feminist scholar in her own right and daughter of the great Jewish philosopher and social activist Abraham Heschel, describes the emotional pain of being shunted aside in many synagogues as she tried to recite the *kaddish*, eleven months of mourning prayers for her father, a role traditionally played by sons rather than daughters. The worst experiences were in Israel, where Orthodoxy prevails: "My experience in Israel, which is supposed to be a place of homecoming for all Jews, taught me that I would have to abandon my Judaism to live there. Not only had I lost my father; I had lost my sense of being a full member of my religion."[21]

But as Heschel explains, Jewish cultural identity is as deep-seated as gender identity; a woman cannot simply throw it away even if she considers the institutions sexist or antagonistic to her inner knowing.

Vivienne Radonsky is now studying to be a rabbi, but previously she didn't want to have anything to do with her Jewish heritage. Slowly she discovered that

INTERVIEW Rabbi Patricia Karlin-Neumann
On Becoming a Rabbi

Patricia Karlin-Neumann serves as the Senior Associate Dean for Religious Life at Stanford University. She works with students and teaches Jewish feminism, rabbinic ethics, and social justice. Like many American Jews, she grew up in a secular context but has come back to the faith as an adult, to the extent of becoming a rabbi, ordained in 1982. She tells her story:

I hadn't intended to be a rabbi. I had been attending a small experimental college in which people put together their own classes and their own graduation contract and curriculum. I majored in nonviolent social change. I spent one summer at Hebrew Teachers' College in Boston, where I learned Hebrew. I was interested in things Jewish, but I didn't grow up in an observant family. After that summer, I went to talk frst to my advisor who was a Presbyterian minister. I told him I was interested in the relationship between the religious community and social justice; he wasn't sure what to do, but he told me about a doctoral program in ethics. I started talking to a number of other people, including Kevin O'Neill, an Irish Catholic philosophy teacher. He said, "What are you interested in?" I said, "I'm interested in the relationship between the individual and the community; I'm interested in education; I'm interested in social justice." He twirled around in his swivel chair and said in a fake brogue, "Become a rabbi."

I laughed and realized I didn't know anything about rabbis, so I sent away for some catalogs to rabbinical school. There were many courses that I'd never heard of, like "Midrash and Homiletics," and "Talmud and Mishnah." I had spent four years in experimental programs, and I thought, "It's time to have someone I can learn from who's the agreed-upon expert." Of course, in retrospect, there were defnite experts in those programs, but I was a haughty undergraduate who thought I knew everything. So I wanted to place myself at the feet of this tradition that I knew very little about.

When I was frst considering the rabbinate, I had a dream about an old man with a beard telling me I couldn't do this. This was in 1975. There was, in fact, one woman ordained as a rabbi, but she was someone in a newspaper. It wasn't at all real to me, so I didn't know what it was going to look like or how it was going to be. When I started in rabbinic school, my class was the frst class where there were numbers of women. For years it had been two or three; some classes had none. My class had about 11 women, so we were starting to fll a room.

My frst year in Jerusalem, I felt like I was failing. The Hebrew teachers were for the most part Israelis who didn't understand American Jews and certainly didn't understand women. A couple of women and I put together a little newsletter in Jerusalem which we called "Dar Dar," which is the word for thorns and thistles. I think we were seen as bristly at the time, but we had a lot of fghting to do. In the early years there was always an attempt to minimize the differentness and the newness of what it meant to be a woman rabbi. It took a long time to be able to say, "No. I really do this differently. It doesn't make it non-authoritative. It doesn't make us less leaders. But we do have to fnd our own way."

There was no help in Israel at all. When I came back to the States to study at the Hebrew Union School in Los Angeles, I became friendly with Laura Geller, who was the second woman to become a rabbi. She had just been ordained, so she didn't know what she was doing either. Through my eyes, since I was just starting out, she seemed like the Goddess. In my second year, we started a women's rabbinic network group, and it still exists. It was helpful to just talk to one another—how much of the resistance we were experiencing had to do with being women and with being acculturated into a very different role.

I worked at UCLA and at Princeton as an intern with senior rabbis who were terrific about opening the tradition and who were committed to egalitarian Judaism. One was an Orthodox rabbi, the other a Conservative rabbi. I learned a tremendous amount and became particularly close to the Conservative rabbi, whom I regard as my rabbinic teacher, a man named Edward Feld. He had a very different rabbinic presence—very soft-spoken, very thoughtful. You would ask him a question and there would be several seconds of silence before you would get an answer. I used to be very bombastic and very strong. He's articulate, but in a soft way, so it was fascinating to have a different model for how to do this. It helped me to realize that I could do it in my own way, too.

About fifteen years ago, I participated in a weeklong workshop of Reform, Conservative, and Orthodox rabbis. A facilitator introduced us to Biblio-drama—psychodrama and the Bible. He asked us to identify with a biblical character. All the men in the room saw themselves as Moses; all the women saw themselves as Miriam, except for me. The image that came to me was Nakhshon ben Amminadav. He was a very little-known biblical character who, according to *Midrash*, was the first person to enter the waters of the Red Sea. He enters the waters, and it is only after he enters that the sea parts. One of the texts is about how he was so eager to enter the waters that he pushed his way in. Another text is about how he was so reluctant that there was a big battle, and he ended up tripping and falling in. The third text is about how there was a negotiation with God until they came to terms about what was acceptable, the impression being that Nakhshon, the surprise leader, finds himself in the waters looking across, and says, "I guess I have to keep going." That was the image I had. I didn't see myself as "bred for power" or expecting as I was growing up that I would have an authoritative position. It has taken me a long time to claim it and to realize, "Yes, there is a way that I do this. I carry the weight of the tradition, and I carry it on different shoulders than the very broad shoulders of men."

Patricia Karlin-Neumann, interviewed November 27, 2004.

6.6 Rabbi Patricia Karlin-Neumann

the hard place in her heart against being a member of the Jewish community was an internalization of the oppression and stereotyping of Jews through the centuries:

I learned the connection between my hard place and how it was connected to how the Jews have been made the scapegoat for centuries and all that hatred and otherness that has been put on us. It was not until I visited Israel in 1997 that I realized how lonely I had been outside of the Jewish community. Then I started to make the giant leaps that ended with me here. I began attending services, joined a Torah study group, took Hebrew lessons, was a bat mitzvah, and yearly immersed myself within a Jewish community for eight weeks. This Rosh Hashanah [Jewish New Year] during *mikveh* I did *teshuvah*, a coming back to my true self. I made a covenant with God and myself to do all I needed to do to be all I could possibly be, and that includes being a Rabbi. As a woman I was not able to be part of the ritual at eight days at which every male *nefesh* makes a covenant with God. But as a 58-year-old woman I can circumcise my heart and make the covenant with God at this different time in my life and with a different consciousness.[22]

Thus women are returning to Judaism, "with a different consciousness." Even though patriarchal texts and traditions remain, since the last quarter of the twentieth century many opportunities have opened for women's spiritual and intellectual participation in Judaism, to the extent that they are actively involved in revitalizing and reshaping the religion itself.

Key Terms

Torah	Talmud
Diaspora	anti-Semitism
Messiah	ghetto
rabbi	*halakhah*
synagogue	*midrash*

Suggested Reading

Adler, Rachel, *Engendering Judaism: An Inclusive Theology and Ethics*, Boston: Beacon Press, 1998. A far-reaching, deep-probing analysis of many aspects of Judaism that are being explored by contemporary feminists.

Baskin, Judith, ed., *Jewish Women in Historical Perspective*, 2nd edn., Detroit: Wayne University Press, 1998. Careful historical analyses of the lives of Jewish women in many times and places.

Biale, Rachel, *Women and Jewish Law: The Essential Texts, their History, and their Relevance for Today*, New York: Schocken Books, 1984, 1995. In-depth analyses of all legal issues involving Jewish women, including women's roles in reshaping Jewish laws.

Glückel, *The Memoirs of Glückel of Hameln*, trans. Marvin Lowenthal, New York:

Schocken Books, 1932, 1977. A great treasury of intimate details from the seventeenth- and eighteenth-century life of a very capable and faithful Jewish mother.

Greenberg, Blu, *On Women and Judaism: A View from Tradition*, Philadelphia: The Jewish Publication Society, 1998. A sincere and sensitive attempt to reconcile Orthodox Judaism with feminist stances in issues affecting women's lives.

Henry, Sondra and Emily Taitz, *Written out of History: Jewish Foremothers*, New York: Biblio Press, 1990. Portraits of notable Jewish women from ancient to contemporary times, as found through extensive research.

Heschel, Susannah, *On Being a Jewish Feminist*, New York: Schocken Books, 1983, 1995. Now-classic examination of old myths about Jewish women, new identities being developed, and Jewish feminist theology.

Peskowitz, Miriam B., *Spinning Fantasies: Rabbis, Gender, and History*, Berkeley: University of California Press, 1997. Careful examination of how the early rabbis shaped Jewish attitudes toward women.

Plaskow, Judith, *Standing Again at Sinai: Judaism from a Feminist Perspective*, 1990. Sensitive, intimate appraisals of themes being explored by contemporary Jewish feminists.

Umansky, Ellen M. and Dianne Ashton, eds., *Four Centuries of Jewish Women's Spirituality: A Sourcebook*, Boston: Beacon Press, 1992. Voices of almost 100 Jewish women telling their spiritual stories, from 1560 to the end of the twentieth century.

7
WOMEN IN CHRISTIANITY

There is no longer male and female

THE APOSTLE PAUL

As Christianity is the largest of the world's religions, its teachings about and treatment of women have played a major role in their global status. The Christian Church is not one unified body—it consists of some 21,000 independent Protestant denominations, 15 independent Orthodox Churches, and the Roman Catholic Church. Within these groupings and within their varied cultural contexts, Christian women have had widely varying experiences. Moreover, the situation of women in Christianity has continually changed over the centuries. Nevertheless, we can look at the broad outlines of those changes and at women who have played significant roles within Christianity, whether its institutions chose to recognize them or not.

The Jesus Movement

Over two thousand years ago, a virgin Jewish woman was reportedly visited by the Holy Spirit and thence became pregnant before her marriage to Joseph, a carpenter. According to the account in Luke, one of the four **Gospel** books in the New Testament of the Christian Bible, an angel appeared to this young woman, Mary (fig. 7.1), with news that she would conceive a child outside of marriage, to be called Jesus, a child to whom God would give the throne of David, the great king of the Jews. Luke says she asked with great concern:

> "How can this be, since I am a virgin?"
> The angel said to her, "The Holy Spirit will come upon you, and the power of the Most High will overshadow you; therefore the child to be born will be holy; he will be called Son of God".... .
> Then Mary said, "Here am I, the servant of the Lord; let it be with me according to your word."[1]

This account of the **virgin birth** is not unique in the world's religions. Myths of virgin birth have been used to elevate the advent of other prophets above worldly sexuality. Buddha, the Egyptian god Horus (who, like Jesus, was also said to have received gifts from three kings as an infant), Zoroaster (founder of

Zoroastrianism), Krishna, even the Egyptian pharaohs, Alexander the Great, and Caesar Augustus were among many other historical and mythological figures said to have been divinely fathered. But many Christians take the story of the virgin birth as a unique and literal fact, and Mary is held up to Christian women as the prime example of piety and self-effacing surrender. (Note: the virgin birth is very frequently miscalled the **Immaculate Conception**. This phrase has nothing to do with Christ's conception without human intercourse—it is a Roman Catholic doctrine that in fact refers to Mary's own conception, by normal means, but without her soul being stained by "**original sin**"—the sin of Adam and Eve.)

Most of Jesus' mission took place within only a few years when he was a young man. At the age of approximately 30, he asked for water **baptism** (the sacrament in which the soul is cleansed of original sin) by his relative, John the Baptist, an ascetic who was proclaiming the imminent coming of the kingdom of God and the appearance of one greater than himself who would bring baptism by the Holy Spirit. The Jews were then under oppressive Roman occupation, and were longing for the apocalyptic coming of a **Messiah** who would save them.

However, the Jesus movement was not political. Jesus called 12 men from various stations of life as his disciples or followers and began an itinerant ministry of preaching, healing, and **exorcism** of demons. The movement that developed

7.1 In European art traditions, such as this painting by Murillo, Mary is usually depicted as an innocent young woman

TIMELINE

*c.*4 BCE	Mary gives birth to Jesus Christ
*c.*30 CE	Crucifixion of Jesus, witnessed by women disciples
*c.*50 CE onward	Paul the Apostle and other missionaries including women spread Christianity
203 CE	Martyrdom of Perpetua
354 CE	Monica gives birth to Augustine, later converts him to Christianity
1054	Orthodox Church breaks with Church of Rome
1098–1179	Life of Hildegard, German prophetess
1195–1253	Clare of Assisi, ascetic founder of the Poor Clares
*c.*1210–1285	Mechtild of Magdeburg, who described inner union with God
1347–1380	Catherine of Siena, "mother of thousands of souls"
1373	Revelations received by Julian of Norwich
*c.*1431	Joan of Arc burned as heretic and witch
1486	*Malleus Malefcarum* condemns women for witchcraft
1515–1582	Teresa of Avila, dynamic founder of Carmelite convents and monasteries
1517	Martin Luther's protest movement begins, supported by his wife Katharina von Bora
1527	Death of Protestant martyr Margaretha Sattler
1591–1643	Anne Hutchison, banished from Massachusetts Bay Colony
1666	Margaret Fell, Quaker, proclaims women's right to preach
1736–1784	Mother Ann Lee, founder of the Shaker movement
1793–1880	Lucretia Mott, Quaker anti-slavery and women's rights activist
1821–1910	Mary Baker Eddy, founder of Christian Science
1858	Bernadette's vision of Mary at Lourdes
1890s	Elizabeth Cady Stanton: *The Women's Bible*
1890–1944	Aimée Semple McPherson, Pentecostal preacher
1897–1980	Dorothy Day, co-founder of Catholic Worker movement
1907–1976	Kathryn Kuhlman, Evangelical preacher
1910–1997	Mother Teresa, founder of the Missionaries of Charity
1923	Birth of Mother Angelica, promoter of conservative Catholicism
1926–1993	Russian Orthodox nun Makaria
1971	Mary Daly writes of threat of women's movement to patriarchal Christianity
1988–1998	World Council of Churches Decade of Churches in Solidarity with Women
1980s to present	Woman-church movement
2002	Seven women ordained as Catholic priests, excommunicated by the Church

around him was unique in its outreach to people from all levels of society, especially those considered unclean by the Jewish temple priests and rabbis, who placed great emphasis on ritual purity and moral piety. These marginal people included the very poor, the physically handicapped, those suffering from skin diseases, the socially despised such as tax collectors, sinners, prostitutes, and slaves, and women. Women had been considered impure because of their bleeding during menstruation and childbirth and were thought of as possessions of men.

Collectively, Jesus referred to them all as the "poor." He invited them all to eat together at the same table, as brothers and sisters in a community that excluded no one from God's grace and recognized no hierarchy. His was a radical gospel of equivalence which ignored the rabbinic and priestly distinctions between "pure" and "impure." He had come to give good news to the poor that all were the beloved children of God. In the kingdom of God whose advent he was proclaiming, the last would be first. The lowly would be recognized before the powerful, the tax-collectors and prostitutes before the proud chief priests and elders. God is most interested in finding the lost sheep, Jesus explained:

> If a man has a hundred sheep and one of them has gone astray, does he not leave the 99 on the mountains and go in search of the one that went astray? And if he finds it, truly I tell you, he rejoices over it more than over the 99 that never went astray.[2]

Again and again, Jesus scandalized the Jewish establishment by the inclusiveness of his mission and his refusal to let rigid laws about ritual purity and observance of the **Sabbath** day of rest take precedence over human compassion. Ultimately one of his male disciples betrayed him, getting him arrested and taken to the supreme Jewish court of elders, chief priests, and interpreters of the law. They accused Jesus of calling himself the Messiah, and took him before the Roman governor, complaining that he was claiming to be a king, opposing payment of taxes to the Romans, and fomenting trouble among the people. Sentenced to death by the Roman governor, Jesus was tortured and **crucified** along with two robbers. Even one of the robbers mocked him on the cross, and he was made to wear a crown of thorns, with the ironic proclamation "Jesus of Nazareth, King of the Jews" set above his head. When he passed away, his body was placed in a tomb with a large stone against the door.

According to all four Gospel accounts, some of Jesus' women disciples visited the tomb on the third day bringing oils and spices to prepare the body for burial—a rite that had not yet been carried out because of Sabbath restrictions. To their consternation, they found the stone rolled away and the tomb empty. Mary Magdalene is said to have seen Jesus standing outside in the garden—or according to another account, she and two other women disciples saw angels proclaiming Jesus' **Resurrection** from the dead. But when they went to tell the male disciples, they were not believed, for they lived in a religious culture that discounted women's credibility as witnesses. Soon after, men also saw and spoke with the risen Jesus, and then they understood and began carrying on his mission as he had instructed them to do.

In time, the Jesus movement became institutionalized Christianity (from "Christ," the anointed, as he was called by his followers), which has spread around the world. Along the way, it has become divided into several major groups with many sub-groups. The Roman Catholic Church is headed by the **pope** in Rome (where the Church was established in the fourth century), and his pronouncements are considered binding on all Catholics. Under him bishops and priests exercise spiritual authority over believers. The Orthodox Church broke away from the Church of Rome in the Schism of 1054. It consists of 15 self-governing Churches such as the Russian Orthodox and the Greek Orthodox, honors the writings of contemplative saints as well as the Bible, and attempts to maintain a conservative tradition modeled on early Christianity. The Protestant **Reformation** began in the sixteenth century in Europe, when reformists such as Martin Luther (1463–1546), Ulrich Zwingli (1484–1531), and John Calvin (1509–1564) urged that Christianity be brought back to Jesus' original teachings and rituals. In place of the authoritarian Roman Catholic structure, the reformers promoted the ideas that there is a "priesthood of all believers" and that authority rests in the Bible, which should be carefully studied and interpreted. The Protestant Reformation was repudiated by the Roman Catholic Church in the Counter-Reformation (mid-sixteenth to mid-seventeenth centuries), and eventually led to thousands of denominations ranging from highly liberal to highly conservative in beliefs and practices.

Women of the Bible

Protestant emphasis on Bible study and interpretation has opened windows for feminist scholars to rediscover women whose stories appear therein. Some of them are well known; others had long been overlooked. In addition to the Jewish women who were followers of Jesus, there are many women in the Hebrew Bible, which Christians consider a foundational scripture linked to their own. Some of these Jewish foremothers were discussed in Chapter 6. Another who is well known among Christians is Ruth. After both her husband and her father-in-law died, Ruth became a model for a woman's loyalty to her husband's family. Instead of going back to her own parents, she famously said to her widowed mother-in-law, "Where you go, I will go; where you lodge, I will lodge; your people shall be my people, and your God my God" (Ruth 1: 6–17). Remarried to her father-in-law's relative, she bore a son who insured the continuation of her late husband's lineage in Jewish patrilineal culture.

The popular semi-fictional story of Judith was excluded by the rabbis from the Hebrew Bible but it appears in the Christian Bible as one of the deuterocanonical ("second-ranking") books of the Old Testament. It is a dramatic tale of a beautiful Jewish widow who rescued the Israelites from the threat of annihilation and desecration of their temple by the huge army of Nebuchadnezzar, the Assyrian king. Advising the Israelites not to surrender, she persuaded the Assyrian general that she was ready to fulfill his desires, and when he was in a drunken stupor, she seized his sword and cut off his head. This deed—and the public display of the severed head—so demoralized his troops that they scattered and abandoned their attack. Judith's prayer is the quintessential statement of faith by the weak and oppressed who believe that God's might is greater than that of human oppressors:

▨ Look at their pride, and send your wrath upon their heads. Give to me, a widow, the strong hand to do what I plan… . Crush their arrogance by the hand of a woman. For your strength does not depend on numbers, nor your might on the powerful. But you are the God of the lowly, helper of the oppressed, upholder of the weak, protector of the forsaken, savior of those without hope.[3] ▨

The same themes emerged with great emphasis in the Jesus movement. Women, included in his mission, appear again and again in the stories of his activities. Many of his followers and supporters seem to have been women, in contrast to their general exclusion from religious participation in the surrounding male-dominant society. He sometimes criticized his male disciples as having little faith, but when a woman who had been hemorrhaging for 12 years touched his cloak with the thought, "If I but touch his clothes, I will be made well," she was instantly healed. Jesus praised her, saying, "Daughter, your faith has made you well" (Mark 5: 34).

There are many conversations recorded in the Bible between Jesus and women. Some seem rather harsh by today's standards. When a foreigner—a Phoenician woman—begged him to exorcise her possessed daughter, Jesus reportedly told her, "Let the children be fed first, for it is not fair to take the children's food and throw it to the dogs" (Mark 7: 27). But because she gave a clever reply, he agreed to bless her daughter, and she was freed of the demon spirits.

One unusually long conversation is recorded with a woman at a well as Jesus was passing through Samaria. When he requested her to draw some water for him, she reportedly replied:

▨ "How is it that you, a Jew, ask a drink of me, a woman of Samaria?" (Jews do not share things in common with Samaritans.) Jesus answered her, "If you knew the gift of God, and who it is that is saying to you, 'Give me a drink,' you would have asked him, and he would have given you living water."[4] ▨

Then followed a lengthy teaching about living water, and Jesus' visionary observations not only about her marital history but also about the locus of worship. For a teacher to talk about theology with a woman was not at all in keeping with the norms established by the rabbis. The Samaritan woman could even be seen as a "proto-missionary," for after speaking with Jesus she went and brought others to him.

Two sisters from Bethany—Mary and Martha—appear repeatedly in the biblical narratives. They seem to have been close disciples of Jesus and welcomed him to stay in their home. The Gospel of John identifies Mary of Bethany as the woman who anointed Jesus on the feet with expensive perfumed oil, a radical act that recalled how prophets recognized kings in the Old Testament. Jesus reportedly explained this to his outraged disciples—who objected to the waste of money—as appropriate preparation for his death. Mary seems to have spent considerable time listening to Jesus' teachings, in defiance of rabbinic custom which disallowed spiritual teachings to women. It was her sister Martha who declared Jesus to be the Messiah, affirming her faith that Jesus could bring their brother Lazarus back to life after he was already four days dead, saying, "I know that God will give you whatever you ask of him" (John 11: 22).

The story of the anointing of Jesus by a woman appears in all four gospels, but three of them do not even record her name, even though, according to the Gospel of Mark, Jesus said, "Truly I tell you, wherever the good news is proclaimed in the whole world, what she has done will be told in remembrance of her" (Mark 14: 9). The Gospel of Luke tells the story of an anonymous prostitute (sometimes identified with Mary Magdalene) who, upon meeting Jesus, wept so much that his feet became wet with her tears, whereupon she wiped them with her own hair, kissed them, and rubbed them with myrrh. When his legalistic host objected to Jesus' allowing this, Jesus praised her for her great love and explained that it was a sign that her many sins had been forgiven.

There were other significant women disciples who accompanied and supported Jesus and his followers. Luke's Gospel—which pays considerable attention to Jesus' mission to the poor and to women—lists Mary Magdalene (Mary of Magdala), from whom seven evil spirits had been exorcised or driven out, Joanna (wealthy wife of the steward of the Roman official Herod), Susanna, "and many others," Luke explains, "who provided for them out of their own resources" (Luke 8: 3), a situation that was highly unorthodox in Jewish society of the time. It is also Luke's Gospel that suggests that women and men are equal in the eyes of God by citing a number of instances in which Jesus tells parallel tales about a man and about a woman. For example, the **parable** about the shepherd with the lost sheep is followed in Luke's Gospel by the parable of a woman who loses one of her ten silver coins and looks in every corner until she finds it and rejoices.

Significantly, it is women who dared to stay with Jesus during the Crucifixion, attempted to tend his body in the tomb, and first witnessed his Resurrection. The Gospel of Mark specifically mentions three women who risked arrest by being present at the Crucifixion—Mary Magdalene, Mary the mother of James the younger and of Joseph, and Salome—whereas Judas had betrayed Jesus, Peter had denied him, and the other male disciples had fled. Influential feminist scholar Elisabeth Schussler Fiorenza asserts:

> Whereas according to Mark the leading male disciples do not understand the suffering messiahship of Jesus, reject it, and finally abandon him, the women disciples who have followed Jesus from Galilee to Jerusalem suddenly emerge as the true disciples in the passion narrative. They are Jesus' true followers who have understood that his ministry was not rule and kingly glory but diakonia, "Service" (Mark 15: 41). Thus the women emerge as the true Christian ministers and witnesses.... Both Christian feminist theology and biblical interpretation are in the process of rediscovering that the Christian gospel cannot be proclaimed if the women disciples and what they have done are not remembered.[5]

Women in Early Christian Communities

The importance of women disciples in the Jesus movement apparently continued for some time after his death as the institution of Christianity began to develop. Early Christianity opened counter-cultural roles for women, but these were gradually withdrawn from the second to fifth centuries. The most influential figure in the shaping of what became Christianity, as opposed to the movement Jesus started during his lifetime, was the **Apostle** Paul. Whereas Jesus had talked about God, Paul's whole theological thrust was Christocentric. His writings marked a shift away from the egalitarian impetus of the Jesus movement toward a more **hierarchical**, institutional faith.

Not meeting with approval in Jerusalem or Jewish synagogues elsewhere, the followers of Jesus began to spread the Gospel to other cities beyond Israel, as **missionaries**. The books of the Bible concerning the Acts of the Apostles and letters to the early Christian churches from the Apostle Paul (or other writers under his name) contain references to many women. Details are sparse, but there is enough material to be sure that women were among the missionaries, and that women offered their homes as places of worship and platforms for missionary work. Since the home was already the social territory granted to women by Jewish tradition, and since table fellowship was a central form of Christian worship, women naturally played a leading role therein. In the Greco-Roman world to which Christianity spread, wealthy women had the economic independence and social leverage to sponsor cult meetings in their homes; furthermore, in the first century CE Hellenistic women were recognized as leaders and priestesses of other religions.

The typical pattern for Christian missionaries was to go out in pairs, some of which were married couples. One of the major missionary couples consisted of Prisca (Priscilla) and Aquila. Of these, Prisca may have been the more important. They were tentmakers and used their income to finance their missionary work. They helped to establish house churches in Corinth, Ephesus, and Rome. They risked their lives to help save their co-worker Paul, and Prisca apparently became the teacher of the eloquent missionary Apollos.

Another missionary pair were Andronicus and Junia, who was probably a woman. Paul refers to them as being imprisoned with him and writes, "They are prominent among the apostles, and they were in Christ before I was" (Romans 16: 7).

Phoebe is praised as a significant leader and probable patroness in the Cenchreae church, though scholars are not sure exactly what role she played. Paul wrote:

> I commend to you our sister Phoebe, a deacon of the church at Cenchreae, so that you may welcome her in the Lord as is fitting for the saints, and help her in whatever she may require from you, for she has been a benefactor of many and of myself as well.[6]

A dramatic story of a female Christian missionary is told in a non-biblical source: "The Acts of Paul and Thecla," which probably existed as an oral tale before being written down late in the second century. The fact that it was widely known and even considered **canonical** by some early churches gives it significance as a clue to women's roles in early Christianity. It was apparently cited as a basis for women's authority to teach and to baptize. In the story, Thecla is engaged but renounces marriage when she is converted to Christianity by the Apostle Paul. At the complaint of her mother and would-be groom about Paul's influence over women, Thecla is ordered to be burned at the stake but is reprieved by a hailstorm. She follows Paul and asks for baptism, but another man falls in love with her. Spurned, he appeals to the governor, who orders Thecla to be thrown into an arena with wild beasts. She is saved by the intervention of the queen, and of a lioness which protects her. More beasts are unleashed against her, but she prays and then plunges into a tank of water to perform self-baptism. A cloud of fire surrounds her and covers her nakedness. The governor, seeing her spiritual power, gives up and releases her to the queen and a group of rejoicing women, whom she then instructs in Jesus' teachings. With her followers, she finds Paul and tells him what has happened, including her baptism, whereupon he sends her out to preach.

Subsequent Subordination of Women

The views of Paul were critical, because of all the missionaries he became the major shaper of Christian theology. Paul's attitude toward women is the subject of considerable contemporary discussion (see box, right), since in some cases he seems to support equality of women and in other cases he argues in favor of patriarchy and hierarchy. The most famous example of his equality statements occurs in Galatians 3: 27–28, in which he is explaining the results of becoming Christians: "As many of you as were baptized into Christ have clothed yourselves with Christ. There is no longer Jew or Greek, there is no longer slave or free, there is no longer male and female; for all of you are one in Christ Jesus."

However revolutionary such a statement of universality must have been in the stratified culture of the times, Paul seemed to have been speaking only about spiritual equality, reflected in the openness of table fellowship to everyone and the promise of the future spiritual kingdom. He was not advocating a social revolution in which existing social distinctions would be completely set aside. As the Christian Church became institutionalized, cultural norms triumphed. In Paul's letters addressed to the new churches, particularly the church in Corinth—which already seemed to be living as though the New Creation promised by Jesus had come—he attempted to correct and limit potentially egalitarian practices. One was the choice of some women to remain celibate. This choice would allow women to maintain control over their bodies and some independence from social control by men. Paul was not enthusiastic about marriage, but he proposed that sexuality should be manifested only within it: "To the unmarried and the widows I say that it is well for them to remain unmarried as I am. But if they are not practicing self-control, they should marry. For it is better to marry than to be aflame with passion" (I Corinthians 7: 8).

Paul's first letter to the Corinthians includes several passages—possibly added later by other authors—that over time became the basis for women's subordination within the family and the institutional Church. For one thing, there is the admonition that women should cover their heads when praying or prophesying rather than letting their hair down during ecstatic experiences. Why? The letter interprets head-covering as a symbol of being under the authority of someone else. Women were to keep their place at the bottom of the order of Creation: God is above Christ, who is above men, who are above women. Furthermore, fellowship should consist not of sharing ordinary meals but only of sharing the symbolic

EXCERPT Equivalence or Subordination
Rosemary Radford Ruether

Conflct between two views, one affrming the equivalence of men and women as human persons and the other defning women as subordinate to men, socially and even ontologically, can be traced through the whole of Christian history. The clash between the two views is rooted in the Christian Bible, or New Testament... . The theology of subordination is based on the notion of "male headship of the order of creation." This notion basically identifes patriarchal social order with the natural or divinely created order. Male headship is thus regarded as rooted in the intrinsic nature of things and willed by God. Any effort to upset this order by giving women autonomy or equal rights would constitute a rebellion against God and would result in moral and social chaos in human society. This notion that male headship is the order of creation usually carries with it the hidden or explicit assumption that God is male or at least properly represented by symbols of paternal authority. Female symbols, therefore, can in no way be regarded as equivalent images for God. Paternal authority, as a power of sovereignty and rule over others, expresses the nature of God... .

Social order, according to this view, demands the sovereign authority of men as husbands and fathers over women as wives and children. The proper relationship between the sexes is one of rule and obedience, however softened it may be by love or kindliness. Women must not initiate ideas or exercise their will independently but essentially must act as obedient followers and complements to the male, carrying out his commands and mediating them to the children (and slaves or servants). Even when the male exercises his power violently, arbitrarily, or sinfully, woman is not justifed in rebellion or autonomous life, but serves the social order and obeys God by silent and prayerful suffering, attempting to better the male by her compliance and good example.

The theology of subordination buttresses this view of male headship as the order of creation by various insinuations that woman is, in fact, morally, ontologically, and intellectually the inferior of the male... . Moreover, her inferiority leads to sin when she acts independently. Thus a key item in the theology of subordination is the scapegoating of woman for the origin of sin... .

Woman's moral status in the theology of subordination, then, is highly ambivalent. On the one hand, woman is called to a kind of heroic ethic of humility and suffering, chastity and self-abnegation which is not required to the same extent of men but which closely approximates the Christian ideal of Christ. On the other hand, woman is regarded as the moral inferior of the male: willful, lacking self-control of her passions and appetites, a temptress to the male, and therefore needing to be kept under control, both for her own good and to prevent her from subverting the higher capacities of male rationality and virtue. This notion is expressed in the bifurcated image of women in Christianity as Mary, the virgin mother obedient to God, and Eve, the disobedient woman who caused sin to come into the world... .

This construct of themes associated with the theology of subordination has never been the sole view of women in Christianity, although for much of Christian history it has been the dominant and official view. A theology of equivalence has also been present, although generally championed only by minority movements... .

The theology of equivalence takes the creation story of Genesis 1: 27, where both male and female are created in the image of God, as normative for its view of male-female relations. Both men and women possess the image of God equally as human persons. Both are given sovereignty over the lower creation. Neither is given dominance over the other. They stand as copartners before God and stewards of creation.

This understanding of shared humanity in the image of God is seen as having been restored in Christ. Galatians 3: 28, where baptism into Christ is seen as making all humanity one, male and female, Jew and Greek, slave and free, is the charter of the Christian theology of equivalence restored in redemption. In the light of Christ, male dominance and all forms of ethnocentrism are seen as sinful. The curse upon Eve, that she should bear children in sorrow and be under the domination of her husband, is read not as divinely intended punishment, but as a historical statement of the fallen state of humanity, which distorts the authentic cohumanity of male and female. This equivalence, restored in Christ, is further extended by the Pentecost text of Acts 2: 17 (Joel 2: 28), where the spirit of prophecy sent by the risen Christ to be with the Church is given to both the "maid servants and the men servants." These three texts form the keystones in the theology of equivalence. One can fnd them cited century after century in movements that seek to affrm women's equal humanity with the male, as well as her calling to the ministry.

From Rosemary Radford Ruether, in Arvind Sharma, ed., *Women in World Religions*, Albany, New York: State University of New York Press, 1987, pp. 208–10.

Eucharist: bread and wine in remembrance of Jesus' sacrifice. Thus women's roles in food preparation were separated from the acts of holiness. What is more, according to what may also be an addition by a later writer, "Women should be silent in the churches. For they are not permitted to speak, but should be subordinate, as the law also says" (I Corinthians 14: 34). Thus women could not even give ecstatic utterances as inspired by the Holy Spirit, much less give rational talks. Even though everyone could be baptized into the Christian Church, hierarchy was to be maintained therein.

Another letter attributed to Paul, but thought by many scholars to have been written by someone else in the second century using his name (a custom of the times), sets out many restrictions on women's religious participation and behavior, using theological arguments relating to the myth of Adam and Eve. The book— which became part of the official canon of the Bible—states that only men should pray in the congregation. As for the other half of humanity:

■ The women should dress themselves modestly and decently in suitable cloth- ing, not with their hair braided, or with gold, pearls, or expensive clothes, but with good works, as is proper for women who profess reverence for God. Let a woman learn in silence with full submission. I permit no woman to teach or to have authority over a man; she is to keep silent. For Adam was formed first, then Eve; and Adam was not deceived, but the woman was deceived and became a transgressor. Yet she will be saved through childbearing, provided they continue in faith and love and holiness, with modesty.[7] ■

Thus women are to be submissive to men because they were created last and because they brought the downfall of humanity by their susceptibility to deception and sin. Their only hope of redemption is through faithfully carrying on the tradi- tional role of motherhood.

Blaming Eve for the "Fall" was an idea circulating in Jewish *midrash* pertain- ing to Genesis 2–3 (the second of the two Creation stories—see Chapter 6). It was given particularly sophisticated form by the Hellenistic Jewish philosopher Philo (*c*.20 BCE–50 CE). To him, Eve's very creation was the beginning of Adam's downfall, because then sexual activity also appeared, leading inevitably from happiness to misfortune. It was better for men to remain celibate and thus retain their original spiritual wholeness, according to Philo.

Restrictive attitudes toward Christian women gradually took precedence over the theoretically universal message of Jesus and the apparent involvement of early Christian women in spreading that message. Historians speculate that in trying to make Christianity more respectable in Greek and Roman society—which was skeptical and often punitive toward the emerging faith—its spokespeople may have tried to avoid scandalizing those they were attempting to convert, by retaining traditional social norms and avoiding comparison with ecstatic mystery cults such as the orgiastic worship of Isis. As the author of Colossians put it succinctly with- in a Christian restatement of the patriarchal Greco-Roman Household Code, "Wives, be subject to your husbands, as is fitting in the Lord. Husbands, love your wives and never treat them harshly" (Colossians 3: 18).

Women's pastoral contributions were increasingly set aside until, at best, they were confined only to ministering to women. This shift took place within a gener- al transformation from the early Spirit-filled charismatic leadership to a more structured institutional arrangement in which officials of the Church took on the teaching roles of the apostles and also the power to make decisions affecting the community. A third-century tract detailing roles and rituals in the Church recom- mended women as deaconesses who would help women spiritually, but only in specified ways. They were to anoint women before baptism, but a male authority was to speak the ritual formulae and bless their heads with his hand. Afterward, the deaconess should instruct baptized women how to remain pure and holy. She was also assigned to visit and tend to the needs of sick Christian women.[8]

For a time, the Gnostic Christian tradition provided women with some leader- ship roles. This complex of religious movements seems to have blended Egyptian, Greek, Jewish, and Persian ideas pertaining to mysterious truths understood only by the spiritual elite. Many Gnostics also referred to Christian scriptural and apostolic traditions and recognized Jesus as a divinity who had descended to earth carrying perfect wisdom that would save those who followed his teachings. They revered secret Gnostic scriptures—such as those buried at Nag Hammadi in Egypt—that were not recognized as authoritative by the Christian Church as it developed. After its peak in the second century, the Gnostic movement dwindled, and its relatively egalitarian vision was not drawn into the mainstream of the institutionalized Church, which attacked it as **heretical**—counter to its teachings.

Martyrs, Saints, and Ascetics

Though relegated to the margins of Church leadership, strong women continued to appear within Christianity. Understanding themselves empowered by Jesus as baptized Christians, a large number of women as well as men during the first three centuries CE fearlessly became **martyrs**—dying for the faith rather than worship the state gods and the emperor. Some were ripped apart by dogs as a public spectacle; some were thrown to wild beasts. The writings of Perpetua, who was martyred in 203 in Carthage, give a clear insight into the extraordinary faith-inspired courage of some of these women. Perpetua, a nursing mother, was begged by her family and even by the governor to worship the emperor and abandon Christianity to save her life, but she refused, for she had seen a vision of mounting a treacherous ladder with a dragon waiting below. In the vision, a fellow-Christian who was also to be martyred called to her from the top of the ladder:

> "Perpetua, I'm waiting for you, but be careful not to be bitten by the dragon." I told him that in the name of Jesus Christ the dragon could not harm me. At this the dragon slowly lowered its head as though afraid of me. Using its head as the first step, I began my ascent.

From a second vision, it was clear that she would die and enter paradise. This foreknowledge increased her willingness to set aside social and familial norms as well as state rule because of her spiritual convictions. When her father begged her to recant for the sake of her infant son, she said to him:

> "Whatever God wants at this tribunal will happen, for remember that our power comes not from ourselves but from God." …
>
> And when my father persisted in his attempts to dissuade me, Hilarion [the governor] ordered him thrown out, and he was beaten with a rod. My father's injury hurt me as much as if I myself had been beaten, and I grieved because of his pathetic old age. Then the sentence was passed; all of us were condemned to the beasts. We were overjoyed as we went back to the prison cell.

The day before the battle in the arena, she had another vision in which she turned into a man with a naked, oiled body ready for hand-to-hand combat, in which she crushed the head of her opponent. Then, she wrote, "I woke up realizing that I would be contending not with wild animals but with the devil himself. I knew, however, that I would win."[9]

Such was the tremendous courage of the early Christians, in their conviction of God's power and saving grace, which had been bestowed upon them thanks to the sufferings of Jesus. Anticipating the coming of the kingdom, they had little concern for worldly life or for traditional gender roles.

In addition to courting martyrdom, some women of the early Christian centuries were known for their great piety. Whether married or virgin, many lived as ascetics and gave away all that they had. Some turned their homes into convents; some converted their marital relationship into a celibate one by mutual consent with their Christian husbands. They devoted themselves to lives of prayer, contemplation, and service to others and thus served as living models of Jesus' teachings. One of the most celebrated of these holy women was Monica, who gave birth to the famous bishop and theologian Augustine in 354 CE. Her Christian forbearance was such that she quietly bore frequent beatings by her husband, until at last she converted him. With her son Augustine she apparently had many elevated spiritual conversations, and succeeded in re-converting him to Christianity from other spiritual and philosophical paths he had adopted. For many centuries, she was held up as a great exemplar of self-sacrificing good works, which became the signature quality expected of Christian women. In his *Confessions*, Augustine wrote to God about his mother Monica:

> She was also a servant of your servants. Whosoever among them knew her greatly praised you, and honored you, and loved you in her, because they recognized your presence in her heart, for the fruit of her holy life bore witness to this. She had been the wife of one husband; she repaid the duty she owed to her parents; she had governed her house piously; she had testimony for her good works; she had brought up children, being as often in labor in birth of them as she saw them straying from you. Lastly Lord, of all of us, your servants—for out of your gift you permit us to speak—who, before she fell asleep in you, already lived together, having received the graces of your baptism, she took care as though she had been mother to us all, and she served us as though she had been a daughter to all of us.[10]

During the Middle Ages, people began to venerate Monica and she was **canonized** as a saint. Organizations of Christian mothers in the Roman Catholic Church regard her as their patron saint.

Perhaps through the influence of the Greek mystery schools, Christian

7.2 Saint Macrina of Cappadocia by Nick Papas. Another saint with family connections, the primary spiritual inspiration of her brother, Pope Gregory

mystical experience became associated with asceticism—with deliberate self-purification and discipline—and this trend has persisted for most of Christian history. By the seventh century, **mendicant** (begging) monks and nuns were wandering through the countryside. As they went along, they established monastic centers to help convert the local people to Christianity. In Frankish culture (broadly that of what is now France in the fifth to eighth centuries), women could inherit and possess property, and many of them used their wealth to establish monasteries for men, convents for women, or joint communities, some of which were headed by women. For those who lived in these areas, the monastic centers brought a daily routine of prayers, a place for people to participate in sacramental worship, Christian education, spiritual counseling for those with problems, and safe places of refuge for those who had nowhere else to turn.

Over the centuries, the ascetic, renunciate life had tremendous appeal to many Christian women. It gave them freedom from traditional social expectations that they marry and live for their families, and fulfilled their inner longing for spiritual union with God or Christ. In some cases this spiritual love reached extraordinary heights. Some of the great mystics went beyond traditional perceptions of Jesus and God in male form; what they experienced was more often an invisible Presence, or Light, in which all things became One. Despite the extreme austerities that some of these women mystics practiced, often they combined their inner life of prayer with an outer life of dedicated service and active social work. In this role, many became great spiritual directors to both men and women. They remained faithful to Christianity, considering Jesus their risen Lord, but by their fresh, original, non-theoretical approach they pushed and stretched the meanings of Christianity as interpreted by men. As visionaries, some were considered spiritual authorities during the Middle Ages. However, they still did their spiritual work and spiritual practice under men's surveillance. In general, only those who had some male supporter within the Church were allowed to express their spirituality in powerful ways.

Hundreds of these mystics have been **beatified** (the first step to sainthood) and revered in the Roman Catholic and Orthodox Churches. Countless others have been declared heretics or witches by male authorities, who alone were credited with the ability to distinguish whether a woman was being guided by God or by Satan.

There have been so many great women mystics in the history of Christianity that we can here examine only a small sample. One of the major periods of Christian mysticism began during the eleventh and twelfth centuries. The first prominent woman mystic during this time was St. Hildegard (1098–1179; fig. 7.3), a German abbess who also became known as a prophetess—the "Sibyl of the Rhine." She experienced God inwardly as Light:

From my infancy until now, in the 70th year of my age, my soul has always beheld this Light, and in it my soul soars to the summit of the firmament and into a different air.... The brightness which I see is not limited by space and is more brilliant than the radiance round the sun.[11]

Hildegard began perceiving what she called the "Living Light" when she was only three years old, but she rarely shared her visions with anyone until, when she was 42, she had a striking illumination experience. The Light thenceforth gave Hildegard direct understanding of the meaning of the Bible and ordered her to share her enlightened understandings with the world. When she diffidently hesitated to do so, she became violently ill. As soon as she acquiesced and began dictating the revelations, her health returned at once. In spite of her ecstatic inner life and periodically weak health, Hildegard was outwardly extremely active. She founded two convents, traveled extensively on preaching tours, wrote books about medicine, flora and fauna, music, and the lives of saints, and was both poet and musician, composing over 60 hymns. She wrote such inspiring, tough, and prophetic letters to many leaders that her direct advice was sought by the German Empire and the Church. For instance, she counseled Henry, the Bishop of Liège, about fighting corruption within the Church:

> The living light says: the paths of the scriptures lead directly to the high mountain, where the flowers grow and the costly aromatic herbs; where a pleasant wind blows, bringing forth their powerful fragrance; where the roses and lilies reveal their shining faces… . But O shepherds, now is the time for mourning and weeping, because in our time the mountain has been covered with a very black cloud so that it no longer sends forth its gentle fragrance. You, Henry, must be a good shepherd, noble of character… . Correct those in error, and wash the mud from the beautiful pearls. Prepare them for the high king. Let your mind pant with great eagerness to call those pearls back to the mountain where the gift of God had its origin.[12]

Some of the European mystics did not live in convents, nor were they officially recognized by the Church hierarchy. An interesting movement of mystical laywomen—the Beguines—arose in Belgium in the twelfth century and spread to Germany. These women were not nuns, did not take permanent vows, and did not live in cloistered monastic settings. Nonetheless, they lived in informal communities, practicing celibacy, devotion, and service to the needy, sometimes turning their city houses into shelters for the sick or poor. To support themselves, they developed cottage industries. But despite their good works, the Beguines were always suspected of heresy, not because of their theology but because of their unconventional lifestyle. One Roman Catholic bishop complained that the Beguines were

7.3 An illuminated manuscript from 1230 depicting Hildegard of Bingen receiving and writing down revelations

too free, not assuming "the yoke of obedience to their priest," or "the coercion of marital bonds."[13] They were eventually forbidden by the Church to practice outside of formal orders. Some had to join groups approved by the male authorities; others were burned at the stake, and thus the movement died away.

The writings of an uncloistered woman mystic who followed such a path and may have been a Beguine—Mechthild of Magdeburg (c.1210–1285)—have survived but have never been well known. One cleric insisted that her book should be burned. God told her to keep writing. She did not write to please the Church. She wrote, "God calls the cathedral clergy goats because their flesh stinks of impurity with regard to eternal truth."[14] Her writings were collected and distributed by her confessor, a Dominican monk, and preserved outside the canon of recognized mystical writings, so that today we can delight in her extraordinarily intimate depictions of the inner union with God. One passage employing extremely sensual imagery was quoted in the first chapter of this book ("Lie down in the Fire. See and taste the Flowing Godhead through thy being… "). Here is another gem:

> And God said to the soul:
> I desired you before the world began.
> I desire you now
> As you desire me.
> And where the desires of two come together
> There love is perfected.
>
> How the Soul speaks to God
> Lord, you are my lover,
> My longing,
> My flowing stream,
> My sun,
> And I am your reflection.
>
> How God answers the Soul
> It is my nature that makes me love you often,
> For I am love itself.
> It is my longing that makes me love you intensely,
> For I yearn to be loved from the heart.
> It is my eternity that makes me love you long,
> For I have no end.[15]

Another path followed by some women mystics was that of extreme renunciation. Such was the case with Clare of Assisi (1195–1253), the friend and greatest disciple of St. Francis. When she was 18, her family arranged for her to marry. She asked the guidance of Francis, who was still a controversial renegade monk, and he advised her to follow God. She gave away all her property to the poor and then on the night of Palm Sunday—the celebration of Jesus' entry to Jerusalem before his Crucifixion—she escaped to the small church in the forest where Francis and his monks were staying. He and his brotherhood cut off her beautiful long hair and gave her their rough tunic to wear. Her outraged family tried to persuade her to come home and get properly married, but she took off her veil, showing them her bare head. She was now the bride of Christ, as nuns understood themselves. Once Francis and his brothers had renovated a dilapidated church in San Damiano, Clare settled there for life. Other women—eventually including her sisters and mother— joined her there in a life of joyful, spirit-filled poverty, as the "Poor Clares." With great determination, Clare cast away all personal desires for even the barest of comforts—sufficient sleep, food, warm blankets. She did not advise the sisters who followed her to live so extremely as she, for she was totally satisfied by "the hidden sweetness that God Himself has reserved from the beginning for those who love Him."[16] She had attained the total detachment experienced by the great mystics of all religions, such that she could continually direct all her attention to God and live as an empty vessel that God would fill with any resources, power, wisdom, or abilities needed. From that Power, she is said to have fed many despite meager material resources, healed many people's ailments, transmitted inner peace, and even saved her convent and the whole of Assisi from attackers.

Another ascetic path chosen by some women was that of anchoress—living such a cloistered life of prayer that they never even left their rooms. They had taken a lifelong vow of being dead to the world, as if shut up with Christ in his tomb. But at the same time, the cell of an anchoress had a curtained window to the outside world, through which she gave spiritual guidance and prayed for anyone who came. Hundreds of English nuns lived like this, some in single cells built against the wall of a church (with a grille through which to hear the services), some in enclosed suites with small gardens. Each would have a servant or two to do the cooking, washing, cleaning, and shopping, and probably also a cat. According to the rules established for this spiritual vocation, anchoresses were not required to wear any special clothing, so long as it was sturdy and simple, and could even go barefoot if they chose, for no one else saw them. They could receive gifts from people they counseled—and sometimes were even named as beneficiaries in wills—but they were to give anything not needed for their personal use to the church or priest with whom they were associated, rather than being besieged by alms-seeking poor.

Such was the life of Julian of Norwich, a fourteenth-century English nun and spiritual director (see box, p. 206). When young, she had prayed fervently for three things: understanding of Christ's sufferings during the Crucifixion, some near-fatal illness, and the three "wounds" of true contrition, loving compassion, and longing of the will for God. In medieval times, Jesus was depicted not as a triumphant victor over death (as in earlier centuries) but as an agonized figure on the cross, with grieving women watching. Julian asked to experience this scene personally, as a "bodily sight, in which I might have more knowledge of our Saviour's bodily pains, and of the compassion of our Lady and of all his true lovers who were living at that time and saw his pains, for I would have been one of them and have suffered with them."[17]

This was not a matter of masochism; it was the prayer of a great lover of Christ, as a way of increasing her sympathetic understanding of his life and his teachings. The second request, for a nearly fatal illness, was because she "wanted to be purged by God's mercy, and afterwards live more to his glory because of this sickness."[18] These prayers were ultimately answered, with an intense vision of Jesus speaking to her from the cross while she was near death. Through such personal

EXCERPT **Our Mother Jesus**
Julian of Norwich

I say that he is to us everything that is good and comforting for our help. He is our clothing, who wraps and enfolds us for love, embraces us and shelters us, surrounds us for his love, which is so tender that he may never desert us... .

The mother's service is nearest, readiest, and surest: nearest because it is most natural; readiest because it is most loving; and surest because it is truest. No one ever might or could perform this office fully, except only for him. We know that all our mothers bear us for pain and for death. O, what is that? But our true Mother Jesus, he alone bears us for joy and for endless life, blessed may he be. So he carries us within him in love and travail, until the full time when he wanted to suffer the sharpest thorns and cruel pains that ever were or will be, and at last he died... .

The mother can lay her child tenderly to her breast, but our tender Mother Jesus can lead us easily into his blessed breast through his sweet open side, and show us there a part of the godhead and of the joys of heaven, with inner certainty of endless bliss.

This fair, lovely word mother is so sweet and so kind in itself that it cannot truly be said of anyone or to anyone except of him and to him who is the true Mother of life and of all things.

Julian of Norwich, "Christ the Mother," in Andrew Harvey, ed., *Teachings of the Christian Mystics*, Boston: Shambhala Publications, 1998, pp. 108–9.

experiences, Julian developed a theology based on the wounded Christ as a manifestation of God's love and the salvation of humanity. Again and again, she insisted, "Love was our Lord's meaning." In her writings, wounded bodies and wounded psyches become paths to healing, deep wholeness, and inner joy.

Many great women spiritual teachers arose in Europe during the Middle Ages. While the Church and papacy were notoriously corrupt, young Catherine of Siena (1347–1380) practiced her devotions in seclusion and became much beloved as "mother of thousands of souls." So intense were her austerities that she died when only 33. But in her short life, she traveled far and wide, imploring clerics and rulers to bring back the purity of Christianity. Hundreds of her spirit-filled letters have been preserved. Another Catherine, of Genoa, overcame her own desire for strict cleanliness and worked among the poor and sick during a deadly plague. She became so fully God-realized that she said, "My me is God." She wrote, "I am so placed and submerged in His immense love, that I seem as though immersed in the sea, and nowhere able to touch, see or feel aught but water."[19]

Visionary women were continually in danger of being declared heretics by the Inquisition or executed as witches. With their direct experience of God, they were regarded as threats by the institutional Church, which was ritual-oriented and run by priests. The support of a high-ranking male in the Church was often critical to

BIOGRAPHY St. Teresa of Avila God's Real Friend

St. Teresa of Avila (1515–1582) defies any stereotype of a saint. She was a beautiful, gregarious, aristocratic Spanish woman, humorous and talkative, who loved the attentions of men. She entered a convent—albeit a rather lax one—apparently as much to protect herself from temptation as to nourish the inner life. But when she was 41, she began having such rapturous experiences of God that worldly pleasures paled by comparison. Desiring for others as well as herself a more dedicated spiritual life that would lead to constant awareness of God, she founded 17 Discalced ("unshod") Carmelite convents and four monasteries. To do so, she traveled through remote mountainous regions by any means available, facing tremendous difficulties. In the midst of one journey by donkey carts, her party tried to ford a flooded river by putting the wooden carts on rafts. The raft cables broke, and all their provisions were swept away. In despair, Teresa complained to God, who replied, "This is how I treat my real friends." Teresa responded, "Then it is no wonder that your Lordship has so few!"[20]

In addition to her demanding activities, Teresa was an excellent writer—one of the best of Spain's prose writers—whose books and letters are full of valuable and intimate details about spirituality. Her autobiography, which she wrote at the request of the men who were her spiritual directors, provides clear descriptions of her early visionary experiences and the degrees of mystical prayer. Her *Book of Foundations* follows in humorous and witty detail the adventures of her life as a religious reformer and founder of convents. *The Way of Perfection* and her magnum opus, *The Interior Castle*, explore the spiritual path, with its pitfalls and God's saving grace, in unsparing detail. A sample reveals her tremendous inner strength and commitment to truth:

> The soul must be virile, not like those soldiers who lie down on their stomachs to drink when they are being led into battle. It must not dream of sweetness and enjoyments at the beginning of its career. Manna does not fall in the first habitations [of the "interior castle"]—we must press on further if we want to gather it! Then alone will the soul find all things to its taste, when it has learned to will only that which God wills. How comic our pretensions are! We are still immersed in difficulties and imperfections, we have virtues that can barely toddle, others hardly born; and we are not ashamed to demand sweetness in prayer, we grumble at dryness! May you never behave like that, sisters. Embrace the Cross—the rest is a mere extra.[21]

their survival and their relative freedom to express themselves. Women mystics were so feared by misogynists that two Dominican inquisitors wrote a hideous document in 1486 called the *Malleus Maleficarum* ("Hammer of Witches"), in which they claimed that women were highly susceptible to witchcraft—consorting with demons rather than communing with God—and described means of executing witches. Their illogical arguments were considered authoritative, and as we noted in Chapter 1, up to four million people, 85% of them women, were tortured and killed on suspicion of witchcraft over a period of several centuries. Among them was Joan of Arc (*c.*1412–*c.*1431), whose visions convinced her that she was to help drive the English invaders out of France. Although she had some military success, the English captured her and gave her to an ecclesiastical court to be tried as a heretic and a witch. During her trial, she was asked if she would accept the authority of the Church. Her answers and the statements of the inquisitors reveal the gap between direct spiritual experience and the institutional "Church Militant":

THEY: "Will you refer yourself to the decision of the Church?"

SHE: "I refer myself to God Who sent me, to Our Lady, and to all the Saints in Paradise. And in my opinion it is all one, God and the Church; and one should make no difficulty about it. Why do you make a difficulty?"

THEY: "There is a church Triumphant in which are God and the Saints, the Angels, and the Souls of the Saved. There is another Church, the Church Militant, in which are the Pope, the Vicar of God on earth, the Cardinals, Prelates of the Church, the Clergy and all good Christians and Catholics: this Church, regularly assembled, cannot err, being ruled by the Holy Spirit. Will you refer yourself to this Church which we have thus just defined to you?"

SHE: "I came to the King of France from God, from the Blessed Virgin Mary, from all the Saints of Paradise, and the Church Victorious above, and by their command. To this Church I submit all my good deeds, all that I have done or will do."[22]

She was burned at the stake, like many of her visionary sisters. By the end of the Middle Ages, the great flowering of Christian medieval mysticism drew to a close.

While the Protestant tradition has not been a primary vehicle for mysticism and asceticism, from the beginning it has included many courageous and influential women. Martin Luther's wife, Katharina von Bora (1499–1552), helped to set the model for married clerical life. She had been an unwilling nun, sent to a convent by her father when young. Interested in Luther's reformist ideas, she and other nuns appealed to him for help, and he arranged their daring secret escape from the convent (at that time, an act punishable by death) in a covered wagon of fish barrels. Having settled the other nuns with families, husbands, or jobs, Luther at last married Katharina herself. Formerly a celibate monk, he now wrote enthusiastically about marriage as a training ground for Christian virtues, such as patience, humility, and charity. He called "my Katie" the "boss of Zulsdorf" (the farm she managed as part of the extensive holdings of the monastery that had been given to him) and also "the morning star of Wittenberg," for she rose at 4 a.m. every day to carry out her many responsibilities: running the farm and a brewery to support the monastery, raising their large family, operating a hospital, and taking care of visitors and Luther's students who lived with them. Respect for the Bible became a hallmark of the Protestant movement, and Katharina became a prime model of this tradition, as Luther encouraged her in biblical studies. She reportedly said on her deathbed, "I will stick to Christ as a burr to cloth."[23]

One of the great martyrs of the Protestant Reformation as it struggled to promote what it considered the original forms of Christianity, rather than Roman Catholic tradition, was Margaretha Sattler (d. 1527) of Germany. She had been a Beguine but left to marry an ex-Benedictine prior, Michael Sattler. They became leaders in the fledgling Anabaptist movement, whose members faced severe persecution; thousands were ultimately condemned to death as heretics. They were considered radical in their insistence upon baptism only of adults who personally professed their faith (rather than of infants), their distrust of clergy as authority figures, their common ownership of property, and their pacifism. After Margaretha and Michael brought Anabaptists together to write their articles of faith, the two were arrested and convicted of heresy. He was publicly tortured and burned to death. For two days afterward, Margaretha remained steadfast in her faith in reformist principles despite threats and persuasion, and then she was killed by drowning.

Several centuries later, some Protestant movements were initiated by women. Mary Baker Eddy (1821–1910) founded Christian Science, with its emphasis on healing by faith; Mother Ann Lee (1736–1784) founded the Shaker movement, in which women and men lived together in celibate communities, dancing and shaking in ecstasy as they anticipated the return of Jesus. The celibate Shaker movement became extinct because it could not perpetuate itself through family lines.

The Orthodox Church, though profoundly mystical, is also thoroughly patriarchal, but has nonetheless quietly given rise to some female as well as male saints. One recent example is the Russian nun Makaria (1926–1993). Crippled when young, she had a dream of Mary, the "Mother of God," when she was five years old. Instead of healing her legs, Mary taught her how to pray. When she was eight, she had a beautiful vision of paradise, with a radiant Mother of God. Later, the Mother of God told her that she had been chosen to take all the people's sufferings and sicknesses on herself, and she agreed. Archangels reportedly taught her prayers and healing blessings for water and oil. Recognizing her as an intercessor, people began coming to her for help, even though Russia was officially committed to atheism at that time. In 1978, she became a nun of the strictest ascetic type: a *schema*. People came to her from early in the morning until late at night, and she prayed for them and gave them blessed oil and water. During the night, she prayed for hours over buckets of water so that they would become vehicles for God's healing grace. She often took others' pains on herself. Makaria was a noted clairvoyant. One person who apparently failed to take her advice was the astronaut Yuriy Gagarin. Makaria reportedly cautioned him not to fly again; he did so anyway and died in a plane crash. At times, the people who took care of Makaria as an invalid were cruel to her, but she prayed for them nonetheless, saying that they did not recognize what they were doing.

The example set by Jesus' self-sacrificial love has thus been carried on over the centuries by countless saintly Christian women, only some of whose names are known.

Christian Women's Institutional Roles

In contrast to the highly personal, unorthodox approaches of mystics, the institutional Christian Church is run by local officials such as ministers or priests, who are under the supervision of higher officials and councils. The Orthodox Church and the Roman Catholic Church still bar women from being priests. However, women can be celibate nuns and so offer services such as education and medical care, as well as living by prayer and devotions. In the Roman Catholic Church, a new situation has arisen. Because so few men now train for the priesthood, or indeed practice their faith (fig. 7.4), many Catholic churches do not have a male priest but rather a female "pastoral associate" who functions as a priest, conducting masses, weddings, funerals, and so forth. But because of Church restrictions, the bread and wine for the mass have to be blessed in advance by an actual priest.

Most Protestant denominations now admit women to full-time ministry, and some have risen to higher administrative posts, such as bishoprics. In many Protestant seminaries, between a third and a half of students are now women. In more humble ways, many women teach children in Bible classes and help carry on the social and charitable work of churches. If church leadership is seen as a

7.4 In many Christian churches, women far outnumber men in devotional activities (as in this Catholic church in Poland), as well as in volunteer work

pyramid, the broad base of least skilled and prestigious work is filled largely with women, while the more skilled and prestigious positions toward the top of the pyramid have traditionally been filled by men, although this is changing.

The initiative for bringing women into the ministry can be traced back to 1666, when Margaret Fell, a leader of the Society of Friends (Quakers), wrote a tract claiming the right of women to preach and teach the biblical message, arguing that the Holy Spirit had blessed women as well as men for the prophetic mission. Quakers continued to support the idea of women's spiritual equality and spoke out on behalf of women's participation. By the later nineteenth century, as women's Christian missionary societies helped to spread the Gospel at home and abroad, and abolitionists and suffragists struggled to promote liberation and voting rights for all in North America, women in some denominations also won the right to be trained for the ministry. Protestant women as ministers became a widespread reality in the 1970s. Given the Protestant emphasis on contextual, historical, and literary study of the Bible, feminist hermeneutics (interpretation of scripture) has helped to uncover the stories and strengths of biblical women, as well as support- ing Protestant principles such as the priesthood of all believers. As the renowned feminist biblical scholar Phyllis Trible wrote in 1982:

Born and bred in a land of patriarchy, the Bible abounds in male imagery and language. For centuries interpreters have explored and exploited this male lan- guage to articulate theology; to shape the contours and content of the church, synagogue and academy; and to instruct human beings—female and male—in who they arc, what roles they should play, and how they should behave. So har- monious has seemed this association of Scripture with sexism, of faith with culture, that only a few have even questioned it.

Within the past decade, however, challenges have come in the name of fem- inism, and they refuse to go away. As a critique of culture in light of misogyny, feminism is a prophetic movement, examining the status quo, pronouncing judgment and calling for repentance. In various ways this hermeneutical pursuit interacts with the Bible in its remoteness, complexity, diversity and con- temporaneity to yield new understanding of both text and interpreter... . In time, perhaps, it will yield a biblical theology of womanhood (not to be sub- sumed under the label humanity) with roots in the goodness of creation, female and male.[24]

Such strands of scholarship and activism have supported the growing demand of Protestant women to be religiously active in significant ways (see box, p. 213). Others have given up on Christianity as an institution. As radical feminist scholar Mary Daly wrote prophetically in 1971:

The women's movement will present a growing threat to patriarchal religion less by attacking it than by simply leaving it behind. Few of the leaders in the movement evince an interest in institutional religion, having recognized it as an instrument of their betrayal. Those who see their commitment to the movement as consonant with concern for the religious heritage are aware that the Christian tradition is by no means bereft of elements which foster genuine experiences and intimations of transcendence… . What will, I think, become possible through the social change coming from radical feminism is a more acute and widespread perception of qualitative differences between those conceptualizations of God and of the human relationship to God which are oppressive in their implications and those which encourage self-actualization and social commitment.[25] ∎

From the last quarter of the twentieth century onward, many Protestant women who chose to stay within the Christian Church thus won the right to be trained and ordained to preach. Nevertheless, they still face considerable difficulties in dealing with patriarchal institutional structures and cultural assumptions. They are still struggling to find full-time employment as ministers, for when congregations seek ministers they tend to prefer men with families—the traditional model. Lesbian women face the greatest difficulty in being hired, for in their social and sexual orientation they are perceived as most threatening to male power. As ministers and as members of Protestant congregations, some women feel alienated from the traditionally male-dominant policies of Church institutions that do not satisfy them spiritually. Married women ministers find it difficult to fulfill all their pastoral duties and also spend time with their families. Women ministers tend to be paid much less than their male counterparts.

In African-American churches, women's position has actually declined. After the Civil War, women and men worked together to develop vibrant church communities that supported their people in the midst of social injustices and economic disadvantages. But as the black Church became the center of African-American

Christian life, men took over the leadership and decision-making and women were relegated to auxiliary roles—educating children, feeding the hungry, helping the poor, organizing health clinics, training mothers, fundraising, and carrying on missionary programs, as well as being active in civil rights efforts. Nevertheless, today some black women are ministers and black women in general have been instrumental in keeping traditional ways of worship alive.

Evangelical and Pentecostal ministries have had many notable female preachers who were recognized as having a genuine spiritual calling, such as Kathryn Kuhlman (1907–1976; fig. 7.5). She preached her first sermon in a small pool hall converted into a mission, and at one time during a revival slept in a turkey house, as no room or inn was available. As a

7.5 Evangelist Kathryn Kuhlman preaching

INTERVIEW Rev. Allison Stokes, Ph.D.

Allison is a clergywoman in the United Church of Christ, former Protestant Chaplain at Ithaca College, New York, and Founding Director of the Women's Interfaith Institute in Seneca Falls, New York. She re flects on the sea change she has seen in Protestant women's ministry:

When I was growing up, I never dreamed of becoming a clergywoman, as some of my younger colleagues and friends did when they were young. Because my childhood and teenage years were in the 1940s and 50s (I graduated from high school in 1960), the closest I ever imagined I would get to ministry was to meet and marry a minister. This was not an unreasonable ambition at the time. But the man I married on the day of my graduation from college was not a minister. I became a housewife and mother, as expected, and did not work outside the home. The breakup of my marriage after 11 years was not in the plan, and also not as common as now. My divorce was soul-wrenching. As the second wave of feminism was breaking in the 1970s, my life took a dramatic and unexpected turn as I entered graduate school. Financial necessity led to what was unthinkable earlier: a career.

Today I look back upon my 25 years as a clergywoman (I was ordained in the United Church of Christ in 1981) and I marvel at the incredible change in the lives and expectations of women during my lifetime. My ministry as chaplain on college and university campuses and as pastor of a church could not have been predicted at the time of my birth in 1942. That I would offciate in 2004 at the legal marriage of two women in Massachusetts was unimaginable then. I feel I have been part of a seismic cultural shift that has brought unanticipated personal growth, fulfllment and blessing—"amazing grace."

I am now retired from active ministry and am working as Founding Director of the Women's Interfaith Institute in the Finger Lakes of upstate New York. Our historic church building is located in Seneca Falls, next door to the Women's Rights National Historical Park. My decision to live and develop our nonpro ft, educational organization in the "birthplace of women's rights" is intentional. Here was where Elizabeth Cady Stanton and other pioneering women called the frst women's rights convention in 1848. Here is where I draw inspiration as I devote my time and energies to encouraging women's leadership in "bringing peace to life."

My progressive Protestant upbringing in the United Methodist Church (my grandfather was a pastor/scholar) and my graduate education at universities founded by Protestant clergy for the training of clergy (Yale and Harvard) profoundly influenced my calling. A college student once formulated his faith for me saying, "Love God. Love others. Nothing else matters." For me, it is almost that simple. Laboring for justice and peace in our world, as a way of making God's love and mercy manifest, is what my faith is about.

My passion as a religious leader is to be a "change agent."

A male role model for my activist faith is the late Rev. William Sloane Coffn. Bill Coffn was the Yale chaplain who became famous in the 1960s when he opposed the war in Vietnam and was jailed as a civil rights "Freedom Rider." Later he worked for worldwide nuclear disarmament. (Rev. Sloan in the Doonesbury comic strip immortalizes Coffn.)

Elizabeth Cady Stanton is a female role model. Her tireless efforts inspire my desire to "sow winter wheat" that will ripen and produce for my six grandchildren and their generation after I am gone. Stanton came to the conclusion that the quest for women's equality could not be won without addressing biblically sanctioned patriarchy. With a team of collaborators in the now classic *The Women's Bible*, she boldly critiqued scripture and challenged traditional religious teachings that God ordains the subordination of women. Just as Stanton broke new ground in her time, along with sisters in ministry I seek to break new ground in our time by creating and promoting interfaith community. We need to transcend the faith boundaries that have long divided people and led to violent conflcts. I labor and pray for "Shalom, Salaam, Peace."

Stokes's book by this title (published by the General Board of Global Ministries of the United Methodist Church, 2006) is a re flection on interfaith peacemaking.

traveling evangelist, she held revival meetings in small churches and buildings throughout Idaho and the American midwest. In 1948 she located in Pittsburgh, Pennsylvania, holding weekly miracle healing services in its Carnegie Auditorium, and ultimately conducted large-scale healing services throughout the United States.

Similarly, Aimée Semple McPherson (1890–1944) heard an inner voice telling her, "Preach the Word!" This was an unimaginable proposition for a woman of her times. After several profound experiences of being anointed by the Holy Spirit, she scheduled a meeting to speak, but no one came. Undismayed, she stood on a chair in the street, held her arms in the air, and prayed silently for an hour. When she stopped, she told the people who had gathered around to follow her, and 50 of them did so. Her spiritual talk was so compelling that more came back the next night, and the next, until the crowds were so large that she had to set up a huge tent—her "canvas cathedral," she called it. Then she bought a big car—her "Gospel Car"— and traveled around the United States, drawing people to Jesus. She had a 5,000-seat church built in Los Angeles for revival meetings and training of people for the ministry—the Angelus Temple. In it, she introduced contemporary music and drama as ways of teaching the stories of the Bible; the services were so popular that they caused traffic jams, and they were broadcast live on the radio. During the Great Depression, she arranged food, clothing, blankets, and shelters for thousands of homeless; her soup kitchen fed 80,000 people a month. The denomination that she founded—the International Church of the Foursquare Gospel—is still going strong, encompassing some two million people in 83 countries, though now with a leadership dominated more by men than women. When Aimée died, 67% of the ordained clergy in her denomination were women. Now there are fewer than 38%, many of them male pastors' wives and few of them senior pastors in their own right. Women are also now scarce within the corporate leadership of the Foursquare Gospel.

There has been a general shift away from the early Pentecostal emphasis on spiritual calling and the authority of the Holy Spirit and toward institutionalization of male-dominated authority structures. Some Pentecostal denominations do not allow women to be fully ordained as ministers. Speaking for Pentecostal women as a whole who are called to ministry, Sheri Benvenuti, who has been a Pentecostal minister for 25 years, says:

> We are women who simply and humbly ask that we be given room to be obedient to the Lord who has called us... . There is also the greater reality of a world desperately needing every anointed person to preach the gospel, while the Church busies itself with unending doctrinal debate over who is qualified to minister in what position. We are, in a sense, watching the house burn down while arguing which fire truck to use. The time has come for Pentecostal women in ministry to leave the arena of debate and simply be who they are and do what God has called them to do.[26]

Many Roman Catholic women feel alienated from their Church because of its traditionalist, male-dominant policies, such as its stands against birth control, divorce, and abortion, its resistance to liberation theology, and denial of priesthood to women. The Vatican insists that women cannot be priests because Jesus chose only men as his disciples (although as we have seen, he had many important women followers and supporters, and there were female post-Crucifixion missionary teachers). When in 2002 seven women had themselves ordained as Catholic priests on a boat in the Danube River by an Argentine bishop, they were excommunicated. The archbishop dealing with this case said that it "attacks the fundamental structure of the church as it was wanted by its founder."[27] At the same time, there is a great shortage of male priests, partly because of the requirement that priests be celibate; moreover, male priests have been implicated in many sexual abuse scandals. Some Roman Catholic women are quite angry. One says: "Vatican arrogance and refusal to even listen to the pain endured by women whose economic, physical, and sexual abuse has been supported by centuries of Roman Catholic theology, philosophy, and practice enrages me."[28] Another Catholic woman speaks of the male leadership as "dysfunctional authority figures who use their role as a means to control rather than *free* others in their relationship with God."[29] Another woman despairs of "the 'watchdog system' imposed on bishops and priests who might want to bring women into new areas of ministry and responsibility... . This obsession with control is so contrary to the spirit of Christianity."[30]

Statistically, far more Roman Catholic women than men are active in the work and worship within their churches. Many Catholic women see the Church as part of the feminization of poverty; much of their work in the Church is voluntary and unpaid, and some feel that their skills are not honored. One Hispanic woman in the American Southwest who worked for 20 years within the church structure but left to work for a non-profit agency asserts:

Women have many gifts that are not recognized or are underutilized in the church. Church hierarchy gives "lip service" to women's contributions while acknowledgements as well as salary increases or other monetary benefits are given to men. The patriarchal system is at times demeaning and humiliating.[31]

Astrid Lobo Gajiwala, an Indian doctor and Catholic Christian journalist, feels the lack of women's participation most keenly with reference to the administering of the Eucharist. She writes of experiencing the Eucharist as served by Lyn Brakeman, an Episcopal priest and pastoral psychotherapist, for whom the cup signifying the blood shed by Christ is a reminder of the blood shed by women. Gajiwala says:

Month after month it flows, this river of energy. No wounds or death in this uniquely woman-experience, only a readiness to receive in order to give till death to oneself brings new life… . Tragically, in the institutional Church, women are reduced to little more than spectators in the eucharistic ritual. They may be the unifiers in families, close and extended, but they are forbidden to preside at the sacrament of unity. They may serve as eucharistic ministers but without any rights of their own, only as substitutes for priests (Canon 910: 1). They cannot be installed as lectors (Canon 230: 1), nor be ordained as deacons. And the final ignominy, these servants of the community cannot even have their feet washed in commemoration of Jesus' call to service. And so they sit in the pew, waiting … hoping … sharing.[32]

Many Roman Catholics have left the Church for greener spiritual pastures; others have deep love for the underlying essence and mysteries of the Church and try to stay on. They are potential agents for change, for there are strong undercurrents within the Church of concern for social justice and support for the contemplative life. Toinette M. Eugene, Professor of Christian Social Ethics at Garrett-Evangelical Theological Seminary, writes as a black Catholic womanist that she does not want to

make the sad and futile mistake of those who seek not to change the structures themselves but only their outward manifestation, resulting in empowerment for only a few—a few more black priests and bishops and, in time, a few black women priests, but leaving the hierarchical, authoritarian entity intact. [Instead,] we can remain to work actively from within to restructure this institution and make it truly inclusive as a model for and an experience of a discipleship constituted of equal human beings… . Given black women's ability to survive under the worst of circumstances and their active commitment to their extended families' and communities' survival, a black Roman Catholic womanist spirituality … must highlight God's role as a principal sustainer of oppressed, struggling, or marginated black women. It must examine the sustaining presences of the Holy Spirit in all black women's lives.[33]

There are also women active in the Roman Catholic Church who take a conservative stance. The most visible of these is Mother Angelica (b. 1923), a feisty, formerly crippled nun who has founded a flourishing monastery in the American South with herself as abbess of the Poor Clare Nuns of Perpetual Adoration, and has also created a broadcasting empire using its own radio and television stations and a website—www.ewtn.com—to broadcast sermons supporting the conservative values of the Vatican, for the "salvation of souls." Mother Angelica had the late Pope John Paul II as Chairman of the Board and Chief Executive Officer of her satellite-based Eternal Word Television Network and her global shortwave radio station WEWN. She built this empire on faith and hard work, starting by assembling fishing tackle, sold as "St. Peter's Fishing Lures." Opposed to feminism, Mother Angelica says:

> Our goal is to serve the Holy Father and the Magisterium of the Church. By doing so we know we are doing God's will. Our network is built on faith and sustained by prayer. I must be God's donkey pulling this load for a while. When God shows us what to do next, well, we will just move on to whatever that is. Imagine! God using me![34]

Recognizing the dissatisfaction and distress of many Christian women who feel excluded and unrecognized, the World Council of Churches devoted ten years to a program called the Ecumenical Decade of Churches in Solidarity with Women. Since it ended in 1998, study has continued on women's ways of "being church," and "how the ministry of the whole church could be renewed to include the gifts for service that God gives to both men and women."[35]

Other Christian women do not expect the institutionalized Church to change significantly, so they are creating their own forms. Many have developed women's spiritual support groups, while at the same time attending a traditional church. Pauline Sykes of England, for instance, grew up very committed to the Methodist chapel which was the center of her family's social life. But by middle age she was forced to re-evaluate her faith, for "it hadn't kept pace with my experience of life." Exposed to Christian feminism while living in the United States and then struggling through four years of depression, she began to recognize that:

> Much of what the Church had taught me about humility, obedience, self-denial, not being angry or resentful ("You are the potter, I am the clay," etc.) was unhelpful when, like most women, I needed to confess to too *little* pride and self-centredness rather than too much! Nevertheless, my local church, All Saints Methodist, has room for the doubter, and the Love so vital in those dear people continued to nourish and sustain me. And I have always seen in individual people how their "traditional" faith gives them courage, the ability to forgive and love, and face illness, hardship, and death with acceptance.[36]

Therefore she has maintained her links with her home church, while at the same time helping to create a dynamic spirituality study group that calls well-known women and men as speakers and explores themes of contemporary interest.

Another growing alternative is the "woman-church" movement. This appeared first in the United States in the 1980s and has now spread to many countries. Diann L. Neu is co-founder and co-director of WATER, the Women's Alliance for

Theology, Ethics, and Ritual, a nonprofit feminist network set up in 1983 to help offer theological, ethical, and liturgical projects, programs, counseling, and retreats by and for women. She explains that the woman-church phenomenon

> signals that women are essentially what patriarchy has denied, namely, religious protagonists able to shape and create the reality called church…. The biblical Mary spoke in the Magnificat of a justice-based spirituality when she experienced God/dess acting to feed the hungry, bring the powerful out of their hierarchies, and offer liberation to those who live under oppression. Women-church communities live this justice-based spirituality by designing rituals that are inclusive, creating myths that portray women as strong doers, not passive receivers, using symbols that express women's life experiences, and encouraging relationships that value women and all oppressed peoples as equals.[37]

Social Activists and Servants of Humanity

Excluded from the higher echelons of institutional power in the Church, Christian women are nonetheless serving God and humanity in many direct ways. Some have been notable as social activists.

One such was Anne Hutchison (1591–1643), who traveled from England to New England as a Puritan to find religious freedom, and held meetings in her new home attended by 60 to 80 people. Guided, she said, by the Holy Spirit, she staunchly maintained that one can communicate with God directly; neither ministers nor Bible are necessary. The male ministers of the Massachusetts Bay Colony considered her position far too radical, for they had made the Bible their civil law, and of course their own authority was threatened. She was tried for her "erroneous opinions"—with the governor himself declaring her teachings "not tolerable" to God and her actions inappropriate for a woman—and was banished from the colony and excommunicated from the Church. Nevertheless, some were sympathetic to her cause, and her brave stance ultimately contributed to the inclusion of the right to freedom of religion in the Constitution of the United States.

The Society of Friends (Quakers) has been the spiritual base of many activist women. It was started in England by George Fox in 1647 and was quickly spread to the Netherlands, North America, and other areas by committed speakers and writers. Among these was Margaret Fell, who became a Quaker in 1652 and donated the large estate of her deceased husband for the use of the movement. She wrote some 24 highly influential tracts, including "Women's Speaking Justified, Proved, and Allowed of by the Scriptures." It is an extensive study of women who spoke in the Bible, used as evidence that two troublesome passages of the Bible saying that women should keep silence (Corinthians 14: 34 and I Timothy 2: 11–12) applied only to women who were spiritually unconverted, "indecent and irreverent." Fell wrote:

> For Christ in the Male and in the Female is one, and he is the Husband, and his Wife is the Church; and God hath said, that his Daughters should prophesie as

well as his Sons: and where he hath poured forth his Spirit upon them, they must prophesie, though blind Priests say to the contrary, and will not permit holy Women to speak.[38] ■

Quakers understand Jesus' message as a radical platform for a just society, rather than mere ritualism, so they have struggled and even been martyred to uphold their beliefs. Between 1662 and 1688, they were severely persecuted. Thousands were imprisoned and beaten; hundreds died, including Mary Dyer, who allowed herself to be hanged in hopes of repealing the death sentence pronounced against Quakers.

It is their spiritual conviction that gives Quakers the initiative to work for social reforms and the calm faith to persist in the face of attacks from the establishment. Their spiritual philosophy allows women to work alongside men as equals. Quaker minister Lucretia Mott (1793–1880) was a brave and persuasive speaker and activist against slavery in the United States, as well as an early proponent of women's rights. During mob violence against antislavery meetings, Mott held interracial gatherings in her Philadelphia home and when such a meeting was threatened with arson, she had black and white women walk out in pairs, arm in arm—a dramatic statement of sisterhood that crossed all social barriers. Together with Elizabeth Cady Stanton (1815–1902), she opened the first Women's Rights Convention in Seneca Falls, New York, in 1848. Her closing resolution proposed the "untiring efforts of both men and women for the overthrow of the monopoly of the pulpit and for the securing to women an equal participation with men in the various trades, professions and commerce."[39] In contrast to "the monopoly of the pulpit," Mott believed in the Quaker principle of the inner light that exists in every-one. She felt that teaching of the Bible had been distorted by the clergy and false-ly used to justify oppression against slaves and women and to wage war. These social evils should be ended by true understanding of religion. She often said, "Take truth for authority, not authority for truth."[40]

All branches of Christianity are full of women who are courageously trying to serve people in need, in accordance with Jesus' teaching that "whatever you did for one of the least of these brothers of mine, you did for me" (Matthew 25: 40). Within Roman Catholicism, Dorothy Day (1897–1980) was a salient example of Christian service to the poor. She helped to found the Catholic Worker movement, reproaching the Catholic Church whenever she felt it supported injustice; she organized housing for the homeless and lived among them. She explained:

> ■ To give what you have for relief, to pledge yourself to voluntary poverty for life so that you can share with your brothers is not enough. One must live with them, share with them their suffering too. Give up one's privacy, and mental and spiritual comforts as well as physical.[41] ■

The sisters of the Medical Missionaries of Mary, based in Ireland, forgo physical comforts and risk their lives in war zones and refugee camps to offer medical aid. Sister Lucy Poulin, a renegade Catholic nun, has organized a cooperative society for homeless people and social rejects in Maine—the HOME Coop. She lives with them, helping to run cottage industries such as horse-logging, milling of lumber, housebuilding, weaving, pottery, and wreath-making. In the face of severe repression and bombing of citizens of El Salvador by the extreme right-wing government in its attempt to root out insurgents, women and men from various Christian denominations in the United States courageously went there to help refugees back to their evacuated, devastated villages. One of them, Carmen Broz, an elderly Quaker teacher born in El Salvador, describes what it means to "walk with the poor." When their caravan of refugees, international supporters, and supplies finally arrived in the ruined city of Aguacayo, nothing was alive except for a few birds. Singing songs of peace and carrying white flags symbolizing neutrality, they were confronted by trucks full of heavily armed soldiers, who separated the internationals from the displaced people and ordered the former to leave immediately. Broz recounts a moment of realization:

> I looked at the Desplazados [displaced persons] and then I felt the military have no power with their little soldiers and their arms and all their colonels and all that paraphernalia. And I looked at ourselves, and I said, we have no power either, and the people of Aguacayo have no power. And I think of the expression that the only power present at that moment was God's power. And that his will was going to be done. It didn't matter what I did, what I said, his will was going to be done, and had nothing to do with me. And then I felt very at peace,

7.6 Mother Teresa of Calcutta won a Nobel Peace Prize in 1979 for her merciful work among the poor

and I was able to sit down, go through the whole motion, and when they lifted me up with my eyes closed, I just went limp. Later on I was told that the little soldiers whose chore was to lift me were very hesitant to touch me, and that when they finally did it, they did it very tenderly.[42] ▪

These and countless other Christian women who have dedicated their lives to the service of others have often met with resistance not only from worldly citadels of power but also from the Church. When Mother Teresa (1910–1997; fig. 7.6) left her more conventional positions as a Loreto Sister and principal of a girls' school in India in order to serve the poorest of the poor—the destitute people and lepers who came to die near a Hindu temple in Calcutta—this tiny Albanian nun had to use her own wits, resources, and deep faith in order to follow Jesus' instructions without institutional support. At last she was allowed by the Archdiocese of Calcutta to found a new order—the Missionaries of Charity. At that time there were only 12 nuns working with her. By the time of her death she was perhaps the most famous female spiritual leader in the world, and was overseeing the work of 4,000 nuns, plus the Missionaries of Charity Fathers, in 123 countries. Steadfastly opposed to abortion and divorce, and accused of accepting donations from questionable sources, she nonetheless won the world's admiration for her simple devotion to the mission Jesus had given her: lovingly caring for Jesus in the "distressing disguise of the poor." A hymn she wrote illustrates her direct approach:

> … Jesus is the Hungry to be fed,
> is the Thirsty to be satiated,
> is the Naked to be clothed,
> is the Homeless to be taken in,
> Jesus is the Sick to be healed,
> is the Lonely to be loved… .
> Jesus is my God and my Spouse,
> Jesus is my Life and my only Love,
> Jesus is my All in All,
> is my Everything Jesus to me.[43]

The Missionaries of Charity continue their work with Mother Teresa's inspiration behind them. Sister Clarice, who had been living and traveling with Mother Teresa since 1974 and is now in a community where only six sisters are taking care of 200 mental patients and conducting sewing classes for poor women, says, "Her spirit is very powerful."[44]

Feminist Theology

Being deeply involved in Christian life, even if not from the pulpits and papacy, contemporary women have tried to redefine the interpretation of Christianity so that it is true to their understanding and their experiences—not necessarily as historically interpreted by men. This effort is linked to the secular feminist movement, which dates back to the nineteenth century, but feminist theology became a distinct theological movement from the 1960s onward, as feminists directed their critiques toward institutions perceived as sexist, including Christianity. In this process, feminist theologians have been instigating re-evaluations of patriarchal language and patterns of power, as well as making their voices heard on other ethical issues. As theologian Mercy Amba Oduyoye from Ghana writes:

> The irruption of women in Church and society is an integral part of the voice of the earth's voiceless majority that is beginning to penetrate the atmosphere and disturb the peace of the principalities and powers that hold the structures of our so-called one world in their hands.[45]

Biblical exegesis or commentary that presents women as equals of men actually goes back to an early understanding among some Christians that—as it is written in Galatians 3: 28, "There is no longer male and female: for you are all one in Christ Jesus," and Acts 2: 17, "In the last days it will be, God declares, that I will pour out my Spirit upon all flesh, and your sons and your daughters shall prophesy"—Jesus' coming, Crucifixion, and Resurrection brought, or will bring, a radical change in society, making "all flesh" equal. This interpretation has come forth again and again throughout Christian history, challenging the hierarchical, patriarchal institutions of the Church and their ways of explaining the Bible.

Theologically, the two different Creation stories in Genesis have been interpreted in various ways. The first, in Genesis 1: 27, is particularly germane for egalitarian interpretation, for it is written, "God created man in his own image; in the image of God he created him; male and female he created them." Both men and women are the image of God, and both are thus equal and intrinsically good. The second Creation account in Genesis 2 introduces the mythical first couple: Adam and Eve. Eve's secondary creation, out of Adam's rib, has often been interpreted as suggesting her inferior status; her acceptance of forbidden fruit from the serpent, as a symbol of woman's natural sinfulness. But Christian women writing in the sixteenth and seventeenth centuries argued that because women were created last, they are the crown of creation. Furthermore, woman and man shared at least equally in the fall of humanity from the Garden of Eden, for both ate the fruit and Adam brought disharmony by blaming Eve. These writers also noted that Jesus had many women disciples and that, unlike his male disciples, they stood with him during the Crucifixion and were the first witnesses to his Resurrection.

These ideas were amplified during the Enlightenment by liberal socialists who described all hierarchies as contrary to "natural order." In the United States, mid-nineteenth-century Quaker feminists such as Sarah and Angelina Grimke staunchly claimed that not only are women and men created as equals according to Genesis 1: 27 but also that suppression of women is contrary to the will of God and the "order of creation." Other nineteenth-century feminists explicitly attacked the Church as sexist. Among them was Elizabeth Cady Stanton, who brought together women biblical scholars in the 1890s to create *The Women's Bible*. Its commentaries on all the texts in the Bible included description of Genesis 2 as a scurrilous attempt to denigrate women; in Genesis 3, woman was shown as having an interest in knowledge, whereas man was described as a weak coward. Thereafter, men tried to dominate women and justify their oppression by blaming them for the fall from God's grace. In the New Testament, Stanton described Jesus as a radical egalitarian, but Paul as ambivalent about women. She felt that the Christian Church was so deeply imbued with its own anti-female interpretations of Judeo-Christian traditions that it could not be reformed; a new, more rational religion was needed.

Other Christian feminists have tried to remain within the Church and reform it from inside. Theological schools now have many female professors, and the academic study of Christianity, as well as the preaching of the Gospel, is now considerably influenced by feminist reconstruction. Some of these scholars understand the Christian message as deeply liberating, but overlaid in the scriptures by male interpretations and practiced by patriarchal institutions. They are trying to weed out the biases of the authors and find within the texts and in early Christian communities the radically liberating message of Jesus. Professor Rosemary Radford Ruether, a pioneering feminist theologian, introduced the "feminist critical principle": that whatever in Christian tradition precludes or diminishes the full humanity of women is not to be considered authoritative.

As we have seen, language about and metaphors for God found in the Bible have a strong impact on one's inner feelings about and relation to the invisible Divine Power. In translation from the ancient original, most of the language in the Christian Bible has been rendered in male terms, by male translators. Astrid Lobo Gajiwala of India writes about Christian translations of the Old Testament:

> The Hebrew God writhing in labour (Deuteronomy 32: 18) has become the God "who gave you birth" (Revised Standard Version), then the God "who had given them life" (Good News Bible), and finally is lost forever in the God who "fathered you" (Jerusalem Bible). "I am El Shaddai" (Genesis 17: 1), says God (Jerusalem Bible). It is a naming that has its roots in the Hebrew word meaning "breast" and evokes feminine images of bodiliness and fertility. Obviously incompatible with our male God image, so the curtain is drawn again to hide her from view with "Almighty God" (Good News and Revised Standard Version).[46]

Many women feel uncomfortable with language and metaphors in which God is portrayed as an aggressive male ruler—patriarchal Father, Lord, Sovereign Power. They prefer images suggesting God's love and tenderness. Sallie McFague looks at God as a lover, a mother, a friend; what happens, she asks, if we regard the world as the body of God? Dorothee Soelle argues that a concept of God as male ruler supports oppression and violence by men against humanity. As a German mindful of the Holocaust, Soelle is keenly aware of how far this can go in creating tacit obedience to evil militarism in the name of obedience to a higher authority. If God is understood as a distant, punitive male figure—rather than a loving Divine presence within everything—then people feel powerless, their spirits crushed by being portrayed as worthless sinners. True Christian conversion, Soelle argues, is becoming free of this belief system and denouncing it as evil; this is the first step toward knowing Jesus and God as they really are. Jesus called people to solidarity with the poor and oppressed rather than compliance with hypocritical religious and political tyrants.

7.7 Chung Hyun Kyung, author of *Struggle to be the Sun Again*, has been a leading figure in the development of Asian women's theology

Some of the most powerful feminist theology today is coming from women in materially poor cultures, the so-called "Third World," which faces increasing poverty, exclusion, inequality, violence, and insecurity as a result of globalization, economic imperialism, and militarism. In the middle of suffering, they are yearning to help transform the world. They find they cannot do so through Christian theology as traditionally created by white Western men. For instance, Chung Hyun Kyung (fig. 7.7), an influential theologian from Korea, says:

The resources for Asian women's liberation theology must come from the life experiences of Asian women themselves. Only when we Asian women start to consider our everyday concrete life experiences as the most important source for building the religious meaning structures for ourselves shall we be free from all imposed religious authority.[47]

Re-reading the Bible from the perspective of the poor, and particularly of poor women, Third World feminist theologians discover it as an affirmation of God as the loving and just companion of the poor in the midst of their sufferings. They see Jesus not as a dominating lord but as a suffering servant of humanity. However, they also discover in the Bible some texts that seem to denigrate women, a fact that brings up the thorny question of biblical authority. Some, such as Elsa Tamez of Costa Rica, dismiss those passages as being reflections of the surrounding culture and secondary to the central message of the Bible. Tamez writes:

A time has come to acknowledge that those biblical texts that reflect patriarchal culture and proclaim women's inferiority and their submission to men are not normative.... The rationale behind this statement is essentially the same as that offered by the Scriptures: the proclamation of the gospel of Jesus calls us to life and announces the coming of the kingdom of justice.[48]

For Hispanic feminist theologians, some of whom now refer to themselves as *mujeristas* (see box, right), there is a need not only to reinterpret the Bible but also to radically change the societies in which they live according to the liberating mission of Jesus. They are turning to a praxis based not on tolerating suffering, but on struggling to bring change. Ada Maria Isasi-Diaz of Cuba explains:

EXCERPT Creating New Liturgies for Women

One aspect of feminist re-visioning of Christian tradition is the creation of liturgies that speak to women from their own experiences, that encourage leadership qualities, and that decentralize power—in contrast to traditional androcentric worship services. The following are excerpts from an Hispanic Women's Liturgy celebrated in San Antonio, Texas, in 1989.

Opening Ritual

Those who have a leadership role in the liturgy sit in silence. As the rest of the women come into the room they become aware of the silent atmosphere and join in it. Once the gathered community is ready, one by one different women go to the altar, light a candle, and while holding it on high say one of the following lines:

> *The power to give life.*
> *The power of being vulnerable without being weak.*
> *The power of believing in a better future.*
> *The power of changing oppressive situations.*
> *The power to face diffcult circumstances.*
> *The power of not giving up.*
> *The power of loving and claiming the need for love.*
> *The power of crying.*
> *The power that is ours because we are women.*

The community is invited to name the powerful women they have known, who have influenced them, while the rest of the candles on the table are lit by two women. Once all the candles are lit another woman says:

> This space in which we have spent these three days is full of the light of our power. We know we are blessed by God and by Mary. Let us call out the different names we give her.

Once they have finished, a different woman says the following:

> And now I ask you to turn to the person on your right and bless her using whatever words and gestures you want.

When the women have almost finished blessing each other, the song starts:

LUCHA, PODER, Y ESPERANZA ("Struggle, Power, and Hope")

Adelante compañeras	Onward, companions,
que a nuestro pueblo asesinan	they are murdering our people
y a la tierra nuestra madre	and our mother, the earth,
el imperio ultraja y viola.	the empire is ravaging and raping.

Al viento nadie lo para	No one stops the wind,
al mar nadie lo encadena	no one chains the sea,
las mujeres solidarias	the women in solidarity
son fuego que nadie apaga.	are a fre no one can extinguish.
Tu causa es causa del Pueblo,	Your cause is the people's cause
tu dignidad es sagrada	your dignity is sacred
mujer color de la tierra	woman, your color is the earth's
arbol de la vida nueva.	you are tree of new life.

La Palabra entre Nosotras ("the word of God among us")
A reading of Exodus 1: 15–21 is followed by a dialogued homily—to last about ten minutes—built around the following points. The homilist walks around among the women gathered.

The homilist asks if there are any midwives present. Who was helped by a midwife to give birth? What was her name? Call on as many women as want to speak.

The homilist gives thoughts on the close relationship between women and giving life.

She talks about the need for us to ask ourselves what kind of life we want for our children.

Blessing Prayer
Each stanza is read by a different woman from where she is in the circle.

The power of the seed from which the wheat grows.
The power of the earth nurtures the seed and makes it fburish.
The power of the sun that gives warmth and light to the wheat.
The power of the campesinas, campesinos, who care for and harvest
    the wheat.
The power of the yeast that even if it is small in quantity makes all the
    dough to rise.
The power of the bread which sustains us and without which there is
    no life.

One of the *campesina* (agricultural worker) women goes to the altar, lifts the bread over her head, and breaks the loaf, saying:

The power of this community which in breaking this bread renews its commitment to the people who struggle for their liberation.

Another woman goes to the altar and lifting the cup says:

This is the milk which comes from our bodies and nourishes life. It is mixed
with honey, for milk and honey was the symbol for our ancestors of the
promised land, of a better future, of liberation. We bless it by drinking of it for
it will sustain us in the struggle.

Another woman helps the woman at the altar fnish breaking the bread. They set several stations around the table with cups, baskets with bread, and plates with dates. Then she says:

> The gifts of God for the people of God, come and eat joyfully, with the resolution and understanding that we will continue in the struggle and that God will always sustain us if we sustain one another. Come and feast.

While the people go to the table and feed themselves all sing:

> … I consecrate you prophet
> Let there be no doubt nor fear
> As you walk through history
> Be faithful to your mission.
>
> … Denounce everything
> That causes oppression
> So that it can be converted
> And return once again to God.
>
> May this be your hope
> May this be your mission
> Be a builder of the Reign
> A society of love.
>
> This is the hour of my grace
> Sacrament of God
> Be a sign of my covenant
> Be the light of a new sun.

Closing Ritual

As participants are given ribbons interlinking the group and confetti and serpentina to throw into the middle of the group, a woman with a guitar sings:

> Blessed is the woman
> Who knows how to be faithful
> To the work of planting
> Justice and peace;
> Happy will be
> The woman who makes an option
> For God's cause
> For the law of love… .

Hispanic Women's Liturgy celebrated at the Las Hermanas Conference in San Antonio, Texas, October 28, 1989, as quoted by Ada Maria Isasi-Diaz, *"Mujerista" Theology*, Maryknoll, New York: Orbis Books, 1996, pp. 179–86.

▨ To do *mujerista* theology is to attempt to live life to the fullest, to be about justice and the self-determination of all peoples... . It enables us to understand that to resign ourselves to what others tell us is our lot and to accept suffering and self-effacement is not necessarily virtuous.[49] ▨

Contemporary Issues

Those Christian denominations that take an authoritarian, controlling approach have created various dilemmas for many Christian women in their personal lives. Those we will examine here are the twin issues of contraception and abortion. These affect a great number of women around the world who are trying to be faithful Christians. The contemporary issue of Mary as a role model for women is of concern largely to feminist scholars but also ultimately affects many Christian women.

Limits on Women's Reproductive Choices

The Roman Catholic Church, Protestant fundamentalists, and some Pentecostal churches take strong stands against women's sexuality outside heterosexual marriage and try to control sexual conduct within marriages as well. Catholic women are told that the only form of birth control they may use is the "rhythm" method, in which conception is inhibited by limiting intercourse to only 17 supposedly "safe" days in each menstrual cycle. This method is one of the least reliable; it sometimes leads to many unwanted pregnancies and to families larger than the parents can properly support. Fundamentalist groups in the United States favor abstinence from sexual activity outside marriage, and have been influential in limiting access to contraceptive information for young unmarried women without their parents' approval. Again, this has led to many unwanted pregnancies for those who can least afford them. Research into more effective, useful means of contraception has been slowed by opposition from Christian fundamentalists, which has restricted funding.

Married or unmarried, women quite commonly get pregnant when they do not want to take on lifelong responsibility for a child—or simply cannot do so, because of poverty, poor health, lack of support from the father, genetic problems, too many children already to care for, rape, incest, or other strongly negative factors. In this predicament, when a woman discovers she is pregnant she may feel strong inner turmoil about the possibility of ending the pregnancy by abortion. Often abortion is accompanied by a deep sense of grief, pain, and perhaps guilt—exacerbated by some Christian churches' strong attempts to ban legal abortion. For the Roman Catholic Church, discussion about allowing abortion in some circumstances has been terminated by the Vatican, which takes the position that all sexual activity— even rape and incest—must allow for procreation, and that life exists and is sacred from the moment of conception. Catholic women seeking abortion have thus often been forced to use illegal, dangerous means. In Latin America, illegal abortion is the highest cause of death of women of reproductive age.

"Pro-life" groups in the United States have attacked abortion clinics, engaged in campaigns against "killing babies," and tried to promote measures to protect the life of the fetus as a person that cannot protect itself. "Pro-choice" groups have responded by trying to protect the right of the woman to make her own ethical choices in her private life, depending on her own circumstances. This right was supported in the United States by Supreme Court decisions—supporting in 1965 the right of married couples to seek contraception, in 1972 the right of unmarried people to contraception, and in 1973, in *Roe vs. Wade*, the right of people to make private decisions to terminate pregnancy up to the third trimester.

Theologically, arguments revolve around the rights of the fetus versus the rights of the mother, and definitions of what is a "person." Is a cluster of cells with no brain or human form a "person"? Does human life begin at conception or birth, or somewhere in between, when the life of the fetus might attain viability? In Christian cultures, a person's age is calculated from birth, rather than from conception. The word used in the Hebrew Bible for "person" is *nephesh*, which also means "breathing." Jesus did not take a rigid legalistic stance toward religious traditions; he took into account the circumstances of the people he met. He was described as forgiving and compassionate toward a prostitute and also toward a woman who had committed adultery, saying to those who cited the law of Moses that an adulteress should be stoned, "If any one of you is without sin, let him be the first to throw a stone at her" (John 8: 7). There is no scriptural record in either the Old or the New Testament of any prohibitions against abortion. This does not mean that abortion did not exist; desperate women have tried to practice it since time immemorial.

In contrast to those Christian traditions that try to regulate private sexual behavior, there are liberal traditions that take the ethical dilemmas seriously but do not prescribe a particular course of action for every woman. Unitarian Universalist minister Dr. Rebecca Edmiston-Lange explains why her tradition supports the right of a woman to choose to end an unwanted pregnancy by abortion:

> Women's choices in reproductive matters are morally complex. Such choices can be very difficult, even the occasion for grieving and profound sense of loss. Nonetheless, the difficulty of such choices does not mean that they cannot also be a faithful and morally affirmative response to what a woman perceives to be holy and just. Women are, inherently, moral agents, as are all people, and they are capable of subtle and sensitive moral discernment.[50]

Mary as a Role Model

Protestants do not project Mary, mother of Jesus, as a figure of worship, for they do not encourage worship of saints; Roman Catholics and Orthodox Christians do not either, theoretically, as only God may be worshiped, though they lovingly venerate her, and outsiders often see this veneration as worship. Innumerable statues, paintings, and icons of Mary—alone, standing in a crescent moon, or with the baby Jesus in her arms—are objects of reverence for Catholic and Orthodox Christians. The canticle attributed to her in the Gospel of Luke, known as the Magnificat (which many scholars see as a reworking of the song of Hannah in I Samuel 2), has inspired many composers of sacred music:

Tell out, my soul, the greatness of the Lord,
Rejoice, rejoice, my spirit, in God my saviour;
So tenderly has he looked upon his servant,
Humble as she is.
For, from this day forth,
All generations will count me blessed,
So wonderfully has he dealt with me,
The Lord, the Mighty One.

His Name is Holy;
His mercy sure from generation to generation
Toward those who fear him;
The deeds his own right arm has done
Disclose his might:
The arrogant of heart and mind he has put to rout,
He has brought down monarchs from their thrones,
But the humble have been lifted high... .[51]

Many are the doctrines enunciated about Mary by the Roman Catholic Church. According to these, she was herself conceived "immaculately," i.e. without original sin. Since she was free from sin all her life, at her death she was instantly "assumed" bodily into heaven. There she continues to be the Mother of all believers, and because she is so holy, she can intercede with God on their behalf if they pray to her.

Mary has been seen at many periods and in many places around the world, reportedly conferring miraculous blessings. In the sixteenth century, she appeared to an Aztec Christian in Mexico and created in his shawl a miraculous image of herself as an indigenous woman surrounded by light. Since then, she has been celebrated as the Patroness of Latin America. In 1858 a 14-year-old peasant, Bernadette, saw her in Lourdes, France, as a beautiful young woman who showed her a fountain of healing holy water. Such sightings continue: in 1981, six young people in Medjugorje, Bosnia-Herzegovina, claimed to have seen Mary and to have begun receiving revelations from her in order to help convert people to lives of peace, love, faith, prayer, and fasting. News of miraculous visions and healings attracts great throngs of pilgrims; Lourdes is visited by over a million people every year, and many miracles of healing are thought to have occurred there.

Some icons of Mary are credited with great healing powers; Russian Orthodox believers venerate hundreds of them. In various parts of the world, "Black Madonnas"—dark-skinned representations of Mary—are likewise credited with similar miracles.

Grassroots adoration of Mary seems to be quite ancient. Drawings of her have been found in the Roman catacombs where the early Christians met secretly. By the third or fourth century CE, devotions were being explicitly addressed to her. Some scholars interpret her appeal as derived from earlier worship of the Mother Goddess; some see her as an embodiment of the feminine aspect of the Divine. In some Christian traditions, she is considered the New Eve. If the first Eve is blamed for the fall of humanity because of her disobedience to God, Mary's willing obedience to God opens the way for the birth of the new creation through Christ.

Mary is held up as a role model of the ideal woman because of her submissiveness to God, humility, and presumed perpetual virginity. In Christian ethics, sexual chastity is ideally to be preserved until marriage, and women's sexuality has generally been seen in a negative light. Even women's natural childbearing functions are thought too lowly to be considered holy, contrary to many women's actual experience of conception, carrying life in the womb, and giving birth as profoundly spiritual. At the same time that Mary is said to be a virgin, she is also known to be a mother—the Mother of God. Thus the ideal set by Mary is unattainable by mortal women: one cannot be both a virgin and a mother. How then do contemporary women see Mary? Aside from the impossible ideal of virgin motherhood, what is her relevance for their own lives as women?

Some of the most critically exact study of Mary is being made by Asian Christian women theologians. On the one hand, they are not happy that Protestant theologians have set aside Marian theology and focused on an all-male version; on the other hand, they feel that the Roman Catholic Church has tried to turn Mary into a male fantasy of an ideal woman, defining her not as a person in her own right but as "daughter of the Father, mother of Jesus, spouse of the Holy Spirit." Therefore in 1987 the Consultation of Asian Women's Theology met in Singapore and issued this "Summary Statement on Mariology":

We must name, and liberate ourselves from, the destructive efforts of two thousand years of male interpretation of Mary.
We must return to the Scriptures as women within our own cultural contexts, to re-discover the Mary who is liberated and liberator.[52]

In this effort, entirely new ways of looking at the meaning of Mary have emerged. Her virginity is being redefined not as a biological reality but as a matter of relationship. After all, some translators of the Bible state that "virgin" is a mistranslation of the word for "young woman." Marianne Katoppo of Indonesia explains Mary's virginity as meaning she is "a liberated human being who—not being subject to any other human being—is free to serve God."[53]

Korean women theologians are concluding that the idea that no human male is included in the conception of Jesus means that the world cannot be saved through the existing patriarchal system. Instead, by believing in herself and believing in God, Mary conceives a child outside of marriage—thus risking social criticism and perhaps even stoning—in order to give birth to the Messiah and open the way for liberation of her people and the potential for a radically transformed world order. Asian women also identify with Mary's agony at the foot of the cross on which her son was crucified, for many have seen their own sons tortured, imprisoned, or massacred for political reasons because they have tried to bring justice and love into the world. They do not see Mary as the obedient servant of male-dominant society but rather as the radical disciple of God alone.

In Latin America, Mary is being reinterpreted through the lens of liberation theology: Christianity's mission as solidarity with the poor and oppressed. In the Magnificat, Mary is said to have stressed God's uplift of the lowly, including herself. Theologians Ivone Gebara and Maria Clara Bingemer write that this message is of great significance to "the great masses of Latin America, the overwhelming majority of whom are poor, enjoy no adequate quality of life, and lack respect, bread, love, and justice." If glorification of Mary is understood as "making God's glory shine on what is regarded as insignificant, degrading, or marginal," then both Mary and Jesus are the protagonists in "the mystery of God's incarnation in human history."[54]

From an impossibly chaste and docile symbol of oppressed womanhood, Mary is being brought to light as a symbol to whom contemporary women can relate and in whom they understand the greatness of God's empowerment. In such ways, women's increasing influence within Christianity is transforming two millennia of male-dominated interpretation of the radical message of Jesus.

Key Terms

Gospel	parable
virgin birth	Apostle
Immaculate Conception	hierarchical
original sin	missionary
baptism	canonical
Messiah	Eucharist
exorcism	heretical, heresy
Sabbath	martyr
Crucifixion, crucified	canonization
Resurrection	mendicant
pope	beatification, beatified
Reformation	

Suggested Reading

Aquino, Maria Pilar, Daisy L. Machada, and Jeanette Rodriguez, *A Reader in Latina Feminist Theology: Religion and Justice*, Austin, Texas: University of Texas Press, 2002. Twelve Latina feminist theologians describe their ways of understanding God and Christian faith.

Christ, Carol P. and Judith Plaskow, *Womanspirit Rising: A Feminist Reader in Religion*, San Francisco: HarperSanFrancisco 1979, 1992. A classic compilation of articles relating to Judeo-Christian women's issues.

Chung Hyun Kyung, *Struggle to Be the Sun Again*, Maryknoll, New York: Orbis Books, 1990. Practical and passionate introduction to Asian women's liberation theology.

Furlong, Monica, *Visions and Longings: Medieval Women Mystics*, Boston: Shambhala, 1997. Life stories and writings of great mystics including Hildegard of Bingen, Julian of Norwich, Catherine of Siena, the Beguines, and Clare of Assisi.

Gilkes, Cheryl Townsend, *If it wasn't for the Women…: Black Women's Experience and Womanist Culture in Church and Community*, Maryknoll, New York: Orbis Books, 2001. The history and sociology of African-American women's significant contributions to religious experience within their community.

Isasi-Diaz, Ada Maria, *"Mujerista" Theology*, Maryknoll, New York: Orbis Books, 1996.

Discussion of solidarity, spiritual empowerment, and liturgical inclusion growing out of the daily lives of Latina Christian women.

Jantzen, Grace M., *Power, Gender and Christian Mysticism*, Cambridge: Cambridge University Press, 1995. A wide-ranging study of ways in which women's mystical experience is subject to institutions and politics surrounding it.

King, Ursula, ed., *Feminist Theology from the Third World: A Reader*, Maryknoll, New York: Orbis Books/SPCK, 1994. Interesting and relevant discussions of Christian beliefs and practices as seen by women theologians from many parts of the world.

MacHaffie, Barbara J., ed., *Readings in her Story: Women in Christian Tradition*, Minneapolis: Fortress Press, 1992. Documents and articles about women in Christianity from the Bible to the present.

McFague, Sallie, *Models of God: Theology for an Ecological, Nuclear Age*, Minneapolis: Fortress Press, 1987. Radical re-interpretation of Christian themes with an appreciation of many metaphors for God, including the world as God's body, and God as lover.

Newson, Carol A. and Sharon H. Ringe, *The Women's Bible Commentary*, Louisville, Kentucky: Westminster John Knox Press, 1998. Women scholars' reflections on women's lives and situations in each book of the Bible.

Ruether, Rosemary Radford, *Women and Redemption: A Theological History*, Minneapolis: Fortress Press, 1998. Thorough examination of the ways in which women became historically linked with sin in the development of Christian patriarchal paradigm, from New Testament time to the present.

Russell, Letty M. and J. Shannon Clarkson, eds., *Dictionary of Feminist Theologies*, Louisville, Kentucky: Westminster John Knox Press, 1996. Interesting and valuable compilation of entries from many parts of the world and many different feminist and liberation theology perspectives, brought to bear on topics such as biblical studies, Christian history, ministry and worship, ethics, social justice, and the like.

Schotroff, Luise, Silvia Schroer and Marie-Theres Wacker, *Feminist Interpretation: The Bible in Women's Perspective*, trans. Martin and Barbara Rumscheidt, Minneapolis: Fortress Press, 1998. Reconstruction of the Old and New Testaments through feminist historical, hermeneutical, and methodological scholarship.

Schussler Fiorenza, Elisabeth, *In Memory of Her: A Feminist Theological Reconstruction of Christian Origins*, second edn., New York: Crossroad, 1983, 1994. Ground-breaking scholarship uncovering clues to women mentioned in the Bible.

Schussler Fiorenza, Elisabeth, ed., *Searching the Scriptures*, 2 vols., New York: Crossroad, 1997. Essays on various aspects of feminist study of the Bible.

Tamez, Elsa, ed., *Through Her Eyes: Women's Theology from Latin America*, Maryknoll, New York: Orbis Books, 1989. Powerful articles about prophetic ministry to those who are marginalized.

Winter, Miriam Therese, Adair Lummis, and Allison Stokes, *Defecting in Place: Women Claiming Responsibility for Their Own Spiritual Lives*, New York: Crossroad, 1995. Report of a study of over 7,000 Christian women who are participating in women's study groups in order to deepen their understanding and practice of Christianity outside the confines of church institutional structures.

8
WOMEN IN ISLAM

Women as well as men have been designated to be God's "khalifah" on earth

RIFFAT HASSAN

In approximately 570 CE, a new prophet—Muhammad—was born into a small clan of one of the powerful tribes in the central Arabian desert. They controlled the town of Makkah (Mecca), a prosperous center for trading caravans traveling between settlements in South Arabia and the Byzantine Empire to the north; it was also an important place of spiritual pilgrimage. Ultimately the religion that the Prophet founded, Islam, spread not only throughout this area but to the whole world, becoming the second largest religion. Its impact on women has been profound; women's impact on the religion was important at first but soon declined. Nevertheless, throughout Muslim history there have been notable women leaders, mystics, and thinkers. Moreover, issues involving women's lives continue to be treated as major factors defining Muslim identity.

Women in Pre-Muslim Arabia

Before the time of the Prophet, women in the area sometimes played powerful social roles, as priestesses, queens, warriors, or wise women. Stories survive of many high-spirited, independent Arab women who were free to choose or deny men as husbands. There were various forms of temporary marriage, including one in which a number of men could get together and share the same woman sexually. Although this was hardly a liberating event for the woman, at least when she became pregnant she could call all the men and declare one of them as the father, and from then on he had to accept responsibility for the child. Three popular shrines near Makkah were dedicated to the daughters of the god al-Llah (Allah)—the goddesses al-Lat, al-Uzzah (the "Mighty One"), and Manat, goddess of fate.

On the other hand, among the Bedouin tribes of pre-Muslim Arabia, female children who were unwanted by their poor families were sometimes buried alive, slave girls were often sexually abused by their masters, women could not inherit property, men kept women as concubines and could take many wives as well, and men could readily beat or divorce their wives. The most important social codes were those designed to protect men's honor by controlling women's sexuality. If a

	TIMELINE
c.570 CE	Muhammad born to Amina
c.610–632	Holy Qur'an revealed
c.619	Death of Khadija, wife and supporter of the Prophet
622	Migration from Makkah to Madinah
630	Prophet returns victorious to Makkah
632	Death of the Prophet and burial under 'A'isha's fbor
632	Death of Fatima, beloved daughter of the Prophet
655	'A'isha one of leaders of Battle of the Camel against 'Ali
680	Battle of Karbala at which Muhammad's grandson Husayn killed
c.713–801	Rab'ia of Basra, the great mystic
1216	Death of Rabi'a bint abi Bakr, "lady of the *faqirs*"
1232	Death of Zaynab, saint of the Rifa'i order
1630s	Jahan-Ara, daughter of Emperor Shah Jahan of India, takes Sufi initiation
c.1806–1931	Hazrat Babajan, famous saint of Afghanistan and India
1866	Deoband reform movement begins, emphasizing subservience of women
1905–1993	Samiha Ayverdi, Turkish *shaykha*
1952	Aga Khan ends veiling of Ismaili women
1977 to present	Revolutionary Association of Women of Afghanistan protects women's rights
1977–1978	Destruction of Fatima's mosque in Madinah
2003	Shirin Ebadi of Iran receives Nobel Peace Prize

woman was suspected of straying beyond the boundaries set by men, she was a great shame to the family, a danger to the all-important honor of a man, and a threat to the purity of tribal bloodlines. Feminist scholar Fatima Mernissi explains that the linking of male "honor" and female virginity are manifestations of

■ a purely male preoccupation in societies where inequality, scarcity, and the degrading subjection of some people to others deprive the community as a whole of the only true human strength: self-confidence. The concepts of honor and virginity locate the prestige of a man between the legs of a woman. It is not by subjugating nature or by conquering mountains and rivers that a man secures his status, but by controlling the movements of women related to him by blood or by marriage, and by forbidding them any contact with male strangers.[1] ■

In contrast to limits on women's sexuality, Arab men were free to treat women as chattels, taking them as wives or discarding them at will. Men could swear that they would no longer have sexual relationships with their wives. Such an oath threw a woman into an unlimited state of suspense, with the right neither to divorce her husband nor to marry anyone else.

The Prophet and Women

What we know of the life of the Prophet Muhammad comes from the **Hadith** literature (reports of his life and sayings), history, and clues in the Holy Qur'an, the scripture that was revealed to him between approximately 610 and 632 CE and written down within 30 years of his death. It is considered perfect and eternal. By contrast, many of the *Hadith*, particularly those regarding women, are now considered inauthentic, and some are contradictory. Feminists point out that they have been interpreted primarily by men, often with anti-female bias. Thus it is difficult to trace the true relationships between the Prophet Muhammad and various women. However, it is clear that many women seem to have been important figures in the Prophet's life and that he treated them kindly, albeit protectively. The stories told about these women are significant in Islamic lore.

Even before the Prophet was conceived, his father Abdallah was reportedly propositioned by a woman while he was on his way to marry Amina. After the marriage was consummated, the other woman was no longer interested, for it is said that she had seen a blazing light between Abdallah's eyes, indicating that he would be fathering a great prophet of the people; another woman would be the mother of that prophet. Amina, now pregnant, said she saw a light radiating from her belly. After the Prophet was born in Makkah, he was given to a Bedouin woman to be wet-nursed, as was customary because of the belief that children would grow up healthier in the desert than in the city. The poorest of women—Halima—offered to take him in. Such was her poverty that she reportedly did not even have milk for her own child, her camel had none, and the donkey on which she had ridden to Makkah was nearly dead. But according to her account in the *Hadith*, once she took the baby:

As soon as I put him in my bosom, my breasts overflowed with milk which he drank until he was satisfied, as also did his foster-brother. Then both of them slept, whereas before this we could not sleep with him. My husband got up and went to the old she-camel and lo, her udders were full; he milked it and he and I drank of her milk until we were completely satisfied, and we passed a happy night. In the morning my husband said, "Do you know, Halima, you have taken a blessed creature!" I said, "By al-Llah, I hope so." Then we set out and I was riding my she-ass and carrying him with me, and she went at such a pace that the other donkeys could not keep up so that my companions said to me, "Confound you! Stop and wait for us. Isn't this the donkey on which you started?" "Certainly it is," I said. They replied, "By al-Llah, something extraordinary has happened." [2]

Since the child brought such good fortune into their lives, Halima wanted to keep him as long as possible, but changed her mind when, according to Muslim lore, he was visited by two men in white who took out his heart and washed it with snow to purify it. Whatever may have happened, he was left in a very weakened condition. Halima took Muhammad back to Makkah to his mother Amina, who is said to have understood that this was a sign of his being a child with a great future. Amina herself died when Muhammad was only six years old. He was sent to live with his grandfather, and then with his uncle, the respected Abu Talib, head of the tribe.

Eventually, Muhammad became a merchant leading trading caravans. In this capacity he was asked by the wealthy widow Khadija to take some goods to Syria for her. When she heard tales of prophecies and angelic appearances about him, and recognized his good character, she proposed marriage to him. Although she is said to have been 40 and he only about 25, he accepted. Khadija became his beloved companion and strongest supporter (see box, p. 238).

Muhammad's financial position would have improved considerably upon his marriage to Khadija, but he gave most of his wealth to the poor. Many times his family had nothing to eat; he kept only a single set of simple clothes. He gave away whatever gifts he received. He was known as an exemplar of charity and also of prayer. It was his habit to take long spiritual retreats from time to time. When he was undertaking such a retreat on Mount Hira, he was visited by an angel who tightly embraced him and ordered him to recite. Muhammad was terrified, for he did not want to be possessed by a *jinn* who would make him a despised soothsayer; he protested that he was illiterate. The angel persisted, and at last Muhammad found himself uttering what became the first revelation of the Holy Qur'an. When the angel was finished with him, Muhammad returned home, extremely shaken by the encounter. With Khadija's encouragement, he finally understood that the revelation was legitimate and that he was destined to be the prophet for whom Arabs had been waiting, giving them a series of revelations in their own tongue. Once others had begun to believe in him, these revelations were collected and later organized into the Holy Qur'an.

First, however, the Prophet Muhammad had waited for three years since the revelations started, sharing them only with Khadija, his young cousin 'Ali whom they had taken into their household to help his poor uncle financially, his friend the trader Abu Bakr, and the freed slave Zayd, who had become his devoted foster-son. These people believed in him, but when he was instructed to share the revelations with others, the Qurayshites (people of his tribe) reviled and stoned him and his followers. They denounced him for preaching allegiance to only one God, Allah, rather than to the rest of the deities, worship of whom was not only traditional but profitable for the Qurayshites who ran the pilgrimage places. Eventually Muhammad and his followers—many of them women and slaves—were exiled for three years to a desolate valley where they barely survived, eating wild foods. When they returned to Makkah, they were again persecuted, and when Muhammad was 50 years old, he lost his two strongest supporters, his beloved wife Khadija and his socially respected uncle. However, he was recognized as a prophet by pilgrims from another city which was later renamed Madinah (Medina, "The City of the Prophet"). At their invitation, Muhammad and his small band of followers secretly migrated to Madinah in 622 CE.

There the Prophet prepared a model constitution for the city and helped the citizens ward off attacks by Makkans, with what seemed to be miraculous help. In 630 he returned triumphantly to Makkah, with so many followers that the city offered no resistance. Muhammad showed his gentle nature by forgiving his opponents, in contrast to the previous tribal customs of revenge. From Madinah, his

BIOGRAPHY Khadija

Khadija bint Khuwaylid is revered by Muslims as a perfect examplar of womanhood, as Mother of Believers, and as the Best of Women (*khair un nisa*). She was a successful merchant from the powerful clan of Asad. She had been twice married and widowed. The state of widowhood not being desirable in her culture, she sought a new husband and made her independent choice of Muhammad, many years her junior. She had hired him to deliver her merchandise to Syria and was impressed by his qualities. According to *Hadith*, she told him, "I like you because of our relationship, and your high reputation among your people, your trustworthiness, and good character and truthfulness."[3]

Khadija and the Prophet apparently had an exceptionally close and monogamous marriage for 25 years until her death in approximately 619 CE. Not only did she bear him six children (four daughters plus two sons who died in infancy), but she was his spiritual supporter and advisor. When Muhammad returned deeply shaken from his visitation by the angel, it was Khadija to whom he turned for shelter. "Cover me! Cover me!" he cried, and she cradled him in her arms, wrapping him in his cloak and soothing his terror. This is said to have happened repeatedly after his intense visionary experiences on the mountain.

After the first such terrifying experience, it was Khadija who reassured Muhammad that he was not being possessed by a *jinn* (a low-level spirit), because Allah would not allow a person of such high moral character to be psychically attacked. She took him to her learned Christian cousin, who declared that Muhammad had been visited by a great angel and that he was the prophet of his people.

Khadija was with the Prophet during all the difficult first years of his mission, and

8.1 A rare photo of Khadija's Tomb in Saudi Arabia, now destroyed

was one of his few staunch believers. She prayed with him in secret. After her death, he always continued to praise her, much to the distress of his later wives. He is said to have defended Khadija's memory before his jealous young wife 'A'isha by saying, "Allah has not replaced her with a better. She believed in me when I was rejected. When they called me a liar, she proclaimed me truthful. When I was poor, she shared with me her wealth and Allah granted her children though withholding those of other women."[4]

A special tomb was built near the Prophet's mosque in Khadija's honor, but it was torn down during the early years of the rather anti-female Saudi Arabian government and now all that remains is a few stones.

spiritual and political center, he undertook campaigns to spread Islam, using its ideals of universal brotherhood to unite people as a community of the faithful that transcended the old tribal identities. He died in 632 CE, leaving no public declaration of his successor, or **caliph**. Islam continued to spread and took with it, perhaps to a lesser extent than during the life of the Prophet, its ideals of social reform.

Over time, issues of succession ultimately divided Muslims (as followers of Islam are called) into two groups. One, the **Shi'as**, followed the fourth caliph, 'Ali, married to Fatima, the Prophet's only surviving child, and thus the closest male kin to the Prophet, who left no son. 'Ali was the Prophet's cousin. The other major group, the **Sunnis**, did not fully recognize 'Ali's legitimacy and after his death nominated a fifth caliph, who was opposed by 'Ali and Fatima's son Husayn. Husayn was killed along with many of the Prophet's family in an historic battle at Karbala in 680 over his opposition to appointment of the fifth caliph's son as the next caliph. The two groups have never been reunited, for the Shi'as recognize a series of **imams** (leaders), whereas the Sunnis, who are in the majority, consider themselves traditionalists and concentrate on the first four caliphs. Nevertheless, both pay homage to the Five Pillars of Islam: 1. profession of belief in the absolute oneness of Allah (God) and the prophethood of Muhammad; 2. prayers five times a day in which men stand shoulder to shoulder, with no distinctions among themselves, and women may stand in back or behind a curtain to avoid distracting the men, or else be excused from prayers because of their duties at home; 3. wealth-sharing; 4. fasting during the month of Ramadan, when the first revelation of the Holy Qur'an occurred; and 5. pilgrimage to Makkah at least once during a lifetime. Both also revere the Holy Qur'an, which upholds ideals of social justice and remembrance of the greatness of God, by whose mercy and power everything is created.

The Prophet himself is revered by both and held up as the most noble model of the practice of Islam, which means "peace" and "surrender" to Allah. He seems to have been very fond of women and children and to have treated them with considerable gentleness. He is often quoted as having said, "God has made dear to me from your world women and fragrance, and the joy of my eyes is in prayer."[5] After his 25-year monogamous relationship with his beloved Khadija, he took a number of wives. One was 'A'isha, the young daughter of his good friend Abu Bakr. She had the distinction of being the only virgin whom he married—female virginity being considered a special prize. The others were widows, divorcees, or former slaves. Like Khadija, they were also called "Mother of Believers."

The Prophet often referred to 'A'isha's scholarship and deep knowledge of Islam. Whereas 'A'isha was apparently a great favorite with the Prophet and had a cheering effect on him, she is also known to have been very jealous of her predecessor Khadija, whom the Prophet continued to praise. 'A'isha was accused of adultery when she was 14, but the accusations have never been fully proven true or false. 'A'isha was the only one of the Prophet's wives to accompany him to a particular battle. Somehow she got left behind when the Prophet's retinue returned; accompanied by a young Muslim man who led her on his camel, she did not catch up with the party until the next day. According to her own recorded version of what happened, the Prophet only halted temporarily for part of the night and then proceeded to Makkah. In the interim, 'A'isha went outside to relieve herself and in the process happened to lose her necklace. While she was searching for it, the troops began to leave, and assuming she was inside her covered litter as was appropriate for the wives of the Prophet, put it on her camel and departed without her. She wrapped herself in her cloak and waited for someone to come back for her. One young man who had been traveling behind the entourage found her and, recognizing her, placed her on his own camel. She claimed she did not speak to him, much less become involved with him in any other way. Nevertheless, people began spreading rumors about her and her rescuer. The resulting scandal threatened the unity between rival tribes who had both accepted Islam. Thus 'Ali reportedly advised the Prophet that there were many women available and one could easily be replaced by another; he also suggested questioning her maidservant who, even after 'Ali beat her, had nothing bad to say about 'A'isha. In that culture, a woman's chastity was considered so important that 'Ali was suggesting to the Prophet that he repudiate his favorite wife even on unproved suspicion of infidelity. The serious dilemma was more or less resolved by a revelation that came to the Prophet and became part of the Qur'an, refuting those who spread lies.

'A'isha was widowed at the age of 18 when the Prophet died, choosing her house as the place of his passing; he was buried under her living room floor. Like other widows of the Prophet, 'A'isha was forbidden by the Qur'an to remarry. She became a major source of stories about him which were ultimately compiled as the *Hadith* and thus served as examples for Muslims to follow. Although Muhammad had a policy of treating each of his wives equally, visiting them turn by turn, special privileges were accorded to 'A'isha which gave her intimate awareness of his personal life. She claimed to have performed her ablutions from the same vessel as the Prophet and to have seen him praying, signs indicating that she herself was ritually pure. She also claimed the special honor of having been present when he received a revelation.

Surviving the Prophet by almost 50 years, 'A'isha remained a central figure in the Muslim community. Her political involvement included an aborted attempt to avenge the death of the third caliph by fighting against 'Ali, who became the fourth caliph. Along with two male conspirators, she went into battle in the first Islamic civil war, riding in a closed litter upon a camel. Before Islam, Arab men had often brought their women into battle to spur their troops to fight harder in order to defend them. The same thing happened: 'A'isha's supporters fought to the death because she was there; both of her co-conspirators were killed and her troops were decisively defeated by 'Ali. Thereafter, Shi'as condemned her for bearing dangerous personal grudges against their beloved 'Ali; Sunnis tried to place the blame for the military action on the men but nonetheless noted that according to the Qur'an she should have remained in her proper place at home. Either way, the "Battle of the Camel" contributed to Muslim males' conviction that women were a threat to political order within the Muslim community.

The third major woman in the Prophet Muhammad's life was his daughter Fatima. She is particularly revered by Sh'ia Muslims, for the Prophet had her married to his cousin 'Ali, from whom Sh'ias trace their tradition and their intimate link with the Prophet's family. Fatima had to suffer the vicious attacks against her father when they lived in Makkah, and accompanied him into the difficult three-year exile, cut off from food and contact with others by the Qurayshites. After Khadija's death, Fatima was a great support to her father. She shared his ascetic and compassionate nature, caring nothing for luxury and giving from her own meager resources to those in need. She and her husband 'Ali barely eked out a living, he by carrying water and she by grinding corn with work-blistered hands. Fatima was a persuasive orator, like her father; when she spoke, her sincerity often made people weep. She was the longest-lived of the Prophet's daughters, all of whom died young, but even then she outlived her noble father by only six months. Still, she insured the continuation of his lineage by having two sons. The Prophet had a particularly affectionate and close relationship with her. When 'Ali asked to take a second wife, Muhammad refused his request—even though he himself had multiple wives—to spare the feelings of Fatima. Her legacy for Muslims is defined by her marriage, motherhood, virtuousness, altruism, and life of poverty. The Prophet reportedly paid her the further honor of telling her on his deathbed that she would soon follow him and become the leader of women in heaven, except for Mariam (Mary, mother of Jesus, who is described with great respect in the Holy Qur'an), to whom she is often likened as a prime exemplar of saintly womanhood. She was given many reverent labels, such as "The Radiant One," "The Virgin," "The Chaste," and "One to whom angels speak." A special mosque was built for her near the Prophet's Mosque in Madinah during the Prophet's time—an extraordinary indication of her importance in the eyes of her father—but it was torn down by the Saudi authorities in 1977–1978 in order to enlarge the Prophet's Mosque, and has never been rebuilt. Another mosque dedicated to her half a mile away, at the place where she led the Muslim women in prayer during a battle, has also been destroyed without explanation or rebuilding.

Increasing Seclusion and Veiling of Women

When the Muslim community was established in Madinah, women apparently were fully engaged along with men in prayers and worship, as public mixing of the sexes was customary at the time. According to one *Hadith*, the Prophet said, "Do not prevent the handmaidens of God from entering the places in which He is worshiped."[6] During the Prophet's time, nothing separated men from women in the mosques except that the women stood in lines behind the men for their prayers. 'A'isha and other female contemporaries of the Prophet used to discuss theological issues with him and his companions. Women's outward involvement in Islamic spirituality continued for some time after the Prophet's death. His great-granddaughter Sayyida Nafisa, for instance, was famous in Cairo for her asceticism, piety, and miracles, and Imam Shafi'i, founder of one of the orthodox schools of law, reportedly used to say his prayers with her.

Nevertheless, in those relatively lawless times in which tribal wars and attacks on Muslims were common, the Prophet seems to have been concerned about preserving the safety of women. The Qur'an allowed men to take up to four widows as wives, for their protection and the protection of their orphaned children, since many husbands and fathers were losing their lives in battle. The Holy Qur'an also advised both men and women to dress modestly and not to stare at each other. In addition, the Prophet's wives and daughters and female believers were advised "that they should not display their adornment except what appears thereof. And let them wear their head-coverings over their bosoms" (Sura 24: 31). When they went out, they were "to let down upon themselves their over-garments. This is more proper, so that they may be known, and not be given trouble" (Sura 33: 59). Following *Hadith*, "what appears thereof" is usually construed to mean the face and hands. In Madinah of the Prophet's time, some men were reportedly molesting Muslim women with the excuse that they thought them prostitutes. Fully covering the body allowed women to transact their affairs without being bothered. The Prophet's wives, "Mothers of Believers," were to be treated especially respectfully, so men were told to speak to them from behind a screen. The implication in such warnings was that men could not be trusted to respect women's chastity; it was not that women were being punished and oppressed.

Veiling of women did not exist among the Arab tribes except for the women in wealthy and powerful families. It was, however, customary in nearby countries such as Persia (Iran), Syria, and Iraq. As Islam spread and became more rigidly defined by theologians after its second century, this custom was imposed on many urban and upper-class Muslim women. In contrast to the mixing of sexes in the Prophet's time, these women became strictly segregated from men except for family members, in enclosed harems. The wives and their children typically lived in a walled compound of rooms arranged around a central courtyard. The enclosed home became not only their special sphere but their only sphere of activity; bread-earning and outer social contacts were the responsibility of men and servants, although in some cultures upper-class women managed the family property as well as the household. There were variations on this pattern, in which women occasionally moved outside the home with their clothes and their whole bodies and hair covered with a *burqa* or *chador* (fig. 8.2). Their faces might be covered by a woven screen or even a mask with only slits for the eyes. Such costumes were like personal tents that allowed them to move in public spaces and to see others without being seen.

Western women view such veiling as an extreme form of oppression, and indeed the veiling and seclusion of women is often a prime objective of Islamization, as we will see later. Muslim-majority countries that had become rather Westernized, with freer dress styles, have in many cases returned to **hijab** (veiling) for women as part of the reassertion of their traditional culture. Where conservative views prevail, *hijab* allows women to take jobs outside their homes when they need an income, or to seek higher education. It is also a way of helping women to cope with a difficult situation: the unfettered lust of some men. Many Muslim women say they do not like men's wanton stares and advances and prefer making themselves publicly

8.2 Muslim women's veils take many forms, such as this mask worn by a woman in Dubai

invisible, reserving their "adornments" only for their husbands. Nevertheless, life inside a heavy black *burqa* can be very hot in summer; women who have some personal choice in the matter may wear one of thinner material.

In some areas, Muslim women wear non-revealing garments such as a long skirt and a headscarf, or the *salwar kameez* of Pakistan and India—a long tunic over loose pants, covering a woman from wrists or elbows to ankles. Such clothing is comfortable and beautiful as well as modest and has therefore been adopted by many women of other religions—such as Hindus and Sikhs—as well.

Feminist Reading of the Holy Qur'an

The foundation of Islam is the Holy Qur'an. Much current scholarship is focusing on the disparities between the revelations in the Qur'an, the collections of *Hadith*, and the decisions of the different legal schools (to be examined later), some of which can be seen as culturally influenced and anti-female. Since the Qur'an is the most authoritative source in Islam, and since it takes a more pro-female approach, this may be a useful way of restoring women's rights and status.

Islamic Studies Professor Riffat Hassan, formerly of Pakistan, has been a pioneer in feminist theology in the context of the Islamic tradition since 1974. By careful and thorough reading of the Holy Qur'an (see box, p. 244), she discerns clear support for women's rights to be respected as a human being, to be treated with justice and equity, to be free of traditionalism, authoritarianism, tribalism, classism, casteism, sexism, and slavery, to have privacy and protection from ridicule, to acquire knowledge, to work, to earn, and to own property, to have a secure place of residence, to leave one's place of origin under oppressive conditions, to develop one's aesthetic sensibilities, and to enjoy the "good life," which is possible only in a just society.[7] These rights comprise a powerful basis for a radically different world order, not to mention improvement of women's position within it.

Negative ideas about women that have no base in the Qur'an have apparently become part of Muslim thinking by assimilation from surrounding cultures, including Judeo-Christian tradition. Women are assumed to be legendarily inferior to men, secondarily created, and naturally "crooked." By contrast, the Qur'an speaks of the creation of humanity in surprisingly biologically accurate language:

> The human being We did create
> From a quintessence;
> Then We placed him
> As sperm
> In a place of rest,
> Firmly fixed;
> Then We made the sperm
> Into a clot of congealed blood;
> Then of that clot We made
> A lump; then We
> Made out of that lump

EXCERPT Human Liberation is Supported by
the Holy Qur'an
Riffat Hassan

Liberating ideas lie at the heart of most enduring faiths, and Islam shares in these. Two themes particularly strike me as being of the highest importance. The first is the fundamental equality of humans before God. The other is religion's revolutionary aim of human liberation. From religion should come freedom to seek understanding of the will of God and life's purpose, and freedom to honor God's creation through self-development and striving toward God's ends.... .

While Muslim women continuously hear the refrain that Islam has given women more rights than any other religious tradition, they continue to be subjected to grossly unequal treatment.... . The dominant, patriarchal interpretations of Islam have fostered the myth of women's inferiority in several ways. They have used sayings attributed to the Prophet Muhammad (including disputed sayings) to undermine the intent and teachings of the Qur'an, which Muslims regard as the Word of God. They have taken Qur'anic verses out of context and read them literally, ignoring the fact that the Qur'an often uses symbolic language to portray deep truths. And they have failed to account for the overriding ethical values of the Qur'an, which stresses that human beings—women as well as men—have been designated to be God's "khalifah" (vicegerent) on earth and to establish a social order characterized by justice and compassion.... .

It is clear to me that, according to the perspective of the Qur'an, women and men are equal, and that women are entitled to an equal opportunity along with men for the actualization of their human potentialities. In fact, because of its protective attitude toward all downtrodden and oppressed classes, the Qur'an is particularly concerned about safeguarding the rights of women, and much Qur'anic legislation is designed to ensure that women are treated with justice in the home and in society.

The Qur'an holds before us a sublime vision of our human potential, our destiny, and our relationship with God. Its vision of human destiny is apparent in the exalted proclamation: "Towards God is thy limit" (Surah 53: An-Najm: 42). With this attitude, the Qur'an seeks to liberate all persons so that we may realize our potential fully. If all Muslims were to pursue the values of the Qur'an, they would create a Paradise of justice and peace on earth.

The means and ends of human liberation are foundational themes of the Qur'an: justice and the duty to strive for it, compassion for all things, the need to strive continuously for the cause of God ("Jihad fisabil Allah"). The most important form of "jihad" for contemporary Muslims is "ijtihad," or the exercise of rational judgment to understand the essential message of the Qur'an and to apply it to particular circumstances. Central to this message is an ethic of responsibility for our lives, for nature, and for the elimination of all inequities and injustices from human society. According to the Qur'an, justice is a precondition for peace: without justice—between men and women, as between classes and between nations—there can be no peace in the world.

Indeed, a large part of the Qur'an's concern is to free human beings from the chains that bind them—above all, authoritarianism and the blind following of tradition. "Let there be no compulsion in religion," says the Qur'an (Surah 2: Al-Baqarah: 256). God tells the Prophet Muhammad, "We made thee not one to watch over [others'] doings, nor art thou set over them to dispose of their affairs" (Surah 6: Al-An'am: 107). The greatest guarantee of personal freedom lies in the Qur'anic decrees that no one but God can limit human freedom (Surah 42: Ash-Shura: 21) and that "Judgment is Allah's alone" (Surah 12: Yusuf: 40)... .

Our right to freedom includes the freedom to tell the truth, as one sees it. Without this, other freedoms are a charade and a just society is impossible. According to the Qur'an, truth is one of God's most important attributes, and the Qur'an emphasizes that standing up for the truth is a right and a responsibility that no Muslim may disclaim, no matter how hard the truth may be to tell (Surah 4: An-Nisa': 135). Further, the Qur'an forbids others to harm those who testify to the truth (Surah 2: Al-Baqarah: 282).

The right to freedom of thought and expression was exercised by Muslims in the early centuries of Islam and was pivotal in the creation of an Islamic civilization characterized by outstanding achievements in diverse fields of knowledge. The early Muslims celebrated cultural diversity and engaged in rigorous intellectual discussion... .

Centered in God and self-critical, the original Muslims believed that although God had given them the Qur'an and the Prophet had exemplified its teachings, it was their responsibility to implement its message in the "Islamic" societies that they were creating. These Muslims read the Qur'an as an "open," rather than a "closed," text and strove continually to understand its deeper meaning. This intellectual striving (*ijtihad*) ... made the Muslims of the first three centuries dynamic and creative peoples who paved the way for the European Renaissance.

It is a profound tragedy and irony that today's Muslims, in large numbers, regard Islam in monolithic terms and regard the **Shari'a** [the code regulating all aspects of a Muslim's life] as fixed. In much of the contemporary Muslim world, we see the substitution of traditionalism for the exercise of *ijtihad*—even a denial of the right of *ijtihad*.

To me, being a Muslim means renewing the cry of the modernists, "Back to the Qur'an and forward with *ijtihad*." ... The Qur'an strongly guarantees all fundamental human rights, without reserving them to men alone. These rights are so deeply rooted in our humanness that their denial or violation is tantamount to a negation or degradation of that which makes us human. These rights came into existence with us, so that we might actualize our human potential. These rights not only provide us with the opportunity to develop all of our inner resources, but they also hold before us a vision of what God would like us to be, what God deems to be worth striving for.

Excerpted from Riffat Hassan, "Members, One of Another: Gender Equality and Justice in Islam," The Religious Consultation on Population, Reproductive Health & Ethics, http://www.religiousconsultation.org/hassan.htm, accessed March 1, 2006.

Bones and clothed the bones
With flesh; then We developed
Out of it another creature.
So blessed be Allah,
The Best to create![8]

Elsewhere, the Qur'an describes Adam, appointed as *khalifah* or vicegerent (one who exercises delegated power) of the earth, and his mate as involved in a collective act of disobedience but also of free choice. After being deceitfully tempted by Satan to transgress the limits set by God, they apologetically admit, "Our Lord, we have wronged our own souls" (7: 23). There is no special blame placed on the woman, nor does she have any separate conversation with the serpent representing Satan. But Muslim folk tradition names Hawwa (Eve), presents her as an eternally flawed secondary creation from the crooked rib of Adam, created for rather than with him, blames her for the fall of humanity, and tends to regard all "daughters of Eve" with suspicion and even hatred. These misogynistic non-Qur'anic ideas have fully penetrated the *Hadith* literature. Both al-Bukhari and Muslim al-Hillaj report various versions of a saying attributed to the Prophet Muhammad, on the authority of a companion called Abu Huraira. One version runs like this: "Woman has been created from a rib and will in no way be straightened for you; so benefit by her while crookedness remains in her."[9]

In contrast to the misogyny that has crept into popular Muslim beliefs, the Qur'an clearly safeguards women's rights to respect and security. If a woman is suspected of sexual relations outside marriage, the Qur'an provides that she cannot be considered guilty unless there are four witnesses to her immoral behavior (4: 15).

According to the Qur'an, all of humanity is created in the "best of molds" (95: 4), for the purpose of serving God. All humans are given the same call to righteousness and the same promise of heavenly reward:

The Believers, men
And women, are protectors,
One of another: they enjoin
What is just, and forbid
What is evil: they observe
Regular prayers, pay
Zakat [charity] and obey
Allah and His Messenger.
On them will Allah pour
His mercy: for Allah
Is exalted in power, Wise.
Allah hath promised to Believers,
Men and women, Gardens
Under which rivers flow,
To dwell therein,
And beautiful mansions
In Gardens of everlasting stay.
But the greatest bliss
Is the Good Pleasure of Allah: that is the supreme triumph.[10]

The Qur'an does make some provision for chastisement of disobedient wives by their husbands. The basic passage from the Holy Qur'an in this regard is:

> Men are the protectors
> And maintainers of women,
> Because Allah has given
> The one more [strength]
> Than the other, and because
> They support them
> From their means.
> Therefore the righteous women
> Are devoutly obedient, and guard
> In [the husband's] absence
> What Allah would have them guard.
> As to those women
> On whose part ye fear
> Disloyalty and ill-conduct,
> Admonish them [first],
> [Next] refuse to share their beds,
> [And last] beat them [lightly];
> But if they return to obedience,
> Seek not against them
> Means [of annoyance]:
> For Allah is Most High,
> Great.[11]

In the past, the Holy Qur'an was interpreted primarily by men, but some female scholars have now begun to dig into its meanings from a woman's point of view. Carefully considering the interpretations of specific words, cultural contexts, and overall intentions of the revelations, Islamic Studies Professor Amina Wadud concludes that the scripture does not make any distinction between women and men in terms of spiritual potential, that woman is not considered just a child-bearer, that no explicit division of labor is specified, that marriage is not meant as a means of oppression of women, and that the social reforms started in the Holy Qur'an are meant to be extended in ever-evolving, changing circumstances. A sample of her exegesis is given here (see box, p. 248), with particular reference to Surah 4: 34, cited above, which has been used to excuse wife-beating.

Laws Concerning Women

The laws that shape Muslim women's personal lives are usually based partly on the revelations of the Holy Qur'an, the **Sunnah** (example of the Prophet), *Hadith* (sayings of the Prophet), traditional jurisprudence, schools of law, and *Shari'a*, and partly on the secular laws of the many countries and cultures in which Muslims live. Even the religious sources have not yielded a unified body of laws. There are

EXCERPT Wives and Qur'an
Amina Wadud

[For cases in which the husband chastises the wife] it cannot be overlooked that verse 4: 34 does state the third suggestion using the word *daraba*, "to strike." According to *Lisan al-'Arab* and *Lane's Lexicon, daraba* does not necessarily indicate force or violence. It is used in the Qur'an, for example, in the phrase "daraba Allah mathalan…" ("Allah gives or sets an example…"). It is also used when someone leaves, or "strikes out" on a journey.

It is, however, strongly contrasted to the second form, the intensive, of this verb—*darraba*: to strike repeatedly or intensely. In the light of the excessive violence towards women indicated in the biographies of the Companions and by practices condemned in the Qur'an (like female infanticide), this verse should be taken as prohibiting unchecked violence against females. Thus, this is not permission, but a severe restriction of existing practices… .

The Qur'an never orders a woman to obey her husband. It never states that obedience to their husbands is a characteristic of the "better women" (66: 5), nor is it a prerequisite for women to enter the community of Islam (60: 12). However, in marriages of subjugation, wives did obey their husbands, usually because they believed that a husband who materially maintains his family, including the wife, deserves to be obeyed. Even in such cases, the norm at the time of the revelation, no correlation is made that a husband should beat his wife into obedience. Such an interpretation has no universal potential, and contradicts the essence of the Qur'an and the established practices of the Prophet. It involves a severe misreading of the Qur'an to support the lack of self-constraint in some men… .

This belief in the need to obey the husband is a remnant of marriages of subjugation and is not exclusive to Muslim history. It has not progressed, although today couples seek partners for mutual emotional, intellectual, economic, and spiritual enhancement. Their compatibility is based on mutual respect and honor, not on the subservience of the female to the male. The family is seen as a unit of mutual support and social propriety, not an institution to enslave a woman to the man who buys her at the highest price and then sustains her material and physical needs only, with no concern for the higher aspects of human development.

If the Qur'an was only relevant to this single marriage type, it would fail to present a compatible model to the changing needs and requirements of developing civilizations worldwide. Instead, the Qur'anic text focuses on the marital norm at the time of revelation, and applies constraints on the actions of the husbands with regard to wives. In the broader context, it develops a mechanism for resolving difficulties through mutual or extended consultation and arbitration.

In conclusion, the Qur'an prefers that men and women marry (4: 25). Within marriage, there should be harmony (4: 128) mutually built with love and mercy (30: 21). The marriage tie is considered a protection for both the male and the female: "They (feminine plural) are raiment for you (masculine plural) and you are raiment for them" (2: 187). However, the Qur'an does not rule out the possibility of difficulty, which it suggests can be resolved. If all else fails, it also permits equitable divorce… .

The continued change which the Qur'an put into motion was not meant to stop when the revelation was completed. Some important social changes not completely instituted by the end revelation (like the total abolition of slavery), were given enough clear indications of the direction that the Qur'an intended. It therefore seems unbelievable that it was only so many centuries after the revelation that they were implemented.

In addition, by extending certain Qur'anic social principles, Muslim communities should have evolved into leading examples of humane and just social systems. Certainly, the Qur'an never intended for institutions like slavery to continue even though it never explicitly prohibited it. There are unlimited possibilities for reform within the parameters of equity, mutual honour, respect, and consultation enunciated by the Qur'an.

Thus I have extended the Qur'anic principles of social justice, equity, mutual honour and moral responsibility, into the context of the present era and at least given some thought to the evolution of those principles in the future. My specific goal was to demonstrate the adaptability of the Qur'anic world-view to the issues and concerns of women in the modern context. If the attitudes of women and men towards each other had not progressed in the last 1,400 years, we would be in a pitiful state… .

The Qur'an encourages men and women to marry as a safeguard of moral behaviour between the sexes. However, some interpretations of the rights and responsibilities between the married couple have so severely restricted woman that marriage becomes an institution of oppression for her. If marriage is the means by which a woman is stripped of her individuality and her self-respect as a human equal in humanity and in spiritual capacity to any man, then this is clearly against the Qur'anic intent for a just and moral social order that encourages the doing of good and forbids the doing of evil. It is necessary to resolve this flaw of interpretation.

Excerpted from Amina Wadud, *Qur'an and Woman: Rereading the Sacred Text from a Woman's Perspective*, New York: Oxford University Press, 1999, pp. 76–8, 101–3.

different collections of the *Sunnah* and *Hadith*; the most respected of these are by Muhammad ibn Isma'il al-Bukhari (810–870) and Muslim bin al-Hallaj (817–875), but even some of their records are probably inauthentic, rooted in prevailing cultural ideas about women. There are also various schools of law and varied interpretations of the Qur'an, all made primarily by men. These laws pertaining to women cannot therefore be seen as absolute, but they have nonetheless been a major focus of attempts to define and impose a Muslim way of life. Within the law codes, those relating to women are the most salient: those concerning marriage, divorce, ownership and inheritance of property, and seclusion and veiling.

In Muslim tradition, the family is an essential social unit. Marriage is treated as mandatory, with few exceptions. According to *Hadith*, the Prophet forbade his followers to be celibate, and also apparently forbade the previous traditions of temporary marriages and extramarital sexual relations. Only one revelation concerning polygamy occurred in the Qur'an. Within the context of frequent battles and a resulting surfeit of widows and fatherless children, men are addressed thus:

> If ye fear that ye shall not
> Be able to deal justly
> With the orphans,
> Marry women of your choice,
> Two, or three, or four;
> But if ye fear that ye shall not
> Be able to deal justly [with them],
> Then only one, or
> That which your right hands possess.
> That will be more suitable,
> To prevent you
> From doing injustice.[12]

The point was the protection of orphans; widows were included so that the rights of the orphans could be protected. Marriage of several wives was not for the sake of male lust.

Women were allowed only one husband. Muslim men could marry Muslim women or other "People of the Book"—generally interpreted as believing Christians or Jews. There was no express permission for a Muslim woman to marry a non-Muslim man. According to the traditions, the man should look at a woman before proposing to her, to be sure that the match will be satisfying. Nothing is said about a woman's looking at a man, but sometimes the marriage proposal is made by the woman, as in the case of Khadija and the Prophet Muhammad. Marriage requires public expression of mutual consent to the marriage as a contract; for a woman, consent is usually given on her behalf by her father or another male guardian. The man is required to offer a dowry to his wife, and thenceforth that property belongs to her. According to the traditions, sometimes when a man was very poor, he gave his bride only an iron ring or two handfuls of meal or dates as dowry, but in general the dowries have been more substantial. Progressive Muslim scholar Kecia Ali suggests that early Sunni Muslim jurists regarded the dowry and financial support by the husband as an exchange for the wife's sexuality, which thus became his possession—an interpretation at odds with the Qur'anic ideals of mutuality, kindness, harmony, and respect within the marriage, instead drawing analogies from cultural laws governing slavery.

Be this as it may, the couple have the right to interpret their marriage agreement in their own terms. Any contractual agreement may be made that is not contrary to Islam. For instance, the wife can specify that she may not be forced to leave the home, that her husband cannot take a second wife, that he will give her a specified allowance, that he cannot prevent her relatives from visiting her, or that she can divorce him for specified reasons.

According to the traditions attributed to the Prophet, marriage involves mutual responsibilities. The wife's traditional sphere is the household, where she is to take primary responsibility for raising the children and managing domestic affairs. It is the husband's responsibility to earn money to support the family. According to sources of Muslim law, the wife must be available to her husband, preserve his property from waste or loss, and avoid doing anything that would disturb the harmony of the household. She is not obliged to cook the food, clean the house, or serve her husband, for she is to be a companion to him, not his slave. Husband and wife are always supposed to be ready to help each other. It is said that the Prophet used to help his wives with domestic chores such as washing the dishes, mending his clothes and his shoes, and milking the goats.

Despite this balanced view of mutual responsibilities, there is widespread belief that when the Prophet's followers asked him if they could bow before him, he refused, but added, "It is not lawful for anyone to prostrate to anyone. But if I would have ordered any person to prostrate to another, I would have commanded wives to prostrate to their husbands." This supposed pronouncement is recorded with many variations, but according to feminist scholar Riffat Hassan, "This *Hadith* is inauthentic and in clear violation of the Qur'an's strict monotheism."[13]

There are many Qur'anic injunctions to men to treat their wives kindly. And in his farewell address, the Prophet is said to have stressed, "O my people! You have certain rights over your wives and so have your wives over you.... . They are the trust of Allah in your hands. So you must treat them with all kindness."[14]

All schools of Islamic law give women the unusual right to financial compensation if they are physically harmed by sexual intercourse. This applies even to marital intercourse, according to some schools of law. When the damage occurs from intercourse to which the woman did not agree, the man has to pay an amount equal to that given as compensation for murder. Given the stigma attached to women who have sex outside marriage, whether by choice or forced, many contemporary Pakistani women consider suicide the best solution to their miserable social condition if they are raped. Therefore, being compensated as if they had been murdered is appropriate.

As we saw earlier, seclusion and veiling of women are practices that have developed within Islamic societies, but are not matters of uniform Islamic law. In fact, women are prohibited from veiling when they are on pilgrimage to Mecca, for the pilgrimage is ruled by principles of social equality, whereas the veil is sometimes associated with higher rank. Nevertheless, in many conservative Muslim societies, when women leave their household, they are expected to wear overgarments—such as the *burqa*—to protect their modesty. This custom is highly variable and has different meanings in different situations. For instance, during the 1979 revolution against the Shah of Iran, many middle-class women covered themselves as a protest against the Shah's introduction of Westernizing tendencies. Afterwards they were forced by the post-revolutionary government to wear *hijab*, which was quite different from wearing it by their own free choice as a political statement. In some societies, women think God has ordered them to cover themselves, so they do so in order to be obedient to God's will. Some educated feminists and professional women wear *hijab* as a protest against capitalism and consumerism, against efforts to enhance their sex appeal and to keep up with the latest fashions. *Hijab* is law in conservative Saudi Arabia, but not in the more liberal neighboring Gulf states.

The Holy Qur'an, tradition, and jurisprudence all support the right of a woman to seek divorce from her husband. Surah 2: 227–240 describes the divorce process in great detail with an emphasis on intelligent and just behavior to prevent misuse of the provision for divorce. Women are clearly given the same rights as men: "Women shall have rights similar to the rights against them, according to what is equitable" (Surah 2: 228), and both husband and wife must wait for three months after declaring their intention to divorce, to make sure there is no pregnancy. A woman is allowed to end the marriage if her husband is missing, but the schools of law vary as to how long she must wait for him to return. The extreme case is the dictate of the Hanafi school that she must wait 100 to 120 years. Other sources of legal tradition specify four to seven years, or even only one year, if the husband is lost in battle.

Husbands can divorce their wives, but the facility to do so is tempered by Qur'anic injunctions about treating wives kindly and by the rule that both husband and wife must be represented by arbiters whose job it is to try to reconcile the two parties. They must wait three months, still living in the same house together unless one has committed some misconduct. The man must three times pronounce his intention to divorce, preferably with some waiting period in between. After the second pronouncement, the husband and wife must make the final decision whether to remain together forever or part forever. However, despite the attempts of the Prophet and Holy Qur'an to provide avenues for retracting the divorce pronouncement and reconciling husband and wife, Muslim men sometimes revert to the pre-Islamic practice of pronouncing the dreaded divorce statement three times at once—"*Talaq! Talaq! Talaq!*"—thus making the divorce irrevocable.

Varied Cultural Settings of Islam Today

Islam is a global brother/sisterhood that crosses all cultural boundaries and includes some of the world's richest and poorest regions. The ideals set forth in the Holy Qur'an and the *Hadith* of the Prophet Muhammad are universally foundational for all Muslims. Yet they have developed their faith within very different cultural contexts, and these cultural factors have always had a major effect on women's status.

In some 44 countries, Muslims form a majority of the population. These countries form a band stretching from west to east of the original home of Islam, now in Saudi Arabia—from northern Africa through West Asia, Arabic and Gulf states, former states of the southern Soviet Union that are now independent republics, to Afghanistan, Pakistan, and Bangladesh, Malaysia and Indonesia. Other areas also have considerable Muslim minorities, such as India, with 120 million Muslims, sub-Saharan Africa, where Islam is growing rapidly, and China, where there may be 40 million Muslims.

Islam has taken hold in the West, with five to six million Muslims living in Europe and seven to eight million in the United States. In the midst of these multi-cultural societies, proliferating mosques are increasingly visible indications of vibrant Muslim communities.

Women's experiences in these areas vary tremendously. One of the most religiously conservative Muslim communities exists in Saudi Arabia, home of the Prophet, now populated by a large Sunni majority. Saudi women are not allowed to drive cars or leave home unless a close male relative accompanies them. The legal system follows Muslim law, and only males can vote.

Many Indian Muslim women live amidst a conservative village culture of poverty and female repression. They are expected to observe extensive restrictions, such as those laid down by the highly regarded Muslim scholar Maulana Ashraf 'Ali Thanawi in the first half of the twentieth century. He was part of the Deoband reform movement, which sought to use the *Hadith* to renew a presumably pure Muslim lifestyle; recent movements such as the Taliban of Afghanistan have drawn their rigid ideas about women's subservience and seclusion from the Deobandi school. Thanawi's guidebook for the comportment of respectable women and girls, *Bihishti Zewar* ("Heavenly Ornaments"), is replete with proscriptions such as these:

On the Customs of Noble Ramazan:
An evil custom during Ramazan is that women will summon a *hafiz* [person who recites the Qur'an by heart] inside the house to have him recite the Glorious Qur'an during *tarawih*, the supererogatory night prayers. There is no harm in this if two conditions are met: first, that the *hafiz* is a near relative and is heard only by women of the household itself; and, second, that the *hafiz* himself offers the required **Namaz** [obligatory five daily prayers] in the mosque before coming to the house. Nowadays, it is common to be careless about this. An unrelated *hafiz* is often summoned into the house, and, although there is a curtain before them for name's sake alone, the women, who are quite careless, begin either:

1   to talk with Hafizji or to call out among themselves. Hafizji hears. Since when is it correct to let an unrelated man hear your voice without necessity?
2   Whoever recites the Qur'an makes his voice as beautiful as possible. The melody of some voices is so good that the hearts of the hearers surely incline toward the reader. In this circumstance, how wrong it is for the melody of the voice of an unrelated man to reach the ears of the women!
3   Women of the whole neighborhood gather day after day. First, it is forbidden for women to set their feet outside their house without necessity. This is not a necessity, for the noble *shari'at* does not require the supererogatory prayer to be read in congregation. To go out is bad—and to do so daily is even worse. Coming home is especially dangerous, for it is late at night, and the streets and alleys are empty and deserted. In such a situation, it would not be surprising if, God forbid, a person was robbed or her honor impaired. To put yourself into such difficulties without thinking is against sense and against the noble *shari'at*.[15]

By contrast, Turkey and Egypt have relatively liberal Muslim majorities. Since modern Turkey was founded in 1923, it has adopted extensive Western-style social, legal, and political changes, such as embracing capitalism, adopting Western law, and secularization. Women have even been refused the right to wear headscarves in universities. Nevertheless, men still tend to be dominant in politics and family life.

Egypt developed a close relationship with the West during the twentieth century, and with it a fairly liberal lifestyle. Its late nineteenth- and early twentieth-century struggles for national independence coincided with the growth of a feminist women's movement. Women left their secluded household environments and became founders and managers of many charitable institutions, running social services such as hospitals. Now, however, Islamic fundamentalism is on the rise. The ideal for womanhood in Egypt is someone who is a selfless servant of her family and her country.

In the oil-rich Gulf states, religion tends to take a back seat to economic interests as former Bedouin tribes adopt a luxurious urban lifestyle. Qatar, for instance, has such rich oil and natural gas reserves that its citizens have one of the highest per capita incomes in the world. Some older Muslim women still live rather conservatively, but the younger generations usually do not.

Other patterns are emerging in the Muslim-majority republics of the former Soviet Union—Azerbaijan, Kazakhstan, Kyrgyzstan, and Tajikistan. Muslims there were cut off from their spiritual heritage during the decades of officially atheist Communist rule. Now they are rediscovering Islam, to varying degrees, but the younger generations have not grown up in an explicitly Muslim milieu. Women for the most part wear Western clothing, without any veiling, and freely work outside their homes. Fatima Adipayeva of Kazakhstan (fig. 8.3), a pediatrician and spiritual healer, did not hear anything about Islam in her youth. She recounts:

My father was a high administrator in the Communist Party. We didn't dare to go to religious places because worship was forbidden and the KGB were in all those places. It was only when my father's brother died that I heard him recite prayers in Arabic. Hearing him sing the traditional prayers, I cried. After he retired, I discovered that he knew Arabic and had gone to a kind of Arabic school in Kazakhstan. My grandfather was under the repression of Stalin and was exiled to Irkutsk, where he died in 1942. He was apparently a very educated scholar of Islam. At that time, people tried to hide such matters. My mother always liked her father-in-law. In my childhood she used to read me fairy tales of Kazakhstan. There were no heroic mythical people—only Allah and the Prophet Muhammad.

Even after my mother's death when I was 32, I did not start reading the Qur'an, because I felt that one could only read it if one was spiritually clean.

After practicing pediatrics for some years, I had a stroke and was utterly motionless for eight months. When I left the hospital, the doctor said that I would only live half a year. But my sister had a vision that I would live a long life. My sister and other relatives went to a sacred Muslim place in Turkestan and prayed for me there.

The young people now [in the formerly Communist Muslim-majority countries] are not so keen on religious traditions. It depends on the family. In our family perhaps the calamities gave us a push toward Muslim traditions.[16]

The pattern is similar in areas of the Russian Federation with substantial numbers of people of Muslim background. In the Ural Mountains, Khalila Saburova (fig. 8.3), a doctor practicing in Ufa, meditates twice a day and reads the Holy Qur'an, but she does not try to do the *Namaz* since "that is a strict discipline that must be followed exactly every day." During Soviet times, her family did not teach her anything about Islam. After *perestroika*, she received a Russian translation of the Holy Qur'an and gave a copy to her mother. Upon starting to read it, her mother began to understand that life is full of lessons, so now she regards difficulties philosophically. Her mother introduced the Qur'an to older women in her village, and now they invite her into their homes to read it to them. In a conversation with the imam of her area, Khalila tried to explain to him that *Namaz* is a means of meditation: full concentration on Allah. The imam told her that she is circling around the outside of Islam and should instead enter it. She replied to him, "I am on the inside. It is you people who are on the outside of the circle."[17]

In the United States, Islam is the second largest religion. Two thirds of the Muslims in the country are immigrants (see box, p. 256); one third are converts, mostly of African background. For African-Americans, conversion to Islam is encouraged both as a matter of pride in their origins and as an alternative to the white-dominated materialistic culture. Converts tend to adopt conservative lifestyles and to teach their children spiritual values.

In addition to national cultural differences, Muslim women's lives are affected by their particular version of Islam. Ismaili Muslims, an offshoot of Shi'a Islam, revere a lineage of Aga Khans, imams who have tended to be progressive and social-minded in their thinking and have been instrumental in many development projects for the sake of humanity. In 1952, the then Aga Khan announced that Ismaili women need not be veiled. Ismaili women and men pray together, side by side.

8.3 Muslim women in former Soviet communist countries, such as Khalila Saburova of Russia (*left*) and Fatima Adipayeva of Kazakhstan (*right*), are now rediscovering their roots

INTERVIEW Sana Shariq *A Journey into the Heart*

Sana Shariq Rafq Warsi is a young Muslim poetess of Indian background, from an extended family that tends the shrine of a great Sufi saint revered by people of all religions. She was raised in Saudi Arabia, and has recently moved to the United States with her parents. She explains her multi-cultural spiritual experience:

> With Indian roots, deeply enmeshed in a Sufi spiritual family, I had an ingrained sense of the Divine existence. I had not yet found a name or words to describe it, yet I knew that we were all under the guidance of enlightened blessings. I was born in Madinah and lived there for 12 years before moving to Riyadh. These years in Madinah found me learning the ways of the people by socializing there, and understanding my own spirituality in the short space of summer vacations when I would visit my grandparents' house in Dewa Sharif, India. I would step into India and wonder at this vast populated and larger-than-life country, so immense in its languages and ways.
>
> Dewa Sharif, home of the shrine of Saint Syed Waris Ali Shah, a nineteenth-century saint from the prophet Muhammad's (Peace Be Upon Him) lineage, held yearly fairs which brought a great number of people as they attended and took part in the nightly Qawwali [Sufi music] programs. It was so interesting for me to sit beside my grandfather and cousins and watch those people losing their senses, so absolutely engrossed in the music and the spiritual voltage of the evening. It was not a gathering divided by religion or sect, but united in soul and heart, in the belief of the eternal and sole God.
>
> India was a new land for my mother too, who had been born and brought up in Madinah, though her ancestors came from Agra in India. Madinah was a small city, the focus being the Prophet's mosque. Her family spoke Arabic and Urdu at home. Her life had been a little different from mine. Girls at that time were made to do what was obligatory and necessary, with little regard to personal space as in freedom of choice and option of intellectual exploration. They were rather bound by family duties and what applied and what didn't.
>
> The difference in our lives as women emerged as I stepped on to the stage. While each phase of time had its own uniqueness and individual dignity, as the years went by, the women gained a different social standing altogether in Saudi Arabia. King Faisal's wife established the first university for women. After that, the country took its own pace, and media gained a feminine voice, expressing a different perspective to the local populace.
>
> Islam gives respect and dignity to women, and advocates justice concerning their rights and proper treatment. While people today might due to misperceptions consider Islam as inhuman and confining, it would be an enlightening discovery were one to actually study deeper with a liberal

8.4 Sana Shariq's cultural influences include her Indian relatives, Saudi Arabian upbringing, and recent exposure to life in the United States

mind—to study what Islam has actually been to women and at what time in history it was brought to the people. It was not the scarf or *burqa* that God wanted to incorporate but the respect that had been long due to this gender which was being buried alive after birth, traded like commodity amongst men, tortured and violated. Thus a purer way of life was accorded.

In all my years in Saudi Arabia, I met Syrian, Lebanese, Egyptian and Saudi women, and realized the universal similarity in each of them. Our foods and language may differ, our clothes may not be the same, yet the common denominator was always humanity and spirituality.

I traveled a lot with my family and vacationed in some Arab countries. Last summer we spent in Syria, and it was such a wonderful experience. The people were gracious hosts, and with the added spiritual essence of the place, the beautiful nature, sea and hills, I did not want to return home. I made friends with a girl who had been staying next door and we shared our life stories. She flled me in on a girl's way of life in Syria—how some people discouraged educating their daughters for the fear of an open mind and independent decision-making power, and on the contrary another part of their society totally encouraged the women in their independent life. This contrast proved that we must each distinguish between religion and personal cultural beliefs. Some may incorporate their own views and social beliefs and term it as part of religion; others may exploit the Holy Scriptures with their own defnitions. Islam rather encourages the seekers of knowledge. It supports truth, meaning, all that we seek from the moment we are born until our soul makes the fnal transition to the spiritual realm.

Moving to the United States was another pleasant surprise, an added chapter in my life. My family and I were respectfully and warmly treated, and my brother's American in-laws were the frst people with whom we were personally acquainted and spent time in their company. The feeling was a spontaneous acceptance of each other, acceptance of universal humanity wearing garbs of salwar kameez, scarves, skirts, jeans, T-shirts and dresses, simply a journey into the heart.

Sana Shariq Rafq Warsi, personal communication, November 2005.

Social Issues and Feminist Activism

Throughout the varied cultures that have embraced Islam, there is as yet no possibility that women can hold positions of spiritual authority in mosques. Many are not even allowed to pray in the mosques. In many cultures, women are frequent attendants at saints' shrines, begging for spiritual intervention to solve their family's problems. In some areas, however, women are not even allowed to approach a saint's tomb and can only look at it and make their entreaties through a grille. Muslim women in some cultures sponsor special meals if their prayer requests are answered, and these become important social as well as religious gatherings. Respected older women may hold classes for children in reading of the Holy Qur'an and religious principles. Although they are in a sense religious leaders, they do not wear any special clothing for public display, unlike male religious leaders. Instead of trying to gain positions of religious leadership, Muslim feminist activism is focusing on more basic issues regarding the quality of Muslim women's lives. Their literacy rate on the whole is among the lowest in the world, so many women continue to be trapped in old patterns falsely associated with Islam, unaware that they have any alternatives.

One of the greatest difficulties adding to women's burdens at present is the fact that as some Muslim societies attempt to reject Westernization, whose influences

8.5 Woman praying privately in Kashmir

they see as corrupt, anti-religious, materialistic, and destructive to family stability, women are bearing the brunt of the attempts to establish "pure" Muslim states. In extreme cases of attempted "Islamization"—such as Taliban rule in Afghanistan— women have been forced to leave their jobs, stop driving cars, stop pursuing their education, and stop venturing forth in public unless heavily covered (fig. 8.5). The basic idea is that veiling and confinement of women will help to prevent modern social ills such as promiscuity, divorce, drug and alcohol abuse, and neglect of children. However, according to the research of feminist scholars, this repressive approach is contrary to the respectful attitude toward women advocated in the Qur'an. Riffat Hassan concludes:

> The Qur'an does not discriminate against women. In fact, in view of their disadvantaged and vulnerable condition, it is highly protective of their rights and interests. But this protectiveness does not change the fact that the way Islam has been practiced in most Muslim societies for centuries has left millions of Muslim women with battered bodies, minds, and souls. Lacking any sense of self-worth, self-esteem, or self-confidence, they find it very difficult to resist the pressure put on them by conservative, widely influential Muslims.[18]

Some Muslim women activists are trying to awake women to their rights and help them lead better lives. During the Taliban years, the Revolutionary Association of the Women of Afghanistan worked underground at great personal risk to run secret schools for girls, provide healthcare for women, help rape victims, document the rape, killing, and kidnapping of women by the Northern Alliance militia who were trying to retake the country from the Taliban, get news of the oppression of women out to the rest of the world, and combat fanaticism through aroused public awareness. However, even after the fall of the Taliban, attacks on girls' schools continued. In 2005, Amnesty International reported that Afghani women and girls were still facing violence including rape, physical and mental cruelty, forced marriages, and exchange of girls as a means of settling disputes. When asked how she and other Afghani women had managed to bear all their difficulties and still work for a better future, Habiba Sarabi, the Minister of Women's Affairs, said simply, "We are mothers."[19] She described the terrible social effects of violence:

> I come from a land where under every tree there is a young one who has shed blood, his blood. Let us pray for no more blood to be shed. I come from a land where a newborn child has never seen the face of his father. Let us pray so there are no more orphans born into this world. I come from a land where the children wake up, not to the songs of birds, but to the sound of guns, and where their mothers have been wounded, neglected, and then perished. We pray to God that peace will come on earth and all guns be silenced, not only in my country but all over the world.[20]

As indicated earlier, women's contemporary experiences and issues vary from country to country and also within countries. In ultra-conservative Saudi Arabia, where veiling is mandatory, Elsie Aljarboa, an American woman married to a Saudi husband, reports from Riyadh:

▦ I must wear a black *abaya* no matter how hot it is. *Abayas* are of different materials. Many are silk, which is light but extremely hot in the summer. Others are cotton, or polyester and cotton. The covering of the head is optional. Of course when I am with my husband I must have it on, even though I leave my bangs out. The reason for this is that he will get in trouble if a *motawah* [religious leader] comes by with a stick in his hand and with the police. This is very common in the malls and the grocery store. You can go to jail if you do not follow the rules. I believe it is good to dress modestly. But I do not believe it is correct for someone to beat you and put you in jail because you do not cover your head. In Riyadh, they do not consider other cultures and religions. The only one that is to be followed is the Islamic religion as they practice it. These rules are not easy. But I have managed to follow them the best I can. All this is with God's help.

I depart for Doha, Qatar, today to visit my sister, and can't wait to shed my *abaya* once I get to Doha. In Doha women can drive. *Abayas* are worn by the native Qataris, yet Westerners can wear their normal clothes. They should be conservative, yet if you want to wear a sleeveless dress it is okay.[21] ▦

In Iran some urban women wear *burqas* but yet work outside their homes, hold public office, run their own businesses, study in universities, travel, and mix with men in business settings. This is a new situation, accomplished through pressure from women's human rights groups during and after the repressive Khomeini regime, which within months of taking over the government of Iran in 1979 and establishing the Islamic Republic directed women to veil themselves, dismissed all female judges, prevented females from studying law, science, or technology, allowed men unlimited right to divorce, and forbade public mixing of men and women unless they were close relatives. Shirin Ebadi (fig. 8.6), one of the first female judges of Iran, was forced to resign after the revolution and was often imprisoned thereafter, but she nevertheless continued defending Iranians' legal rights based on new interpretations of Islam. In 2003 she received the Nobel Peace Prize for her courageous activities.

In rural areas, the status of women has been more resistant to political change, for women are a major workforce and their movements cannot be so strictly confined. As they have for centuries, tribal women in Iran dress in colorful clothes, sometimes without veils, are related to most of the men in their villages and thus move freely

8.6 Judge Shirin Ebadi of Iran has steadfastly fought for human rights

among them, do hard physical work outdoors, and have significant social influence, even though they do not hold political or economic power. However, whereas up to 100 percent of women are literate in some urban areas, only about 50 percent are in rural areas, and in any case they cannot read Arabic, the language of the Qur'an. Rural women are too busy working to watch television, which carries religious programs giving messages from the Qur'an and Muslim history, or to attend ceremonies in mosques. The young women who go to high school study the Qur'an and rituals, but when they return to their villages there is little provision for them to worship formally. Rural women are more likely to visit the shrines of saints to ask for divine help. Many regard themselves as sinful, for in the course of their daily work they may gossip, have an argument with a neighbor, curse their children for misbehaving, ignore a baby who is crying, forget to feed the animals, or do something without their husband's permission, such as visiting their own relatives. These are all considered sins. Oppressed with the idea of their own weakness and sinfulness, as well as overwhelmed with problems, many women commit suicide.

Part of Muslim women's burden is the large families they have to care for. Contraception is not widely practiced, except for the withdrawal method ("coitus interruptus"), fairly ineffective but permitted by all five major schools of law in Islam. Family planning programs have not had much effect, partly because many Muslim women are heavily influenced by misogynistic cultures and partly because family planners from outside their cultures fail to understand and grapple with the religious issues involved. Although the Qur'an does not explicitly speak about contraception, Riffat Hassan concludes that the human rights it underlines would make contraception a legitimate option, in the interests of limiting family size and therefore improving the quality of life. Hassan suggests:

> The right to use contraceptives, especially by disadvantaged masses whose lives are scarred by grinding poverty and massive illiteracy, should be seen— in the light of the Qur'anic vision of what an Islamic society should be—as a fundamental human right. This is particularly applicable to Muslim women, who, although more than 500 million in number, are among the most unrepresented, or voiceless, and powerless "minorities" in the world.[22]

Genital mutilation (a topic discussed more fully in Chapter 2) is another issue around which women's rights activists have been pitted against ultra-orthodox Islamists. In Egypt, for instance, the grand sheikh of the great Muslim university al-Azhar ruled that every Muslim woman should be circumcised to curb her sex drive and thus make her virtuous. However, after a lawsuit was launched against him by the Egyptian Organization of Human Rights, the highest court of Egypt in 1997 supported the existing ban on genital cutting of girls and women.

Women have often suffered terribly when their societies are in political turmoil, losing their family members, homes, means of survival, and often being victims of violence themselves. In the midst of social violence in their embattled region, Muslim women in Palestine are seeking to curb domestic violence and honor killings. In the Muslim-minority state of Gujarat, India, the International Initiative for Justice in Gujarat has tried to bring to public awareness the fact that rape of Muslim women was commonly used as a means of intimidation during anti-Muslim riots and massacres in 2002, in which thousands of women, children, and men were murdered. In 2004 the Initiative claimed that this pattern of using rape as a political weapon was still continuing, with the complicity of the police and state government.

The aftermath of September 11 has created tremendous suffering for Muslim women and men in many parts of the world. Not only governments but also individuals are responding with ignorance and hatred because of fear of terrorist attacks. Women in Iraq have seen many of their loved ones killed or wounded. Nations that are retaliating against those behind September 11 have seen a great increase in anti-Muslim feelings. Professor Sharifa Alkhateeb, President of the North American Council for Muslim Women, reports:

> I have been spat upon and told to go home, right in downtown Washington, along with thousands of other Muslim women. And people at airports take their children and move them away from me. I had spent my whole life trying to create good feelings among people, but I felt all that work was falling to pieces. But the sincere people have intensified their interfaith work, knowing that it may be a Muslim being persecuted in America, but tomorrow it could be a Christian or a Jew or Hindu or Buddhist. They are realizing that prejudice and stereotyping and discrimination are bad no matter whom they affect.[23]

Women also bear the brunt of attempts to make conservative versions of *Shari'a* the social norm. Incurring protests against exposure of women's bodies, beauty pageants have set off rioting in some conservative Muslim regions; in Nigeria, an estimated 100 people were killed in riots in 2002 between Muslims and Christians over a newspaper article suggesting that the Prophet Muhammad would have approved of the Miss World contest. When Nigeria made *Shari'a* the basis of its legal code, Amina Lawal, who had allegedly confessed to having a child while divorced, was sentenced by a *Shari'a* court to death by stoning. Amnesty International and the Oprah Winfrey Show aroused so much public opinion against this order that some 1.2 million people sent messages of protest to the Nigerian government. The death sentence was rescinded, on the grounds that neither the confession nor the conviction was valid.

At the same time, some traditional Muslim women are suffering from attempts to introduce more liberal or secular norms. In France, Muslim girls have been forbidden to wear headscarves in public schools. Western feminists' views of Muslim family matters are not necessarily welcomed, even by progressive Muslim women, because they come from different cultural and religious contexts. Many Muslim women are deeply concerned about the breakdown of traditional family values and by Western cultural hegemony.

Progressive Muslim scholars today are looking not to Western individualistic ideas about personal freedom but to their own Muslim heritage to envision and move toward a more ideal, harmonious, spiritually oriented world (see box, right). In the life of the Prophet and in the revelations of the Holy Qur'an they are discovering many basic principles by which women, men, and children might live qualitatively better lives. Just as misinterpretation of Islam has brought misery to many Muslim women, reinterpretation of Islam could lead to a happier future.

EXCERPT Alternative Views of Islamic Ideals
Amina Wadud

Much of Western scholarship and media coverage asserts or implies that Islam itself oppresses women. Muslims have responded to this portrayal by defending the name of "Islam," even to the extent of defending practices that are harmful to women. These responses and the dominant Western perspectives on Islam make no attempt to address the disparities among Islamic primary sources, intellectual developments, and Muslim cultural practices. Some Muslim response is called for in the context of Western hegemonies and their political and economic monopolies for they pose a threat to the preservation of an autonomous Islamic identity... .

The more conservative neotraditionalist perspective seems ill prepared to face and accept the effects of the new global economies on local lifestyles. The effort to preserve the dignity of Islam from the disintegration of the encroaching Western culture and secularism often proves only to create a rigid barrier between what is perceived as Western modernity and what is perceived as Islam. In this conservative approach a strong emphasis is placed on a symbolic return to the Madinan model. The Prophet established a comprehensive Muslim community at Madinah based on the Qur'anic ethos.

Today's conservative strategy concretizes those symbols by literally mimicking the original community at Madinah. Women may be heavily veiled, including the face veil, and they are rarely called upon to perform competitive public duties such as wage-earning employment outside the home. In some cases, the women in the groups who adhere to this perspective may also fall below the national trends toward higher education because educational institutions themselves are viewed as vehicles of corrupt Western or un-Islamic values... .

The second neotraditionalist perspective might be seen as a reaction to the consequences of the global economy. Paid employment for women is no longer simply necessary for the lower classes. More Muslim women leave their homes for paid employment than did directly after the end of colonialism. A decent and comfortable lifestyle increasingly depends on a woman's contributions to the family income... .

As women continue to increase their part of the trend toward higher levels of education, professional training, and valuable public contributions, they face a contradiction in their lives. Women continue to fulfll the bulk of household duties and child care. The notion that the honored woman does not have to compete in the public domain because it is the Islamic duty of the male to maintain and protect her creates a double bind: her professional life offers little or no relief from domestic duties, whereas her fulfllment of home and family responsibilities does not relieve her from providing the additional income. As a further reaction to this double bind, symbolic forms of Islamic dress imply that a woman maintains tradition and should be honored as such. Although the dress symbols are present in both neotraditionalist perspectives, here there is less rigidity and little or no confnement... .

Both of the neotraditionalist approaches address the issue of Muslim women's identity, experiences, and concerns over equitable rights and responsibilities by asserting that "Islam" provided women their full rights more than 14 centuries ago. They offer little concrete consideration or analysis of the innumerable instances when those rights are denied to women in the real contexts of lived Islam. Such a consideration would require a critical examination of the way the word Islam is used. When "Islam" is applied to the status quo, it makes it difficult for women to address this ambiguity of usage without being seen as recalcitrant... .

At the other end of the spectrum is a perspective also clearly articulated by Muslim women and various women's groups. I considered this left-winged perspective a secularist approach because the women who represent it are adamantly opposed to all consideration of religion in the discourse over women's human rights. In their quest for rights they have become pro-Western, pro-modern, and anti-tradition, even though they fail to distinguish between lived Islam, the intellectual legacy of the Muslims, and Islam as a reflection of the primary sources.

Furthermore, the secularists express little or no concern over the centrality of Islamic spirituality to Muslim women nor over the importance of Islam as a dimension of identity... . Although they address serious infractions of the rights of Muslim women in the context of some Muslim governments and conservative religious thinkers, they ignore the negative consequences of this approach... . In the secularist perspective not only are many of the standards of measurement external to Islamic cultural ethos but they also bear no resemblance to the primary sources of Islam. Although these standards are promoted as "universal," they continue to support other ethnic, class, and gender-based stereotypes... . Under the guise of "equality," women are offered opportunities to do the same as, or be like, men... . Ideally, Islam promotes an equitable experience of complementarity between women and men, who enhance the humanity of each other through sharing experiences and perspectives... .

Despite opposition and backlash from both sides, a new and forceful perspective has developed in response to the issue of Muslim women and human rights. Those that adhere to this perspective claim that Islam is a dynamic relationship of engaged surrender between Allah and the khalifah, or trustee, on earth. Allah is known by the articulations of the Qur'an, its embodiment in the sunnah of the Prophet, and through the hearts of those engaged in surrender. Islam can never be reduced to any mere historical development, intellectual debate, or other limitation of its adherence no matter how much authority they might wield and how much legitimacy they might claim over Muslim sentiments, resources, and institutions.

Paramount for this new perspective is the definition of Islam. Islam is not a historical phenomenon that came into being at one place and time, like Madinah, which must then be followed blindly by one who adheres to notions that one has not experienced. Rather, Islam is a dynamic process within all creation that is in accord with the cosmic order established by the Creator, articulated in the Qur'an, and embodied by the Prophet.

Amina Wadud, "Alternative Qur'anic Interpretation and the Status of Muslim Women," in Gisela Webb, ed., *Windows of Faith: Muslim Women Scholar-Activists in North America*, Syracuse, New York: Syracuse University Press, 2000, pp. 6–10.

Women as Mystics

Whether living in repressive or more open, worldly cultures, Muslim women have sometimes reached great heights in transcendent spheres. As in other religions, they are the main practitioners of popular piety, praying for their families at the shrines of saints, giving charity to the poor, warding off evil spirits, and preparing the special meals for breaking fasts during the month of Ramadan. Women have often been the patrons who built shrines in memory of saints and served pilgrims therein. And throughout the centuries, there have been many great female mystics in Islam.

The mystical tradition in Islam, *tasawwuf*, is traced back to the Sufis who lived in the Prophet's mosque in Madinah in voluntary poverty and continual prayer. Rather than concentrating on outer rituals, theirs was a life of inner devotion and surrender to God. Their poverty was a matter of ascetic renunciation, following the example of the Prophet himself. It was within the Sufi movement that women's spirituality became evident.

Sufi asceticism soon became joined with intimate love for God because of the tremendous influence of the great Iraqi mystic Rabi'a al-'Adawiyya of Basra (*c.*713–801). She was born into a poor family and was captured by a slave-trader. During her enslavement she managed to worship God by staying awake at night. It is said that one night her master happened to wake and see her praying in the courtyard. He saw a lamp mysteriously appear over her head, suspended from space by a chain and illuminating the entire house. Deeply shaken, the next morning he offered Rabi'a her freedom, and she left to pray in the desert, continuing her lifelong habit of staying awake throughout the night in devotion. She was a great ascetic, living in extreme voluntary poverty, accepting only what God might provide for her. Many pious Muslim men kindly tried to offer her material help, but she turned away their offers. Once when she was sick, for instance, one asked if there was anything she wanted. She replied that for 12 years she had desired fresh dates, which were commonly available, but had never eaten one. She explained:

> I am a servant, and what has a servant to do with desire? If I will (a thing) and my Lord does not will it, this would be unbelief. That should be willed which He wills, that you may be His true servant. If He Himself gives anything, that is a different matter.[24]

Being so close to God, Rabi'a was involved in miraculous occurrences but paid them no particular regard, because she had no desire for fame, her whole attention being on her Beloved. Many stories told about her make this point. Once, for instance, the proud ascetic Hasan of Basra is said to have cast his prayer-mat on the river near where she was praying and to have invited her to sit on it over the water with him to say two *rakats* (ritual prayer-rounds). She said to him, "O Hasan, was it necessary to offer yourself in the bazaar of this world to the people of the next? This is necessary for people of your kind because of your weakness." Then she threw her own prayer-mat into the air and sat upon it, calling, "O Hasan, come up here that people may see us." He could not follow her. To console him, she said,

"O Hasan, that which you did, a fish can do just the same, and that which I did, a fly can do. The real work [for the saints of God] lies beyond both of these, and it is necessary to occupy ourselves with the real work."[25]

Some of the early female mystics of Islam were so God-intoxicated that they forgot all proprieties; sometimes this caused them to be sent to madhouses. Others wept constantly, always mindful of God. A prime exemplar was the ninth-century Persian ascetic Sha'wana. It was her fear of God that caused her to weep. Her friends begged her to stop, lest she should go blind or lose all her strength, but she insisted, "Verily to be blind in this world through much weeping is better, to my mind, than to be blind in the next through the fires of Hell."[26] Sha'wana was apparently a famous *pir*, or Sufi teacher, with numerous disciples.

Whereas the early Sufis practiced by themselves and shared spontaneously with others, by the end of the twelfth century there were noticeable *tariqahs*, brother/sisterhoods of those following the path laid out by a particularly illustrious teacher, as well as the Prophet Muhammad and the Qur'anic revelations. These schools were usually transmitted through men but there were many "radiant women" conveying the practices and guiding disciples. There were also a few female *shaykhas* who could initiate either men or women. Some were learned scholars of the mystical traditions. The *shaykh* or *shaykha* took responsibility for guiding the disciple through intense spiritual retreats and through the many and sometimes perplexing stages of spiritual progress toward the desired state of self-annihilation and utter immersion in God-realization.

The first recognizable Sufi *tariqah* was the Qadiri order, started by a teacher who had been spiritually inspired by his aunt and his mother. This order, which first spread through northern Africa, emphasized education of women, and still includes many learned women who run the communities of disciples and informally teach Islam and spiritual practices to both men and women.

The Rifa'i order grew up around a teacher whose wife, Rabi'a bint abi Bakr (d. 1216; see box, right), was the daughter of a famous *shaykh* and was so pure-hearted and awestruck by the awareness of God that her husband called her the "lady of the *faqirs*" and "mother of the *faqirs*" (those who are materially poor but spiritually rich in their attachment only to God). Her daughter Zaynab (d. 1232) was so remarkable for her spirituality, piety, and ascetic lifestyle that an author writing several centuries later about the lives of saints described her as "the one who took precedence over saintly men, through her lofty qualities and her illustrious spiritual states."[27] The Rifa'i order still includes many spiritually blessed women, including the Turkish *shaykha* Samiha Ayverdi (1905–1993), author of 35 books on spirituality and Turkish culture and one of the great mystics of recent times. Samiha wrote, for instance, about the essential role of spiritual teachers in keeping people attuned to the high ideals of Islam:

Fourteen centuries ago, Islam brought to humanity a unity of faith, in common moral values, in a sublime moral order, and in the spiritual elevation which this created. However, many people diverged from that, entangled their skirts in thorns during the long march, and strayed far afield. From time to time some heroic figures have pierced the enveloping darkness and have tried to make people remember and realize what they have lost. These noble natures, archi-

EXCERPT Prayers of Rabi'a

My God and my Lord:
eyes are at rest, the stars are setting,
hushed are the movements of birds in their nests,
of monsters in the deep.
and You are the Just who knows no change,
the Equity that does not swerve,
the Everlasting that never passes away.
The doors of kings are locked
and guarded by their henchmen.
But Your door is open to those who call upon You.
My Lord, each lover is now alone with his beloved.
And I am alone with You.

O my Lord, if I worship Thee from fear of Hell, burn me in Hell, and if I worship Thee from hope of Paradise, exclude me thence, but if I worship Thee for Thine own sake then withhold not from me Thine Eternal Beauty.

Rabi'a al-Adawiyya, as quoted in Marcus Braybrooke, ed., *The Bridge of Stars*, London: Duncan Baird Publishers, 2001, p. 111; and as quoted in Farid al-Din 'Attar, *Tadhikirat al-Awliyd*, I, ed. Nicholson, London, 1905, p. 73, reprinted in Margaret Smith, *Rabi'a*, Oxford: Oneworld Publications, 1994, p. 50.

tects of souls, have tried to awaken to nobler goals the masses of people who had abandoned their goals to enemies and to petty purposes.[28] ■

Another strong Sufi order—the Chistiyya order—spread in India from the thirteenth century onward. Women have always been accepted as initiates. In the early days, there was a special initiation for them: the woman would put her hand in a cup of water, and so would the *pir*, and thus the spiritual power and blessings were transmitted to her through the water without his touching her. Among the many famous saintly women associated with the Chisti lineage, there was the thirteenth-century Bibi Fatima Sam, adopted sister of the great mystic Farid-ad-Din Ganj-I Shakkar. She gave an extraordinary explanation for the power of the Muslim saints, which far transcends that of ritual observances: "The saints will cast away both worldly and religious blessings to give a piece of bread or a drink of water to someone in need. This state is something one cannot obtain by one hundred thousand fasts and prayers."[29]

So detached from worldly concerns are the saints—whether female or male—that events that would disturb others do not ruffle their absorption in the Beloved. A typical story is told of the great twentieth-century Sufi saint of Afghanistan and India, Hazrat Babajan. She was so ready to share with the needy anything given to her that once, when she was sleeping under a very expensive shawl presented by a devotee, and a thief tried to snatch it, she moved slightly, without even opening her eyes, so that it could easily be removed.

Some who chose to renounce worldly treasures for the sake of spiritual wealth were of royal or ruling families. One such was Fatima, or Jahan-Ara, of seventeenth-century India. She was the favorite daughter of the Mughal Emperor Shah Jahan, who built the Taj Mahal as a memorial to his beloved wife Mumtaz Mahal. Jahan-Ara and her brother shared a desire to follow the mystical Way and were both initiated into the Path by the famous saint Mulla Shah. She reached the heights of spiritual union with God, and with it such exalted wisdom that Mulla Shah considered her worthy of being his deputy.

At the other extreme, there have been innumerable poor and simple Muslim women who by sheer faith have attained communion with God. Mimunah, who became a greatly loved saint of North Africa, is said to have been such a simple-minded old woman that she could not properly remember the ritual prayer that a boat captain attempted to teach her, so she ran across the water as his boat departed, in order to ask him to repeat it once more. She knew only one prayer: "Mimunah knows God, and God knows Mimunah."[30]

In general, the mystical way has offered Muslim women more opportunities than the orthodox path to express their spirituality. There have been special communities solely for women ascetics, and shrines to female saints that only women can enter. Even within the home, carrying out their household tasks, women have sung devotional songs while they worked and thus spread the mystical dimensions of Islam. Many of the female saints were married, and they raised their children steeped in love and faith. The Prophet Muhammad himself is often quoted as having said, "Paradise lies at the feet of the mothers."

So clear is the association between women and mystical union that in India and Pakistan Muslim poets have long personified the soul as a woman longing for her Beloved. Contemporary efforts to rediscover the great female mystics in Islam have turned up evidence of many highly spiritually evolved women from the time of the Prophet onward. Today, many of the teachers of the mystical path in Islam are women, and the truths they are exploring are profound and relevant. After describing the rigors of the traditional spiritual retreat and the subtleties of awakened inner vision, the American Sufi Rabia Terri Harris, founder and coordinator of the Muslim Peace Fellowship, concludes:

We are lame ants on the [pilgrimage] road in the midst of a breaking storm [of the mind]. But fortunately this road is not about faith, nor about vision either. Attractive and desirable as those may be, the Divine Presence does not depend on them in any way. It is not our business to seek ecstasy and secret knowledge. It is our business to seek servanthood, what Hazrat Ibn al-'Arabi calls "the station of no station." And to such a quest, time and circumstance neither present any impediment nor bestow any advantage. Wherever it is we find ourselves, it is to that place that we have been taken, and in that place our responsibility may be found.[31]

Key Terms

Hadith	*hijab*
caliph	*Sunnah*
Shi'a	*Shari'a*
Sunni	*Namaz*
imam	

Suggested Reading

Ali, Maulana Muhammad, *The Religion of Islam*, 6th edn., Columbus, Ohio: Ahmadiyya Anjuman Isha'at Islam, 1994. A classic reference work describing all aspects of Muslim life, offered by the Ahmadiyyah Movement in their attempt to present a true picture of Islam both for Muslims and for non-Muslims.

El Fadl, Khaled Abou, *Speaking in God's Name: Islamic Law, Authority and Women*, Oxford: Oneworld, 2001. A Muslim lawyer's research into Islamic jurisprudence and its contemporary tendencies to authoritarianism, often with negative results for women's lives.

Helminski, Camille Adams, *Women of Sufism: A Hidden Treasure*, Boston: Shambhala, 2003. Rich collection of writings and songs of women mystics, with biographical material.

Safi, Omid, ed., *Progressive Muslims on Justice, Gender, and Pluralism*, Oxford: Oneworld Publications, 2003. Leading progressive thinkers explore the sensitive issues facing Muslims today.

Schimmel, Annemarie, *My Soul is a Woman: The Feminine in Islam*, trans. Susan H. Ray, New York: Continuum, 1999. A wide-ranging exploration of spiritual dimensions of women's roles in Islam.

Smith, Margaret, *Rabi'a: The Life and Work of Rabi'a and other Women Mystics in Islam*, Oxford: Oneworld Publications, 1994 reprint. A classic study of Sufi mysticism, its greatest early female exemplar, and other women mystics.

Spellberg, D. A., *Politics, Gender, and the Islamic Past: The Legacy of 'A'isha Bint Abi Bakr*, New York: Columbia University Press, 1994. An exploration of early Muslim culture, as examined through stories about the young wife of the Prophet.

Thanawi, Maulana Ashraf 'Ali, *Perfecting Women*, trans. Barbara Daly Metcalf, New Delhi: Oxford University Press, 1990. Fascinating and informative window into social expectations of Muslim women in early twentieth-century India, many of which still shape women's lives.

Wadud, Amina, *Qur'an and Woman: Rereading the Sacred Text from a Woman's Perspective*, New York: Oxford University Press, 1999. Landmark exegesis of the Qur'an from a non-patriarchal point of view.

Webb, Gisela, ed., *Windows of Faith: Muslim Women Scholar-Activists in North America*, Syracuse, New York: Syracuse University Press, 2000. Profound revisionist scholarship pertaining to many women's issues in Islam.

9
WOMEN IN NEWER RELIGIONS

We can create a more just, peaceful, and harmonious world

CAROL CHRIST

Over time, religious movements come and go. Relatively few have become global movements with millions of followers. In the past few centuries, many spiritual messengers have appeared; some have developed a large and sustained following. Women's status within these organizations varies considerably, but some have room for them in leadership positions and have enhanced appreciation of women in general. Nonetheless, cultural patterns of patriarchy are deeply entrenched and not readily overcome.

We will be sampling in this chapter only a few of these more recent religious movements in which women are playing significant roles: Sikhism, Baha'i, the Theosophical Society and associated New Age movements, Neo-Paganism, Goddess worship, and Afro-Caribbean mixtures.

Sikhism

In the midst of patriarchal Indian culture, a new religion began developing in the sixteenth century around a wise spiritual master who became known as Guru Nanak (1469–c.1539). His seat of spiritual authority was passed down through a series of nine other enlightened masters, all of them men. The transmission of spiritual power was then given by the Tenth Sikh Guru, Guru Gobind Singh (1666–1708), to the scripture that the Gurus had assembled, the Guru Granth Sahib. The movement is now the fifth largest of all world religions, with over 22 million followers. It has had an empowering influence on women, as well as on people from lower castes, but the oppressive cultural effects of patriarchy and casteism still have not been overcome.

Guru Nanak was a spiritual and social reformer. Having reportedly been blessed with a transformational experience of the presence of God, he thenceforth set out to teach people that God pervades everywhere, all beings, all places. No distinctions should therefore be made on the basis of gender, caste, or even religion. From his male point of view, he sang women's praises:

Of woman are we born, of woman conceived;
To woman engaged, to woman married.
Women are befriended, by woman is civilization continued.
When woman dies, woman is sought for.
It is by woman that the entire social order is maintained.
Then why call her low of whom are great men born?[1]

Guru Nanak rejected the prevalent idea that women are sources of spiritual pollution, especially during the period after they have given birth. He advocated marriage rather than celibacy, and envisioned marriage as an equal partnership. Sexual loyalty was to be the norm for both partners—husband as well as wife.

The Guru Granth Sahib is a treasury of mystical hymns not only from Sikh Gurus but also from Hindu and Muslim saints of medieval India. In these hymns, the ideal devotee of God is often depicted as a woman longing for her Beloved. God is known as formless, and therefore without gender, but for devotional purposes, God is personified as the only Male; devotees are all like females who love Him. For instance, Guru Nanak sang:

Come my sister
Let us embrace!
Come beloved friend
Let us speak of love!
Let us sit together
And talk of our Husband
Our perfect, powerful Lord... .
Go ask the happy spouse,
"What virtues earned you favor of the Lord?"
"It's the gentle path of calmness of manner and sweetness of tongue."
If you hearken unto the guru's word
You will meet your Husband, the Lord of Love.[2]

The goal of spiritual practice is union with God, metaphorically referred to as a marriage, with the devotee as the bride: "She who, night and day, abides with her Beloved, obtains truth and goes to sit in her own Home."[3] With such imagery so prevalent in Sikh scripture, there is no possibility of claiming that women cannot obtain enlightenment.

The relatively positive attitude toward women continued throughout the history of the Sikh Gurus, even though it was not a primary focus. Female infanticide was prohibited in the code of conduct; *sati* (widow-burning) was prohibited in the Guru Granth Sahib. To raise the poor social status of widows, Sikhs allowed them to remarry.

Sikhs have often lived during times of social disorder and brutality. The Gurus themselves often faced attacks, caught as they were between warring Hindu landlords and Muslim invaders and rulers. By the time of the Sixth Guru, Sikhs were being trained in martial arts to help defend their community. Guru Gobind Singh, the Tenth Guru, also took strong measures to develop his followers' inner strength. With his *amrit* (spiritual nectar) ceremony, he turned both men and women of all castes into **Khalsa**: brave warriors pledged to defend anyone in need, to stand always on the front line against injustice, to regard all women with respect as their own mothers or sisters (in the case of males), to fight against their own inner weaknesses (desire, anger, attachment, greed, and ego), and to always remember God and encourage others to do likewise. The Tenth Guru firmly discarded all previous caste divisions by giving all the men the same last name, "Singh" ("lion"), and the women the name "Kaur" ("princess"), thus ennobling them all. Women who have taken *amrit* wear the same symbolic dress as men: the long hair of a spiritual ascetic, but bound and covered by a veil, a small comb to keep the hair neat, loose underpants for modesty, a steel bracelet symbolizing union with all and dedication to God, and a small dagger in a sling, symbolizing readiness to stand up for justice and to defeat one's own inner weaknesses.

In the annals of Sikh history, many women are beloved and remembered for their courageous actions as well as their spiritual devotion. Guru Nanak faced heavy criticism from his father because of his mystical leanings, and it was his devoted older sister Nanaki who stood up for him and became the first to believe in his spiritual potential. When his father at last gave up trying to make Nanak behave normally, he was sent to live with Nanaki and to work for her husband. She arranged his marriage to Sulakhni, who bore the Guru two sons and waited patiently while he went off on long preaching journeys each lasting many years.

Khivi was the wife of the second Guru, Angad. She became a famous model of Sikh hospitality and service, helping to establish a continuing tradition of loving attention to guests. Just as Guru Nanak had chosen Angad rather than one of his own sons as his successor, Guru Angad chose not a son but Amar Das as the third Guru. One son did not accept this choice, and after Guru Angad's passing, he tried to establish himself as the next guru with his own followers. Khivi, his mother, was able to convince him that the headaches he was experiencing were the result of his having taken on too much responsibility, and she took him to Guru Amar Das to apologize. Her son's headaches disappeared, and Sikhism was saved from a potential schism.

Guru Amar Das had actually come to Sikhism through the preaching and spiritually touching singing of Khivi's daughter, Amro, which radically changed his life. When Guru Amar Das later organized the Sikhs into districts, he put Amro in charge of one of them. She was given full responsibility for the content of preaching, for maintaining equality, for collecting funds, and for making decisions for the sake of her district.

Guru Amar Das had taken under his wing an orphaned boy with severe leprosy. This boy, whom he renamed Murrari ("destroyer of the demons"), could only crawl around at first, but the Guru himself washed and clothed him, and slowly he was cured. One of the Guru's followers offered his beautiful daughter Matho to be married to Murrari. The Guru called the couple "Matho Murrari," thus giving her unusual recognition. She and her husband both took spiritual training from the Guru, and he placed Matho in charge of one of the districts, with Murrari to assist her—a clear reversal of traditional gender roles.

The Guru taught that all people are equal, irrespective of caste, and particularly tried to free women from oppressive traditions such as *purdah* (seclusion and veiling) and *sati*. He encouraged women to be participants in religious and social life.

The wives of the Sikh Gurus often played important religious and social roles. Mata Gujari was the wife of Tegh Bahadur, whom she married in 1633. In 1644, after the death of the Eighth Guru, she accompanied her husband into his voluntary life of seclusion while the Sikhs sought their next Guru, basing their search on an obscure reference to Bakala, where Tegh Bahadur had gone into spiritual retreat. Once he was discovered and acclaimed as the Ninth Guru, he traveled east to Patna with his mother and wife, leaving them there. According to Sikh historians, Guru Tegh Bahadur willingly sacrificed his life to help save Hindus from forced conversion to Islam. Mata Gujari was reportedly very courageous when she said goodbye to her husband as he left for certain execution in Delhi, and it was she who helped to manage affairs until their son was old enough to take full charge as the Tenth Master, Guru Gobind Singh. She faced another extremely difficult period in 1705 when the citadel built by Guru Gobind Singh was besieged by Hindu chieftains and Mughal troops. At last the Guru's disciples persuaded him to leave with his family under cover of darkness. In the process, Mata Gujari and her two younger grandsons got separated from the Guru's party and were led by a traitorous servant into Mughal captivity in a cold tower. (The eldest grandson had been killed aged 15 fighting a Mughal attack.) Mata Gujari reportedly urged her surviving grandsons to be strong in their faith, and they were bricked up alive for refusing to abandon their religion. Mata Gujari herself died on the same day, having been imprisoned in the December cold without any warm clothing. She, too, had remained steadfast, singing hymns of the Gurus. Sikhs pay special homage to her memory in Gurdwara Mata Gujari, a temple that was later built on the site where she was imprisoned.

Guru Gobind Singh himself had three wives, as was not unusual in Indian culture, but there is some confusion over the facts. The first woman he apparently married, in 1677, was Mata Jito. Their three sons were raised on the stories of the martyrdoms of their grandfather, the Ninth Guru, and great-great-grandfather, the Fifth Guru. Mata Jito is also remembered in Sikh tradition as the person who brought sugar crystals to be stirred into the holy water by which Guru Gobind Singh baptized the first Khalsa members, symbolically rendering them sweet as well as courageous. She herself died in 1700, before her sons were martyred. Sikhs pay great respect to their martyrs, and to the women who raised them, and the place of Mata Jito's cremation is marked by a shrine.

The second woman that Guru Gobind Singh married was Mata Sundari. Their wedding apparently took place in 1684. Their one son was martyred along with his elder half-brother, Mata Jito's son, in the battle against Mughal attackers. The third wife, Mata Sahib Devan, was offered in marriage to the Guru by her parents, but the marriage was not consummated, the Guru having apparently agreed to allow her only to stay with his family to spare her social embarrassment. Some Sikhs consider her the "Mother of the Khalsa" and think that it was she who put the sugar crystals in the holy water. Both Mata Sundari and Mata Sahib Devan were evacuated along with Guru Gobind Singh from his besieged citadel; separated from him as they crossed the river by night, they were taken to Delhi by one of his followers. After the Guru passed away in 1708, it was Mata Sundari to whom his followers looked for guidance. She had his writings collected, arranged for management of the sacred shrines, and issued orders to the Sikhs under her own seal.

There were many brave Sikh women who took major roles in the defensive battles that Sikhs had to fight in order to protect themselves from attacks by both Hindu chieftains and Muslim forces. Because Sikhs place great value on dedication and courage as spiritual virtues, these heroic women are highly honored. Perhaps the most well-known of them is Mai Bhago. When Guru Gobind Singh's citadel at Anandpur Sahib was besieged, 40 of his male followers decided that the situation was hopeless, and agreed to accept the demands of the attackers that anyone who renounced Guru Gobind Singh would be allowed to leave unharmed. The 40 signed a document to this effect and went back to their villages. Their wives were so disgusted that they reportedly refused to let them back into their homes. One woman, Mai Bhago, rallied the deserters and led them on horseback to where the Guru with a few followers was being pursued by the forces of the Mughal emperor. Mai Bhago and the deserters intercepted the Mughal troops and fought so furiously that they routed them. All the deserters, however, were killed; they were pardoned and blessed by the Guru. Mai Bhago was wounded, and Guru Gobind Singh allowed her to remain as one of his bodyguards, dressed in man's clothing. She stayed near him until he passed on, and then shifted to a southern state, where she lived in deep meditation for the rest of her life. Her hut has been turned into an historic **gurdwara** (Sikh temple), and there is also a hall dedicated to her memory in the place where the Guru passed away.

The tradition of strong women has continued among Sikhs (see box, right). Like the men of Punjab, they tend to be taller and larger than other Indians, and to be hugged by a Sikh village woman is to be nearly crushed. As Sikhs faced attacks from Mughals, Hindus, and later English colonialists over the years, many brave women were martyred. They also had to face the tortures of relatives, including their own children. In 1753, Mir Manu (Mir Muin-ul-Mulk), the Mughal Governor of Punjab, grew so ruthless in his attempt to wipe out Sikhs, whom he perceived as a threat to his rule, that he had cartloads of Sikh men clubbed to death daily and filled the wells with their heads. He captured their women and children and threatened them with torture if they did not convert to Islam. The women steadfastly carried on their duties of grinding grain, murmuring remembrance of God and the verse "Manu is our sickle, we are a crop for him to mow; the more he cuts us, the more we grow." Their children were tossed into the air and impaled on spears. Their bodies were cut into pieces before their mothers' eyes, and the parts were strung around their mothers' necks. But the women bore it all without crying or complaint and refused to abjure their faith. They themselves were hideously abused or died in self-defence. Such women are remembered every day in Sikh prayers.

The tradition continues. In 1984 a very brave woman, Nirlep Kaur (d. 1990), stood up to Jarnail Singh Bhindrawala, who was using the Golden Temple—holiest of Sikh shrines—as a separatist stronghold. He was so popular and so powerful that no one dared to challenge him. Yet Nirlep Kaur, daughter of the Chief Minister of one of the states that became Punjab, and an influential Member of Parliament in her own right, was very concerned about what would happen to Sikhs if this situation continued. She prepared a strong statement asking him to leave the Golden Temple, and gave it to all the media throughout India. She herself went to the Temple in person, with only a few unarmed men. Along the way, she asked many other leaders to support her or issue their own statement. No one was brave

BIOGRAPHY   Bibi Sahib Kaur

There have been so many strong women in Sikhism's short history that it is hard to single one out for special consideration. But as an exemplar, we will look at the greatness of Bibi ("Lady") Sahib Kaur (1771–1801). She was born a princess in a royal clan that had established strong and compassionate rule over a large territory with its center in Patiala, Punjab. Her father, the Maharajah, died when she was only 15, leaving her younger brother in titular control, but with actual power in the hands of an advisor who soon began machinations to destroy the empire for his own gain. Bibi Sahib Kaur had been married at a young age, but when she learned that her younger brother's empire was crumbling, she left her happy married life and joined him to protect Patiala. He gave her the post of Prime Minister.

As Bibi Sahib Kaur began trying to re-establish order in the kingdom, word came that a force of 100,000 soldiers of the Maratha clan was advancing on Patiala. The Sikhs there were badly outnumbered, with no hope of defending their kingdom. But Bibi Sahib Kaur had taken the *amrit* of Khalsa. She ordered the sounding of battle drums and gathered all the men of the area to meet the impending onslaught. With powerful words, she gave them the confidence to make a brave stand:

> Brothers, the enemy, thinking of you as few and weak, is advancing to snatch your freedom. Our freedom is a blessed reward of our Gurus… . You are Sikhs of the Guru and I am confident that you will not allow the enemy to advance any further. The remaining issue is that of numbers. But remember, our Tenth Guru engaged 125,000 against each Sikh. You are Sikhs of the same Guru. Thus don't worry about the huge numbers of the enemy force. We are within our rights and following the truth… . Take an oath with me that we may die but not allow the enemy to advance even a foot.

Thus rallied, the Sikh men raised the Khalsa victory cry: "Who is ever happy? The one who knows that Truth is deathless."

The Marathas advanced with their large force, armed with heavy cannons. The few Sikhs had no cannons. The Maratha commander sent a message to Bibi Sahib Kaur, "Why are you bent upon getting your men killed for nothing? Give up and surrender." Her reply: "Guru's Sikhs know no surrender. Go tell your gentlemen that if they have any desire to live, they should return immediately. If not, Khalsa's sword awaits them. They may approach with their coffins."

Angered, the Marathas began firing their cannons. The Sikhs courageously moved forward in the face of cannon shelling, with only swords in hand. Bibi Sahib Kaur was dressed in men's clothing and directing them from horseback with an unsheathed sword. The Sikhs moved right into the enemy's fortified positions and engaged them in hand-to-hand combat. In this situation the cannons were useless, and the few Sikhs, being famous for their skilled swordsmanship, were able to fight for an entire day. However, they grew tired, and with half their number dead on the battlefield, they had no reinforcements. The enemy had surrounded them. Again, Sahib Kaur stirred them on by finding a weak segment and breaking through.

Both sides then stopped fighting, since it was too dark to see. The Maratha camp was celebrating; the Sikh camp was mourning its dead. The men hesitantly approached Sahib Kaur, saying that there seemed no chance of winning the battle. But in the face of her composure, they said they would bravely fight to the death. However, they begged her to leave, since they could not bear her to be captured and harmed by the enemy. She reportedly replied:

> Brothers! No one can live forever in this world. One day we all have to die. Sahib Kaur is prepared for this. Granted, I am a woman and surely weak. But brothers! I too have partaken of the *amrit* of the same Guru of which you have partaken. Then why would I hesitate facing death? Don't even think about it. If I leave here, I shall leave in victory or I shall not leave at all. You say we have no hope of victory. I cannot accept this. We are fighting the battle of truth and righteousness. Wahe Guru [God] is with us. I am confident of our victory. Don't get discouraged.

Then Bibi Sahib Kaur walked to and fro in silence, listening for inner guidance. After a bit, she announced that the Guru had shown her the strategy that would lead to victory. They would attack the Maratha forces that very night, while they were off-guard celebrating their seeming victory. At midnight, the reinvigorated Sikhs launched a surprise attack on the Marathas. Between the suddenness of the attack and the darkness, the Marathas were in total confusion and many died fighting against their own troops. In the turmoil, the Maratha commanders gathered whatever soldiers they could and ran away, leaving behind not only their dead but also all their cannons, ammunition, food, and money. Sahib Kaur distributed the money among her soldiers and took the cannons and ammunition back to Patiala, where she was welcomed with the greatest celebration ever held there.

Quotes from Karam Singh, "Daughters of the Khalsa," *Adarshak Singhnia*, trans. Baldev Singh, http://allaboutsikhs.com/women/bibi_sahib_kaur.htm, accessed November 14, 2005.

enough to do so except she. She met Bhindrawala face to face within the Golden Temple. He and his men were armed, and the situation was extremely tense. Yet in the face of her courage, he quietly turned away. (Despite her challenge, he did not vacate the Golden Temple, and soon government troops attacked it, an outrage for Sikhs and ultimately the cause of tremendous loss of Sikh lives.) Nirlep Kaur was known as a very intelligent and outspoken woman and an excellent administrator. She had contested—and won—an election to Parliament against her own father-in-law. She also led agitations against corruption in two historical Sikh *gurdwaras* in Delhi, and her bold actions there were ultimately successful.

Many of the contemporary Sikh-based communities known as Gobind Sadan ("The House of God") have women as managers. There, women are given significant spiritual duties by their teacher, His Holiness Baba Virsa Singh, who often praises their management abilities. Bibi Gurcharan Kaur, the manager of Gobind Sadan's central community outside Delhi, gets up every morning at 12.30 a.m. to bathe, sit in meditation, cook the *prasad* (sweet food offering), ceremonially open the Guru Granth Sahib, offer prayers at two places, sing the first prayer of the day, read scripture for two hours, and then sing the last morning prayer at 4 a.m., in addition to her daytime duties, which include attending people, managing the *langar* (free community kitchen, where hundreds of people are fed at each meal), keeping accounts, and ironing the precious cloths that surround the Guru Granth Sahib. She says, "This is just routine. It's not difficult."[4] Another strong Gobind Sadan woman, Bibi Jaswant Kaur (b. 1921), is the chief singer of sacred hymns or *kirtan*—a role that usually belongs to men. At her advanced age, her voice is still extremely powerful, and she has won many awards for her classical *kirtan*. Once she played the role of one of the Panj Piare (Five Beloveds) for a Khalsa initiation ceremony, a role in which women are rarely found.

At present there are many female Sikh scholars and social activists, and in recent times the head of the Sikh Gurdwara Management Committee was a woman. However, in 2005 she had to resign, in the face of allegations that she had misappropriated *gurdwara* funds.

Despite the openness of Sikhism to the recognition of women's strengths, patriarchal cultural traditions are still very strongly entrenched in India. Women sit separately from men in *gurdwaras* and usually keep their heads veiled in public. There are no hymns by women in the Guru Granth Sahib; its egalitarianism transcends divisions of caste and religion but not of gender. Women do not serve as *granthis*, or chief priests. *Gurdwara* management committees usually consist of men; the women are more often found in such subordinate roles as making *chapatis* (flat bread) in the free kitchen. The heavy demands on a bride's family for dowry make it so disadvantageous to support daughters that many are still killed as fetuses or infants in Punjab. The current sex ratio there is only 780 females for every 1,000 males, even though the Gurus strongly criticized anti-female practices and in 2001 the Sikh leaders issued an order that anyone who aborted female fetuses or killed baby girls should be ostracized from the community: there should be "no liaison or relationship with any person, man or woman, who is guilty of female foeticide or infanticide." This ruling has been largely ignored; female foeticide and infanticide continue, with Punjab having one of the highest rates of female foeticide in India.

The Sikh Gurus also condemned polygamy and *sati*, but Maharajah Ranjit Singh (1780–1839), the benevolent and popular ruler of the egalitarian, non-sectarian, but short-lived Sikh empire, had many wives and some of them and their maidservants voluntarily threw themselves on to his pyre when he died. Among them were Hindu and Muslim women as well as Sikhs; the Maharajah had permitted each one to worship in her own way.

In Sikhism's holiest shrine, the Golden Temple, women have requested to be allowed to help carry the scripture when it is reverently brought out on a covered platform every morning and returned every evening, to sing *kirtan*, and to share in the voluntary cleaning service. The latter two rights already belonged to them by previous rulings, but until a new ruling in 2005 by the Sikh Gurdwara Management Committee they were not granted for the pre-eminent shrine. The general feeling seems to be that for women to be involved in these activities is immodest and provocative.

Many Sikh women suffer from the traditional Indian expectation that they leave their own family and become little more than servants of their husband's. Some of them have to bear alcoholism, drug abuse, and violence from husbands who have become physically inactive rather than farming to earn their living, as they did in the time of the Gurus. Thus the social reforms initiated by the Gurus, including equality of the sexes, are still a long way from being fully realized. Narinder Kaur, a Sikh writer and businesswoman living both in Punjab and in Thailand, says:

We are suppressed by men for the sake of being "respectable." I think Sikh women are very strong, whether due to religion, or genetics, or environment, I don't know. But I think they are very strong—mentally and physically also. They do what they want to do. If they decide, they will do, and they can do everything—nothing is impossible in front of them. But politics are every-where. That is why women cannot do. They want to do, but they cannot do, because they are women. A lot of pressure is there from male dominance. If we step beyond our place, men have ways of suppressing us. Instead of following our Gurus' teachings, men are doing many wrong things.

I want to write about this, but I have been stopped because in the future there might be some damage not only to me but also to my daughters and my extended family. Women are much stronger than men, and they can make more changes. But when the issue of our "respect" is raised, we can't do anything. Someone is always there to suppress and frighten us. I want to write and speak the truth, but it's difficult because of the children and the family. If we want to live in this male-dominant Indian society, there are again and again attacks on our respect. Even those who are close to us do not support us. Thus we have to stop ourselves. When we stop ourselves from writing, from speaking, from doing—but we want to do—a lot of things are trapped inside us.[5]

Baha'i Faith

Of the global religions, the Baha'i Faith is unique in promoting equality of the sexes as one of its fundamental principles. The faith had its roots among Shi'a Muslims in Persia (present-day Iran) in 1844, with the announcement by a young man called the Bab ("gate") that a new prophet would soon appear with a message from God for all people in the world. Shi'a Muslims anticipate the coming of a messenger from God who will appear at the end of time, bringing truth and justice, so he attracted some followers. As the movement grew, it was opposed by ortho-dox leaders. In the face of their attempts to oppress it, it became more fanatic and militant, and the Bab and many of his followers were persecuted and killed. One of the Babis, the aristocrat Baha'u'llah (1817–1892), was ultimately banished to

Turkey. He declared himself the messenger foretold by the Bab, and in fact the Promised One expected by all religions. From the prison city of Akka, he wrote letters proclaiming that a new global civilization was dawning in which there would be just distribution of wealth, harmony of science and religion, equality of men and women, an end to prejudice, and the development of a global government. He considered the teachings of all religions as progressive revelations, destined to result ultimately in a single world religion.

Most of the remaining Babis became Baha'is—followers of Baha'u'llah—and their missionary efforts carried the faith to other regions, including Europe and North America, so that there are approximately five million followers throughout the world today. The largest population of Baha'is is now in India, where Mrs. Shirin Boman Meherabani initiated a mass movement to convert illiterate villagers to the faith in the 1960s and 70s. Recognizing that women were being left out, the leadership established the Baha'i Vocational Institute for Rural Women in 1985, to help empower women to earn some money, to become functionally literate, to improve their families' health, hygiene, and nutrition, and to become agents of social change.

Baha'u'llah had placed great emphasis on justice and equality for all humanity. He had written clearly, "Women and men have been and will always be equal in the sight of God."[6] The most salient example of women's strong position in Baha'i is Tahirih (Fatimih Bigum Baraghani, c.1817–1852). She was prominent in a sect that anticipated the imminent appearance of the messianic figure, and in the mid-nineteenth century the Bab appointed her one of his own 18 chief disciples without even meeting her. Even though her own father was a prominent Muslim cleric, she was radically anti-clerical. Well trained in traditional Muslim knowledge, she argued that standard Muslim practices did not apply to Babis. She even refused to perform the daily Muslim prayers. Although she normally wore a veil, sometimes she took it off at public gatherings when she wanted to make a point of breaking away from Muslim tradition. At times she purposely provoked the Shi'a clerics by her actions, such as wearing gaily colored clothes during the traditional period of mourning for the violent death of Husayn (grandson of the Prophet Muhammad), and asserting that it should be a time for celebrating the Bab's birthday instead. On that occasion, an outraged mob tried to attack her, after which she was sent to exile in Baghdad along with her male and female followers. There she continued her radical activities, giving speeches from behind a curtain until she was confined to the house of the leading cleric of Baghdad. Her father, because of his own standing, was able to order her return to Iran. On the way, masses of people turned out to hear her talk and join the movement.

As attacks against the Babis increased, Tahirih took shelter with Baha'u'llah and traveled with him to a meeting of movement leaders to determine what to do about the imprisonment of the Bab. Tahirih was the leading radical voice, advocating a total separation from Islam and a militant posture. She utterly scandalized the moderates in favor of working for Islamic renewal by such actions as running out of her tent during prayer time waving a sword and yelling, "Now is not the time for prayers and prostrations; rather on to the battlefield of love and sacrifice!"[7] She had originally been named after Fatima, beloved daughter of the Prophet Muhammad, and was regarded as her holy incarnation, such that some people did not dare to look even at her shadow. Therefore, when she appeared unveiled and vigorously criticized the ordinances of Islam, proclaiming a new religion, one man in the stunned group was so upset that he cut his throat and ran away so that he would not see her face. Nevertheless, she eventually persuaded the leader of the moderates to adopt her radical position, and many women came to hear her talks. After the Bab's execution in 1850, some Babis tried to assassinate the Shah of Iran. They failed, and the massacre of Babis by Iranian government forces began. Tahirih was strangled, but before she died, she reportedly cried, "You can kill me as soon as you like, but you cannot stop the emancipation of women."[8]

Another woman who is held up as an example for Baha'i women was Bahiyyih Khanum (1846–1932), daughter of Baha'u'llah. Her brother, 'Abdu-l-Baha, was appointed by their father to be the official interpreter of his teachings after his death. When 'Abdu-l-Baha was away, he left Bahiyyih Khanum in charge, and when he himself died, Baha'is turned to her for leadership until his successor, Shoghi Effendi, arrived. Shoghi Effendi in turn entrusted affairs to her whenever he traveled. Because of her leadership roles, Bahiyyih Khanum was called "The Greatest Holy Leaf."

The writings of Baha'u'llah generally support a liberal attitude toward women. For instance, he wrote that adulterers—whether male or female—should be fined, rather than killed, and women are allowed to perform the routine prayers during their menstrual period if they want, rather than being considered polluted. Understanding the importance of women as the people carrying on the foundation of society, he said that if a family could educate only one child, it should be a girl. Nevertheless, Baha'u'llah's writings generally seem to assume a male audience and a traditional family structure, with men as breadwinners and women as homemakers, though neither is seen to be higher than the other. Over time, women have more and more been participants and decision-makers in the local and national governing bodies, but to date they still have not been included in the nine-man highest body, the Universal House of Justice, in Haifa, Israel. Their exclusion is currently a matter of discussion among Baha'is, for it is not clear whether the founder intended to exclude them or not. Linguistically, when he used the Arabic word *rijal*, which is usually interpreted to mean "men," he may have meant it in a more generic, non-gendered sense. He even explicitly referred to women as *rijal* if they had recognized him and worked in his cause. But uncertainty about his intentions and the cultural reluctance of men to allow women to advance quickly—especially in Iran, where the status of the Baha'i faith has always been tenuous—have thus far debarred women from the highest rank. Women who object have either left the organization or kept quiet, for those who question the authority of Baha'i institutions are considered expelled from the faith.

Otherwise, contemporary Baha'is, especially in the West, place great emphasis on social transformation through the cooperative efforts of women and men, and they see the advancement of women as a naturally evolving part of social transformation. Unity across all social divides is a cherished feature of the faith. Joyce Jackson, an editor of educational material in Nashville, Tennessee, explains, "To walk into a Baha'i Unity Feast is like seeing a microcosm of the world. There is tremendous love, peace and hope in the Baha'i community, and it feels like a safe haven from the troubles of the world at large."[9]

In a 1986 statement on peace, "To the Peoples of the World," the (all-male) Universal House of Justice wrote:

■ The emancipation of women, the achievement of full equality between the sexes, is one of the most important, though less acknowledged prerequisites of peace. The denial of such equality perpetrates an injustice against one half of the world's population and promotes in men harmful attitudes and habits that are carried from the family to the workplace, to political life, and ultimately to international relations. There are no grounds, moral, practical, or biological, upon which such denial can be justified. Only as women are welcomed into full partnership in all fields of human endeavor will the moral and psychological climate be created in which international peace can emerge.[10] ■

Theosophy to New Age

In recent centuries, women have developed more direct spiritual authority in the field of the occult, bypassing male-led institutional structures in favor of esoteric communications with unseen forces which can presumably be contacted only by high-level initiates. This idea was particularly developed by a highly independent woman born into the Russian aristocracy in 1831: Helena Petrovna Blavatsky (fig. 9.1). Strange things seemed to happen around her as a child. Servants heard knocking sounds and she spoke of past lives and spirits that no one else could see. After her mother, a novelist, died, she often stayed on the estates of her maternal grandfather, immersing herself in his libraries of occult literature. She was married briefly as a teenager, but soon left her husband in favor of freedom to do what she wanted. According to her, she spent the next 20 years traveling in search of esoteric wisdom; she claimed she was initiated by hidden Tibetan masters during this period. She said the Masters told her to spread the ancient teachings of the East in the West—including ideas of reincarnation, karma, spiritual evolution, and subtle energies. In 1873, she traveled to the United States, where she became temporarily associated with Spiritualism, a movement seeking contact with the dead. Then in 1879, she and Henry Steel Olcott (1832–1907) went to India in pursuit of the "Ancient Wisdom." There they founded the Theosophical Society to study clues to what they believed were the eternal Wisdom Teachings which have appeared since time immemorial as an esoteric tradition within each religion.

9.1 Madame Helena Blavatsky, founder of the Theosophical Society, had mystical tendencies from her childhood in Russia

Brilliant, gifted as a clairvoyant, charismatic as a weaver of stories, stormy in temperament, and steadfastly dedicated to the mission she felt had been given to her by the Masters, Madame Blavatsky attracted followers—such as Frank Baum, the author of *The Wizard of Oz*—as well as attackers. The media opposed her; even the Society for Psychical Research proclaimed her a fraud. She was said to be able to manifest objects out of thin air and to exchange mysterious letters with the invisible Masters. Although she emphasized the setting aside of personal considerations and the attempt to evolve metaphysically for the sake of others whose spiritual power was undeveloped, she was apparently hurt by the accusations. Mocked and unhealthy, she struggled to finish writing her magnum opus, *The Secret Doctrine: The Synthesis of Science, Religion, and Philosophy*, a huge and obscure tome of esoteric sciences from both East and West. She predicted that twentieth-century scientists would begin to regard its contents as factual truths after her own death, which occurred in 1891.

The Theosophical movement had considerable appeal for intellectual upper-class women. Blavatsky had described the Creative Power in nature as androgynous—both male and female. She had identified the potential for spiritually-inclined women to move beyond the constraints of traditional religions in the search for metaphysical knowledge, and in the process, to develop as personally powerful individuals. In this quest, she affirmed, gender is irrelevant.

Blavatsky's successors in the Theosophical movement were both women: Annie Besant (1847–1933) and Katherine Tingley (1847–1929). They each had something of Blavatsky's charismatic spiritual gifts and Olcott's administrative ability, but they had different visions and soon the movement split into two factions, both convinced that they were ushering in a New Civilization. Their ideas fed into the stream that became the "New Age" movement, the term used by Alice Bailey (1880–1949), leader of the Arcane School. Despite the leading roles of women in such movements, the Arcane School often uses male-oriented language, such as "men" for "people." On the other hand, it is now promoting the idea of "The New Group of World Servers," defining the group as "every man and woman in every country who is working to heal the breaches between people."[11]

The term "New Age" was also used by the South African visionary Johanna Brandt (1876–1965), founder of the World Harmony Movement, which seems to have some roots in Theosophy, as well as Christianity, occult traditions, and New Thought (which emphasizes the positive power of the mind). Brandt's movement aims to promote "Harmony between races; the sexes; religion and politics; spirit and matter; mysticism and intellect; faith and reason; nature and science etc.—Harmony in one world, between God and Man."[12] Married to a Christian leader, she received radical revelations that went beyond the Bible to assert that the coming Paraclete ("Comforter") promised by Jesus would be a wise and beautiful South African woman who would be called "God the Mother." She wrote that the Mother would first be recognized by women, but that through them all humanity would then grow in mysticism, imagination, and intuition. Brandt foretold great earth changes during the transition from the astrological age of Pisces to the present age of Aquarius and emphasized self-development rather than obedience to old authoritarian structures—themes that have become familiar parts of all New Age movements.

9.2 Helena Roerich encouraged women's spiritual liberation, calling them to lead humanity into a new era

Theosophy has spawned many other offshoots, and women continue to play significant roles in several of them. One important Theosophy-inspired female leader was another Russian aristocrat, Helena Ivanovna Roerich (1879–1955; fig. 9.2). As a child, she had unusual dreams and fiery spiritual experiences. Her husband, the artist Nicholas Roerich, was one of many symbolist artists and poets such as Mondrian and Yeats who were influenced by Theosophy during its heyday in the late nineteenth and early twentieth centuries. The couple were both fascinated by Oriental philosophy, and Helena translated Madame Blavatsky's complex book, *The Secret Doctrine*, into Russian. She set up many women's organizations and in her letters encouraged women to abandon their old passive roles. Helena felt that women were destined to play a leading part in the spiritual development of humanity, and she wrote that most world problems were caused by the enslavement and humiliation of women. To her, Love, Beauty, and Knowledge should be the hallmark of woman's rise in the world and with it the elevation of civilization, "because

from the very beginning she was chosen to link the two worlds, visible and invisible."[13] Helena and Nicholas said they were in communication with the Mahatmas,
or great souls, living in their subtle bodies somewhere in the Himalayas, who gave
them a new spiritual path: "Agni Yoga," an esoteric synthesis of ancient wisdom,
science, and culture. Helena was called "The Mother of Agni Yoga," because the
teachings were given mostly to her. She accompanied her husband on difficult
expeditions through Central Asia and the Himalayas in search of ethnographical,
linguistic, religious, scientific, and cultural material. They then settled in the
Himalayan foothills in India. After Nicholas's death, Helena continued writing to
people in many countries, encouraging them in their spiritual quest, and her writings are still of interest to spiritual seekers.

Another woman influenced by Theosophy—Elizabeth Clare Prophet (b. 1939
in New Jersey)—has developed a following who believe she is guided by invisible
"Ascended Masters," who have dictated over 1,800 messages to her. Among them
are Master Morya (who was also reportedly guiding Madame Blavatsky, Helena
Roerich, and many other Russian mystics even today), Buddha, Jesus, Saint
Germain (a mysterious European who is said to have moved in royal circles up to
the eighteenth century and to have been an adept at alchemy), and Mary, mother of
Jesus. Prophet wrote of the profound impact of her first encounter with Mary, and
the understanding that she reportedly received:

The love of her heart poured out to me. It melted my soul, my self. In the presence of her immense compassion I was being wrapped in the swaddling
garment of her understanding.... Mother Mary explains that it is the hatred of
Mother, or "anti-Mother," that denies the source of that Christ consciousness in
all. That denial effectively closes off to the children of this generation the rising fountain of purity that is the Mother light within their own temples.[14]

With her husband Mark, Prophet founded Montessori International, a worldwide
system of children's schools based on the creative educational methods of Dr.
Maria Montessori. Elizabeth Clare Prophet is now President of the Summit
Lighthouse, Summit University Press, and Summit University, and spiritual leader
of the Church Universal and Triumphant. She has also founded a spiritual community in the U.S. in the Rocky Mountains with a reputation for being politically
right-wing. It was said to be storing armaments in anticipation of a catastrophic
apocalypse, but these were reportedly removed by the staff in 1993 after the U.S.
government moved against another apocalyptic community.

Numerous other New Age movements are based on messages said to be coming from invisible spiritual masters. The "channels" for these messages are most
often women. Sometimes these women keep themselves in the background. This
was especially the case with Helen Schucman (1909–1982), who channeled *A
Course in Miracles*, with teachings that subtly lead one to understand they are
coming from Jesus. Schucman was a highly unlikely medium, for she was a
tenured professor in medical psychology in New York City. In 1965, after a series
of spiritual dreams and visions, she heard an inner voice, which she eventually
identified as Jesus, saying to her, "This is a course in miracles, please take notes."
As she later explained:

The Voice made no sound, but seemed to be giving me a kind of rapid, inner dictation which I took down in a shorthand notebook. The writing was never automatic. It could be interrupted at any time and later picked up again. It made obvious use of my educational background, interests and experience, but that was in matters of style rather than content. Certainly the subject matter itself was the last thing I would have expected to write about... . It made me very uncomfortable, but it never seriously occurred to me to stop. It seemed to be a special assignment I had somehow, somewhere agreed to complete... . On the one hand I still regarded myself as officially an agnostic, resented the material I was taking down, and was strongly impelled to attack it and prove it wrong. On the other hand I spent considerable time in taking it down and later in dictating it to Bill [Dr. William Thetford, her medical colleague and eventually popularizer of the Course], so it was apparent that I took it quite seriously... . I was in the impossible position of not believing my own life's work.[15]

To protect her professional and social reputation as a scientist, as well as to keep the focus on Jesus rather than herself, Schucman concealed her identity as the "scribe" for *A Course in Miracles* from most of her friends, relatives, and colleagues. The Course became quite popular in the West, with many people forming study circles based on its teachings.

The New Age channeling phenomenon has also included Jane Roberts (d. 1984), who channeled a "personality" known as Seth who taught "You create your own reality," Pat Rodegast, who has served as channel for "Emmanuel" for over 30 years, using books, workshops, and the Internet to convey messages such as "Wherever the voice of Love calls you, follow it. However Truth knocks upon your door, open to it,"[16] and JZ Knight (b. 1946), who has channeled messages from Ramtha, said to be a 35,000-year-old warrior from the lost culture of Lemuria. When Knight, an attractive blonde woman, is supposedly channeling Ramtha, she takes on an entirely different, masculine persona, often speaking and moving provocatively and aggressively. Ramtha's School of Enlightenment website asserts that this is not JZ's alter ego or a case of personality disorder or fakery. According to the School:

Ramtha, while being channeled through JZ Knight, has the ability to open his eyes, walk, dance, eat and drink, laugh, speak, converse, and teach his students personally. JZ Knight is the only channel he has chosen and uses to deliver his message. Ramtha's choice to channel his message through a woman rather than using his own physical body is making the statement that God and the divine are not the prerogative of men alone and that women have always been worthy expressions of the divine, capable of genius and of being God realized... . It is also making the statement that the true essence of the human person is not limited to the physical body or a specific gender.[17]

In general, the metaphysical Theosophical approach to spirituality, including channeling of presumed invisible teachers who are typically male, has made it possible for numerous gifted women to operate outside the constraints of established religious organizations. It arose largely within Christian countries, challenging the idea of Christian superiority by introducing Eastern philosophies and challenging entrenched patriarchal structures by making room for nonprofessional and female leadership.

Wicca

Another arena in which many women have found a significant spiritual niche is Neo-Paganism. Its practitioners feel they are modeling their rites on those of ancient people with a close relationship to the sacredness of the natural world. One of its expressions—Wicca—is usually traced to an English civil servant, Gerald Gardner (1884–1964), who was much influenced by the writings of Margaret Murray (1863–1963). She was an eminent anthropologist, archaeologist, and Egyptologist with a special interest in the history of witchcraft. Her research led her to the conclusion that witchcraft was of pre-Christian origin, a continuous stream that led back to the fertility rites of matriarchal Paleolithic tribes in Europe. She was mocked by other scholars, but she persisted in her research, saw her writings published by prestigious academic presses, and wrote the story of her life at the age of 100. Gardner first published his beliefs and practices in 1954; the rites he used were derived not from ancient rituals—of which there is of course no written record—but perhaps from the works of another early twentieth-century Englishman, Aleister Crowley, whose book *Magick in Theory and Practice* is still popular. Another strand of Wicca—Alexandrian Wicca—was developed by a husband-and-wife team, Alex and Maxine Sanders. Both Gardnerian and Alexandrian forms of Wicca tend to be patriarchal. A more recent version has arisen called Dianic Wicca, which is feminist and non-hierarchical.

Gardnerian Wicca was originally a mystery religion available only to those who had been initiated into an existing coven of up to 13 people (13 being the number of phases of the moon in a year). Each coven had its own presiding priest or priestess, who was expected to be skilled in rituals and the use of magic after having passed through several degrees of initiation. This systematic approach, modeled on late Victorian occult traditions, has been creatively revised to allow for solitary witches, and includes modern rituals as well as those considered to be of ancient origin, shamanic practices, and Buddhist and Hindu beliefs.

Wicca is a rather formalized religion, as opposed to witchcraft, which is an individual skill including the practice of magic and casting of spells rather than a particular spiritual path, and may involve using black magic, which Wicca does not support. Because countless women were killed in earlier times on suspicion of witchcraft, the label "witch" carries dangerous connotations, but many contemporary women have nonetheless adopted it to explain their spiritual path. Others use the label "Pagan," equally anathema in Christian tradition, which tried to stamp out earlier nature-oriented spiritual ways and gave their adherents the pejorative labels "pagan" (meaning a non-religious person) or "heathen" (an unenlightened person living on the heaths, on the margins of presumably civilized society).

In general, Wiccans believe in a divine force that both pervades and encompasses the entire cosmos. Everything that exists is therefore sacred, and the natural environment is to be revered rather than destroyed. To commune with this all-pervading force, Wiccans conduct rites within a circle. It is ritually demarcated, cleansed, and blessed for this purpose. In some groups, the participants are naked; others may wear robes, medieval costumes, or ordinary clothes. Many rites celebrate points of the solar year—the two solstices and two equinoxes (known as the "Minor **Sabbats**"), and the "Major Sabbats": Imbolc (February 2), Beltane (May 1), Lughnasadh (August 1), and Samhain (October 31). Another set of rituals follows and honors the phases of the moon.

Many Wiccans see the divine force as both masculine and feminine, Goddess and God, and emphasize the natural balance of opposites—night and day, summer and winter, light and dark, life and death. Some Gardnerians practice sexual rituals in which the male ritually honors the female in order to call up the power of the Goddess. After surveying many Neo-Pagan or modern Wiccan groups in the United States, radio producer and journalist Margot Adler came to the conclusion that despite the differences, all agree on several basic principles:

The world is holy. Nature is holy. The body is holy. Sexuality is holy. The mind is holy. The imagination is holy. You are holy. A spiritual path that is not stagnant ultimately leads one to the understanding of one's own divine nature. Thou art Goddess. Thou art God. Divinity is immanent in all nature. It is as much within you as without.

In our culture which has for so long denied and denigrated the feminine as negative, evil, or, at best, small and unimportant, women (and men too) will never understand their own creative strength and divine nature until they embrace the creative feminine, the source of inspiration, the Goddess within.

While one can at times be cut off from experiencing the deep and ever-present connection between oneself and the universe, there is no such thing as sin (unless it is simply defined as that estrangement) and guilt is never very useful. The energy you put into the world comes back.[18]

In its contemporary manifestations, Wicca has become interwoven with environmental and political activist movements that are not based in any religion as such; these newer expressions of Wicca are less patriarchal than the earlier occult forms. By word of mouth and the Internet, which bypasses the corridors of entrenched power, the informal Neo-Pagan network has been drawn into helping with various causes, such as anti-war demonstrations and disaster relief. When the U.S. government failed to help the poor people of New Orleans after Hurricane Katrina in 2005, some of the volunteers who came forth were witches. They used natural methods to try to clean contaminated soil, served as grief counselors, and were among the critics of the racism that was exposed when the survivors were neglected. One of the most powerful witches who has taken a pro-active political stance is Starhawk (fig. 9.3). She travels around the world from her home in California, teaching magic, ritual, and nonviolent direct activism, as well as organizing and participating in courageous actions for peace, the environment, economic problems, and justice. Her writings have helped to develop the Neo-Pagan and Goddess movements (see box, p. 289), and she herself has co-founded Reclaiming, an activist version of Neo-Paganism. She concluded her 2002 book *Webs of Power* with a discussion of the pros and cons of mixing spirituality with politics.

Goddess Spirituality

Neo-Paganism is deeply interwoven with contemporary Western worship of the Goddess. This movement is also considered by its followers to be a revival of ancient ways. It can be traced back to the pioneering research of Marija Gimbutas (1921–1994), a respected Lithuanian expert in eastern European archaeology who conducted her studies under the aegis of Harvard University and UCLA. By digging into linguistics, ethnology, symbols, and folklore as well as unearthing goddess figures from prehistoric archaeological sites, she decided that beneath the remains of patriarchal warrior Indo-European cultures there appeared to be older matristic cultures that worshiped the divine in female forms as well as male. Symbols and sculptures dating back to 35,000 BCE show goddesses as creatrixes with emphasis on their swelling breasts, bellies, buttocks, and vulvae. The cultures are thought to have been peaceful, for people had no weapons except for hunting implements. Having advanced beyond hunting and gathering as a way of life, they lived in settled agricultural communities, usually in beautiful environments. According to Gimbutas's theory, women seem to have been on an equal footing with men, and the women seem to have run the temples. The cultures were more advanced in many ways than the nomadic warrior tribes that eventually invaded them, bringing domineering sky gods. There were two-story houses and temples with painted walls. In Çatal Hüyük, Turkey, for instance, archaeologists have found 140 sophisticated wall paintings from an urban civilization of the seventh millennium BCE that lasted a thousand years. This settlement is the earliest clear indication found so far of Goddess worship. In the many shrines built among the houses she is often depicted naked at the moment of giving birth, with the baby's head showing. Other images show her as a young maiden or an old woman. She is also

9.3 Starhawk, social activist and leader in earth-based spirituality

EXCERPT Spirit and Action
Starhawk

For 30 years and more, I've been walking that edge where the spiritual meets the political. For me, the two have always been integrated. My spirituality is rooted in the experience of the earth as a living, conscious being, and names this world, nature, human life, sexuality, and culture as sacred. And so I feel compelled to take action to protect the earth and to work for a world in which human freedom and creativity can fburish.

The edge where two systems meet can be a place of great fertility in nature. But edges and borders can also be sites of enormous conflct. Spirituality can bring life and vibrancy and imagination into activism—but the mixture of religion and politics can also fuel the most extreme and destructive acts and lead to systems of great repression... .

We should be rightly suspicious of religion when it means a belief system, a dogma, a set of standards for determining who are the Worthy People and who are the Others. The root meaning of the word "re-ligio"—"relinking"—has more to do with connection than with discrimination. Still, it's far too formal and systematic to convey what I'm talking about. Language is always a problem, because the English language doesn't have the word I want, a word that doesn't split "spirit" from "matter" or "nature" but integrates the sacred and the mundane, the high and the low, the dark and the light—a word that conveys the sense of living in an animate and generous universe. I am left with the word "spirit" or "spirituality" by default.

The type of spirituality I embrace is one that encourages us each to have our own relationship with the greater creative powers, that teaches us not what we should believe but how we can learn to listen, that sees spirit embodied in nature, and that honors the body, the earth, and the everyday. While we draw from the past and respect the wisdom of the ancestors, we are not trying to live in yesterday or abandon the post-modern world, but rather to fnd those practices and modes of awareness that can lead us into a viable future... .

Why bring ritual, magic, spirituality into action? Why mix up a clear-clean militant critique of the world with woo-woo, mumbo-jumbo, New Age fluffy stuff? The frst reason is that a part of our humanity needs symbols and myths and mystery, yearns for a connection to something broader and deeper than our surface life. That part of us is powerful and dangerous: it can call us to the most profound compassion or justify the worst intolerance, lead us to sacrifce for the greater good or to commit mass murder in the name of our ideals, open us to a wider experience of life or imprison us in a narrow moralism, inspire our liberation or function as an agent of our repression. Progressive movements are understandably wary of it, for we have all seen the religious impulse fuel hatred and holy wars and justify extreme oppression. But we ignore it at our peril, for if a movement of liberation does not address the spiritual part of us, then movements of repression will claim that terrain as their own.

The events of 9/11 showed us how deep our need for expression and communal connection in moments of deep pain really is. When normality is shattered, when we face death and loss, when we encounter great fear or great hope as we do in activism, we need some framework within which to fnd meaning in our experiences. Fundamentalisms of all sorts, whether religious or political or academic, appeal because they provide a coherent system of meaning. We need alternative ways of thinking, feeling, and understanding that lead to tolerance, compassion, and freedom. And we need to express them in ritual as well as in rhetoric if they are to touch the aching wounds of the soul... .

I admit that I do experience the world as alive and speaking. Forces and energies that have yet to be described by science are real to me. The birds, the trees, the rocks, the winds, the land itself have voices, and part of my work in changing the world is to listen deeply to them. The ancestors are present, and aid me in my work. When we cast a web of magical protection for an action, I can feel its power.

And I would rather live in an animate world. I believe we are likely to create a healthier, more dynamic, freer, and more balanced culture if we perceive ourselves as living cells in a living body imbued with an underlying consciousness than if we perceive the world as dead, exploitable matter.

The tools of magic—the understanding of energy and the power and use of symbols, the awareness of group consciousness and of ways in which to shift and shape it—are also the tools of political and social change. Dion Fortune's defnition of magic as "the art of changing consciousness at will" is also a fne defnition of transformational political praxis. We construct our world through the stories we tell about it, and the practice of magic is the art of cultural storyshifting, the conscious dreaming of a new dream... .

Without a spiritual base for my activism, without regular practices that renew my energies and my sense of hope, and without a community to share them with, I might long ago have succumbed to frustration and despair. Political work is hard. Results are rarely immediate and sometimes barely evident. The forces we contest are immensely powerful. To carry on for a lifetime, we need faith in something, whether it is the perfectibility of human nature, the ultimate withering of the state, or the belief that the universe is on the side of justice, as Martin Luther King said. My connection to the earth helps me believe that loss can lead to transformation, that decay can be food for something new, that all energy moves in cycles, that the universe is flled with immense creativity which is stronger than violence, and that hate is ultimately not as powerful a force as love... .

When we know what we stand for and are willing to risk ourselves for, what the standard is by which we measure our actions and choices, what is most deeply important to us, and what most profoundly nourishes and inspires us, we know what is truly sacred. All we need to do, then, is to put our life energies and time and creativity at its disposal, however we name or describe it. Then the great powers of the universe, inner and outer, seen and unseen, move in alignment, and as agents of embodied love we are fed and sustained.

Starhawk, *Webs of Power: Notes from the Global Uprising*, Gabriola Island, British Columbia, Canada: New Society Publishers, 2002, pp. 261–5.

worshiped as an intimate of animals such as leopards. Many efforts have been made to deduce from such clues the religious beliefs and practices of those early people, particularly with reference to the obvious worship of the Goddess. Marija Gimbutas concluded near the end of her decades of research:

> I cannot see that the Goddess as she was can be reconstructed and returned to our lives, but we have to take the best that we can seize. The best understanding is of divinity itself. The Christian God punishes and is angry and does not fit into our times at all. We need something better, we need something closer, we need something that we can touch and we need some compassion, some love, and also a return to the nature of things. Through an understanding of what the Goddess was, we can better understand nature and we can build our ideologies so that it will be easier for us to live. We have to be grateful for what we have, for all the beauty, and the Goddess is exactly that.[19]

Evidence gathered by Gimbutas and others has led to many attempts to reconstruct the existence of widespread worship of the Goddess by our ancient ancestors. Merlin Stone published her classic book *When God was a Woman* in 1976, proposing that Judaism, Christianity, and Islam had violently suppressed worship of the Goddess, replacing her with awe of the jealous male God who in the Hebrew Bible commands, "You must completely destroy all the places where the nations you dispossess have served their gods, on high mountains, on hills, under any spreading tree; you must tear down their altars, smash their pillars, cut down their sacred poles, set fire to the carved images of their gods and wipe out their name from that place."[20] Stone proposes that "Ashtoreth," the main deity to be eliminated according to such instructions, was actually Astarte, the Queen of Heaven as she was known to the Canaanites (see illustration in Chapter 6). According to Stone, her identity as Goddess was hidden even in the scriptural accounts. She had been worshiped by many names in West Asia, which became the center of the patriarchal Abrahamic faiths, as well as elsewhere around the world.

The theory of a matriarchal prehistory in which women played leading roles and the Goddess was worshiped has not necessarily been academically accepted as fact. Cynthia Eller, Assistant Professor of Women and Religion at Montclair University, has devoted years to study of the phenomenon of this myth, only to conclude that it is surprising that anyone takes it seriously. She writes, "Poking holes in the 'evidence' for this myth was, to rely on cliché, like shooting fish in a barrel."[21] At the same time, the myth has a powerful psychological effect. Redefining the divine as Goddess has helped contemporary Western women to reject the patriarchal Western portrayal of women in general as dangerous, weak, and ignorant. In many historic cultures for which evidence does exist, the Goddess was worshiped as a wise, powerful, and prophetic being. She becomes an empowering symbol; women can turn to her for strength or discover her within themselves. Another major shift is the attitude of women toward their own sexuality. Contemplating the full-figured naked goddess statues, they cannot help understanding that they were made with a positive, appreciative attitude toward women's ability to create and nourish life with their own bodies. And the statues show that not only chaste young maidens are singled out for worship, as in Christian depictions of the Virgin Mary.

As is evident in the art of the older cultures, in which the Goddess is depicted as a young woman, a full-bodied mother, and an old crone, women are fully and naturally involved in the cycles of birth, life, death, and regeneration.

Women and also some men in many countries are trying to develop contemporary ways of worshiping the Goddess, celebrating rather than suppressing what lies within women. Carol Christ received her doctorate in Religious Studies from Yale, pioneered the development of "thealogy" (study of the meanings of the Goddess), and lives in Greece as Director of the Ariadne Institute for the Study of Myth and Ritual. She describes her vision of reclaiming the Goddess today:

> The Goddess is the power of intelligent embodied love that is the ground of all being. The earth is the body of the Goddess. All beings are interdependent in the web of life. Nature is intelligent, alive, and aware. As part of nature, human beings are relational, embodied, and interdependent. The basis of ethics is the feeling of deep connection to all people and all beings in the web of life. The symbols and rituals of Goddess religion bring these values to consciousness and help us build communities in which we can create a more just, peaceful, and harmonious world.[22]

Some contemporary feminists do not directly worship the Goddess, for they reject any attempts to worship an anthropomorphic deity. Nevertheless, in the informal "feminist spirituality" or "women's spirituality" movement—in which a seeker may blend many religious threads in her own spiritual life—there is often an underlying assumption that ancient civilizations were matriarchal and Goddess-worshiping, and that these qualities created more peaceful and environmentally respectful societies.

Afro-Caribbean Mixtures

Religious boundaries are more fluid than is suggested by the separate names for each faith, and some seemingly dissimilar religions have been merged to form new **syncretic** mixtures (combining diverse practices). This has happened in many times and places under varying circumstances. For example, syncretic mixtures of different African spiritual traditions, local indigenous practices, European Spiritualism, and Roman Catholic devotion to saints developed around the Caribbean as millions of slaves were brought from Africa to the Americas between 1540 and 1850. The slaves had their own religious ways, but those who survived the trauma of the boat passage were baptized as Christians when they arrived and their own practices were suppressed. Some of the slaves used secret symbols to continue worshiping their deities as best they could, such as tying a red string around bananas or placing a bit of white cloth over a door. They also drew links between their gods and goddesses and the Catholic saints—for instance, worshiping the Yoruban god Shango in the form of St. Barbara, who is associated with thunder, lightning, and fire. In Cuba, the resulting fervent devotions to the saints earned the pejorative label "Santeria," from the Spanish word for saint (*santo*), but the preferred name for this path is Lukumi. Other varieties of this path have evolved in Brazil, where they are known as Candomble or Umbanda. In Haiti, the syncretic mixture is called Vodou or Voodo. There is some evidence that such syncretism already existed in Africa, particularly in the Kongo Empire. In all cases, these newer versions are creatively combining fragments of older traditions and understanding them in new ways.

Santeria is based on an understanding that the world is a network of beings, both visible and invisible, all sharing the same energy, known as **ashe**, which is always dynamic, moving, growing, connecting everything. Oludumare is the invisible, mysterious source of all things, whose knowable aspects are called the **orishas** (see Chapter 2). These gods and goddesses are not remote deities; although invisible, they are actively involved in the life of the visible world. They need constant nourishment and praise, and only humans can offer these, thus keeping *ashe* flowing properly through the web of life. The particular energy pattern of each woman or man is related to the energy of a particular *orisha*, who thus "owns one's head."

The highly structured rituals of Santeria are conducted by initiated priests (**santeros**) or priestesses (**santeras**). Women are not allowed to undergo the highest initiations—these are reserved only for men. The *santeros* and *santeras* become the physical counterpart of the deity who "owns their head," and they have the power to initiate others similarly. A *santera* who has initiated one or more men or women as priests or priestesses is an *iyalocha* (mother of an *orisha*); a *santero* who has done the same is a *babalocha* (father of an *orisha*); their homes become houses dedicated to the saints where ceremonies and celebrations may be held. They may also initiate people into lower levels of practice as their godchildren.

Marta Moreno Vega, an Afro-Puerto Rican professor in New York and a Santeria priestess and godmother, teaches her godchildren the stories of the *orishas* as spiritual guidance for their lives. She reports:

Every 15 days, my godchildren and I sit and conduct a *misa*, a ceremony in honor of our ancestors. Before and after these sessions, we discuss the role of the *orishas* in our lives, and the differences we are experiencing in our lives as we become one with our spirits. Our sessions, like all new experiences, began tentatively as I struggled to accept that my long years of study would prepare me to take on a greater level of responsibility.

When at last I placed the chairs for my godchildren in a circle in front of my *boveda*, my ancestral altar table, I began to feel the spiritual energy fill my living room. The rays of the afternoon Sunday sun seemed to brighten as I set my *boveda* in the center of the room. My hands shook as I tried to light the match for the candle to be placed before the ancestor altar. Suddenly the flame soared higher than it should have, and as the room filled with the luminous energies of my spirit mothers I knew then everything would be fine.[23]

In addition to such teaching sessions, divination by means of cowrie shells may be employed, and singing and dancing are used to evoke possession of the *santera* or *santero* by his or her *orisha*. Offerings to the *orishas* include animal sacrifices, a practice which was controversial in the United States. However, in 1993 a landmark case in Florida allowed such sacrifices on the basis of freedom of religion, and the secrecy that had surrounded the practice of Santeria in the United States decreased.

Similarly, all of the Afro-Brazilian religions were labeled as criminal by the Brazilian government and condemned as "devil worship" by the Catholic Church until the second half of the twentieth century, when they became more visible aspects of the popular culture. It is estimated that in Brazil alone, millions of people practice Roman Catholicism in public but worship the *orishas* in private. Umbanda is now attracting not only people with African roots but also women of European ancestry, who see it as an appealing nature-based religion that offers personal empowerment and healing.

In Benin, West Africa, Vodou (or Vodun, as it is called there) is the national religion, practiced by the majority of the population. Haitian Vodou is practiced not only in Haiti (where it is popularly said that there are 85 percent Catholics, 15 percent Protestants, and 100 percent Vodou followers) but also in places to which Haitians have moved to escape poverty and oppression, including New York City, now home to some 450,000 Haitians. Alourdes, a Vodou priestess in Brooklyn known as "Mama Lola," has become famous through the research of Karen McCarthy Brown, who is both Professor of the Sociology and Anthropology of Religion and also a participant-observer in Vodou rites. She observes that most people come to Mama Lola for healing:

She adheres to a tradition that discourages making large profits from healing work. Her reputation, spread by word of mouth, has led to invitations to perform "treatments" throughout the eastern United States and Canada and in several places in the Caribbean and Central America... . She deals both with health problems and with a full range of love, work, and family difficulties. Like healers in related traditions found throughout the Caribbean and South America, Alourdes combines the skills of a medical doctor, a psychotherapist, a social worker, and a priest... .

[On saints' celebration days in her home] Clients, friends, and relatives gather around a decorated "niche," whose centerpiece is a table laden with food. Here they pray, clap, and sing until the crowd is sufficiently "heated up" to entice a Vodou spirit to join the party, to "ride" Alourdes. In a trance state from which she will later emerge with little or no memory of what has transpired, her body becomes the "horse" of the spirit, her voice the spirit's voice, her words and behavior those of the spirit.

These possession-performances, which blend pro forma actions and attitudes with those responsive to the immediate situation, are the heart of a Vodou ceremony. The spirits talk with the faithful. They hug them, hold them, feed them, chastise them. Group and individual problems are aired through interaction with the spirits. Strife is healed and misunderstanding rectified.[24]

The most women-centered of the Afro-Caribbean mixtures is Candomble, in which women tend to be chosen for the highest positions and to form the majority of the adherents (fig. 9.4). A major festival of the water goddess Yemanji, who is linked to the Christian Virgin Mary, is held every year on January 1 throughout Brazil. Great crowds of celebrants dressed in white wade into the ocean at sunset, setting

9.4 A Candomble priestess presiding over the Casa Branca, a ritual house in Salvador, Brazil

afloat little boats containing spiritually meaningful objects to carry their prayers to the goddess. New priestesses and priests are also initiated by high priestesses. One of the best-known Candomble high priestesses is Mae Beata (b. 1931), who was formally initiated by a traditional matriarch at the age of 25 but learned the religion as a child from descendants of slaves on a sugar cane plantation. Now she is in continual demand for her spiritual services and advice. Not only a charismatic spiritual leader, she is also a social activist who has had to defend the legitimacy of Candomble as a religion. Although Brazilian social and religious hierarchies have long been run by men, Mae Beata is one of the women who have, in Candomble, turned this structure upside-down.

In all Afro-Caribbean religions, women are playing significant roles, in part because the religions are operating as folk alternatives behind the scenes even while the Catholic Church is the dominant visible religious institution. In contrast to the strong patriarchal institutions, in these syncretistic folk mixtures women can be more self-directed, answering the calls to their spirits. Yet they are still operating within frameworks largely headed by men. In the final chapter of this book, we will look at another alternative: women ignoring any kind of institution and simply striking out on their own spiritually.

Key Terms

Khalsa
gurdwara
prasad
langar
Sabbats

syncretic
ashe
orisha
santeros/santeras

Suggested Reading

Adler, Margot, *Drawing Down the Moon*, New York: Penguin, 1979, 1986. An early survey of Neo-Pagan groups in the United States.

Brown, Karen McCarthy, *Mama Lola: A Vodou Priestess in Brooklyn*, Berkeley: University of California Press, 1991. Intimate account of the life and work of a Haitian Vodou priestess in New York City.

Christ, Carol P., *Rebirth of the Goddess: Finding Meaning in Feminist Spirituality*, New York and London: Routledge, 1997. Discerning exploration of the rebirth of Goddess worship in western cultures.

Eller, Cynthia, *The Myth of Matriarchal Prehistory: Why an Invented Past Will Not Give Women a Future*, Boston: Beacon Press, 2000. Informed skepticism about the widely circulated theory that prehistoric cultures were matriarchal goddess-worshipers.

Gadon, Elinor W., *The Once and Future Goddess*, San Francisco: Harper and Row, 1989. Illustrated historical examination of Goddess worship, with extension into its contemporary manifestations.

Gonzalez-Wippler, Migene, *Santeria: The Religion*, St. Paul, Minnesota: Llewellyn Publications, 1996. An anthropologist and initiate describes many aspects of the practice of this usually secret religion.

Puttick, Elizabeth, *Women in New Religions*, New York: St. Martin's Press, 1997. A social history of women's involvement in new religious movements.

Sered, Susan Starr, *Priestess, Mother, Sacred Sister: Religions Dominated by Women*, New York and Oxford: Oxford University Press, 1994. Attempt to find common features in women-dominated religions from widely different cultures.

Starhawk, *The Spiral Dance: A Rebirth of the Ancient Religion of the Great Goddess*, San Francisco: HarperSanFrancisco, 1979, 1999. A classic exploration of contemporary Goddess worship, by one of its major practitioners.

Starhawk, *Webs of Power: Notes from the Global Uprising*, Gabriola Island, British Columbia: New Society Publishers, 2002. Stories of a diverse global justice movement that finds much of its strength in earth-based, Goddess, and Neo-Pagan spirituality.

Stone, Merlin, *Ancient Mirrors of Womanhood*, Boston: Beacon Press, 1979. Global survey of Goddess stories.

Stone, Merlin, *When God was a Woman*, San Diego: Harcourt Brace Jovanovich, 1976. Classic survey of archaeological evidence of ancient Goddess worship.

Vega, Marta Moreno, *The Altar of My Soul: The Living Traditions of Santeria*, New York: Ballantine Books/Random House, 2000. A professor and Santeria priestess gives an intimate account of her spiritual experiences within the faith.

Wessinger, Catherine, ed., *Women's Leadership in Marginal Religions: Explorations Outside the Mainstream*, Urbana/Chicago: University of Illinois Press, 1993. Explorations of the thesis that American women are finding personal empowerment and freedom from authoritarian oppression in religions outside mainstream Christianity.

10
WOMEN BEYOND RELIGIONS

A peaceful revolution is going on

JEAN SHINODA BOLEN

Increasing numbers of women are expressing their spirituality outside the constraints of institutionalized, often patriarchal religious structures. In the past, there
was strong social and family pressure to be a member of the religious tradition of
one's family and one's community. Today, particularly in hyper-individualistic
Western cultures, there is somewhat less social resistance to making one's own
choices, choices that transcend community boundaries. Some women are converting to other religions; some have abandoned religion; some are exploring outside
traditional religious structures, searching for meaning, searching for experience of
an invisible reality, searching for self-identity. In her poem "The Journey," Mary
Oliver expresses this search succinctly:

> ... But little by little
> as you left their voices behind,
> the stars began to burn
> through the sheets of clouds,
> and there was a new voice,
> which you slowly
> recognized as your own,
> that kept you company
> as you strode deeper and deeper
> into the world,
> determined to do
> the only thing you could do—
> determined to save
> the only life you could save.[1]

Contemporary women beyond religions may not be famous, for they are not supported by large, fund-raising, publicity-generating, power-holding organizations.
But they are finding personal satisfaction and useful opportunities to be agents of
change. Their ways are many and varied. In this final chapter, we will look at a few
patterns as exemplars: personal spirituality, mystics and healers, eclectic approaches, and groups without hierarchy or dogma.

Personal Spirituality

According to its Latin root, *re-ligio*, religion is that which re-ties us to some invisible reality. Failing to reconnect authentically with this reality through organized religions, many women have tried to do so in personal, idiosyncratic ways.

Some women have discovered the underlying reality through spiritual experience of the natural world. As the child of a Protestant evangelical family in the prairies of Winnipeg, Canada, Marianne Worcester kept a secret scrapbook of pictures of and poetry about nature. She did so secretly because, as she explains:

▨ Our belief system abhorred external aids to devotion and was suspicious of such expressions of passion for the natural world that might detract the created from the Creator. Although I faithfully and even passionately searched the Bible for the divine revelation hidden there, I did not abandon the sacred texts of the earth itself or the intuitive knowledge I carried of my connection to the things of this world. I was always in danger of being misunderstood.... And yet the connection between beauty and spirit in landscape itself had been made. This connection lay in a reality outside of metaphor or analogy. I knew that the natural world did not just point to something else, it was complete in itself, and I was part of it, like stars and grass. I learned the term pantheist and applied it to myself like a small stigmata, marveling in secret. ▨

As the new bride of an outdoor man in Vancouver, Marianne was suddenly catapulted from the prairies into the wildernesses that she had previously idealized, and she was terrified—terrified of mountains, terrified of the sea. But gradually, very gradually, she came to terms with her fears and discovered the reality, not the romanticism, of spirit in nature. Living on a small island surrounded by ocean, she found that:

▨ Everything here resonated with spirit, with meaning, with its own life. I marveled and built altars on my sacred sites—circles of stones to which I brought humble offerings—returning to the gestures of my child-self, the cycle complete. Light, dark, sound, silence, tide, wind and water are my unteachers. I learn to bear the beauty, to submit to silence as to joy, to tolerate the ambiguity of half-light or the unvarying remittance of green. I unlearn the craving for variation and the cold comforts of a small-scale world.... I am simply here, awake and alert, where the sheltered moist places are, where water seeps perpetually out of the earth onto velvet mosses and galaxies of microbes break everything down and reform it again. I know I have come for benediction, begging absolution, yearning to be home.[2] ▨

Octagenarian Dorothy Maclean from Canada says that for many decades she has been receiving communications from the spirits of plants, minerals, and animals. These communications gave information that was used to develop flourishing gardens, yielding huge vegetables on the bleak, sandy northeast coast of Scotland. Those gardens became the basis of the Findhorn Community, now a famous center for spiritual workshops teaching "co-creation with nature and attunement to the divinity within all beings." The Community explains:

> We believe that humanity is engaged in an evolutionary expansion of consciousness, and seek to develop new ways of living infused with spiritual values. We have no formal creed or doctrine. We recognize and honour all the world's major religions as the many paths to knowing our own inner divinity.[3]

Before receiving the communications, Maclean had been sitting in meditation several times a day as a spiritual discipline. Otherwise, she feels:

> We get too caught up in whatever it is, the world's ways and so on. Each time we make a choice we learn something. We get a result and we learn from the result what satisfies us.… . So we keep on choosing until we find what really makes us joyful, and that's the connection with the divine in all things… . To me God is the life energy in everything… . If we get past our excuses and have a self-discipline, we'll just love doing it. It will change us mightily, because the more we bathe ourselves in these wonderful vibrations, the more they're part of our lives and the more they change the world.[4]

Women's personal spiritual disciplines may take any form, in the midst of their other social roles. Young mothers, for instance, may find breastfeeding their babies a calming and meaningful spiritual "practice" that takes them beyond mundane thoughts and feelings. As we saw in Chapter 1, nurses and doctors may encounter spiritual experiences in the midst of medical practice. For the well-known Jungian psychiatrist Jean Shinoda Bolen (fig. 10.1), her spiritual "rituals" include her morning cup of coffee and her sessions with clients:

> If spiritual practice is a quality of timelessness and openness to others, then I have two unorthodox spiritual practices. One is my morning coffee meditation. I live on the side of a mountain overlooking the San Francisco Bay area. I see the sun rise over the eastern hills every morning and I usually awake before, or around, dawn. My house is quiet, I have a couple of cups of coffee, so with a coffee cup in one hand, I look out of my window and see the perspective of the beauty in the distance, or I get fogged in and I am in what I consider the equivalent of being by the side of a pool in which things rise to the surface and I notice them.
>
> The other unorthodox practice—if it has to do with a quality of attentiveness and compassion and a wider view of putting myself and this person that I am with into a field—it is that as a Jungian and as a psychiatrist I spend "50-minute hours" with people in my office. I listen to what they tell me and I respond from my heart, consciousness, etc. Since my work has a great deal to do with listening to the dreams and images, much of what comes to mind is metaphoric or it touches on a feeling through which I can connect with the feeling in the other person. Or it's a quality where I am focused on the other person and my psyche is bringing up associations to what they are telling me, so I'm not just diffused, thinking about other things. It revolves around what I

10.1 Jean Shinoda Bolen, Jungian psychiatrist, author, and workshop leader

am hearing, what my associations are to them and the history I know to previous images and dreams that have come up, to feelings I have had that have been similar to what they are telling me, so that I have access to a similar level of feelings or whatever it is that then suggests some response from me to them. So I consider the analytic session a compassionate, creative spiritual practice which takes in the realm of both light and shadow and which actually, in Jungian terms, is a *temenos*, which is Greek for "sanctuary." This is a safe place, it is a temple space.[5] ■

Another unique spiritual path was that taken by "Peace Pilgrim," an elderly woman who walked many miles every day for 28 years, crossing the United States seven times, up to her death in 1981 (fig.10.2). Wherever she walked, she talked to individuals and groups about peace. She carried only a comb, toothbrush, and writing materials in her tunic; she never asked for money, passed through many dangerous situations, and slept wherever she was at night. Thousands whom she met along the way were reportedly touched and transformed by meeting her. She was not a leader in or founder of any religious movement; she spoke simply from the heart. She explained her choice:

■ As I looked about the world, so much of it impoverished, I became increasingly uncomfortable about having so much while my brothers and sisters were starving. Finally I had to find another way. The turning point came when, in desperation and out of a very deep seeking for a meaningful way of life, I walked all one night through the woods. I came to a moonlit glade and prayed.

I felt a complete willingness, without any reservations, to give my life—to dedicate my life—to service. "Please use me!" I prayed to God. And a great peace came over me.

I tell you it's a point of no return. After that, you can never go back to completely self-centered living.[6] ■

Mystics and Healers

All religions have produced mystics and spiritual healers, but some women have grown their own versions of mysticism, with no basis in any particular organized

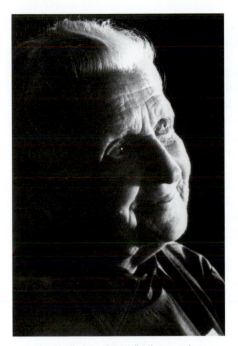

10.2 Peace Pilgrim, who walked across the United States for almost three decades carrying a simple message of inner peace

religion. This has always been the case, but women in highly individualistic Western societies are now freer to follow their inner calling. The mystical impulse may begin at any point in their lives, leading them along solitary paths into unknown territory.

Some women with mystical gifts have gone through great life crises before becoming spiritually sensitized. Elena Polyakova of Ukraine weighed only a little over a pound when she was born prematurely. Her twin brother was attended by the medical staff, but she was so small that they did not see her, and they threw her away. The cleaning lady just happened to see her moving in the tub with the placenta. At the age of 15 Elena became responsible for supporting her large family when her father died. She cleaned dishes in a canteen, lived on the maize she gathered there, and slept on the canteen floor. When she was 24 her mother and then her son died, sending her into such depression that she attempted suicide. After being declared clinically dead, she somehow survived but was paralyzed for a year, during which her husband left her. Amid all these difficulties, she found God and a gift for healing. She remarks,"I was so small that God had to take care of me. That's why I had to live."[7] As Elena recovered from paralysis, she discovered that she could diagnose and heal people spiritually. Now she is the busy director of a large medical center treating handicapped children, combining her spiritual healing gifts with degrees in psychology and clinical psychiatry.

The phenomenon of the "wounded healer" (in Father Henri Nouwen's phrase) is apparent in the lives of many deeply spiritual women. The renowned Bulgarian clairvoyant and healer Vanga (1911–1996) was blinded as a girl when she was carried for over a mile through swirling sand and dust by a tornado. She nonetheless could see with her inner vision things that sighted people could not see. She was sought out for her political predictions and information about missing people, and she helped anyone who came to her with a problem. They came in crowds, people of all sorts. As they stood in line outside her closed door, she would sometimes call someone by name out of turn if she saw s/he needed immediate attention. If anyone else tried to come in at that moment, she would know his/her name as well and send him/her to the end of the line. Scientists attempted to videotape her secretly at work, but after three days of being filmed with a hidden camera, she called to the video operator and asked him, "Do you think that being blind, I see nothing?" The film turned out to be blank.

INTERVIEW Koshi *Uncharted Ways*

A great contrast to the routine ways of organized religions is presented by the extraordinary life of a small and joyous woman from Kazakhstan who calls herself Koshi—or anything else that occurs to her. On meeting her, one cannot be sure whether she is a saint, a madwoman, a child, an ancient wise woman, or someone totally beyond categorizing. Before this interview, she had been traveling for five years without money, on an uncharted spiritual pilgrimage according to spiritual instructions. She had crossed the Gobi Desert twice on foot (and had become nearly blind in one eye); she had also traveled through India (where she was imprisoned for five months on false charges), Turkey, Syria, Nepal, Tibet, China, Pakistan, Bulgaria, and small former Soviet republics. She is a free and spontaneous soul dedicated to God (to whom she speaks as her Father), and amazing things happen to her.

Koshi had been a journalist and television personality before she started her pilgrimage through the unknown, but when she met the man whom she considered her Guru, he told her instead to sell sunfbwer seeds in the marketplace, like a peasant. She relates:

I said, "You are crazy. Everybody knows me; I'm very famous in the city." He said, "No, you are wrong. Nobody knows you. It is your mind that tells you that you are very famous, that you are very popular." Before that, I had become very tired of the life of the external world. I didn't want to stay in this world. There is nothing. I started to pray, "If Somebody exists, please send me a master. My heart is ready to receive some knowledge. If nobody exists, then give me death." In one day, my friend came with one man. At first, I remembered him, but I didn't know from where or when. He told me that my memory was closed. I asked many people why. They said, "If you know who you are, then you will be much crazier than you are now." My Guru told me that it is not important who you were in a previous life. The most important is who you are now and here. He also told me, "It is not necessary to read books or to stay in an occult religious school to study some spiritual technology. You have everything, but you just need to remember."

Twice my teacher burned money in front of me—thousands of American dollars. I said to him, "You are crazy. You know we can give this money to poor people; you can give this money to an old age home; you can give it to orphans." He said, "I don't give you energy to be proud that you help people. After that, you will be proud and say, 'I helped old people whom I gave this money to.' No, it is a sacrifce to God." After he burned the money I checked my pocket and I also put the money in the fre. He laughed and said, "Now I see you are ready to travel without money." So after this experience I crossed nine countries without money. I never thought about money, because I knew that it is not my problem. My Guru, my God, my Father told me to go. It is my only goal. Where will I sleep or eat, or who will give me money? It is not my problem. It is my Father's problem.

I recognized that all people whom I have met on my way are people whom God was working through. For me, they are divine messengers, a courier from my Father. And every situation gave me a lesson. In jail, I studied being grateful for everything—for a cup of tea, for milk, for a letter. Every morning I say, "Universe, I am very grateful for your kindness. Oh my Father, I am very grateful to you for your kindness and love." Sometimes I just imagine everyone's face whom I have met in my life and say, "May God bless you. May God give you happiness and prosperity, and what you need."

My Guru told me never to look for popularity and fame. He said, "It's not our mission. We come to this place to do our mission. It may be a very small mission, but we must do it and go. We never have followers, we never have an ashram. Our way is very narrow. In this way, somebody could kill you. It will be very painful, but you must be very strong. This way is very dangerous, but you must be very brave." I know that somebody can kill or harass me, but it's okay. It's my way and I know that. Everything is in the hands of God. I know that everything can change, and the Father can change it. We cannot know our destiny.

As I was crossing the Gobi Desert, one day I started to die. My skin was like a tomato—like a tomato's color, and this skin was peeling off. I lost my vision— one eye was burned. I said, "Okay—everybody please forgive me. Whoever I have thought wrong of or did something wrong to, please forgive me." I prepared myself for death. At this moment, a very tender breeze came. It was such an amazing breeze that I cannot describe it. This breeze went only around me, and my shirt was flapping in the wind. I looked around and it was still. This breeze went on for about ten to fifteen minutes. It gave me a lot of power. I forgot about death. I got up and walked about 12 to 15 miles that day. I felt like I was Hercules.

It was also in Mongolia that I met a wolf on the mountain. It was very wet weather; it had just rained. I sat near a rock and my whole dress was wet, my whole backpack was wet, everything I had was wet. At that moment a wolf came. I looked at him very tiredly. I said, "Oh, my God, you see it is raining and everything is wet." I complained to the wolf. He looked at me, and I realized that he understood me. I looked at his eyes, and they were like human eyes. He was a very clever wolf, and I saw that he understood me. He was very quiet and compassionate. He stayed for maybe ten minutes, then he went. I said, "Okay wolf, I will sleep now." I was very tired and leaning against a rock, but it was an amazing meeting. It was like I met a Guru, some saint, or some sage—it was the same feeling.

Really speaking, it is very hard work with the ego and very hard work with ourselves, because we must be very attentive and very careful. We must control, control our senses, our mind. It is easier to do rituals and go to temples.

I hope that everybody will reach God. I don't know my future, but I feel that now I have a possibility to speak. I speak very willingly. My Guru's future prediction of me is that I will become a *muni*—someone who never speaks and just keeps silent. I will smile like crazy, but I will emanate vibrations of happiness and

10.3 Koshi of Kazakhstan, traveler and mystic

love. I said, "Okay—I know it is just an instrument or channel of God. It is not possible to persuade. Everything is not ours, everything is God's. Okay, my Father—if you want me to be your instrument, you can take my tongue and language. You can make me whatever you want. If it emanates, then emanate."

The Dalai Lama gave me audience in his home in Dharamsala for more than one hour. People were saying that I was a very great incarnation of a Tibetan lama. The day after the meeting with the Dalai Lama, some Tibetan people were doing prostrations in front of me. I was thinking, "What should I do?" I realized that if I started to explain that I am not an incarnation of a Tibetan lama, they would say that I was very modest. Then the Voice gave me an idea. I went to a tailor, and he made for me a pink pirate suit—a very joyful design with frills at the knee. I wore a headdress like a pirate. After that I took a drum and started playing a Russian Revolution song. In Dharamsala there are just five small streets. So there I was with the drum playing this song. All the Tibetans were standing near their doors, observing and thinking that not one great Tibetan lama would do that.

Another time six Hindu *sadhus* came to me in orange dress. They said to me, "We see in you the incarnation of the Mother of India." "What?" They were very serious. "Yes, you know the Mother in Pondicherry died. Mother Teresa in Calcutta died. This place is vacant. We will travel together and collect food for you. After two or three years you will be very famous. We will go by foot from the North to the South. We will say that the Mother of India has come back." At this moment, the Voice told me to play Mata Ji. So I said, "Okay, Mata Ji, so Mata Ji." They made me a long black *sadhu* dress and a turban. I was walking with six *sadhus* as an escort, and for two weeks I played Mata Ji. After that, I said, "I'm sorry—I must go back." They said, "You won't stay in India? We must go to such and such city." I said, "No, my time in India is finished and I must go back." The Voice had told me, "Take any possibility—it is only your attitude toward it that matters. Take it easy and take any opportunity, any possibility. Never say, 'No, it is not for me.'" It was a very high opportunity to be Mata Ji. I took it and I just played it for two weeks and took advantage of this opportunity. Why do some people only take small or middle opportunities? Why don't they take high opportunities?

"Koshi," a.k.a. Svetlana Otrebekova, interviewed August 20, 2004.

Eclectic Ways

In Eastern cultures, there has long been mingling of many spiritual ways. Japanese families may use elements from Buddhism, Confucianism, and Shinto for various spiritual needs; members of Hindu families may worship different gods and goddesses. Such mixtures were not the norm historically in Judeo-Christian-Islamic cultures. But in today's open spiritual marketplace, many Western women are picking and choosing elements from various religions to create their own spiritual path. In the process, they remain relatively free, without committing themselves absolutely to any organization. It is quite usual for women from Judeo-Christian backgrounds to dabble in other traditions such as Sufism, Tibetan Buddhism, Daoism, and yoga. The phenomenon is so common these days that the label "spiritual seekers" has been applied to these people. This term can be understood as suggesting that they have not found what they are looking for, and that their search is superficial, or it can be understood as a deep personal odyssey into the unknown for the sake of inner transformation and enlightenment.

Consider the example of Margaret West, born into a Christian family in Canada in 1939. As a young adult, she explored shamanic traditions and went to England to learn about Celtic traditions. Back in Canada, she worked as a shaman and psychologist, often helping women who needed healing of severe childhood trauma and who were searching for inner peace. As she worked with women's groups, she began performing women's ceremonies with the earth, drumming in sacred circles (an indigenous practice), and honoring the indigenous North American myths. Margaret says she also felt the presence of Mary Magdalene, around whom contemporary women have developed a body of woman-empowering myths. Margaret's search ultimately led her to Russia, where she was introduced to Agni Yoga and says she felt a connection to the "Ascended Masters." She began intensive study of the writings of Nicholas and Helena Roerich, who foretold a new epoch of women. As the new millennium opened, Margaret was invited to collaborate with a group of women psychologists in Russia to conduct family camps. They called the camps "Creating a New Story." The activities were indeed eclectic, among them invoking the spirits of the Four Directions, smudging for purification, reciting Hindu mantras, reading Helena Roerich's writings about the importance of the Feminine Principle, chanting the Great Invocation (from Alice Bailey, reportedly working in combination with the Ascended Master Djwhal Khul of Tibet), mask-making, guided meditations, healing with sound and dance, exploring relationships with power animals, empowerment workshops to honor the chief stages of women's lives—maiden, mother, and crone—and celebrations such as "wild woman" workshops with face paints and costumes.

Have women such as Margaret West, drawing upon so many different spiritual strands, been less successful in delving deeply into religion than those who attempt to be faithful to a single religious tradition? Many such seekers would deny this. Another issue is the sensitivity of indigenous people—in particular, Native Americans—to having their sacred ceremonies appropriated by outsiders, as we saw in Chapter 2. It is unlikely that people coming from a different culture can fully grasp the highly complex spiritual lifeways and perspectives embedded in indigenous communities and histories; as we have seen, indigenous peoples themselves are struggling to remember traditions that have almost been lost. For outsiders, it is more likely that the forms are being used in creative ways for the sake of inner spiritual experiences.

There are women who find their own spiritual path closer to home. In every religion it is usually the women who have maintained the family altars, caring for the ancestral spirits, praying to the deities to help their families and others in need, and praising and thanking the Divine. Today this tradition of creating a sacred space continues even among women who have no specific religion. Many spiritual women around the world create private altars in their homes with pictures or statues of deities, saints, or spirits whom they adore—perhaps from different traditions—along with idiosyncratic collections of objects that have personal meaning for them. There may be twigs, shells, stones, feathers, leaves, candles, mementoes of loved ones, all carrying specific meaning and creating a private spiritual world into which a woman moves when she prays at her altar. Not only the sacred objects but also the prayers may be eclectic, drawn from fragments learned from religions but also from their hearts. Mexican-American Soledad "Chole" Pescina (d. 1986) prayed sincerely at her altar devoted to Our Lady of Guadalupe and St. Anthony (which included a photograph of John F. Kennedy and another of her cousins) rather than at the church, and thus many friends were helped and healed. She explained the importance of prayer to women:

> Let me tell you, prayer is important for us. For women. The men, they should do it, too. But the world was not made for women. You know that. The world was not made for us. I stopped going to church because they accused me of witchery…. But a woman who knows the saints is what? A bad one? No, I tell you we need them. And they know that we have the faith.[8]

Non-hierarchical, Non-dogmatic Groups

Finally, many women are finding their spiritual place within groups that attempt to diffuse leadership and are not dogma-based. Such groups provide them with ways to join their efforts with those of others, without the fixed belief systems and power issues of organized religions.

Sometimes these groups are drawn from women of all religions, in an attempt to help bring social harmony into their respective communities. These women have a deep commitment to their own faith, but are willing to cross its political and idealistic boundaries for the sake of peace. Often such interfaith work is being carried on in regions that have been terribly scarred by inter-religious violence. The Jerusalem Women's Interfaith Encounter, for instance, draws together women of Muslim, Christian, Jewish, and Druze (a tenth-century outgrowth of Ismaili Islam, mixed with Greek philosophy, Gnosticism, and esoteric Christianity) faiths to explore what they have in common and to learn more about each other's religions. In intimate, personal ways they study topics such as life-cycle events in each religion, scriptures, the status and problems of women, intermarriage, stereotypes about their religions, and teaching their religion to their children. They pray together, eat together, and visit each other's holy places. One such group of 50 women, which included some of their daughters, devoted a day to "How Religion Gives Strength to Women." After listening to passages from scriptures and the lives of the prophets, they broke into small discussion groups. They report:

One discussion got into the suffering of women in war resulting from the distortions of religious teachers. A Muslim woman told how in the Koran it is forbidden to harm children, women, and old in war—it is only permitted to attack somebody who has weapons and can defend himself. A Druze woman told us that in their religion, somebody who takes life, even by accident, is not allowed to come into the religion. A Christian said that Jesus was against war, preaching about love also to the enemy. The Jewish women spoke about the strict laws of war that are written in the Bible, and how we must be careful not to vandalize or damage accidentally the innocents, property, and the animals of the enemy.

Another discussion covered the difference between what the Holy Books (Bible, New Testament, Koran, the Druze Book of Wisdom) say about women—and the gap created by the interpretations that male religious commentators have given through the years. They agreed about the importance of the true intentions of the Holy Books, and about the right and the obligation of women to find the right interpretation for us. They also agreed that we must empower ourselves via the religion, not by trying to be like the men, but by deepening our understanding of what is our real mission on earth as women, and what we can do that men can't, in order to bring peace and compassion to our loved ones and to our land.[9]

Such encounters always end with loving hugs, and are extended to include expressions of mutual support when people in any of the communities are killed. Coordinator Elana Rozenman explains, "We are all bound together in the mutual suffering of our situation."[10]

In addition to visible movements linking women, there are many working quietly behind the scenes to strengthen and increase the global network of spiritual women. Elinore Detiger of the Netherlands and Scotland has been doing so for decades, catalyzing conferences, supporting women with a cause, and bringing forth women's inner wisdom. She always hides herself away before the spotlight can fall upon her. She explains:

The Nameless Ones (a category I fall into comfortably and a part of this global unfolding which is much larger and more active) mentor and guide all those who emerge as personas, feed and nurture the ideas which the front-line and onstage individuals eventually bring more articulately and in greater focus to the world at large, all anonymously, as spirit works that way when it first appears and integrates into society. Behind the scenes there are many unnamed ones with no face. If you would put any one of these in the spotlight, they would not look that good or might not read that well. In fact, it never fits into the focus of our senses and how our mind works. We are understudies to the

10.4 Members of a rural women's prayer group or circle in Kenya

greater ones amongst us who do have a face and whose words are vibrational-
ly so elevated that whether we listen or not is beside the point. Their very
embodiment in our midst shifts the field and also opens our capacities to be
more like the great archetype which created us all in the first place.[11] ■

Another growing manifestation of the desire for religion without power structures
is the phenomenon of sacred circles (fig. 10.4). A circle is round; there is no top or
bottom. Some of these welcome both men and women; some are composed only
of women, for the sake of more intimate communication. Circles of women are
gathering at many places around the globe to facilitate open and honest communication and a sense of community without hierarchy. Ann Smith, who has helped
give birth to many women's circles, writes:

■ My experience with most women in religion is that they are in bondage to these
bureaucracies. They get just enough attention and perks to keep them in a code-
pendent relationship, and it is very difficult to break loose. Sacred circles are
like a twelve-step program for breaking the addiction of power-over.[12] ■

Women's circles may gather to support each other through life passages, to develop inner compassion and outer service work, to understand each other across cultural and age differences, to bring forth women's sacred roles, and to take action
beneficial to the community and the world. The main thing they have in common
is a commitment to shared leadership, and to listening with respect and non-judg-
mentally to every voice. Beverly Engel has studied the Women's Circle movement
and has found that the circles are of many types, including Peer Spirit, Wisdom,
Empowerment, Simplicity, Peacemaking, Crone, Shamanic, Women's Spirituality,

and Medicine Wheel Circles. A sacred circles movement known as Circles of Ten is developing a database of peacemaking stories. Director Sarah Hartzell explains, "The purpose is to make visible the existing culture of peace which we believe is known by the vast majority of women."[13] Jean Shinoda Bolen shares her dream of a million circles of women around the planet:

> Each one is like a pebble thrown into a pond. The effect on women in them, and the effect women in them have, send out concentric rings of influence. A peaceful revolution is going on, a women's spirituality movement, hidden in plain sight. Through circles of women, healing women, might the culture come around? In myths and dreams and in our collective memory, women are remembered as they once were and could be: carriers of the sacred feminine. If the patriarchy is to be healed and the planet restored, might women's wisdom be needed?[14]

Whether in women's circles or on solitary paths or in the midst of social justice actions or in pulpits or temples, women are expressing their deep spirituality in myriad ways as never before. According to all indications, this is a trend that will only grow with time. As women discover their own spiritual power and the stories of those who have preceded them, women's contributions to the spiritual life of humankind may be expected to increase exponentially.

Suggested Reading

Bolen, Jean Shinoda, *The Millionth Circle: How to Change Ourselves and the World*, Berkeley, California: Conari Press, 1999. A short book about women's circles, drawn from decades of the author's experiences of their transformational effects.

Dillard, Annie, *Pilgrim at Tinker Creek*, New York: HarperPerennials, 1985, 1998. Intimate observations of the dramas within the natural world, as a path that sometimes leads through terror to awe.

Edwards, Wynne and Dianne Linden, eds., *Running Barefoot: Women Write the Land*, Alberta, Canada: Rowan Books, 2001. Prose and poetry celebrations of the spirituality of the natural world by Canadian women.

Peace Pilgrim, *Peace Pilgrim: Her Life and Work in her Own Words*, Santa Fe, New Mexico: An Ocean Tree Book, 1983. The simple words of an extraordinary woman whose spiritual path was walking for peace.

Sewell, Marilyn, ed., *Cries of the Spirit: A Celebration of Women's Spirituality*, Boston: Beacon Press, 1991. Passionate, deeply felt poems from the souls of many Western women writers.

Turner, Kay, *Beautiful Necessity: The Art and Meaning of Women's Altars*, New York: Thames and Hudson, 1999. Exploration of the phenomenon of women's altars, as found in Goddess, Celtic, African, Hindu, Buddhist, Catholic, Greek Orthodox, and eclectic spiritual paths.

West, Margaret, *Circle of Wisdom: A Journey with the Glastonbury Grandmothers*, Chieveley, England: Capall Bann Publishing, 2001. A grandmother's far-ranging personal shamanic journey, intimately described.

NOTES

Quotations heading the chapters are each drawn from a longer quotation within the chapter—see relevant note for details.

The notes include details of all copyright permissions/credits for quoted material. Permissions for quoted material in the boxed excerpts are listed at the end of the notes, on p.318. The interviews are reproduced with the permission of the subjects.

Every effort has been made to contact copyright holders, but should there be any errors or omissions, Laurence King Publishing Ltd would be pleased to insert the appropriate acknowledgment in any subsequent printing of this publication.

Chapter 1

1   Sue Woodruff, "Women's Words: Wisdom, Power, Beauty," in Theresa King O'Brien, ed., *The Spiral Path*, St. Paul, Minnesota: Yes International Publishers, 1988, pp. 425–6. The newer, 1992 edition of *The Spiral Path* is ed. by Theresa King. www.yespublishers.com. Reprinted by permission of the publisher.
2   Chandra Patel, M.D., "Woman's Body and Spirituality," in O'Brien, *op. cit.*, pp. 73–6.
3   Annie Dillard, *Pilgrim at Tinker Creek*, New York: HarperCollins Perennial Classics, 1974, 1999.
4   Georgia O'Keeffe, "Some Memories of Drawing," Atlantis Editions, New York, 1974, Georgia O'Keeffe, *Georgia O'Keeffe*, New York, 1976, and Laurie Lisle, *Portrait of an Artist: A Biography of Georgia O'Keeffe*, New York, 1981, as quoted in Roger Lipsey, *An Art of our Own: The Spiritual in Twentieth Century Art*, Boston: Shambhala, 1989, pp. 375–8.
5   Lyla Yastion, personal communication, December 3, 2002.
6   Pema Chodron, *When Things Fall Apart*, Boston: Shambhala, 1997, repub. London: Element Books/HarperCollins, 2003, pp. 122–3, 125.
7   *The Malleus Maleficarum of Heinrich Kramer and James Sprenger*, p. 47, as quoted in Serinity Young, *An Anthology of Sacred Texts by and about Women*, New York: Crossroad, 1995, pp. 79–80.
8   Mechthild of Magdeburg, "The Flowing Light of the Godhead", 6.29, in Lucy Menzies, trans., *The Revelations of Mechthild of Magdeburg*, London: Longmans, Green, 1953.
9   Mirabai, "Money's no good here," in Andrew Harvey, ed., *Teachings of the Hindu Mystics*, Boston: Shambhala Publications, 2001, p. 78. Reprinted by permission of the publisher.
10 Barbara Sargent, "The Role of Spirituality in the Healing of the World Community," presentation given at the Global Peace Initiative of Women Religious and Spiritual Leaders, Geneva, Switzerland, October 6–9, 2002, pp. 2–3 of transcript.
11 Carol Lee Flinders, *Enduring Grace*, San Francisco: HarperSanFrancisco, 1993, p. 23.
12 *Sunday* Magazine, January 9–15, 1994, as reported in Madhu Kishwar, *Off the Beaten Track: Rethinking Gender Justice for Indian Women*, Oxford: Oxford University Press, 1999, 2002, p. 200.
13 Oyeronke Oyewumi, *African Women and Feminism: Reflecting on the Politics of Sisterhood*, Trenton, New Jersey and Asmara, Eritrea: Africa World Press, 2003, pp. 2–3.
14 Amina Wadud, "Alternative Qur'anic Interpretation and the Status of Muslim Women," in Gisela Webb, ed., *Windows of Faith: Muslim Women Scholar-activists in North America*, Syracuse, New York: Syracuse University Press, 2000, pp. 8–9.
15 Lenett Partlow, personal communication, February 23, 2003.
16 Ursula King, *Women and Spirituality: Voices of Protest and Promise*, University Park, Pennsylvania: Penn State Press, 1993, pp. 89–90. Pierre Teilhard de Chardin, *Toward the Future*, 1975, London: Collins, p. 84.

17 Sallie McFague, *Models of God: Theology for an Ecological, Nuclear Age*, Philadelphia: Fortress Press, 1987, p. 39.
18 Dadi Janaki, talk in Geneva, October 6, 2002.
19 Karen Armstrong, speech in Geneva, October 7, 2002.
20 Chung Hyun Kyung, "Your Comfort vs. My Death," in Mary John Mananzan *et al.*, eds., *Women Resisting Violence: Spirituality for Life*, New York: Orbis Books, 1996, p. 132. Reprinted by permission of the publisher.
21 Right Reverend Vashti Murphy McKenzie, speaking in Geneva, October 7, 2002.

Chapter 2
1 Cecilia Montero, personal communication, October 2002.
2 Mark St. Pierre and Tilda Long Soldier, *Walking in the Sacred Manner: Healers, Dreamers, and Pipe Carriers—Medicine Women of the Plains Indians*, New York: Touchstone, 1995, p. 81. Reprinted by permission of Simon & Schuster, Inc.
3 Alice Papineau, De-wa-senta, quoted in Sally Roesch Wagner, *Sisters in Spirit: Haudenosaunee (Iroquois) Influence on Early American Feminists*, Summertown, Tennessee: Native Voices, 2001, p. 46.
4 Paula Gunn Allen, *The Sacred Hoop: Recovering the Feminine in American Indian Traditions*, Boston: Beacon Press, 1986, 1992, pp. 2–3. Reprinted by permission of the publisher.
5 Ursula King, *Women and Spirituality: Voices of Protest and Promise*, 2nd edn., University Park, Pennsylvania: Pennsylvania State University Press, 1989, 1993, pp. 38–9.
6 Quoted by Sheila Moon, *Changing Woman and Her Sisters: Feminine Aspects of Selves and Duties*, San Francisco: Guild for Psychological Studies Publishing House, 1984, pp. 172–3.
7 M. A. Jaimes Guerrero, "Native Womanism: Exemplars of indigenism in sacred traditions of kinship," in Graham Harvey, ed., *Indigenous Religions: A Companion*, London: Cassell, 2000, pp. 38–9.
8 Manuel Red Bear, quoted in St. Pierre and Long Soldier, *op. cit.*, pp. 39–40.
9 Judith Gleason, *Oya: In Praise of the Goddess*, Boston: Shambhala Publications, 1987, p. 1. Reprinted by permission of the publisher.
10 Pierre Verger, *Notes sur le culte des orisa et vodun. Mémoires de L'Institut Français d'Afrique Noire*, no. 51 (1957), pp. 414–21, as rendered in English by Judith Gleason, *op. cit.*, p. 2–3.

11 From the Thanksgiving Address, "Condensation of the Opening Address sent by the Mohawk Nation and the Haudenosaunee Grand Council to the Fourth Russell Tribunal, Rotterdam, The Netherlands, November 1980," *Northeast Indian Quarterly*, Fall 1987, p. 8.
12 Lucy Swan, quoted in St. Pierre and Long Soldier, *op. cit.*, p. 48.
13 In Ronald M. Berndt, *Djanggawul: An Aboriginal Religious Cult of North-Eastern Arnhem Land*, Routledge and Kegan Paul, 1953, p. 41.
14 St. Pierre and Long Soldier, *op. cit.*, p. 166.
15 Lenore Keeshig-Tobias, "Not Just Entertainment," *Whole Earth Review*, 1991, as quoted by Mariah Jones, "Spiritual Commodification and Misappropriation," on www.sonomacountyfreepress.com, May 17, 2003.
16 Diane Bell, "Aboriginal Women's Religion: A Shifting Law of the Land," in Arvind Sharma, ed., *Today's Woman in World Religions*, Albany: State University of New York Press, 1994, p. 49.
17 John S. Mbiti, *African Religions and Philosophy*, 2nd edn., Oxford: Heinemann, 1990, p. 127.
18 Mercy Amba Oduyoye, "Spirituality of Resistance and Reconstruction," in *Women Resisting Violence: Spirituality for Life*, Mary John Mananzan *et al.*, eds., Maryknoll, New York: Orbis Books, 1996, p. 164.
19 Charlotte Johnson Frisbie, *Kinaalda: A Study of Navajo Girls' Puberty Ceremony*, Middletown, Connecticut: Wesleyan University Press, 1967, p. 11.
20 Ines M. Talamantez, "The Presence of Isanaklesh: The Apache Female Deity and The Path of Pollen," in Nancy Auer Falk and Rita M. Gross, *Unspoken Worlds: Women's Religious Lives*, 3rd edn., Belmont, California: Wadsworth/Thomson Learning, 2001, p. 296.
21 Ruth Underhill and Maria Chona, *The Autobiography of a Papago Woman*, Memoirs of the American Anthropological Association, no. 46, Menasha, Wisconsin: Krause Reprint Co., 1936, 1974, p. 31. Reprinted by permission of Stanford University Press.
22 Luanna Neff, personal communication, October 2002.
23 Sweet Honey in the Rock, from the song "Breaths," *Breaths* CD, Cambridge, Massachusetts: Rounder Records, 1992.
24 Lenett Nefertiti Myrick, "The Journey Continues: The Trail of Dreams Team Goes to

Africa," www.nowtimeprophecies.com, March 31, 2002.

25 Audri Scott Williams, "Returning through the doors of no return," www.nowtimeprophecies.com, August 15, 2002.

26 Te Urutahi Waikerepuru, talk at Global Peace Initiative of Women Spiritual and Religious Leaders, Geneva, October 2002.

27 Gunn Allen, *op. cit.*, p. 2.

Chapter 3

1 Veena Talwar Oldenburg, *Dowry Murder: The Imperial Origins of a Cultural Crime*, New York: Oxford University Press, 2002.

2 Manjula Krishnan, personal communications May 16, 2003 and June 7, 2003.

3 Ashok Bararoo, *Call of Nine Goddesses*, Jammu: Pustak-Sansaar, 1994, p. 33.

4 Madhu Khanna, "The Ritual Capsule of Durga Puja," in Christopher Key Chappel and Mary Evelyn Tucker, eds., *Hinduism and Ecology*, Cambridge: Harvard University Press, 2000, pp. 490–1.

5 Ramprasad, "Abandon whatever limits you cling to," in Lex Hixon, *Mother of the Universe: Visions of the Goddess and Tantric Hymns of Enlightenment*, Wheaton, Illinois: Quest Books, 1994, p. 180. Reprinted by permission of Theosophical Publishing House.

6 Akka Mahadevi, Chennaiah: 1974:39, in Vijaya Ramaswamy, *Walking Naked: Women, Society, Spirituality in South India*, Shimla, India: Indian Institute of Advanced Study, 1997, p. 165.

7 Mirabai, in A. J. Alston, *The Devotional Poems of Mirabai*, Delhi: Motilal Banarsidass, 1980, pp. 72–3. Reprinted by permission of the publisher.

8 Akka Mahadevi, as quoted in Swami Ghanananda and Sir John Stewart-Wallace, eds., *Women Saints East and West*, Hollywood: Vedanta Press, 1955, 1979, pp. 31–2. Reprinted by permission of the publisher.

9 Akka Mahadevi, in Vijaya Ramaswamy, *Divinity and Deviance: Women in Virashaivism*, Delhi: Oxford University Press, 1996, p. 74.

10 Madhu Purnima Kishwar, "Women, Sex and Marriage: Restraint as a Feminine Strategy," *Manushi*, Issue No. 98: March–April 1997, on http://free/freespeech.org/manushi/99/sexuality.html. Reprinted by permission of the author.

11 Sri Sarada Devi, as quoted in Swami Ghanananda and Stewart-Wallace, *op. cit.*, p. 113.

12 Swami Vivekananda, as quoted in www.srisaradamath.org/about_srisaradamath.htm.

13 www.bkwsu.com/about/leaders.html.

14 Neelu Kumari, personal communication, December 7, 2002.

15 Veena Sharma, personal communication, May 24, 2003.

16 The Mother, *Words of the Mother*, vol. 13, p. 95, quoted in www.miraura.org/bio/herself/html.

17 Ramsukhdas, *How to Lead a Householder's Life*, 1992, p. 50, as quoted by Amrita Basu, "Hindu Women's Activism in India and the Questions it Raises," in Betsy Reed, ed., *Nothing Sacred: Women Respond to Religious Fundamentalism and Terror*, New York: Thunder's Mouth Press, 2002, p. 198.

18 Arundhati Roy, "The Common Good," on www.altindia.net/gujarat/roy1.htm, p. 3.

19 Mathioli R. Saraswati, as interviewed by Vijaya Ramaswamy, March 2006.

Chapter 4

1 *Lalitavistara*, Chapter 18, from *Voice of the Buddha: The Beauty of Compassion*, trans. into French by Edouard Foucaux and thence into English by Gwendolyn Bays, Dharma Publishing, 1983, p. 407.

2 Rita M. Gross, "Buddhism," in Arvind Sharma and Katherine K. Young, eds., *Her Voice, Her Faith*, Boulder, Colorado: Westview Press, 2003, p. 66.

3 As summarized in Narada Thera, *A Manual of Buddhism*, Kuala Lumpur, 1971.

4 *Culla-Vagga*, X.1, as reprinted in Serinity Young, *An Anthology of Sacred Texts by and about Women*, New York: Crossroad, 1995, p. 330.

5 Ven. Zhaohui Shi, "Buddhist Women's Movement in The New Century: The Taiwanese Experience of Contemporary Nuns' Defiance of The 'Treaty of Non-Equality,'" summary of paper given at Sakyadhita Conference in Taipei, 2002, on www.sakyadhita.org/conferences/taipei 2002/summary.htm.

6 Kisagotami, *The [female] Elders' Voices*, vol. 2, *Therigatha*, trans. K. R. Norman, London: Pali Text Society, 1971, p. 24.

7 *Anguttara Nikaya*, vol. II, *Thai Tripitaka*, p. 8, quoted in Chatsumarn Kabilsingh, *Thai Women in Buddhism*, Berkeley: Parallax Press, 1991, p. 34.

8 Ven. Bhikshuni Wu Yin, *Choosing Simplicity: Commentary on the Bhikshuni Pratimoksha*,

Ithaca, New York: Snow Lion Publications, 2001, p. 32.

9   *Ashtasahasrika* VII, 170–1. In Edward Conze, I. B. Horner, David Snellgrove, and Arthur Waley, *Buddhist Texts through the Ages*, Oxford: Oneworld Publications, 1995, p. 146.

10 Dogen, *Taisho*, vol. 82; 2582, p. 35, as quoted in Paula Kane Robinson Arai, *Women Living Zen*, New York/Oxford: Oxford University Press, 1999, p. 38.

11 *Ta-hui Chueh Ch'an-shih p'u-shuo, Dainihon zokuzokyo* 2, 31, 5, p. 433b, as cited by Miriam Levering, "Lin-chi (Rinzai) Ch'an and Gender: The Rhetoric of Equality and the Rhetoric of Heroism," in Jose Ignacio Cabezon, ed., *Buddhism, Sexuality, and Gender*, Albany: State University of New York Press, p. 139.

12 *Taisho shinshu daizokyo*, 46, p. 196a, as quoted in Miriam Levering, *op. cit.*, p. 145.

13 Janet Gyatso, "Down with the Demoness: Reflections on a Feminine Ground in Tibet," in Janice D. Willis, *Feminine Ground: Essays on Women and Tibet*, Ithaca, New York: Snow Lion Publications, second edition, 1995, p. 43.

14 From "Praise to the Twenty-one Taras," trans. Bokar Rinpoche in *Tara: the Feminine Divine*, San Francisco: Clear Point Press, 2000. Reprinted by permission of the publisher.

15 Machig Lapdron, quoted in W. Y. Evans-Wentz, ed., *Tibetan Yoga and Secret Doctrines*, New York: Oxford University Press, 1935, 1967, pp. 303–4. Reprinted by permission of the publisher.

16 Keith Dowman, *Sky Dancer: The Secret Life and Songs of the Lady Yeshe Tsogyel*, Ithaca, New York: Snow Lion Publications, 1996, p. 16. Reprinted by permission of the publisher.

17 Dowman, *op. cit.*, p. 82.

18 Dowman, *op. cit.*, p. 86.

19 Samaneri Dhammananda (Chatsumarn Kabilsingh, now Bhikkhuni Dhammananda), personal communication, 25 June, 2003.

20 Ven. Huynh Lien, quoted in Ven. Tri Lien, "Nuns of the Mendicant Tradition in Vietnam," www.sakyadhita.org/conferences/taipei2002/summary.htm.

21 Hiuwan Fashih, "Enlightened Education," in Martine Batchelor, *Walking on Lotus Flowers*, London: Thorson/HarperCollins, 1996, pp. 87–8.

22 Paula Kane Robinson Arai, *Women Living Zen: Japanese Soto Buddhist Nuns*, New York/Oxford: Oxford University Press, 1999, p. 162.

23 Ajahn Candasiri, "Why come to a monastery?" in *Freeing the Heart: Dhamma Teachings from the Nuns' Community at Amaravati and Cittiviveka Buddhist Monastery*, Hemel Hempstead, England: Amaravati Publications, 2001, pp. 162–7. Reprinted by permission of the publisher.

24 *Anguttara Nikaya* I, p. 1.

25 Chatsumarn Kabilsingh (now Bhikkhuni Dhammananda), "Women in Buddhism," Manila: Isis International and Institute of Women's Studies, monograph, pp. 20–1.

26 *Anguttara Nikaya* III, p. 77.

27 Rita Gross, "Strategies for a Feminist Revalorization of Buddhism," Arvind Sharma and Katherine K. Young, eds., *Feminism and World Religions*, Albany: State University of New York, 1999, pp. 81, 88.

28 Rita Gross, *Buddhism After Patriarchy: A Feminist History, Analysis, and Reconstruction of Buddhism*, Albany: State University of New York Press, 1993, pp. 176–7.

29 Tsultrim Allione, "The Tibetan Principle in Tibetan Buddhism," in Marianne Dresser, ed., *Buddhist Women on the Edge: Contemporary Perspectives from the Western Frontier*, Berkeley: North Atlantic Books, 1996, p. 107.

30 Myongsong Sunim, "The Water and the Wave," in Batchelor, *op. cit.*, pp. 78, 81.

31 Roshi Jiyu Kennett, in Lenore Friedman, *Meetings with Remarkable Women*, Boston: Shambhala, 1987, p. 168.

32 Chatsumarn Kabilsingh (Bhikkhuni Dhammananda), *Thai Women in Buddhism*, Berkeley: Parallax Press, pp. 83–4.

33 Rita Gross, "Strategies for a Feminist Revalorization of Buddhism," *op. cit.*, pp. 94–5.

34 Daw Aung San Suu Kyi, "Freedom from Fear," 07.10.1990, www.dassk.org/contents.php?id=416, accessed March 5, 2006.

Chapter 5

1   *The I Ching or Book of Changes*, trans. Richard Wilhelm, English trans. Cary F. Baynes, Princeton, New Jersey: Princeton University Press, 3rd ed., 1967, pp. 10–11.

2   *The I Ching*, *op. cit.*, pp. 143–5.

3   "The Texts of Confucianism," trans. James Legge, in Max Mueller, ed., *Sacred Books of the East*, vol. 27, Oxford: Oxford University Press, 1885, reprinted by Delhi: Motilal Banarsidass, 1968, pp. 454–5.

4   "The Texts of Confucianism," trans. Legge, in Mueller, *op. cit.*, vol. 28, pp. 430–2.

5   Alber Richard O'Hara, trans., *The Position of Women in Early China According to Lieh Nu Chuan, "The Biographies of Chinese Women,"* Taipei: Mei Ya Publications, Inc., 1971, p. 105.

6   Terry Woo, "Confucianism and Feminism," in Arvind Sharma and Katherine K. Young, eds., *Feminism and World Religions*, Albany: State University of New York Press, 1999, p. 129.

7   Confucius, *The Analects*, XVII: 6, trans. D. C. Lau, London: Penguin Books, 1979, p. 144.

8   *Reflections on Things at Hand: The Neo-Confucian Anthology Compiled by Chu Hsi and Lu Tsu-ch'ien*, trans. Wing-tsit Chan, New York: Columbia University Press, 1967, as quoted by Serinity Young, ed., *An Anthology of Sacred Texts by and about Women*, New York: Crossroad, 1993, p. 365.

9   Mao Zedong, "Overthrowing the Clan Authority of the Ancestral Temples and Clan Elders, the Religious Authority of Town and Village Gods, and the Masculine Authority of Husbands," 1927, as quoted in Deborah Sommer, ed., *Chinese Religion: An Anthology of Sources*, New York and Oxford: Oxford University Press, 1995, p. 305.

10   16th National Congress of the Communist Party of China, 2002, trans. Chen Lin, November 11, 2002, www.china.org.cn/english/features/49206.htm.

11   Livia Kohn, *The Taoist Experience*, Albany: State University of New York Press, 1993, pp. 11–12. Reprinted by permission of the publisher.

12   Ellen Chen, *The Tao te Ching: A New Translation with Commentary*, New York: Paragon House, 1989, verse 78, p. 225.

13   Sun Bu-er, Secret Text: "Unexcelled True Scripture of Inner Experiences of Jadelike Purity," in Thomas Cleary, ed. and trans., *Immortal Sisters: Secret Teachings of Taoist Women*, Berkeley, California: North Atlantic Books, 1996, p. 47. © 1989, 1996 by Thomas Cleary. Reprinted by permission of the publisher.

14   Lao-tzi, *Daode jing*, trans. Livia Kohn, in Kohn, *op. cit.*, verses 6, 8.

15   Sun Bu-er, "Facing a Wall," in Cleary, *op. cit.*, p. 38.

16   Sun Bu-er, in Cleary, *op. cit.*, pp. 77–8.

17   See Eva Wong, "Taoism," in *Her Voice, Her Faith: Women Speak on World Religions*, Arvind Sharma and Katherine K. Young, eds., Boulder, Colorado: Westview Press, 2003, pp. 136–42.

18   Catherine Despeux and Livia Kohn, *Women in Daoism*, Cambridge, Massachusetts: Three Pines Press, 2003, p. 22.

19   As quoted in Cleary, *op. cit.*, pp. xi–xii.

20   Karen Laughlin and Eva Wong, "Feminism and/in Taoism," in Sharma and Young, *Feminism and World Religions*, *op. cit.*, pp. 174–5.

Chapter 6

1   Genesis 25: 23.

2   Judith Plaskow, *Standing Again at Sinai: Judaism from a Feminist Perspective*, San Francisco: HarperCollins Publishers, 1990, p. 54. Reprinted by permission of the publisher.

3   Lynn Gottlieb, "The Secret Jew," in Susannah Heschel, ed., *On Being a Jewish Feminist: A Reader*, New York: Schocken Books, 1983, 1995, p. 275. Reprinted by permission of Random House, Inc.

4   Jeremiah 44: 15–19.

5   Midrash Proverbs 30, 10, as quoted in Sondra Henry and Emily Taitz, *Written out of History: Jewish Foremothers*, New York: Biblio Press, 1990, p. 56.

6   Sambathe, *The Sibylline Oracles*, trans. from the Greek by Milton S. Terry, New York: Hunt and Eaton, 1890, p. 82, as quoted in Henry and Taitz, *op. cit.*, p. 42.

7   Rebecca Tiktiner, *Meneket Rivka*, Cracow, 1618, trans. from the Yiddish by William Ungar, Courtesy of the Jewish Theological Seminary, New York.

8   Henrietta Szold, "Letter to Mrs. Julius Rosenwald," New York, 17 January 1915, reprinted in Ellen M. Umansky and Dianne Ashton, eds., *Four Centuries of Jewish Women's Spirituality: A Sourcebook*, Boston: Beacon Press, 1992, pp. 166–7.

9   "Reviews," *Ha-Isha* ("The Woman"), The Federation of Hebrew Women, vol. 6, 1928, p. 11.

10   Proverbs 31: 25–27.

11   Tova Hartman and Tamar H. Miller Halbertal, "Our Tradition Ourselves," *JOFA* [Jewish Orthodox Feminist Alliance] *Journal*, www.jofa.org/social_htm.php?bib_id=790, accessed 4/29/2006.

12   Dvora Weisberg, "The Study of Torah as a Religious Act," in Umansky and Ashton, *op. cit.*, pp. 276–8.

13   In Ellen M. Umansky, "Feminism in Judaism," in Arvind Sharma and Katherine K. Young, eds., *Feminism and World Religions*, Albany: State University of New York Press, 1999, p. 184.

14   Laura Geller, "Reactions to a Woman Rabbi,"
     in Susannah Heschel, ed., *On Being a Jewish
     Feminist: A Reader*, New York: Schocken
     Books, 1983, 1995, pp. 212–13. Reprinted by
     permission of Random House, Inc.

15   Plaskow, *op. cit.*, p. 199.

16   Blu Greenberg, *On Women and Judaism: A
     View from Tradition*, Philadelphia: The Jewish
     Publication Society of America, 1998, p. 112.

17   Lynn Gottlieb, "Spring Cleaning Ritual on
     the Eve of Full Moon Nisan," in Heschel,
     op. cit., pp. 278–9. Reprinted by permission
     of Random House, Inc.

18   Rachel Adler, *Engendering Judaism*, Boston:
     Beacon Press, 1998, p. 75.

19   Gail Shulman, "A Feminist Path to Judaism,"
     in Heschel, *op. cit.*, p. 108.

20   Erin E. Arvedlund, "A Russian Rabbi's First
     Task: Teach Jews to be Jews," *New York Times*
     in *Asian Age*, January 15, 2005, p. 2.

21   Susannah Heschel, in *Her Voice, Her Faith*,
     Arvind Sharma and Katherine K. Young, eds.,
     Boulder, Colorado: Westview Press, 2003,
     p. 147.

22   Vivienne Radonsky ("Tzipi"), personal
     communication, 13 November 2001.

Chapter 7

1   *The New Oxford Annotated Bible: New Revised
     Standard Version with the Apocrypha*, Oxford:
     Oxford University Press, 2001 (this translation
     is used throughout this chapter; reprinted by
     permission of the publisher). Luke 1: 34–35.

2   Matthew 18: 12–14.

3   Judith 9: 9–11.

4   John 4: 9–10.

5   Elisabeth Schussler-Fiorenza, *In Memory of
     Her*, New York: Crossroad, 1994, p. xliv.

6   Romans 16: 1–2.

7   I Timothy 2: 9–15.

8   "On the appointment of Deacons and
     Deaconesses," *Didascalia Apostolorum
     [Teaching of the Twelve Apostles]: The Syriac
     Version Translated and Accompanied by the
     Verona Latin Fragments*, in Barbara J.
     MacHaffie, ed., *Readings in Her Story: Women
     in Christian Tradition*, Minneapolis: Fortress
     Press, 1992, pp. 17–18.

9   Perpetua, in *A Lost Tradition: Women Writers
     of the Early Church*, by Patricia Wilson-
     Kastner, G. Ronald Kastner, Ann Millin,
     Rosemary Rader, and Jeremiah Reedy,
     University Press of America, 1981, pp. 20–25.

10   Augustine, *The Confessions of St. Augustine*,
     Book 9, Chapter 9, in Serinity Young, *An
     Anthology of Sacred Texts by and about

     Women*, New York: Crossroad, 1995, p. 49.

11   St. Hildegard of Bingen, as quoted in Evelyn
     Underhill, *The Mystics of the Church*, New
     York: George H. Doran Company, n.d., p. 76.

12   Letter from Hildegard to Henry, Bishop of
     Liège, 1148–1153, Letter 37R, in *Hildegard
     of Bingen: Selected Writings*, trans. Mark
     Atherton, London: Penguin Books, 2001, p. 67.

13   Bishop Bruno of Olmütz, in R. W. Souther,
     *Western Society and the Church in the Middle
     Ages*, Middlesex, England: Penguin Books,
     1970, p. 329.

14   Mechthild of Magdeburg, "The Flowing
     Light of the Godhead," 6.3, as quoted in
     Carol Lee Flinders, *Enduring Grace: Living
     Portraits of Seven Women Mystics*, San
     Francisco: HarperSanFrancisco, 1993, p. 51.

15   Mechthild of Magdeburg, "God Speaks to the
     Soul," *Teachings of the Christian Mystics*, ed.
     Andrew Harvey, Boston: Shambhala
     Publications, 1998, p. 82. Reprinted by
     permission of the publisher.

16   St. Clare of Assisi, as quoted in Flinders,
     op. cit., p. 23.

17   Julian of Norwich, "The Long Text" con-
     tained in E. Colledge OSA and James Walsh
     SJ, *Julian of Norwich: Showings*, London:
     SPCK and New York: Paulist Press, 1978, as
     quoted in Grace Jantzen, *Julian of Norwich*,
     New York: Paulist Press, 2000, p. 58.

18   *Ibid.*, p. 59.

19   St. Catherine of Genoa, as quoted by
     Underhill, *op. cit.*, p. 166.

20   St. Teresa of Avila, as quoted in Flinders,
     op. cit., p. 174.

21   St. Teresa of Avila, *The Interior Castle*, as
     quoted in Underhill, *op. cit.*, p. 180.

22   Joan of Arc, from *Jeanne d'Arc, Maid of
     Orleans: As set forth in the Original
     Documents*, trans. T. Douglas, New York:
     McClure, Phillips & Co., 1902, excerpted in
     Young, *op. cit.*, p. 82.

23   http://en.wikipedia.org/wiki/
     Katharina_von_Bora, accessed 4/19/2006.

24   Phyllis Trible, "Feminist Hermeneutics
     and Biblical Studies," http:// www.
     religion-online.org/showarticle.asp?title=1281,
     accessed 4/19/2006.

25   Mary Daly, "After the Death of God the
     Father: Women's Liberation and the
     Transformation of Christian Consciousness,"
     in Carol P. Christ and Judith Plaskow, eds.,
     *Womanspirit Rising: A Feminist Reader in
     Religion*, 1979, 1992, p. 57.

26   Sheri R. Benvenuti, "Pentecostal Women in
     Ministry: Where Do We Go From Here?",

Cyberjournal for Pentecostal-Charismatic Research, http://www.pctii.org/cyberj/cyberj1/ben.html, 12/9/2003, p. 1.

27 Archbishop Tarcisio Bertone, in "Women priests against Church structure," Associated Press, Vatican City, in *Asian Age*, August 7, 2002, p. 6.

28 In Miriam Therese Winter, Adair Lummis, and Allison Stokes, *Defecting in Place: Women Claiming Responsibility for Their Own Spiritual Lives*, New York: Crossroad, 1995, p. 105.

29 *Ibid.*

30 *Ibid.*

31 Winter *et al.*, *op. cit.*, p. 71.

32 Astrid Lobo Gajiwala, "The Passion of the Womb: Women Re-living the Eucharist," Francis Gonsalves, S.J., ed., *Body, Bread, Blood: Eucharistic Perspectives from the Indian Church*, New Delhi: Vidyajyoti, 2000, pp. 124–5.

33 Toinette M. Eugene, "No Defect Here: A Black Roman Catholic Womanist Reflection on a Spirituality of Survival," in Winter *et al.*, *op. cit.*, p. 219.

34 Mother Mary Angelica of the Annunciation, in "Mother Angelica," http://www.dailycatholic.org/issue/archives/1999Dec/232dec7, vol. 10, part II, pp. 3–4.

35 "What are Women Saying after the Decade?", World Council of Churches, http://www.wcc-coe.org/wcc/what/jpc/women.html, p. 2.

36 Pauline Sykes, personal communication, May 2003.

37 Diann L. Neu, "Women-Church on the Road to Change," in Winter *et al.*, *op. cit.*, pp. 242–3.

38 Margaret Fell, "Women's Speaking," http://ccat.sas.upenn/edu/~kuenning/fell.html, p. 7.

39 Lucretia Mott, at Women's Rights Convention, Seneca Falls, New York, 1848, as quoted in Rosemary Radford Ruether, *Women and Redemption: A Theological History*, Minneapolis: Fortress Press, 1998, p. 168.

40 *Ibid.*, p. 172.

41 Dorothy Day, *The Long Loneliness*, Garden City, New York: Doubleday, 1952, p. 210.

42 Carmen Broz, *Friends Bulletin*: Pacif, North Pacific and Intermountain Yearly Meetings of the Religious Society of Friends, November 1986, p. 49.

43 Mother Teresa, "Jesus is my Life," in *Beatificazione di Madre Teresa di Calcutta*, Piazza San Pietro, 19 October 2003, pp. 48–9.

44 Sister Clarice, personal communication, July 24, 2005.

45 Mercy Amba Oduyoye, "Doing Theology from Third World Women's Perspective," in Ursula King, ed., *Feminist Theology from the Third World: A Reader*, Maryknoll, New York: Orbis Books/SPCK Press, 1994, pp. 24–5.

46 Astrid Lobo Gajiwala, "Putting Back the Womb of God," *In God's Image*, vol. 24, no. 2, June 2005, p. 11.

47 Chung Hyun Kyung, *Struggle to Be the Sun Again: Introducing Asian Women's Theology*, New York: Orbis Books, 1990, p. 5.

48 Elsa Tamez, "The Bible as a Source of Empowerment for Women," in King, *op. cit.*, p. 195.

49 Ada Maria Isasi-Diaz, "The Tasks of Hispanic Women's Liberation Theology—*Mujeristas*: Who We Are and What We are About," in King, *op. cit.*, pp. 89, 101.

50 Reverend Dr. Rebecca Edmiston-Lange, "Unitarian Universalism," http://www.rcrc.org/faith/choices/unitarian_universalism.htm.

51 Luke 1: 46–52.

52 "Summary Statement on Mariology," Consultation of Asian Women's Theology, Singapore, 1987, in Kyung, *op. cit.*, p. 76.

53 Marianne Katoppo, *Compassionate and Free: An Asian Women's Theology*, Maryknoll, New York: Orbis Books, 1980, p. 17.

54 Ivone Gebara and Maria Clara Bingemer, "Mary—Mother of God, Mother of the Poor," in King, *op, cit.*, pp. 277, 280.

Chapter 8

1 Fatima Mernissi, *Women and Islam: An Historical and Theological Enquiry*, Oxford: Blackwell, 1991, p. 183.

2 Muhammad Ibn Ishaq, Sira 104–5, in A. Guillaume, trans. and ed., *The Life of Muhammad: A Translation of Ishaq's Sirat Rasul Allah*, London, 1955, p. 71.

3 Muhammad ibn Ishaq, Sira 120, in Guillaume, *op. cit.*, p. 82.

4 Muhammad Ibn Hanbal, *Musnad*, Cairo, 1895, vol. 6, p. 154.

5 The Prophet Muhammad, as quoted in Annemarie Schimmel, *My Soul is a Woman: The Feminine in Islam*, New York: Continuum Publishing Company, 1999, p. 26.

6 Quoted by Schimmel, *op. cit.*, p. 31.

7 Riffat Hassan, "Is Family Planning Permitted by Islam?" in Gisela Webb, ed., *Windows of Faith: Muslim Women Scholar-Activists in North America*, Syracuse: Syracuse University Press, 2000, pp. 230–1.

8   Surah 23:12–14.
9   A. H. Siddiqui, trans. of *Sahih Muslim*, vol. 2, Lahore: Shaikh Muhammad Ashraf, 1972, p. 752.
10 Surah 9: 71–72.
11 Surah 4: 34.
12 Surah 4: 3.
13 Riffat Hassan, personal communication, March 1, 2006.
14 Imam Abu Husaan Muslim ibn al-Hajjaj, *al-Sahih al-Muslim*, 16: 17, as quoted in Maulana Muhammad Ali, *The Religion of Islam*, Delhi: Motilal Banarsidass, 1994, p. 481.
15 Maulana Ashraf 'Ali Thanawi, *Bihishti Zewar*, trans. Barbara Daly Metcalf as *Perfecting Women*, Delhi: Oxford University Press, 1990, pp. 155–6. Reprinted by permission of the translator.
16 Fatima Adipayeva, interviewed by author April 11, 2005, translation by Galina Ermolina.
17 Khalila Saburova, personal communication, February 23, 2006.
18 Riffat Hassan, "Is Family Planning Permitted by Islam?", in Webb, *op. cit.*, p. 236.
19 Interviewed by author in Geneva, October 7, 2002.
20 Her Excellency Habiba Sarabi, prayer at the Global Peace Initiative of Women Religious and Spiritual Leaders, Geneva, October 6, 2001.
21 Elsie Aljarboa, personal communications to author, July 30–31, 2003.
22 Riffat Hassan, in Webb, *op. cit.*, p. 231.
23 Sharifa Alkhateeb, interviewed by author, October 7, 2002.
24 Rabi'a, in Farid al-Din 'Attar, *Tadhikirat al-Awliyd*, I, ed. Nicholson, London, 1905, p. 71. Uyghur version, trans. De Courteille, Paris, 1889. Quoted in Margaret Smith, *Rabi'a*, Oxford: Oneworld Publications reprint, 1994, p. 44.
25 Rabi'a al-Adawiyya, in Attar, I, *op. cit.*, p. 65, quoted in Smith, *op. cit.*, p. 57.
26 As quoted in 'Abd al-Rahman b. al-Jami, *Nafahdt al-Uns*, Calcutta, 1859, p. 718, cited in Smith, *op. cit.*, p. 175.
27 Abu Muhammad al-Witri, *Garden of the Guardians and the Extract of the Deeds of the Upright*, in Carl W. Ernst, trans., *Teachings of Sufism*, Boston: Shambhala Publications, 1999, p. 190.
28 Samiha Ayverdi, *The Friend ["Dost"]*, trans. Ismet Turnturnk, Istanbul: Kubbealti Nesriyati, 1980, pp. 149–50.
29 Bibi Fatima Sam, in Ernst, *op. cit.*, p. 187, and Camille Adams Helminski, *Women of Sufism:*

A Hidden Treasure, Boston: Shambhala, 2003, p. 79.
30 Annemarie Schimmel, *Mystical Dimensions of Islam*, Chapel Hill, North Carolina: University of North Carolina Press, 1975, p. 430.
31 Rabia Terri Harris, "The Relevance of Retreat," a talk delivered at the University of California, Berkeley, at the annual U.S. symposium of the Muhyiddin Ibn 'Arabi Society in 1994, as excerpted in Helminski, *op. cit.*, pp. 167–8.

Chapter 9
1   Guru Nanak, *Asa di War.*
2   Guru Nanak, Sri Rag, Guru Granth Sahib.
3   Guru Nanak, Guru Granth Sahib, p. 689.
4   Gurcharan Kaur, personal communication, February 22, 2006.
5   Narinder Kaur, interviewed May 6, 2006.
6   *Women: Extracts from the Writings of Bah'u'llah, 'Abdu'l-Baha, Shoghi Effendi and the Universal House of Justice*, Thornhill, Ontario: Baha'i Publications Canada, p. 26.
7   H. Nugaba'i, *Tahirih*, Teheran: 128 Badi/1972 ACE, p. 60, as cited in Arvind Sharma, *Religion and Women*, Albany, State University of New York Press, 1994, p. 216.
8   Shoghi Effendi, *God Passes By*, Wilmette, Illinois: Baha'i Publishing Committee, p. 75.
9   "Woman loves diversity of Baha'i Faith," www.tennessean.com/local/archives/03/09/40 010712, accessed May 6, 2006.
10 Universal House of Justice, "To the Peoples of the World: A Statement on Peace," Thornhill, Ontario: Baha'i Peace Council of Canada, p. 8.
11 www.lucistrust.org/goodwill/ngws.shtml, accessed December 14, 2005.
12 Johanna Brandt, *The Order of Harmony, founded at Pretoria in 1916 by Dr. Johanna Brandt*, p. 1, as quoted in Christine Steyn, "Johanna Brandt and the New Age Movement," *Dialogue and Alliance*, vol. 13, no. 1, Spring/Summer 1999, p. 19.
13 Helena Roerich, March 1, 1929, *The Letters of Helena Roerich*, vol. 1, 1929–38, New York: The Agni Yoga Society, 1954, p. 6.
14 Mark and Elizabeth Prophet, *My Soul Doth Magnify the Lord! New Age Rosary and New Age Teachings of Mother Mary*, The Golden Word of Mary Series, Book 1, Los Angeles: Ashram of the World Mother, 1979, pp. x–xi.
15 Helen Schucman, as quoted in http://64.77.6.149/about_acim.section/scribes.html, accessed January 19, 2006.

16 http://www.emmanuelandfriends.com/
    welcome.html, accessed January 19, 2006.
17 http://www.ramtha.com/html/aboutus/
    about-jz.stm, accessed January 19, 2006.
18 Margot Adler, *Drawing Down the Moon*, 2nd
    edn., New York: Penguin Press, 1986, p. ix.
19 Marija Gimbutas, interview in
    www.levity.com/mavericks/gimbut/htm,
    accessed December 20, 2005, p. 8.
20 Deuteronomy 12: 2–3.
21 Cynthia Eller, *The Myth of Matriarchal
    Prehistory: Why an Invented Past Will Not
    Give Women a Future*, Boston: Beacon Press,
    2000, p. 5.
22 Carol P. Christ, *Rebirth of the Goddess*, New
    York and London: Routledge, 1997, p. xv.
23 Marta Morena Vega, *The Altar of My Soul:
    The Living Traditions of Santeria*, New York:
    Ballantine Books/Random House, 2000, p. 11.
24 Karen McCarthy Brown, *Mama Lola: A Vodou
    Priestess in Brooklyn*, Berkeley: University of
    California Press, 1991, pp. 4–6. Reprinted by
    permission of the publisher.

Chapter 10
1   Mary Oliver, "The Journey," in Marilyn
    Sewell, ed., *Cries of the Spirit*, Boston: Beacon
    Press, 1991, p. 32. Reprinted by permission of
    the publisher.
2   Marianne Worcester, "Holy Ground," in Wynne
    Edwards and Dianne Linden, eds., *Running
    Barefoot: Women Write the Land*, Canada:
    Rowan Books, 2001, pp. 93, 98.
3   www.findhorn.org/about_us/display_new.php,
    accessed May 19, 2006.
4   Dorothy Maclean, "Choosing Love," an
    interview by Michael Bertrand,
    www.banyen.com/INFOCUS/MACLEAN.>
    HTM, accessed December 10, 2003.
5   Jean Shinoda Bolen, interviewed October
    2002.
6   *Peace Pilgrim: Her Life and Work in Her Own
    Words*, Santa Fe, New Mexico: An Ocean Tree
    Book, 1983, p. 7.
7   Elena Polykova, interviewed October 10, 2004.
8   Chole Pescina, in Kay Turner, *Beautiful
    Necessity: The Art and Meaning of Women's
    Altars*, New York: Thames and Hudson, 1999,
    p. 140.
9   Elana Rozenman, Mara List, Ibtisam
    Mahamid, and Piera Edelman, "IEA Report:
    Women's Interfaith Encounter of Northern
    Israel—Day of Learning at Yemin Orde on
    June 3," from msyuda@phys.huji.ac.il, June
    19, 2003.
10 Elana Rozenman, "Women's Interfaith

Encounter: Tuesday March 4 in Druze village
    of Daliat haCarmel," from
    msyuda@phys.huji.ac.il, March 21, 2003.
11 Elinore N. Detiger, personal communication,
    October 16, 2002.
12 Ann Smith, personal communication, August
    19, 2002.
13 Sarah Hartzell, sarah@peacecircles.net,
    December 20, 2005.
14 Jean Shinoda Bolen, *The Millionth Circle:
    How to Change Ourselves and the World*,
    Berkeley, California: Conari Press, 1999,
    pp. 83–5.

Excerpts

pp. 42–3, Paula Gunn Allen.
Reprinted by permission of the publisher

pp. 82–3, Vijaya Nagarajan.
Reprinted by permission of the publisher

pp.99–100, Maechee Pathomwan.
Reprinted by permission of the publisher

pp. 124–6, bell hooks.
Reprinted by permission of the author

pp. 134–5, Pan Chao.
Reprinted by permission of the University
of Michigan Press

pp. 143–5, Chung Hyun Kyung.
Reprinted by permission of the publisher

pp. 161–2, Tanakh.
Reprinted by permission of the publisher

pp. 165–6, Tanakh.
Reprinted by permission of the publisher

pp. 170–1, Glückel of Hamelin.
Reprinted by permission of Random House, Inc.

p. 178, Judith Plaskow.
Reprinted by permission of the publisher

p. 181, Mierle Laderman Ukeles.
Reprinted by permission of the publisher

pp. 197–8, Rosemary Radford Ruether.
Reprinted by permission of the publisher

p. 206, Julian of Norwich. Reprinted by
permission of the publisher

pp. 225–7, New Liturgies. Reprinted by
permission of the publisher

pp. 244–5, Riffat Hassan. Reprinted by
permission of the publisher

pp. 248–9, Amina Wadud. Reprinted by
permission of the publisher

pp. 263–4, Amina Wadud. Reprinted by
permission of the publisher

pp. 289–90, Starhawk. Reprinted by
permission of the publisher

GLOSSARY

androcentric Male-centered, as of language ("he," "his" when referring to humanity generally).

anthropomorphic As though in human form. To anthropomorphize is to treat an animal or object as though it were human.

anti-Semitism Hatred of or hostility towards the Jews.

Apostle Specifically, one of the 12 disciples who were Jesus' most intimate followers; also applied to Paul, who spread Christianity with his writings.

ascetic Living without worldly comforts, in extreme self-discipline, for instance with only enough food to stay alive.

ashe The energy that connects everything and is always dynamic.

ashram A place of religious retreat.

baptism The Christian sacrament that removes the stain of **original sin** from the soul.

beatification, beatified The act of declaring someone "blessed," the step before **canonization**.

bhakti Movement whose followers practice devotional adoration of a deity or **guru**.

bodhisattva A saintly figure in Buddhism, destined to become enlightened, who dedicates his or her own spiritual practice to helping all suffering beings.

Brahman, Brahmin The highest caste in India, the only one considered ritually pure enough to conduct religious ceremonies.

caliph A successor to the Prophet Muhammad.

canonical Of scripture, accepted as authoritative by religious leaders.

canonization The act of declaring someone a saint.

Ch'an The Chinese branch of **Vajrayana** Buddhism.

Crucifixion, crucified The death of Jesus on the cross; Roman method of putting criminals to death by fixing them to a wooden cross.

dakini An enlightened female energy from the celestial realm who may appear on earth in human form as a **yogini**.

Dao The intrinsic power and pattern of the universe.

Dharma In Hinduism, the all-pervading ideal of duty, moral order, righteousness. In Buddhism, the doctrine and code for living, as defined by the Buddha.

Diaspora In Judaism, the body of Jews scattered across the world, separated from Zion.

Eucharist Bread and wine symbolizing the body and blood of Jesus, eaten and drunk in remembrance of his sacrifice. Roman Catholics hold that the bread and wine actually become Jesus' body and blood (transubstantiation) at the moment of consecration.

exorcism The rite of casting out demons that possess a person.

feminism The belief that women should have the same opportunities as men, and that relationships should be based on mutuality rather than oppression and hierarchy.

gender Femaleness or maleness defined by cultural ideas, including what a female or male is allowed and expected to do.

ghetto Jewish-only walled urban area, locked at night.

Gospel The four books, attributed to Matthew, Mark, Luke, and John, of the New Testament in the Christian Bible.

gurdwara Sikh temple.

guru Spiritual teacher.

Hadith Literature that reports the life and sayings of the Prophet Muhammad.

halakhah Jewish legal system, formulated from the Hebrew Bible and from elaborations and clarifications of rights and obligations developed by post-biblical rabbinical traditions.

hatha yoga The ancient Indian art of physical postures and breathing exercises to help the devotee achieve inner concentration, often taught in the West outside its religious context.

heresy, heretical Belief held by followers of a religion but counter to its orthodox doctrine.

hierarchy, hierarchical A system, society, or organization in which classes of authority are ranked one above another.

hijab The veiling of Muslim women.

imam Leader or teacher in Islam.

Immaculate Conception Roman Catholic doctrine referring to the conception of Mary, by normal human means, but without her soul being stained by **original sin**.

karma The effects of a person's thoughts and actions, felt in this life and in the next, after reincarnation.

Khalsa Sikhs pledged to defend anyone in need and to stand against injustice.

kundalini The power of **shakti** that spirals serpent-like up the spine, awakening the latent energy of all the subtle centers of the body.

langar Free community kitchen.

Mahayana One of the three major forms of Buddhism, which emphasizes compassion and loving kindness; it contains theistic elements as well as highly abstract constructs. See also **Theravada, Vajrayana**.

martyr One who dies for his or her religion.

matriarchal Society or group led by women, with descent through the female line.

matrifocality The tradition by which households consist only of a mother and her children.

matrilineal, matrilinearity Lineage traced through the mother's side rather than the father's.

matrilocality The tradition by which the husband lives with the wife's community.

mendicant Wandering, begging monk or nun.

Messiah The long-awaited savior of the Jews; also applied to Jesus Christ as the savior of his people, and hence of all Christians.

midrash Interpretation of the Bible, an ongoing process.

misogyny Hostility to or hatred of women.

missionary One who spreads his or her religion to societies that have no knowledge of it.

myth A story used by a community to make sense of the universe and to place itself therein.

Namaz Five daily prayers, obligatory for a Muslim.

nirvana The ultimate egoless state of bliss.

original sin The sin of disobedience committed by Adam and Eve, and passed down to all humanity, washed away only by the sacrament of **baptism**.

orisha An elemental force of specified or unspecified gender, considered a divinity in the Yoruba society of Africa and in the Caribbean; a knowable aspect of the invisible, mysterious source of all things.

parable Story told by Jesus to point a moral or reveal God's purpose.

patriarchal A society or institution led by men as father figures.

patrilineal Society or group based on kinship through the male line.

pope The spiritual leader of Roman Catholics.

prasad In Sikhism, an offering of sweet food.

puja Worship rituals, often carried out in a special room.

qi Vital energy, promoted through the balancing of *yin* and *yang*.

rabbi Jewish teacher of the scriptures, decision-maker, and prayer-leader.

Reformation Protestant movement begun in the sixteenth century in Europe by reformists urging that Christianity be brought back to Jesus' original teachings and rituals.

reified Concrete; materialized or made into an object.

religion A particular response to sacred dimensions as shaped by institutionalized traditions, encompassing beliefs, practices, ritual objects, scriptures, or oral traditions.

Resurrection The rising of Jesus from the dead, three days after his **Crucifixion**.

ritual A religious or solemn rite carried out in a prescribed order.

Sabbath The day of rest: in Judaism, Saturday, in Christianity, Sunday.

Sabbats The eight points of the solar year: Minor Sabbats, the two solstices and two equinoxes; Major Sabbats, Imbolc (February 2), Beltane (May 1), Lughnasadh (August 1), and Samhain (October 31).

samadhi Transcendent absorption in spiritual matters.

samaneri A novice monk or nun who has limited duties and rights.

samsara The endless cycle of death and rebirth.

Sangha The community of monastics, perhaps including laypeople.

santeros/santeras Initiated priests and priestesses of Vodou.

sati Practice in which widows were cremated alive on their husbands' funeral pyres.

sex The biological fact of being female or male.

shakti Awesome creative power.

shaman Visionary woman or man with direct access to the spirit world, called and trained to interact with spiritual forces on behalf of the people.

Shari'a Code regulating all aspects of a Muslim's life, sometimes enshrined as law.

Shi'a One of the two major branches of Islam (see **Sunni**), which followed the fourth caliph, 'Ali, the Prophet's cousin, married to Fatima, the Prophet's daughter.

spirituality Any personal response to dimensions of life that are considered sacred.

Sunnah Collected examples from the life of the Prophet Muhammad.

Sunni One of the two major branches of Islam (see **Shi'a**), which did not fully recognize the fourth caliph 'Ali's legitimacy and followed a fifth caliph.

synagogue Meeting place for Jewish worship.

syncretic Combining diverse practices from several religions.

Talmud Body of commentaries and oral traditions gathered together by rabbis. Of the two major versions, one was written down in Israel about 400 CE, the other in Babylonia from 500 CE onwards.

Tantrism, Tantric Mystical writings setting out doctrines involving mantras, meditation, and yoga, emphasizing worship of the divine feminine; the practice of these.

Theravada One of the three major forms of Buddhism, which claims to be closest to the original teachings of the Buddha; meditation is its chief focus. See also **Mahayana**, **Vajrayana**.

Torah (1) The laws by which the Israelites are to live righteously in order to uphold their side of the covenant with the Lord; (2) the first five books of the Hebrew Bible; (3) the whole body of Jewish teaching and law.

Vajrayana One of the three major forms of Buddhism, which includes esoteric Tantric spiritual practices from India and elements from indigenous Tibetan shamanism. See also **Theravada**, **Mahayana**.

Vedas Ancient sacred literature of the Indian subcontinent.

vipassana Mindfulness meditation.

virgin birth The birth of Jesus Christ as a result of Mary's impregnation by the Holy Ghost.

womanist Term used by women of color in preference to "feminist," which they feel is associated with a white Western point of view.

yang The assertive, bright, creative, "male" aspect of the cosmic impersonal force, in eternal interplay with its female counterpart *yin*.

yin The dark, receptive, "female" aspect of the cosmic impersonal force, in eternal interplay with its male counterpart *yang*.

yogini A female with spiritual powers and enlightened wisdom because of her meditation practice, the human form of a **dakini**.

Zen The Japanese branch of **Vajrayana** Buddhism.

ILLUSTRATION CREDITS

Preface: Photo Mark Henley/Impact Photos

Chapter 1
1.1 Photo by Mary Pat Fisher
1.2 Georgia O'Keeffe, *Black Iris III*, 1926. Oil on canvas, 36 x 29⁷/₈ in. (91.4 x 75.9 cm). The Metropolitan Museum of Art, New York, Alfred Stieglitz Collection, 1969 (69.278.1). © ARS, NY and DACS, London, 2006
1.3 Photo by Alexandra Engel
1.4 Courtesy of Galina Ermolina
1.5 Courtesy of the Nicaraguan Cultural Alliance, www.quixote.org

Chapter 2
2.1 Photo by Bert Gunn
2.2 Photo © Medford Taylor/National Geographic/Gettyimages
2.3 Courtesy of the artist
2.4 Photo by Galina Ermolina
2.5 Photo © Marc Garanger/CORBIS

Chapter 3
3.1 Photo K.L. Kamat
3.2 Courtesy of Mary Pat Fisher
3.3 Courtesy of Mary Pat Fisher
3.4 Photo by Mary Pat Fisher
3.5 Photo by Alexandra Engel
3.6 Photo © Avinash Pasricha
3.7 Photo M.A. Center

Chapter 4
4.1 Antique porcelain figure. Photo © Araldo de Luca/CORBIS
4.2 Courtesy of Mary Pat Fisher
4.3 Drawing by Eva van Dam
4.4 Courtesy of Amaravati Buddhist Monastery
4.5 Courtesy of Allen & Unwin
4.6 Photo © Aubert Dominique/Corbis Sygma

Chapter 5
5.1 Photo V&A Images/Victoria and Albert Museum
5.2 Photo by Jane Bown, courtesy of Random House, Inc.
5.3 Photo © Peter Turnley/CORBIS
5.4 From *Zengxiang Liexian Zhuan*

Chapter 6
6.1 Photo Private Collection/Peter Willi/The Bridgeman Art Library
6.2 Nude goddess figurine (late 8th–early 7th century BCE), excavated at Tell el-Duweir (ancient Lachish), southern Levant. Ceramic, ht. 7¹/₈ in. (18.1 cm). The Metropolitan Museum of Art, New York, Gift of Harris D. and H. Dunscombe Colt, 1934 (34.126.53)
6.3 Courtesy of the Jewish Museum of Maryland, 1992.242.7.178
6.4 Courtesy of Judith Plaskow
6.5 Photo © Richard T. Nowitz/CORBIS
6.6 Photo by Linda Cicero

Chapter 7
7.1 Bartolome Murillo, *La Concepción del Escorial*, 1656–60. Oil on canvas, 81 x 56 in (206 x 144 cm). Museo del Prado, Madrid. Photo © Oronoz
7.2 Courtesy of the artist
7.3 From Hildegard von Bingen, *Liber divinorum operum simplicis hominis*, Italian illuminated manuscript, *c.*1230. Biblioteca Governativa Statale. Photo akg-images
7.4 Photo by Alexandra Engel
7.5 Courtesy of the Kathryn Kuhlman Foundation
7.6 Photo © Bettmann/CORBIS
7.7 Photo by Lynn Saville, courtesy of Union Theological Seminary in the City of New York

Chapter 8
8.1 Courtesy of Mary Pat Fisher
8.2 Photo by Alexandra Engel
8.3 Photo by Mary Pat Fisher
8.4 Courtesy of Sana Shariq
8.5 Photo by Alexandra Engel
8.6 Photo © Jkaveh Kazemi/CORBIS

Chapter 9
9.1 Siberian Roerich Society, Nicholas Roerich Museum, Novosibirsk
9.2 Courtesy of the Nicholas Roerich Museum, New York
9.3 Courtesy www.starhawk.org
9.4 Photo © Barnabas Bosshart/CORBIS

Chapter 10
10.1 Photo by Lisa Levart
10.2 Photo by Carla Anette, Courtesy Friends of Peace Pilgrim
10.3 Photo by Mary Pat Fisher
10.4. Photo by Sarah Hartzell, Circles of Ten: Women for World Peace

INDEX